LITERATURE, EMOTIONS, AND PRE-MODERN WAR

War and Conflict in Premodern Societies

Series Editors
John D. Hosler, *US Army Command & General Staff College*
Kathryn Hurlock, *Manchester Metropolitan University*
Louisa Taylor, *Universitet i Oslo*
L. J. Andrew Villalon, *University of Texas, Austin*

See further: www.arc-humanities.org/our-series/arc/wcp/

LITERATURE, EMOTIONS, AND PRE-MODERN WAR

CONFLICT IN MEDIEVAL AND EARLY MODERN EUROPE

Edited by
CLAIRE MCILROY and **ANNE M. SCOTT**

ARC HUMANITIES PRESS

British Library Cataloguing in Publication Data
A catalogue record for this book is available from the British Library.

© 2021, Arc Humanities Press, Leeds

The author asserts their moral right to be identified as the author of this work.

Permission to use brief excerpts from this work in scholarly and educational works is hereby granted provided that the source is acknowledged. Any use of material in this work that is an exception or limitation covered by Article 5 of the European Union's Copyright Directive (2001/29/EC) or would be determined to be "fair use" under Section 107 of the U.S. Copyright Act September 2010 Page 2 or that satisfies the conditions specified in Section 108 of the U.S. Copyright Act (17 USC §108, as revised by P.L. 94–553) does not require the Publisher's permission.

ISBN (print): 9781641893084
eISBN (PDF): 9781641893091

www.arc-humanities.org
Printed and bound in the UK (by CPI Group [UK] Ltd), USA (by Bookmasters), and elsewhere using print-on-demand technology.

CONTENTS

Preface
    ANDREW LYNCH vii

Introduction: The Long Reach of War
    CLAIRE MCILROY and ANNE M. SCOTT 1

Chapter 1. Love in Times of War: Some Shakespearean Reflections
    ROBERT S. WHITE 9

PART ONE:
THE EMOTIONAL COSTS OF WAR

Chapter 2. "she shal bryngen us the pees on every syde": The Ceremonial Restoration of Women in Late Medieval Culture
    STEPHANIE DOWNES and STEPHANIE TRIGG 29

Chapter 3. Emotions and War in Chaucer's *Knight's Tale*
    RALUCA L. RADULESCU 45

Chapter 4. Making Dole in Malory
    KAREN CHEREWATUK 65

PART TWO:
VOICING CONLFICT

Chapter 5. The Hero "Remembers": The Verb *Gemunan* in *Beowulf* and *The Battle of Maldon*
    AD PUTTER 83

Chapter 6. The Hard Parting: Conflicting Codes of *fin'amors* and Christian duty in the Old French *chansons de croisade*
    HELEN DELL 101

Chapter 7. Christ versus Lucifer in *Piers Plowman*
ANNE M. SCOTT 119

Chapter 8. Breathing in Peace and War: Malory's *Le Morte Darthur*
CORINNE SAUNDERS 131

Chapter 9. Giving and Gaining Voice in Civil War: Alain Chartier's
Quadrilogue Invectif in Fifteenth-Century England
JAMES SIMPSON... 151

PART THREE:
THE IMPACT OF WAR

Chapter 10. Oriental Despotism and the Reception of Romance
JOHN M. GANIM 167

Chapter 11. Belon, Palissy, Ronsard, and the War for the Forests of France
SUSAN BROOMHALL 179

Chapter 12. Holy War, Cold War: War, Comedy, and the Lessons of History
in the Films of Mario Monicelli
LOUISE D'ARCENS 199

Select Bibliography... 213

Index 219

Abbreviations

MED	*Middle English Dictionary*. Edited by Hans Kurath and S. M. Kuhn. Ann Arbor: University of Michigan Press, 1952–. http://quod.lib.umich.edu/m/med/
OED	*Oxford English Dictionary*. Edited by John Simpson and Edmund Weiner, 20 vols, second edition. Oxford: Clarendon Press, 1989.
The Works of Sir Thomas Malory	Sir Thomas Malory, *The Works of Sir Thomas Malory*. Edited by Eugène Vinaver, vol. 3, third edition, P. J. C. Field. Oxford: Clarendon Press, 1990.

PREFACE

Andrew Lynch

I AM HONOURED to be asked to contribute a preface to this collection of twelve chapters by long-term friends and colleagues. I deeply appreciate such a kind gift from a set of scholars whose store of cultural reference, scholarly information, and specialist expertise I admire so much. Thank you all! The editors are providing the Introduction to the volume, and giving a broader context to the individual chapters. They have suggested that I write a less formal piece for it, and I am taking the opportunity to reflect a while on what is involved, for me, in the business of studying medieval and medievalist war literature in the contemporary world.

The chapters gathered here are connected by their involvement in the literature and culture of medieval and early modern war in England and France, with a final study of its afterlife in Italy. They range in time from the eighth century to the twentieth, and cover multiple genres: epic; *chanson*; romance; religious satire; political and social treatise; chronicle; theatre and film. They are by no means all about actual wars, real or imagined, but the literal and metaphorical variety of their subjects gives a good indication of how omnipresent both the idea and the impact of war have been in the long history of Western Europe and its cultural influence. They show that "war" extends far beyond the battlefield or the delineated years of military campaigns.

I am interested in how written and cultural forms of all kinds communicate war: how they conceive what it is, how they structure understandings of its rationale and execution, and evaluate its effects. Some kinds of writing on war, such as treatises and advice literature, address these matters consciously and directly, but most do not, and one must pick up their sense of "war" more obliquely from the analysis of textual practice: from the welter of formal and generic tendencies, rhythms and soundscapes, speech habits, obsessions, emphases and omissions that make up the overall action of this literature to inform our thoughts and emotions. I have always liked Pierre Macherey's idea that literature destroys ideology by using it, and in this context I think of literary criticism—attentive to the ideological fault lines and contradictions of texts, along with all their other qualities—as both a way of seeing better what war means in texts and a modest means of resisting attempts to recycle it in simplified versions.

I should explain more. My whole working life as an academic has been in Australia, and I study past war literature, in good part, with an eye to the cultural labour that the imaginary of war performs in my own country, where both government policy and conservative press influence have ensured it dominates historical consciousness, in highly selective ways. In Australia, very much more has been written, more films and documentaries made, more museums and monuments erected, and more public money spent in order to commemorate wars than for any other formative national events: the arrival of Europeans on the land; the great Gold Rush of the mid-nineteenth century; the Federation of six separate states into one Commonwealth in 1901; the Great Depression; the continuing transformation of Australia by new waves of immigration. And more is heard by the public about Australia's part in international wars than about the more than 60,000-year-old history and culture of our Indigenous peoples.

The Australian War Memorial in Canberra, the chief national institution in this area, does not commemorate fighting between Aboriginal Australians and military, police, and citizen militia forces. From 1770 up to 1930, at least, many thousands died in these conflicts, but they are not recognized as "wars." As a result, this part of the national history receives less public recognition. The situation is quite different from what applies in New Zealand, for example, where the "New Zealand Wars" (formerly called the "Maori Wars") are widely acknowledged.

Accordingly, in the Australian public mind war refers to military service overseas, not to the European conquest of Australia. Unlike in many former colonies, war did not provide Australia with a means of liberation from colonial control. Rather, war became emotionally important to settler Australians after our existence as a sovereign country was achieved. Then in 1914, entry into the Great War was welcomed as a chance to show that the new nation was a loyal part of the British Empire. That imperial rationale has long since been replaced by another, as shown by the words of the then Prime Minister, Tony Abbott, writing for a News Corp publication on ANZAC Day, 2015 (ANZAC Day commemorates Australia's part in the Dardanelles campaign of 1915 and in all overseas wars):

> In the magnificent failure at Gallipoli, the successful advances in the Middle East and the terrible victory on the Western Front, our soldiers embodied the commitment to freedom, the spirit of adventure and the bonds of mateship that we hold dear to this day. Their values helped to forge our nation's identity. Their sacrifice has helped to ensure that to be an Australian remains "the greatest privilege that the world has to offer."[1]

Under such conditions, I have unsurprisingly become a suspicious and politicized reader of war literature, conscious of my difficulty in "knowing what to feel" about war, not through lack of imagination or knowledge, but through awareness of the more recent political sponsorship of its public profile. It is hard to acknowledge one's natural respect and compassion for the courage and sufferings of combatants in a context where those very qualities are now exploited to affirm war as a character-building national "adventure" and to treat its mass killings as a fight for "freedom." To that mindset it would seem blasphemous to point out that our soldiers were not actually sent off to "sacrifice" themselves but to kill enemy soldiers. But in any case, where are the "values" and the sufferings of the enemy, of women, or of non-combatants on all sides in this narrative of accrued national "privilege"? It is truly a "forged" identity for Australia.

In its more metaphorical applications, "war" is now normalized as a proper activity. Even in the time of relative Western peace in which I and most of the writers in this book

---

[1] Tony Abbott, "Anzac Values Forged Our Identity at Gallipoli," *The Australian*, April 25, 2015.

have largely lived—when our countries' wars have largely been exported elsewhere or directed at identified "others" within their power—war's oppositional structures of thought and its thematics of worthy struggle have influenced many aspects of our lives. Our societies "fight" poverty, homelessness, and cancer. The culture of aggressive competition that permeates business is increasingly applied in other areas, including education. In Australia, universities once understood to "serve" their local communities now battle it out for global rankings. In a strange irony, it is now mainly veterans—those who have fought in actual wars—who are simply honoured for "service." We need to keep thinking hard about where the imaginary of war, with all its applications and symbolic transformations, is taking us. What we do with the legacy of medieval and early modern war literature is an important part of that.

At the present time, when non-violent approaches to global problems are increasingly replaced by militarized strategies—Australia's mandatory imprisonment of refugees arriving by boat is an instance—and racist organizations across the world fantasize about links with the Middle Ages, the study of Western medieval and early modern war literature clearly involves dangers and responsibilities. Whether or not it has been recognized, that has been the case for a very long time. Ever since the end of the Middle Ages, when continuing claims to personal nobility and honour, national virtue, and military tradition survived other religious and cultural rejections of the past, medieval war literature has constituted a resource for which succeeding ages have found uses. Positive adaptations of medieval and early modern war and warriors have been strangely protected from the otherwise dominant story of continuing historical progress from a barbarous past to a civilized present, even while the notion of "violence" often defines the Middle Ages *per se* for modernity.

In an earlier era of medievalism, the main appeal of "chivalry" was the idealism, fair play, and lack of personal animosity that writers like Walter Scott could see in its best practices. Such a view allowed war to be seen as an undertaking in which gentlemen could participate, and has been critiqued for presenting it as a theatre for shows of disinterested magnanimity. At the other end of the spectrum, some modern versions of the medieval warrior offer patterns of uninhibited masculine aggression and dominance, like the thug Beowulf of Robert Zemeckis' 2007 film—"I am lust! I am power!"—so different in manner and outlook from his early English namesake. More dangerously than these individualist models, the medievalization of war, or the staging of extremely aggressive actions as "medieval" war, often invoke as their context a supposedly age-old national, racial, or religious struggle, always simultaneously a moral struggle, against natural enemies. The imagined great cause is seen to summon the "medieval" warrior and his violence, and to give modern agents an enhanced identity and a special destiny. We have seen the perpetrators of two atrocious massacres in recent times stage themselves as resistance fighters in the context of a civilizational crisis, and both claim a connection to the "Knights Templar." One could easily multiply current examples of such appropriations of the medieval for bad causes, from Eastern and Central Europe to America and Australia.

It must be admitted that medieval and early modern literature would provide plenty of material to anyone looking for these purposes, including in canonical authors. The stark anti-Semitism of Chrétien de Troyes' *Conte du Graal*, written at a time when persecution of Jews in Northern France was on the upsurge, is one example.[2] Chaucer's *Prioress's Tale*, which epitomized his charm for Wordsworth and Matthew Arnold, has a story premised on the murderous envy of "cursed Jues," "[h]ateful to Crist and to his compaignye"—the rationale for many pogroms. For Spenser, as Suzanne Conklin Akbari shows, the "Turk" and the Pope together make up Antichrist, and "[b]y describing English Catholics as 'Turkes and Sarazins', Spenser makes his own countrymen seem to be aliens, people wholly excluded from the community ... in the context of a religious war, when shared national identity competes with religious difference."[3] The seemingly endless adaptability of this kind of apocalyptic reading of the world, quite ahistorical but exercising great symbolic power, is one of its most worrying features, along with its millenarian insistence that "something must be done."

Similarly, investment in medieval and early modern war literature is a feature of many modern prejudices and atrocities. Richard Utz, Martin Shichtman, and Laurie A. Finke have investigated the intimate involvement of Hitler's Germany with the medieval.[4] One could equally note the "Teutonic" supremacism fundamental to the medievalism of Charles Kingsley, a Cambridge professor of history and mainstream author in Victorian England.[5] Louise D'Arcens has shown how the colonial Australian novelist Rolf Boldrewood adapted *Ivanhoe*'s story of Saxon liberation from the "Norman yoke" to occlude reference to the enslavement of Aboriginal Australians, allowing the colonists to "retain the righteousness reserved for the injured, as well as asserting their right to regain their historical destiny through conquest."[6] There could be very many such examples listed.

In the face of all this worrying knowledge, why should we continue to "learn war" through the medium of medieval and medievalist texts? I would argue that our awareness of the dangers makes even more urgent the need for informed reading of the medieval and early modern literature of war, because to apprehend this writing in its long-range, historicized complexity of utterance and reception is a step towards weakening

---

2 Lisa Lampert-Weissig, " 'Why Is This Knight Different from All Other Knights?' Jews, Anti-Semitism, and the Old French Grail Narratives," *Journal of English and Germanic Philology* 106, no. 2, Master Narratives of the Middle Ages (April, 2007): 224–47.

3 Suzanne Conklin Akbari, "The Rhetoric of Antichrist in Western Lives of Muhammad," *Islam and Christian-Muslim Relations* 8, no. 3 (1997): 297–307 at 305.

4 Richard Utz, *Medievalism: A Manifesto* (Bradford: Arc Humanities, 2017); Martin Shichtman and Laurie A. Finke, "Exegetical History: Nazis at the Round Table," *Postmedieval* 5, no. 3 (2014): 278–94.

5 Andrew Lynch, "Mediating English Historical Evolution in Charles Kingsley's *Hereward the Wake* (1866)," in *Emotions in Late Modernity*, ed. Roger Patulny et al. (London: Routledge, 2019), 161–75.

6 Louise D'Arcens, "Inverse Invasions: Medievalism and Colonialism in Rolf Boldrewood's *A Sydney-Side Saxon*," *Parergon* 22, no. 2 (July 2005): 159–82 at 175.

the power of the false doctrines and bogus symbolic analogies it is sometimes used to support—the Christchurch terrorist linked his murders to the Siege of Acre (1189) and the Siege of Vienna (1683). Prejudicial violence thrives on generalities—taking a part for the whole—and on monomyths of "age-old" causes and confrontations—as then, so now. Medieval scholars, I hope, can make a helpful contribution here. Careful reading of the literature of the past in its own context alerts us to its stubborn differences from the present, to features that do not satisfy present-day readerly needs of "relevance" of whatever kind. It shows how contemporary weaponizing and instrumentalizing of the medieval distorts the history it cites.

"Relevance" has a powerful call for medievalists, who see that our expertise can be important to aspects of contemporary life. One good way of showing that right now would be to use our knowledge to put critical limits on the notion that we are still living the Middle Ages, or living in a new Middle Ages, as Umberto Eco variously put it. We need to articulate the specificities that disrupt a sense that modern prejudices are mystically rooted in the medieval past, while keeping keenly aware of medieval literature's dark side and its remaining openness to bad uses. To return to the example of Chaucer, the anti-Semitic strain in the *Prioress's Tale* is "age-old" in one way, but also specific to a vindictive kind of popular Christian hagiography, admittedly one with a horribly long afterlife. It does not relate, for example, to the later conspiracy theory of a Jewish cabal seeking to dominate world finance, which has a very different aetiology. We falsify the nature of anti-Semitism, or of any forms of racial and religious prejudice, if we treat them as undifferentiated matters to which all examples contribute alike. Such ahistorical ways of thinking unwittingly mimic the racial and religious essentialism of prejudiced outlooks.

Crusades literature offers the most extreme medieval examples of prejudicial violence, claiming a moral right to invasive warfare, in which the Christian forces are styled as defenders or liberators of foreign places already identified as their own. Here a total absence of "love" for the enemy is justified, because they are "enemies of the cross of Christ."[7] Only Christ's side has any right to receive love.[8] This kind of thinking is prevalent in medieval and early modern war literature directed at identified religious enemies, whether "pagans," Jews, Muslims, or heretics. Yet the wars based, or supposed to be based, on these grounds, are also clearly specific to contemporary cultural and political requirements. They were not, for instance, wars undertaken in defense of modern ideas of "Western Civilization" or Western "freedoms," and those who enlist them in those contexts can be shown to be wrong. Nothing palliates the horror of medieval and early modern atrocities and of the texts that supported them. But it remains important to show that certain modern atrocities are not "medieval," however

---

7 Beverly Mayne Kienzle, "Preaching the Cross: Liturgy and Crusade Propaganda," *Medieval Sermon Studies* 53 (2009): 11–32.

8 Jonathan Riley-Smith, "Crusading as an Act of Love," *History* 65 (1980): 177–92.

they are dressed up, and so to remove the prestige that medievalist cultural associations seem to provide them in some eyes.

We can make a parallel but inverse kind of intervention by analyzing earlier instances of modern medievalism. To continue my earlier example, by examining Australian literature of the period 1914–1918 we find that the Great War was then much more about Empire than Nation, that there was no simple national unity but fierce debates about participation, and the public mind of the period was bombarded by stupidly propagandist views of causes and effects, designed to spread national hatreds. These last found their way into medievalist literary expressions, in which France became Joan of Arc, the Australian army was exhorted to "Do the last Crusaders' work/On the bastard Teuton-Turk," and it was "the holiest task to slay ... Yon blatant heathenrie."[9] Studying this literature today offers an instructive contrast to the Great War of "mateship," "sacrifice," and new national identity that Australians now hear so much of. It also shows the spurious short-term opportunism of aligning contemporary conflicts with medievalist archetypes. Up until the war much British-oriented culture had been decidedly Germanophile and suspicious of France; the supposedly "timeless" medieval archetypes were actually created to suit the occasion. Overall, the study of past war literature within its own time reveals many features that weaken its applicability to current situations, while the study of its reception history and influence shows up radical changes in the demands of meaning that successive ages have made on it, and in the uses to which it has been put. Together, these historical specificities deny the idea that a sensible function of this literature can be to enlist modernity in ancient struggles, or summon a modern hero to join the old fight on behalf of his beleaguered tribe.

War literature, like war itself, is a messy business, but its failure to execute ideological agendas with perfect precision should be one of its saving graces, because it makes the wars it relates less easily reduced to partisan readings, or to simplifying symbols and slogans. Many of the core war narratives in medieval European literature and its early modern afterlife—Thebes, Troy, Rome, Alexander, Arthur—are left to us in multiple forms and genres, and in contested and hybridized historiographical traditions. They tell different stories, and often enlist very mixed sympathies. They differ, in effect, from the influential model of medievalist war in writers like Tennyson and Tolkien, who tend to treat the subject allegorically. Tolkien once wrote that "romance" has grown out of allegory and its wars are still derived from the "inner war" of allegory in which good is on one side and various modes of badness on the other. In real (exterior) life men are on both sides.[10] In the medieval wars of Thebes and Troy, including the twelfth-century *romans antiques*, that kind of "romance" division does not apply: as in Tolkien's "real life," villains and heroes fight and die on each side, so readers' sympathies are divided. These are avoidable conflicts arising out of reckless greed, pride, and dishonesty, and

---

[9] Quotations in this paragraph are from Christopher Brennan, *A Chant of Doom* (Sydney: Angus and Robertson, 1918).

[10] *The Letters of J. R. R. Tolkien: A Selection*, ed. Humphrey Carpenter with assistance from Christopher Tolkien (London: George Allen and Unwin, 1981), 82.

they do the participants no good. Medieval Troy stories also often acknowledge that traditions of war writing are themselves partisan, pushing the agenda of a particular side rather than respecting truth. Above all, there is not much suggestion that these wars, however famous for the deeds of their heroes, or their long-term results, are good things in themselves, or that the outcome is a providential dispensation to let good triumph over evil. Trauma and grief are the outcomes, great cities destroyed. Survivors, like Aeneas, are led into years of new strife. Many of the "victors," like Ajax, Achilles, and Agamemnon, also come to bad ends.

In allegorical treatments like Spenser's *Faerie Queene* and Tennyson's *Idylls of the King*, opponents of the "right" side tend to be symbolic embodiments of evil—the "Beast"—beyond redemption, and with no legitimate interests of their own or right to exist. Partly through the continuing effects of racial, religious, and ethnic hatred, sometimes in medievalist guises, and partly through the moral archetypes of medievalist fantasy—what can you do with Orcs except kill them?—these attitudes towards opponents are thought to be generally characteristic of medieval and early modern war literature. But that is misleading. Questions of the "right" to war and of right conduct in war are usually operative in medieval writing, even if not directly addressed in principle. Even the romances of Alexander's conquests contain rebukes of the hero's pride and contrast his outlook with higher, "philosophical" views of life. The Alliterative *Morte Arthure* qualifies its praise for Arthur as a warrior with a sense of the destructiveness of his ambition, both to the lands he invades and to his own regime. Notable later medieval English writers—the *Gawain*-poet, Gower, Chaucer, and Hoccleve—pointedly avoid describing battle in detail—they clearly have better material to relate. Shakespeare hedges his apparent support for a national hero like Henry V with all kinds of questions about whether the king's campaign is justified, and lays Henry's arguments for it open to the charge of "Machiavellian fraud."[11] The interests of the victors are not necessarily the interests of God. Writers also often make a clear distinction, as Malory does, between brave conduct in the field of battle once a war starts, and the "dolorous" nature of war itself, where "good men" die on both sides. Similarly, not all medieval and medievalist war literature treats its warriors as the supporters of a sacred cause, however brave they are. It is acknowledged that war and fighting often involve people quite against their own inclinations in bad causes, and that these are often the best characters: Hector in medieval Troy narratives, Gunnar in *Njáls saga*, Lancelot and Arthur in the close of the French Vulgate Cycle, and Malory's *Le Morte Darthur*. Those most willing to have trouble start are often amongst the worst: Paris, Mord Valgardsson, Agravain, and Mordred. Malory's book was not written to show the failures of chivalry, as some have claimed, and cannot be read as the anti-war manifesto T. H. White wanted it to be, but despite all its enthusiasm for "worship in arms," Arthur expresses the sadness and human waste of the last war, and a deep

---

11 John S. Mebane, "'Impious War': Religion and Ideology of Warfare in Henry V," *Studies in Philology* 104, no. 2 (2007): 250–66.

sense that there are no winners: "Alas, alas, that ever yet this war began." Close reading of many medieval texts uncovers resistance in them to idea of "glorious" or "holy" war, forming a basis for our proper scholarly resistance to their modern instrumentalization in those terms.

Over many years now, I have been drawn back to the beautiful passage in Laʒamon's *Brut* (lines 11338–345) where the poet praises the happiness of a twelve-year period of peace in Arthur's reign, a time in which nothing happens in the adversarial and acquisitive terms of his ultimate source text, Geoffrey's *Historia*, yet everything good— unimaginable happiness—happens for the king and his people. If I have a regret about my long-term involvement in medieval and medievalist literature, it would be not having written more often about peace. Another notion is that since the thematics of war and aggressive competition now seem to control so many areas of our lives, it would have been good to connect the study of medieval and medievalist literature with critique of other kinds of contemporary war—on the environment, on human rights, on education and the arts, and on the intrinsic values that uphold humane societies. That might provide some ideas for the future. Meanwhile, I wholeheartedly thank the editors again for preparing this book, and express again my very deep gratitude to the contributors for their work.

Andrew Lynch is Emeritus Professor of English and Literary Studies at The University of Western Australia, and an Honorary Senior Research Fellow there. He has published widely on medieval literature and its modern afterlives, including *Malory's Book of Arms* (1977). Recent publications include two co-edited collections: *The Routledge History of Emotions in Europe, 1100–1700* (2019) and *A Cultural History of Emotions*, 6 vols. (2019). Amongst his current projects are co-editorship of the journal *Emotions: History, Culture, Society* (Brill) and *The Cambridge History of Arthurian Literature and Culture*.

INTRODUCTION: THE LONG REACH OF WAR

Claire McIlroy and Anne M. Scott[*]

War is not severed from time but comes from the past and renders uncertain the future.

So writes Robert S. White in the opening chapter of this collection, epigrammatically justifying the title of our Introduction: "The Long Reach of War." Our focus in this volume is on a range of factors that affect the lives of human beings who are impacted by war and conflict. The wars under consideration range from historical events, such as the Battle of Maldon, the Crusades, the wars between England and France, and the French civil wars of religion, through literary replications of war such as the Trojan War and the battles fought by Arthur's knights, to the metaphysical conflict between Christ and Lucifer, truth and sin, in *Piers Plowman*.

The chapters pay tribute either obliquely or directly to the work of Andrew Lynch who has made his own the study of Thomas Malory, opening up the text of *Le Morte Darthur* to subtleties of interpretation based on human attributes to do with name, vision, blood, emotion, and gesture as they relate to the battles and wars of the text. In the context of this volume, his work on the way medievalism has been harnessed into the service of glorifying war has had a major impact on scholars in the field, as the chapters show. Lynch has also deepened and broadened the way emotions are read, leading new generations of scholars to an explicit recognition and understanding of emotions in history and literature. This volume is presented in recognition of his wide-ranging scholarship, skilful mentoring, and strong collegiality.

This volume is not exclusively concerned with Malory, nor emotions, although several chapters do use *Le Morte Darthur* as a point of reference. Instead, the collection as a whole takes an extended look at the many ways in which the processes of war and conflict impact human life. The chapters select literary texts of poetry, drama and song, discursive texts concerning the landscape, and, in the final chapter, modern medievalist film satire, to explore the many ways in which human beings and their lives are touched, given heightened meaning, or changed by experiences stemming from war and conflict.

---

[*] **Claire McIlroy** is an Honorary Research Fellow in the School of Humanities (Medieval and Early Modern Studies) at The University of Western Australia and the Reviews Editor of *Parergon*, Journal of the Australian and New Zealand Association for Medieval and Early Modern Studies. She is the author of *The English Prose Treatises of Richard Rolle* (2004) and was the series co-editor, with Andrew Lynch, of the Brepols Publishers series Early European Research for more than a decade. **Anne M. Scott** is an Honorary Research Fellow in English and Literary Studies at The University of Western Australia. She studied under Andrew Lynch who she greatly admires as scholar, mentor, and friend. She has published a monograph on *Piers Plowman*, seven essay collections, and several articles on late Middle English literature. She was, for ten years, Editor of *Parergon*, Journal of the Australian and New Zealand Association for Medieval and Early Modern Studies.

The chapters are arranged thematically, under headings of "The Emotional Costs of War," "Voicing Conflict," and "The Impact of War."

While within the sections the chapters are arranged in, generally, chronological order, an exception is made for White's Shakespearean study, "Love in Times of War: War Wives and Widows in Shakespeare." This chapter encapsulates many of the issues taken up in the course of the following chapters; just as Shakespeare ostensibly writes for all times and peoples, White's chapter points out the universality of themes concerning war, themes which will be picked up and applied to specific times and texts by the later chapters. In choosing to consider war wives and widows, White concentrates on characters who are often so marginal as to make a single, brief appearance in a play, speaking no more than a few lines, yet those are fraught with intense though scarcely articulated emotion. He shows how, in a few broad strokes, Shakespeare portrays women's keenly felt experience of severance, loss, or, as in the case of Henry V's war bride Catherine, forced surrender to an unsympathetic victor/husband. Importantly for this collection, which references the modern in its connection to the pre-modern, White draws attention to the way Shakespeare speaks to modern times, pointing out resonances which anticipate in his plays the genre of the modern "war movie." Referencing Paul Fussell's classic study *The Great War and Modern Memory*, White speaks of war as an "experience" which has enough similarities from age to age to confer some kind of continuity and human significance through each occurrence. As the subsequent chapters unfold, the themes addressed by White are picked up and applied to works written in different ages and genres, always addressing the human impact of conflict or war.

The Emotional Costs of War

The following three chapters in this first section concern themselves directly with emotional disjunction caused by the circumstances of war or conflict. Stephanie Trigg and Stephanie Downes write of the emotions experienced by three women, two fictional characters and one historical person, who are used as tools through which men believe they can make a truce between warring nations. Their reasoning is that "when war concludes with a marriage alliance, the symbolic and practical involvement of women in securing peace is paramount." Symbolic and practical the involvement may be; however, this chapter analyzes closely the emotional cost the women must bear so that the men may make the peace. Chaucer's heroine in *Troilus and Criseyde* finds her life torn apart by her severance from Troilus when she is sent to the Greek camp in a hostage exchange for the Trojan, Antenor; the chapter portrays her extreme vulnerability, preyed upon by Diomede who poses as her only protector within a hostile camp. A second damaged woman, Isabelle, the young widow of the assassinated King Richard II, is returned to France by Richard's successor in the hopes of securing peace between the two nations. Contemporary chronicle accounts paint a picture of distress and indignation on the part of Isabelle and both grief and joy among her French and English followers, differently interpreted according to the chronicler's own political sympathies. The third woman, Queen Guenevere, is returned to Arthur by Lancelot ostensibly in order to maintain the peace of the Round Table. Conflicted though the emotions of Guenevere, Lancelot and Arthur may be between shame, love, and injured loyalty, as Trigg and Downes say,

> in the act of restoration women are reduced—or elevated—to their status as ceremonial symbols; ideally as symbols of peace, but often in practice as symbols of more complex external relationships or internal feelings ... The primary social symbolism of each woman ... is as a promise of peacetime in the midst of war.

In all these instances, the complex feelings of the women who are the focus of the peace negotiations are of no consequence in practice, and the fact that the sought-for peace is in each case either short-lived or a downright failure only heightens the poignancy of these war-damaged women's wasted emotions.

Following with a study of another Chaucerian text, the *Knight's Tale*, Raluca Radulescu addresses the notion of "roaming" as an indicator of emotional expression and development among three young people, each of whom is a prisoner of war. Confined within their respective spaces, Palamon and Arcite in their prison tower, Emelye in her garden, each one suffers more from the emotion of love than from the imprisonment that war has caused, albeit an imprisonment which is the instrument that enables them to fall in love. Yet as the tale unfolds, it is this love that Palamon and Arcite both feel for Emelye that changes their personal relationship. From being loving cousins and sworn brothers in warfare, they change to being enemies and rivals in love, with fatal consequences. The confined "roaming" of the three young people inverts the normal expectations of knights who roam freely in landscapes seeking adventure and the love of a lady. Radulescu suggests that the emotions the knights display in the pursuit of Emelye "show how the trauma of both war and incarceration has altered their perception of reality and their response to stimuli."

Underlying the emotional content of all the examples already mentioned is the massive component of grief experienced by all: lovers, hostages, and the women treated as political pawns. Karen Cherewatuk in the next chapter addresses grief as a common and indeed a major emotional experience in *Le Morte Darthur*. She closely examines the grief and mourning that result from armed combat and shows how grief is moved from the edges of the narrative to the centre in the death scenes of the final huge conflict. By doing so, she distinguishes grief as an individual reaction, producing effects of swooning, weeping, and sometimes enraged action in search of revenge, while mourning, equally intense, is more communal. In conclusion, she writes that "In material culture, tombs are sites that merge love, loss, grief, and mourning. So too in the textual culture represented in the *Morte Darthur*. Malory achieves this effect by employing rhetoric that heightens the sorrow expressed there."

Voicing Conflict

Rhetoric enables the poet to give voice to the complexity of emotion and so the second section of the volume, "Voicing conflict," moves from the analysis of emotions to broader concerns related to human behaviour in war and conflict. Ad Putter's study, *The Battle of Maldon* and of *Beowulf*, addresses an aspect hitherto unnoticed by critics of Old English poetry: the remarkable emphasis the poets place on the need to "remember." Arguing that it is inaccurate to think of warriors in these poems acting according to a preordained code of conduct, Putter suggests instead that they make choices informed by loyalty. In the Old English heroic context, to remember is more than a cognitive impulse, it is a call to action, to recall and to fulfil in action the promises made in peacetime. "Voicing" invokes loyalty through vows made in the mead hall and remembered on the battlefield. As Putter says, "This form of 'remembering' is about 'overt action' that makes present behaviour consistent with past behaviour." Those who remember in this way become heroes; those who forget are cowards.

Helen Dell finds that codes of conduct reflected in the *chansons de croisade* express loyalties conflicted between duties owed to God and duties owed to the lady. Given voice in the chansons, tropes that recur draw upon ideas of loyalty to God to whom the soldier is bound by feudal ties as a Christian vassal and by the ties of gratitude for his sacrifice in the crucifixion. In this, the crusaders resemble the heroes of Old English poetry discussed in the previous chapter; but service of God in the Crusades may conflict with service of the lady who, in the tradition of *fin'amors*, sometimes rivals the pull of God. Dell teases out the complexities set up when the lover has to break the code of *fin'amors* by placing service to God above service to his lady. In these songs, the reward afforded by the lady is distant, indefinite, always in the future, whereas the reward promised by God is defined and attainable. Service in the crusade will bring heavenly reward and perhaps a martyr's crown; service to the lady brings the agonizing delight of unfulfilled but potentially exquisite love. In terms of the *chanson de croisade* genre, as Dell says, "to have two supreme figures, God and the Lady, in opposition but very differently positioned in relation (or non-relation) to the lover and his desire, was obviously a gift to the genre in the complexities it offered."

The conflict between Christ and Lucifer in *Piers Plowman* takes the idea of warfare onto the metaphysical plane, and Langland voices the opposition between Christ and sin through powerful images. Anne M. Scott traces the many occurrences of the image of Christ as a knight and his conflict with sin and death as a joust, images particularly germane to the themes covered in this volume. It is through imagery that Langland finds a voice to elucidate the mysterious union of divinity and humanity in Christ and his vanquishing of sin, imaged as the devil. Langland's understanding of God is of a triune being, and his poem makes sense of God's presence in the mundane world by imaging the ways in which the deity became human. The logic flowing from this truth is that only God can vanquish sin, and only a God who understands human nature can understand the reality of sin. But the overall impact of the imagery is to bring into clear focus Langland's portrayal of Christ as the embodiment of love, that all-pervasive attribute of God that he shares with human beings to their eternal benefit. The poem demonstrates convincingly that the crucifixion of Christ, though apparently inglorious, is an act of triumph in the battle between Christ and Lucifer. Of all the wars that are dealt with in the course of this volume, this one is absolutely necessary. Love can do no other than joust to vanquish evil. The poem presents this understanding as something to be embraced by the reader for the good of the soul; the text is one which invites a response of the mind and heart.

Stressing embodiment in valour and emotion, Corinne Saunders draws on recent research to show the significance of breath in *Le Morte Darthur*. The chapter explores the treatment of breath (and breathlessness) in *Le Morte Darthur* within its wider late medieval medical, literary and cultural contexts, looking in particular at breath in relation to war and peace, knightly prowess, and emotion. Linking with earlier chapters in this collection which discuss the tears and swooning connected with grief, Saunders more fully explores *Le Morte Darthur*, finding that breath articulates and makes visible emotion, in joy, but most of all in laments, sighs, and swoons. Breath, she explains, is also integral to knightly prowess; the movements of breath mark the greatness in love and war of Malory's protagonists, Launcelot, Tristram, Lamorak, Palomides. And in the Grail Quest, the spiritual is seen and felt in the movements of the air and the embodied experience of vision, through tears, sleep, and swoon.

The last chapter in this section, by James Simpson, discusses drama as a way of giving voice to those who suffer the ills of civil war, and gaining voice for the different members of the polity whose lives are impacted by civil war. Political theory and historical fiction are two possible ways of gaining voice and gaining traction in a civil war context. Another is drama, which gains voice by giving voice. Both England and France were affected by civil war in the fifteenth century, and Alain Chartier's *Quadrilogue Invectif* was translated from French into English in two versions. Where *Piers Plowman* is written in a register that invites shared contemplation of divine mysteries, the *Quadrilogue* registers that three estates, knights, clergy and people, have been given voices in order that a parliamentary, national voice be gained. Both of these texts set out to cause change, the *Quadrilogue* within a disturbed national polity, *Piers Plowman* within a universal need for spiritual coherence.

The Impact of War

The final section, "The Impact of War," contains three chapters which highlight some unexpected consequences of the impact of war. John Ganim outlines the way the Crusades reemerge in European national romances in the fifteenth century giving rise to literary forms of the new romance and epic. In these romances, the historical frame of reference is not the loss of Jerusalem in 1187, but the fall of Constantinople in 1453. Hosts of warriors set off to defeat what Ganim describes as a "disturbingly refashioned infidel," with the Ottoman Empire representing an absolutist sovereignty that resembles those developing in Western Europe which threaten the political existence of the knightly classes: "The Ottoman empire, under Western eyes, seems to loom as an absolute state, which it is not, while the regalia of the Christian feudal west increasingly disguises and often abets a radical centralization of power that dissolves both the knightly class and the hope for a universal Christianity." Ganim sees the thrust of the new romances as expressing the clash of nation versus empire, with the Saracen representing the power of the Ottoman Empire, and the knights often conflicted between adherence to an older variant of civilization and the reality of the newer one whose political status is, nevertheless, often indistinguishable from that of the Saracen "other."

Susan Broomhall focuses specifically on place, namely the forests of France ravaged during the course of the sixteenth-century wars of religion between Huguenot and Catholic factions. Looking at three textual sources, horticultural, political, and poetic, she explores the way the ideals of silviculture were systematically ignored and forests destroyed under the guise of expediency, by both warring factions. She writes that "France's forests supplied the firepower for numerous technologies of war, were destroyed in its crossfire, and enlisted as a financial resource to fuel partisan politics." Her chapter takes a fresh look at the complex relationships between faith behaviours and the environments, natural and constructed, in which they were practised. She refers to the works on forestry management by Pierre Belon and Bernard Palissy, the latter a Protestant self-taught natural philosopher and theologian, who stresses the need for productive management of forests in tune with their existence as gifts of God and nature. But the strongest arguments are made by the poet Pierre de Ronsard, who had first-hand experience of his own forests and wrote with scathing satire against the politically motivated destruction of forests sanctioned by the religious leaders. Conceptual notions of "taming" forests for man's needs, the forest as a victim of war, and as a material manifestation of God's design and His providence are explored in this chapter to unlock both the spiritual and physical impact of war on a natural resource.

The final chapter acts as a type of coda, and demonstrates how medieval memories, symbols, and literary genres permeate modern thinking and give scope for creating a retrospective view of history that both romanticizes the medieval past and equally gives rise to nationalistic, ethnocentric, and Christocentric interpretations of the past that continue into the present. Louise D'Arcens explores how the anti-war satirical films of Mario Monicelli present a strong rebuttal to such medievalist triumphalism, offering themselves as "a meta-parody in which medieval chivalry and medievalist representation are lampooned by depicting a Middle Ages that is manifestly not real, but nevertheless aims to be true." Monicelli aims to show the impact of war from the point of view of "the humble people, the little guy."[1] D'Arcens discusses in detail *The Great War* and the *Brancaleone* films. In these, mordant comedy shows the audience world-historical events "as experienced by those who gain little and lose much from the wars waged by authorities and institutions, such as churches, armies, and governments." D'Arcens uses these films to demonstrate how war has, over the centuries and continuing into modern times, exposed to danger and destruction those with little say over the political and economic forces that determine their lives. Her chapter cleverly exposes the medievalist war depicted in the films as "a world which, despite being amusingly distant, was also unsettlingly familiar."

---

[1] Deborah Young, "Poverty, Misery, War and Other Comic Material: An Interview with Mario Monicelli," *Cinéaste* 29 (2004), quoted on page x.

Conclusion

The collection of essays in *Literature, Emotions, and Pre-Modern War* allows critical exploration of a wide range of textual and historical sources, some widely known and others of a more obscure nature. Under the broad monikers of emotion, voicing, and impact, they examine and explicate the many subtleties of how war and conflict can affect the human condition. The single work of literature that characterizes the dominant influence of Andrew Lynch on studies of war and emotions is Malory's *Le Morte Darthur*. This work is referenced by many authors throughout the volume as a work that celebrates courage, heroism, and great love: filial, fraternal, and romantic. Yet it is also a work that evokes immense sadness in the reader who witnesses and shares in the catastrophic destruction of the Round Table and all its lofty ideals.

The chapters in this volume offer reflections on the past, exploring how people's lives and environments have been impacted by battles and war. Taking texts as far apart as the Old English heroic poem *The Battle of Maldon*, and twentieth-century war movies such as the Olivier *Henry V* which sets out to glorify war, and Mario Monicelli's *Brancaleone* films which satirize it, the authors demonstrate the long reach of war. It becomes clear that heroism, grief, politics, and empire are enduring components in war and conflict. These chapters demonstrate that pre-modern texts can give voice to experiences of war which are both culturally distant from the present day, and yet recognizable in their effect on the vulnerable, both lands and people. Following on from recent works on the experience of war, particularly *Writing War: Medieval Literary Responses to Warfare*, *Emotions and War: Medieval to Romantic Literature*, and *Writing War in Britain and France, 1370–1854: A History of Emotion*,[2] and in line with the sentiments expressed in the Preface, this volume seeks to place experience of the long tentacles of war as a continuum altogether "unsettlingly familiar."

---

[2] Corinne Saunders, Françoise Le Saux, and Thomas Neil, ed. *Writing War: Medieval Literary Responses to Warfare* (Woodbridge: Brewer, 2004). Stephanie Downes, Andrew Lynch, and Katrina O'Loughlin, ed. *Emotions and War: Medieval to Romantic Literature* (Basingstoke: Palgrave Macmillan, 2015); and Stephanie Downes, Andrew Lynch, and Katrina O'Loughlin, ed. *Writing War in Britain and France, 1370–1854: A History of Emotions* (London: Routledge, 2018).

Chapter 1

LOVE IN TIMES OF WAR: SOME SHAKESPEAREAN REFLECTIONS

Robert S. White*

THE SUBJECT OF war in Elizabethan literature, and Shakespeare's plays in particular, has attracted attention from a variety of perspectives.[1] However, it is usually treated in the light of military manuals, as a technical subject which is "men's work," and the masculine discourse dominates. There are many books on Shakespeare containing the words "military" and "war," but accounts using peace as touchstone for discussion are few and far between.[2] The question is rarely raised: what happens to love in times of war? In discussions of the comedies, the existence of war is either ignored altogether or regarded as background;[3] in tragedies, the loss of love is seen as inextricably part of the male protagonist's fate; history plays, while keeping war in the foreground, downgrade love to moments of contrast. However, with the renewed critical interest in emotions, the nexus between war and love emerges as a subject inviting closer attention.

Shakespeare's treatment of love in times of war poses new questions. How important is the disturbing setting of military conflict to the vision of a play as a whole? How central is the imagery of war to the foregrounded love in such plays as *The Comedy of Errors*,

---

* **Robert S. White** (FAHA) has been Winthrop Professor of English at UWA, and a Chief Investigator in the Australian Research Council Centre of Excellence in the History of Emotions. He has held an Australian Research Council Professorial Fellowship, and visiting research fellowships, most recently at Magdalen College, Oxford. Publications are mainly on Shakespeare, Keats, and the history of emotions, recently including *John Keats: A Literary Life* (2010), *Pacifism in English Literature: Minstrels of Peace* (2008), *Avant-Garde Hamlet* and *Shakespeare's Cinema of Love* (2016), and *Keats's Anatomy of Melancholy: "Lamia, Isabella, The Eve of St Agnes and Other Poems (1820)"* (2020). He co-edited *Shakespeare and Emotions, The New Fortune Theatre: That Vast Open Stage*, and *Hamlet and Emotions* (2018).

1 See especially C. G. Cruickshank, *Elizabeth's Army* (London: Oxford University Press, 1946); Paul A. Jorgensen, *Shakespeare's Military World* (Los Angeles: California University Press, 1956); Theodor Meron, *Bloody Constraint: War and Chivalry in Shakespeare* (Oxford: Oxford University Press, 1998); Nick de Somogyi, *Shakespeare's Theatre of War* (Aldershot: Ashgate, 1998); Charles Edelman, *Shakespeare's Military Language: A Dictionary* (London: Athlone, 2000); Simon Barker, *War and Nation in the Theatre of Shakespeare and his Contemporaries* (Edinburgh: Edinburgh University Press, 2007).

2 See Robert S. White, *Pacifism and English Literature: Minstrels of Peace* (London: Palgrave, 2008) and John S. Garrison and Kyle Pivetti, *Shakespeare at Peace* (London: Routledge, 2019).

3 Among exceptions which analyze war in the comedies are the chapters by Helen Wilcox and Ruth Morse in *Shakespeare and War*, ed. Ros King and J. C. M. Franssen (Basingstoke: Palgrave Macmillan, 2008).

Much Ado about Nothing, and *All's Well that Ends Well* among comedies, in *Othello*, *Antony and Cleopatra* and *Troilus and Cressida* among tragedies, and civil "brawls" in *Romeo and Juliet*? Is it important that a play framed within a military or belligerent context may be paradoxically and centrally about love? Even the chronicle plays, which are invariably focused on war at some stage, contain inset scenes demonstrating the different ways in which public belligerence affects private, marital relationships based on marriage and love. The respective war wives, eventually widows, Kate, Lady Percy (wife of Hotspur), Queen Isabel (Richard II), Calpurnia (Caesar), and Portia (Brutus), are just a few of the innocents who suffer "collateral damage" in an emotional sense during times of national conflict.[4] Is the often stark conjunction of love or marriage on the one hand, and war on the other, an interdependence, or an antithesis, an alternative resolution of conflict, or simply a narrative coincidence? Answers to such questions differ from play to play, as I hope to show. It is, however, revealing that Shakespeare chooses to touch so often on these chords if only in small cameos, glimpses of a larger, menacing linkage between violent war and fragile emotional relationships.

The subtitles in this chapter, reprising movies from the Second World War, might help by allusion to suggest comparisons with a more familiar, modern context yoking love and war. Whether Shakespeare anticipated these ways of seeing, or alternatively whether the conditions of war remain depressingly unchanging or recurrent through history, at least resonances in his plays anticipate the genre of the "war movie." Paul Fussell, in his classic study *The Great War and Modern Memory*, speaks of war as an "experience" which has enough similarities from age to age to confer some kind of continuity and human significance through each occurrence.[5] Either that, or Shakespeare's history plays laid down a generic blueprint for later depictions of love in war. The development of sympathetic sensibility in the eighteenth century inescapably governs modern treatments, but we find in Shakespeare sparer, unsentimental treatments of similar emotional material, embedded sometimes so unobtrusively in his narratives that commentary and performance have neglected them.

In Which We Serve

War affects all levels of society, provoking a whole gamut of often extreme emotional states such as courage, elation, fear, shame, pride in one's nation or hostility against its government, anger at a constructed enemy or at the violence itself, trauma, grief for the lost ones, and many others. Some are collective states, others personal, and some, such as the persecution and hostility endured by conscientious objectors, lonely. Some are typically felt by men or by women, by combatants or non-combatants, by a particular class or community. However, one way or another, to some degree war touches the emotional lives of each and every person living in a country at war, whether international or civil.

---

4 Ruth Morse discusses the semantics of "civilian" and "casualty" in her fine essay, "Some Social Costs of War," in *Shakespeare and War* (Basingstoke: Palgrave Macmillan, 2008), 56–68 at 60–61.
5 Paul Fussell, *The Great War and Modern Memory* (Oxford: Oxford University Press, 1975), *passim*.

Noel Coward's classic wartime film *In Which We Serve* (1942), like Shakespeare's chronicle plays based on historical sources, is structured to show that war affects the lives of whole populations, irrespective of gender, age, or especially class. This was part of a conscious "nation-building" intention behind the film which was supported by the British Navy, as it was behind Olivier's *Henry V* (1944) with the blessing of the RAF and the British War Office. In the former, flashbacks to family life before the War and flash-forwards to the men perilously stranded on a raft after their ship has been sunk show that war is not severed from time but comes from the past and renders uncertain the future. War is a state in which *all* "serve" and all suffer, suspending expectations of "normal" emotional lives. Equally and inevitably, war alters the course of emotions that in peacetime would run peacefully—love, marriage, and child-rearing—and war is a rent in family security, as the commoner Williams in *Henry V* sagely points out, questioning the legitimacy of the king's military invasion of France:

> But if the cause be not good, the King himself hath a heavy reckoning to make, when all those legs and arms and heads chopped off in a battle shall join together at the latter day, and cry all, "We died at such a place"—some swearing, some crying for a surgeon, some upon their wives left poor behind them, some upon the debts they owe, some upon their children rawly left. I am afeard there are few die well that die in a battle, for how can they charitably dispose of anything, when blood is their argument?
>
> (4.1.127–36)[6]

The subject of love in war crosses boundaries of Shakespeare's dramatic genres and also tears across dramatic genres. Writing on war in *All's Well that Ends Well*, Helen Wilcox points out that genre influences the presentation and ideological attitudes to war.[7] In comedies, "conflict is almost always located in the past and often coloured by symbolic or amorous purposes," whereas the tragedies "construct war as integral to their mood of crisis." Meanwhile, the so-called "problem plays" pit against each other satire and romance, optimism and pessimism, weaving "good and ill together" in the manner of the "mingled yarn" of life itself. Wilcox examines "the tragicomedy of war" in *All's Well* as an example. While not contesting these useful distinctions, in this chapter I hope to further argue that, in the majority of Shakespeare's plays, armed conflict is implicated in "amorous purposes" and that the course of true love in such cases is, at the very least, contingent on wars that may rage elsewhere or even in the past.

The War Widow

Although no trace remains of the plot in the silent, one-reel movie, *War and the Widow* (1911), the title gives some indication of its subject-matter, its date showing that the war widow is a perennial casualty of every war, not exclusively of the "Great" wars of the twentieth century. War separates families, most poignantly young wives from their husbands, first by the enforced absence of military service and then by death. *The*

---

6 Quotations are from *The Complete Oxford Shakespeare*, ed. Stanley Wells and Gary Taylor (Oxford: Oxford University Press, 1987).

7 Helen Wilcox, "Drums and Roses?," in *Shakespeare and War*, 84–95.

Two Noble Kinsmen, based on Chaucer's the *Knight's Tale*, opens with a moving scene, universally accepted as written by Shakespeare though the play was co-authored with Fletcher, depicting the circumstances of two wars. Three Theban queens, widowed in civil war by the tyrant Creon, plead with Theseus, himself newly returned victorious from the war against the Amazons and sporting his own bride-to-be Hippolyta, to make war against Creon and recover the bodies of their husbands to give them burial rites. Significantly, the queens appeal to the feminine empathy of Hippolyta and her sister Emilia to intercede with Theseus, lamenting the fate of their husbands on the battlefield:

> Tell him, if he i'th'blood-sized field lay swollen,
> Showing the sun his teeth, grinning at the moon,
> What you would do.
> (1.1.99–101)

The play draws a contrast between Athens, in which a war has ended with a conciliatory marriage between the victor and vanquished, and fratricidal Thebes which has generated grief-stricken widows, and the cameo of war's destructiveness is presented from the female point of view. Hippolyta and Emilia later perform the same function by persuading Theseus not to execute the Theban prisoners of war, Palamon and Arcite.

The fate of the war widow can be anticipated even when it lies in the future. In *Henry IV Part One* Sir Henry Percy (Harry Hotspur) manages the moment of separation from his wife with characteristically abrupt bluntness: "How now, Kate! I must leave you within these two hours" (2.4.36). Lady Percy is more fully conscious of the divided claims of war and love in their emotional lives. Her harrowed description, longer than it needs to be for its narrative function, powerfully evokes the heavy toll taken on married life by war even before death itself strikes, describing herself as "a banished woman from my Harry's bed":

> Why hast thou lost the fresh blood in thy cheeks,
> And given my treasures and my rights of thee
> To thick-eyed musing and curst melancholy?
> In thy faint slumbers I by thee have watched,
> And heard thee murmur tales of iron wars,
> Speak terms of manège to thy bounding steed,
> Cry "Courage! To the field!" And thou hast talked
> Of sallies and retires, of trenches, tents,
> Of palisadoes, frontiers, parapets,
> Of basilisks, of cannon, culverin,
> Of prisoners ransomed, and of soldiers slain,
> And all the currents of a heady fight.
> ... O, what portents are these?
> Some heavy business hath my lord in hand,
> And I must know it, else he loves me not.
> (2.4.37–64)

Lady Percy's attentive and detailed cataloguing of her husband's behaviour, awake and asleep, marks her out as one already in effect widowed to war, since war is already internalized as a third, adversary presence in the marriage. She has been placed in the position of the modern "golf widow," effectively abandoned to her husband's passion. Andrew Hiscock points out that her imagery suggests that, although "determined not to submit to the prevailing *zeitgeist* of warfare," the wife's suffering is conspicuously marginalized:

> If she repeatedly attempts to challenge with unfailing eloquence the military ambitions of her husband, it is revealing that even she is unable to purge her language of the lexis of the battlefield. Hotspur's night-time catechism "of sallies and retires, of trenches, tents/ Of palisadoes, frontiers, parapets" is clearly deeply engraved in her consciousness and remains her only means of mental navigation through the war-torn landscape.[8]

Hotspur is unresponsive to his wife's eloquent and anxious pleas. To Kate's persistent questioning, "But hear you, my lord," he is distracted, and callously facetious in response to her cry, "What is it carries you away?:" "Why, my horse,/My love, my horse" (2.4.73–5). Reproving his levity, she teases, again using imagery of violence, however meagre: "In faith, I'll break thy little finger, Harry,/An if thou wilt not tell me all things true." His reply is even more brutally final, unsoftened by any hint of domestic affection:

> Away, away, you trifler! Love? I love thee not,
> I care not for thee, Kate. This is no world
> To play with maumets and to tilt with lips.
> We must have bloody noses and cracked crowns,
> And pass them current, too. God's me, my horse!
> (2.4.87–91)

Love and marriage are central to the woman's world, an integral part of her identity:

> Do you not love me? Do you not, indeed?
> Well, do not, then, for since you love me not,
> I will not love myself.
> (2.4.92–6)

Hotspur evasively downgrades love to a status below horse riding: "Come, wilt thou see me ride?" (2.4.97). In the gentlest tone he can muster, he explains that no matter how "wise" his wife is, "constant you are,/But yet a woman" and therefore (in his view) not to be trusted with knowledge of war. His promise that she will follow him meets with a resigned fatalism: "Will this content you, Kate?/LADY PERCY It must of force" (2.4.111–14).

We see the couple once more (3.1) in Wales. Hotspur is ill-at-ease and contemptuous in this bucolic context, in the familial company of his wife's brother, Mortimer, and her uncle Glendower whose daughter sings and plays the harp. Theatrically, the music sets up a strong tonal contrast to the tumult of war raging elsewhere, though Hotspur is

---

8 Andrew Hiscock, "Shakespeare and the Fortunes of War and Memory," *Société Française Shakespeare* 30 (2013): 11–26 at para. 12.

mockingly unable to appreciate the moment of rare harmony and stasis: "LADY PERCY Lie still, ye thief, and hear the lady sing in Welsh./HOTSPUR I had rather hear Lady my brach howl in Irish." (3.1.223–32). Hotspur, mentally as much a victim of the imagery of war as his wife, impatiently urges the men to leave for battle. He is later to win a grudging eulogy from the victorious Hal, but his wife is left to suffer in silence, unseen and offstage, though it is clear the loss of emotional intimacy with her husband happens long before his death in battle. He has so compulsively identified with his profession that his emotional life and capacity to love are stunted, and Shakespeare implicitly gives a prospective insight into the war widow's fate.

The Best Years of Our Lives

The title of William Wyler's classic film made in 1946 is deeply ironic and has multiple reverberations. Depicting the return to civilian and family life of three veterans after the Second World War, the emphasis is on the damage sustained by them which incapacitates them from social re-assimilation. In one case this is physical impairment, in the others psychological or marital, all caused by war. These "veterans" (though they are still little more than youths) return from war in the promised expectation of "the best years of their lives," to enjoy peacetime and stable relationships in "homes built for heroes." However, it becomes clear that "the best years" are behind them, for they now carry debilitating scars, visible and invisible, frequently afflicted with mental conditions like post-traumatic stress disorder. In yet another, more homely sense, the phrase "the best years of our lives" has been worn into a cliché by many nostalgic for the ways in which communities were brought together in times of war, by the remembered camaraderie between soldiers and sometimes the heightened intensity of emotional liaisons and love affairs overshadowed by the ever-present spectre of violent death for combatants. However, as the Wyler film shows, war is aberrational and has continuing and lifelong consequences for individuals and communities. Likewise, Shakespeare reflects an understanding of these different and contrasting perspectives on victims of war.

War in Shakespeare's plays is a ubiquitous presence, though its significance is obscured. A point about *Hamlet* in particular made by Paola Pugliatti in her book *Shakespeare and the Just War Tradition* can be applied to most of the plays, even the comedies. She describes *Hamlet* as "the play in which war, although absent as staged event, is most insistently present both as topic of discussion and as metaphor.... Although war is visually absent from the action, the pressure of the threat of war does not relent throughout the whole play."[9] Indeed, England itself must have struck commoners as in a state comparable to Elsinore's war-footing. Ever since Elizabeth had been on the throne, the nation had been prepared for invasions or war of some kind, though despite conflicts at sea culminating in the defeat of the Spanish Armada, military engagement did not reach its shores. The bellicose language directed at the Spanish and constant fears of

---

9 Paola Pugliatti, *Shakespeare and the Just War Tradition* (Farnham: Ashgate, 2010), 139.

Scottish marauders and Irish rebels created a prevailing atmosphere of impending siege, while English men were also conscripted into armies on foreign service in the ongoing European conflicts between Catholic and Protestant nations which threatened to engulf their own country. Meanwhile, mercenaries choosing or forced into military service in foreign wars were returning in a continual stream, not only bearing tales and all-too-obvious wounds, but also often posing threats to law and order in civilian society:

> soldiers returning maimed from Continental wars found themselves adrift when their services were no longer required. The consequences were an increase, real or perceived, in rates of crime and civil disorder.[10]

Such individuals and groups were socially conspicuous enough to find their way into plays such as the one these days attributed to Dekker, *A Larum for London, or the siedge of Antwerpe: with the vertuous actes and valorous deedes of the lame Soldier* (1602). The "lame Soldier" is Lieutenant Stump:

> *Enter a Soldier*
> *Sol.* Arme you my Lord, and to the fight againe,
> A crew of stragling Soldiers (lately vanquisht)
> Haue gathered head, and in the heate of rage,
> Giue fresh assault: the leader to the rest,
> Is a lame fellow that doth want a legge,
> Who layes about him like a deuill of hell.
> ...
> It is impossible to passe the streetes,
> They are so pesterd with this brainsicke crew.
> (1054–60; 1066–67)

More compassionate voices were raised against the lack of adequate aid for returned soldiers who had, for example, left to "fight for *Antwerps* libertie" against the Spanish:

> A swettie Cobler, whose best industrie,
> Is but to cloute a Shoe, shall haue his fee;
> But let a Soldier, that hath spent his bloud,
> Is lam'd, diseas'd, or any way distrest,
> Appeale for succour, then you looke a sconce
> As if you knew him not.
> (609–14)[11]

Soldiers, then, could be victims, especially when they had no say in their conscription. The sight of soldiers returning from various conflicts without a leg or an arm was common enough to be figured in stage plays in characters like lame Ralph in Dekker's

---

10 *Broadview Anthology of Sixteenth-Century Poetry and Prose*, ed. Marie Loughlin, Sandra Bell, and Patricia Brace (Ontario: Broadview, 2012), 377, citing Paul Griffiths, *Lost Londons: Change, Crime, and Control in the Capital City, 1550–1660* (Cambridge: Cambridge University Press, 2008).

11 Quotations from Thomas Dekker, *A Larum for London, or the Siedge of Antwerpe: with the vertuous actes and valorous deedes of the lame Soldier*, ed. W. W. Greg. Malone Society Reprints (Oxford: Oxford University Press, 1913).

The Shoemaker's Holiday, Captain Bowyer in *The Trial of Chivalry*, Lieutenant "Stump" in *A Larum for London*, and the emblematic, unknown veteran evoked by Boult in Shakespeare's *Pericles*:

> What would you have me do? go to the wars, would you, where a man may serve seven years for the loss of a leg, and have not money enough in the end to buy him a wooden one? (4.6.185–87)

In one of several curious loose ends in *Twelfth Night*, Orsino is reminded that his "young nephew Titus lost his leg" on a naval vessel called the *Tiger* (5.1.58). The physical plight of such figures drew attention to their grievances and to the pitifully inadequate welfare made available to disabled veterans by successive Acts of government.[12]

There are, likewise, returned soldiers with other problems, such as the culturally misplaced Armado in *Love's Labour's Lost*, who may have been originally a prisoner of war. There are those suffering from what we would call post-traumatic stress, amongst whom would be the gun-happy Pistol in *2 Henry IV*. He appears to be clinically shell-shocked into anti-social violence and suicidal impulses ("Then death rock me asleep, abridge my doleful days" [2.4.194]). He enters the tavern indiscriminately offering to "discharge" his gun, and is mocked by Doll Tearsheet as a "poor, base, rascally, cheating, lack-linen Mate," drunk, idle, and "mouldy," a "fustian rascal," ridiculing his military status. His "choler," which Mistress Quickly malapropistically begs him to "aggravate," threatens a brawl until Falstaff drives him out with his sword, restoring a tenuous peace which allows a kind of love scene to be played out between Falstaff and Doll.

This tavern scene reflects conditions in which courtship would have proceeded against the ever-present, palpable threat of impending battle and future insecurity, verbalized in Falstaff's already elegiac fears (see below). At the same time, the conditions provide matter for later nostalgia, as people recall how emotionally close they were brought in times of peril, and the scene is marked by a kind of proleptic or anticipated nostalgia. Falstaff himself, in his obesity and age, may not have been a typical lover, but the circumstances are exemplary, since poverty and uncertainty in England created a constant sense that fit young men could face unemployment which allowed no alternative but to enlist in the army, or be dragooned unwillingly. Falstaff's effort to raise a rag-tag group of soldiers in Gloucestershire, however comic and satirical in presentation, was also no doubt a common experience in villages throughout England.[13] Intriguingly, Shakespeare's own father, as an alderman in Stratford, was responsible for recruitment to put down a rebellion in 1569. While those conscripted were likely to include some who were poor, feeble, or ill, like Mouldy, Shadow, and Feeble, as in all wars it would have been mainly the Peter Bullcalfs of the world, able-bodied young men ripe for marriage, who would have been conscripted, especially if they were unemployed

---

12 de Somogyi, *Shakespeare's Theatre of War*, 8, 11ff.

13 See Edelman, *Shakespeare's Military Language* under entries such as "Levy," "Muster," and "Press."

victims of agricultural changes happening at the time. War is also always a generational matter since young men are invariably placed first in the firing line. Of necessity, as Bardolph points out, "a Soldier is better accommodated than with a wife," but equally, as Mouldy spells out, there could be disastrous consequences for whole families, when unmarried economic breadwinners were siphoned off into often unpaid military service. Mouldy pleads on behalf of his mother: "She has nobody to do anything about her when I am gone, and she is old and cannot help herself" (3.2.227–29). Some would not return alive, others would come back to families and relationships in no fit state to sustain amatory adventures, but instead maimed, incapacitated, poverty stricken, and traumatized.

The recruiting officer is not innocent of damages wrought by war. Falstaff himself in *2 Henry IV* is very different from the resilient and bombastic character bearing his name in *1 Henry IV*. Blaming the war for the fact that he is no longer adroit and active enough to evade trouble, he is also dogged by creditors and the Chief Justice for unpaid debts, and living in fear of the consequences of the Gadshill exploit which had been plotted by Poins and Hal but is potentially cause for Falstaff to be impeached and hanged. He is ill with "more diseases than he knew for" (*2 Henry IV*, 1.2.4). And, in his own particular way, he is in love and loved, since both he and Doll Tearsheet are haunted on a music-filled night before armed conflict, by fears he may die on the battlefield.

> SIR JOHN Sit on my knee, Doll ...
>
> DOLL TEARSHEET ... Thou whoreson little tidy Bartholomew boar-pig, when wilt thou leave fighting o' days, and foining o' nights, and begin to patch up thine old body for heaven?
>
> SIR JOHN Peace, good Doll! do not speak like a death's-head, do not bid me remember mine end.
>
> (2.4.227–37)

"Kiss me Doll ... I am old, I am old," he intones, provoking Doll's touchingly understated admission of affection, "By my troth, I kiss thee with a most constant heart ... I love thee better than I love e'er a scurvy young boy of them all" (2.4.271, 275). But Falstaff is determined at least temporarily to stave off melancholy:

> SIR JOHN
>
> ... A merry song! Come, it grows late; we'll to bed. Thou'lt forget me when I am gone.
>
> DOLL TEARSHEET
>
> By my troth, thou'lt set me a-weeping, an thou sayest so. Prove that ever I dress myself handsome till thy return—well, harken a'th'end.
>
> (2.4.276–83 *passim*)

Ironically, Falstaff's cowardice—or "discretion" as "the better half of valour"—will save him from the soldier's fate. To close the tavern scene, insistent knocking at the door comes as a call to arms, disrupting the atmosphere of deferred grief with forced bravado:

SIR JOHN

[To the Page] Pay the musicians, sirrah. Farewell, hostess; farewell, Doll. You see, my good wenches, how men of merit are sought after. The undeserver may sleep, when the man of action is called on. Farewell, good wenches. If I be not sent away post, I will see you again ere I go.

DOLL TEARSHEET [*weeping*]

I cannot speak. If my heart be not ready to burst—well, sweet Jack, have a care of thyself.

SIR JOHN

Farewell, farewell!

(2.4.376-85)

Contrasting with this tender parting, the farewell from one who is emotionally little more than a "scurvy young boy," Prince Hal, is perfunctory, and without a hint of regret that the seedy but warm-hearted conviviality in the tavern is now over forever. They are fated never to meet again there, given Hal's decision not "So idly to profane the precious time": "Give me my sword and cloak, Falstaff, good night." The knocking on the door is a call to arms and Hal's regal destiny, and for him war is incompatible with love and even friendship. For Doll and Falstaff, however, war is the immediate occasion, or at least threatening backdrop, for a love all the more precious in the face of possible death.

The War Bride

Among the expected spoils of war is a trophy wife, as Theseus triumphantly acknowledges in *A Midsummer Night's Dream*: "Hippolyta, I wooed thee with my sword,/And won thy love, doing thee injuries" (1.1.16-19). Social reasons for the existence of the figure of war bride in modern times are many, including marriages of local women with soldiers from an occupying army. *The War Brides* (1916), an interesting, pacifist film made in the United States during the First World War, shows that home governments and military authorities not only condoned but actively encouraged such liaisons. The cynical policy was to turn war widows into war brides, thus replacing the young men killed in battle. In the movie, the heroine leads a demonstration against the practice by women dressed in black to signify their grief as widows, and angrily protesting against war itself and militarism in general. The heroine kills herself as a martyr for this cause. The example reminds us that the figure of war bride has no doubt always been ambiguous, and once again, Shakespeare's treatment of the theme was prescient in ambivalence. There is the disastrous marriage between Richard III and Anne Neville, who was widowed in a civil war, and her father-in-law executed under Richard's orders (in Shakespeare's version), but we have another, more complex example.

One character who could make Theseus' claim is the victorious Henry V in his robustly jocund courtship of Catherine of France. Ringing still in the audience's ears is Henry's brutally worded demand, conveyed by Exeter to Catherine's father, to give up his throne to the invader. Henry knows, just as well as writers like Erasmus, how victory in war can be used to destroy families of the vanquished, and threateningly adapts this apparent cause for pacifism to his own militaristic purposes:

> Deliver up the crown, and ... take mercy
> On the poor souls for whom this hungry war
> Opens his vasty jaws; and on your head
> Turns he the widows' tears, the orphans' cries,
> The dead men's blood, the pining maidens groans,
> For husbands, fathers and betrothed lovers,
> That shall be swallowed in this controversy.
> (2.4.103–9)

Shakespeare leaves us in little doubt in the later "wooing scene" (5.2) that love is subsidiary to affairs of state. The serried ranks of queens, kings, dukes and duchesses, and *"other French, among them Princess Catherine and Alice"* (stage direction) assemble. Queen Isabel is under no illusions that Henry may demand what spoils he wishes, and she is acutely aware that these include an enforced, political wedding between Henry and her daughter Catherine, a situation in which she must tread diplomatically herself. Speaking of Henry's eyes as "fatal balls of murdering basilisks," Queen Isabel hopes,

> QUEEN ISABEL
> The venom of such looks we fairly hope.
> Have lost their quality, and that this day
> Shall change all griefs and quarrels into love.
> (5.2.12–20)

Burgundy's lengthy, diplomatic speech emphasizes the sheer waste of war in every sense, in its destructive effects on the agricultural seasons, its distractions from the occupations of a population normally in tune with the diurnal course of civil society in a state of "gentle peace." Henry, to drive home his advantage, relentlessly blames France for the war, and in his curt reply to Burgundy insists that the French must "buy that peace" by deferring to his "just demands" (5.2.70–73). The terms are already a "done deal," offering only limited opportunities to "Augment, or alter" the schedule, an exercise which Isabel hopes will benefit from the woman's touch: "Haply a woman's voice may do some good/When articles too nicely urged be stood on" (5.2.92–4). However, Henry's legalistic vocabulary and tone do not waver:

> Yet leave our cousin Catherine here with us.
> She is our capital demand, comprised
> Within the fore-rank of our articles.
> (5.2.95–97)

On this somewhat unpromising note, one of the best-known wooing scenes in literature ensues.

> Fair Catherine, and most fair,
> Will you vouchsafe to teach a soldier terms
> Such as will enter at a lady's ear
> And plead his love-suit to her gentle heart?

CATHERINE
Your majesty shall mock at me. I cannot speak your England.
(5.2.97-101)

Despite the almost universal rendition of this scene as charming, romantic, and comic, on closer inspection there are some questionable aspects. At no stage does Catherine unequivocally acknowledge or return Henry's protestations of love. In turn, he exploits his self-image as a plain-speaking soldier, in phrases like the curious vow to love Catherine "cruelly" (200), his stated preference in love to "lay on like a butcher" (142), and his hope that she will prove "a good soldier-breeder" (203): "take me, take a soldier; take a soldier, take a king" (166-67). To Henry's persistent questions as to whether she can love or even like him, she replies first noncommittally and later with stunning frankness: "Is it possible dat I sould love de enemy of France?" (170). Henry predictably uses a black joke to claim: "I love France so well that I will not part with a village of it; I will have it all mine" (173-75). The offensive humour is lost on Kate, who replies, "I cannot tell vat is dat" (177). He will not leave her alone: "But, Kate, dost thou understand thus much English, canst thou love me?" but she will not give him the satisfaction of a straight answer: "I cannot tell" (192-93). The only closure Kate allows is to say that she will do what pleases her own father ("Dat is as it sall please de roi mon pere," 245). Actual consent is not verbalized, and there is no certainty in the text that the kiss which Henry forces on her is received with any mutual warmth or repulsed. After the kiss, upon which Henry comments that there is "witchcraft" in her lips (275), the other political figures bustle back onstage and Kate says not one more word in the play. Instead, we hear a lengthy, misogynistic exchange between Henry, Burgundy, and the king of France, in which women are likened to summer flies, until the negotiations are finalized. Olivier and Branagh in their filmed productions do everything possible to mute the notes of reluctant capitulation, political bargaining, and menacing threats, presenting the scene instead as full of charm and physically reciprocated love, where language differences between English and French are harmlessly amusing rather than signaling imposed cultural dominance and masculine manipulation. However, Catherine, like Hippolyta, can be seen as less a willing lover than a spoil of war.

Dad's Army

Like many cities, Perth has a "Shakespeare in the Park" season every year. Given the outdoor venue in which families picnic beforehand, the ambience is always mildly carnivalesque, the plays usually comedies or the most studied tragedies. Under a skilled director, performances can reveal challenging themes. In 2013 *Much Ado About Nothing* was set after the Second World War. Extra-textual loudspeaker announcements and popular 1940s songs established the period. Musical and visual reference was made to the post-war British television series, *Dad's Army* (1968-1977), an echo carried most obviously by Dogberry's group of watchmen, likened to the incompetent and eccentric members of Britain's Home Guard in the fondly recollected programme. Reminding audiences that the play begins with soldiers returning victoriously from a war, there were allusions also to Kenneth Branagh's film version (1993) which, set during the period of Waterloo, began with the stirring sight of English soldiers riding home in triumph; and Branagh's less celebrated *Love's Labour's Lost*, set during the Second World War. These movies and the production in the Park provoke thought about Shakespeare's setting a comedy as aftermath of war.

The actual war in *Much Ado* seems more like a local football derby designed for masculine display of men in uniform, comparable to Helen Wilcox's description of the war between armies of the Tuscan city-states in *All's Well that Ends Well* as "a sort of boys' game" in which bored young gentry are in search of "exploit" (1.2.16–17).[14] There are no significant casualties. However, in its own cryptic way, this triumphant starting point suggests the truism that the end of one war is simply the beginning of the next, or as Milton was to put it, "For what can war, but endless war still breed?"[15] Don John, Don Pedro's illegitimate half-brother Don Pedro, pursues a grievance by plotting to separate the lovers, Claudio and Hero, as revenge for his social ostracism and a form of civil war by other means. His gull is described sarcastically by Don John as "the exquisite Claudio ... a proper squire," a young courtier mentioned initially in his role as a returning soldier, doing on the battlefield, "in the figure of a lamb, the feats of a lion." Don John's resentment seems fueled by Claudio's promotion ahead of him (a direct parallel of Iago and Cassio in *Othello*): "That young start-up hath all the glory of my overthrow: if I can cross him any way, I bless myself every way" (1.3.52–53).

The tonal allusion to the comic *Dad's Army* may not seem out of place in turning war into comedy. However, the military frame of reference raises less cosy aspects of *Much Ado*, as the vocabulary of war carries over into a battle between the sexes.[16] The two love relationships are, on close examination, neither ideal nor idealized. Between Beatrice and Benedick there is initially "a kind of merry war" (1.1.159). Beatrice's jocular but premonitory preoccupation is with Benedick's conduct in war: "I pray you, how many hath he killed and eaten in these wars? But how many hath he killed? for indeed I promised to eat all of his killing." The metaphor is to return, with chilling effect. The Messenger responds that Benedick had "done good service, lady, in these wars," adding that he is "a good soldier too," to which she ambiguously quibbles, "And a good soldier to a lady." Hero's father Leonato diplomatically intervenes, speaking of "a kind of merry war betwixt Signior Benedick and her: they never meet but there's a skirmish of wit between them." The words in the play unmistakably if lightly link conflict of war with "skirmishes" of love. The apparently harmonious resolution is the result, first, of a trick,

---

[14] Wilcox, "Drums and Roses?," 85.

[15] Milton, Sonnet 15, "To Fairfax." *Milton's Sonnets*, ed. E. A. J. Honigmann (London: Macmillan, 1966).

[16] See Susan Harlan, "'Returned from the wars': Comedy and Masculine Post-War Character in Shakespeare's *Much Ado About Nothing*," *Upstart: A Journal of English Studies* (June, 2013), online text, no page numbers, accessed November 18, 2020. https://upstart.sites.clemson.edu/Essays/returned-from-the-wars/returned-from-the-wars.xhtml.

and, second, declaration of an armistice between the representatives of a segregation along gendered lines over the issue of the slandered Hero:

> BENEDICK
> Come, bid me do anything for thee.
> BEATRICE
> Kill Claudio.
> BENEDICK
> Ha! Not for the wide world.
> BEATRICE
> You kill me to deny it. Farewell.
> (4.1.286–89)

To Benedick's plea to be "friends," Beatrice retorts, "You dare easier be friends with me than fight with mine enemy," referring to the deluded Claudio, "O that I were a man! ... O God, that I were a man! I would eat his heart in the market-place" (4.2.285–307). In performance, the violence of the repeated words here usually provokes un uneasy audience reaction.

The other emotional liaison, between Claudio and Hero, is also disturbing, lacking direct communication between man and woman. In amatory affairs Claudio's image is the reverse of his persona in war, acting instead like a lamb with the appearance of a martial lion. Critics note Claudio's silence, "a soldier unprepared for the fashions of civilian life."[17] He asks Don Pedro to woo on his behalf in a mask, suggesting imperfect emotional contact between the lovers. Claudio's violent language at the broken wedding ceremony shows him preferring to believe in a false, reported appearance than trust his lover: "Give not this rotten orange to your friend/She's but the sign and semblance of her honour." "Honour," as both Hotspur and Falstaff in *I Henry IV* confirm, can hold different meanings in war and in peace. In this instance, military prowess is to the fore: "Don Pedro hath bestowed much honour on a young Florentine called Claudio" (1.1.9). When the issue of Hero's "honour" as chastity is traduced, the *machismo* group of returning soldiers are quick to believe the slander since it undermines the masculinist reputation of Claudio. The implication is that this man, who has had no pre-marital knowledge of the woman as an individual, also has little ability to abandon military attitudes. The habitual male collusion is comparable to Othello as soldier choosing to believe his male comrade-in-arms rather than Desdemona. Don Pedro's priority is merely honour and reputation: "I stand dishonour'd, that have gone about/To link my dear friend to a common stale" (3.5.64–5). More generally in *Much Ado*, issues of conflict, slander, "rancour," entrapment, and domination carry over into love relationships, evolving from the opening situation depicting soldiers returning victorious from war. This at first seems to clear the way for love to thrive in peacetime, but instead we witness instances of the psychic cost to soldiers unable to relinquish masculine wartime bonds to build more socially acceptable relations with women. The whole play can be seen to depict an unravelling and then reweaving of the men's emotional tapestries, and the process is

---

[17] Garrison and Pivetti, *Shakespeare at Peace*, 41.

painful for the women, almost fatal for Hero, since they must fight for trust in a suspicious society. When, as genre requires, the double weddings are finally announced, the comic denouement seems predicated not on open-eyed love but on a series of tricks played on characters, and an ultimate biological imperative—"the world must be peopled" (2.3.233). These accidentally linked couples are fortunate they are placed in the comic world where "all's well that ends well," and not the morally unforgiving, tragic world of *Othello*, another play where war provides the catalytic setting, gendered differences of perception, "reputation," and male jealousy.

Brief Encounters

As well as being a progenitor of cultural violence, war is also paradoxically the mother of melodrama. *Casablanca* and *Brief Encounter*, in their different ways, point to how love in times of war can be arbitrarily contingent, turning on chance encounters driven by a sense of urgency that would not operate in peacetime. Emotional lives become playthings of historical circumstances, and unfettered, free choice may not operate as it should. Again, modern films centralize and sometimes sentimentalize the fate of women in love during wartime, but Shakespeare understood the predicaments four centuries ago. Inevitably, if our perspective changes from the logistics of war to personal lives of lovers yearning for peace, then the experience of women whose lives are caught up in military events becomes more revealing than that of their male counterparts. Women in love, such as Desdemona who follows her husband into the battle zone of Cyprus, and Bianca who seems sincerely in love with Cassio but reputed to be a courtesan, camp-follower, and "strumpet" (a slander which she vigorously denies),[18] are tragic examples of indirect casualties of love in times of war. So is Cressida.

Troilus and Cressida has been seen as one of the great anti-war works, its emotional range identified as satirical, bitter, and angry. Rhetoric which espouses values such as national pride, honour, just war, courage, military glory, and masculine stereotypes is relentlessly undermined. The cause of the war between Troy and Greece, in the most reductive and jaundiced view, is inherently related to sexuality, since the trigger is the abduction, if not rape, of Helen:

> The ravished Helen, Menelaus' queen,
> With wanton Paris sleeps—and that's the quarrel.
> ...
> Now, good or bad, 'tis but the chance of war.
> (Prologue, 9–10, 31)

According to Thersites, the play's most cynical commentator, the analogy for war as a form of legitimized rape is venereal disease: "After this, the vengeance on the whole camp—or rather, the Neapolitan bone-ache, for that methinks is the curse dependent on those that war for a placket" (2.3.17–19). Earlier critical evaluations of Cressida as weak,

---

18 Robert S. White, *Innocent Victims: Poetic Injustice in Shakespearean Tragedy* (London: Athlone, 1986), chap. 7.

promiscuous, or a "whore" began to shift under the influence of feminist readings from the 1970s, seeing her more as a victim of circumstances, though we still find unsympathetic accounts. Sharon M. Harris provides an economical review of the matter.[19] Needless to say, my argument turns on the war, which unfairly shapes the destiny of Cressida when she finds herself haplessly swept up in its morally destructive ethos.

Even before she appears onstage, Cressida is unwittingly enmeshed in the sexualized context established by this dubious war. She is being "groomed" by her uncle Pandarus (from whose name "pander" is derived) as the target of Troilus' attentions, which, despite his protestations of love, can be described as infatuation and a desire for conquest. There are discussions (1.1.109–12) that she must follow her father "to the Greeks" as a political pawn in a prisoner swap, the fate which does overtake her (4.3). Neither Pandarus nor Troilus is sympathetic to her refusal, nor to her vehemently expressed wish to renounce her father and stay with Troilus, threatening to

> Tear my bright hair, and scratch my praised cheeks,
> Crack my clear voice with sobs and break my heart
> With sounding "Troilus." I will not go from Troy.
> (4.3.20–35)

Under coercion, she follows this assertive speech with a grief-stricken outburst, leaving no doubt that she is not complying with the plan (4.5.1–10). Troilus himself is delegated to break the news and escort her to the enemy side, and he does so with a fatalistic acceptance of "the rude brevity and discharge of one." His primary feeling is what he calls "a kind of godly jealousy" that the "Grecian youths ... flowing and swelling o'er with arts and exercise" will tempt her to break her vow to him. He is the one who introduces the subject of infidelity: "But be not tempted," to which she replies indignantly, "Do you think I will?" (4.5.92–3). His rhetoric reveals a mistrusting compulsion to insist that Cressida reiterate her vow of constancy, rather than protesting his own love with as much passion as she does hers. Clearly uncomfortable in the situation, Troilus tries to hasten the departure with the peremptoriness of Hotspur: "Come kiss, and let us part" (4.5.98). He himself delivers her to Diomedes, and the finality of this gesture in itself must reawaken Cressida's earlier fear that, for women, "Things won are done" (1.2.283). She is identified as an imminent spoil of war, like Helen.

Next, vulnerable and lonely in the enemy camp, Cressida is paraded before the Greek soldiers who aggressively compete for turns kissing her in a kind of gang violation. Given her clear resistance ("Therefore no kiss"), the scene is humiliating to her, and she is increasingly coerced to join the banter only because she is given no choice. Ulysses' arrogantly dismissive and judgmental speech has the force of the rapist blaming the victim:

> Fie, fie upon her!
> There's language in her eye, her cheek, her lip;

---

[19] Sharon M. Harris, "Feminism and Shakespeare's Cressida: '*If* I be false ...,'" *Women's Studies: An Interdisciplinary Journal* 18 (1990): 65–82.

> Nay, her foot speaks. Her wanton spirits look out
> At every joint and motive of her body.

He stereotypes her as representative of camp-followers, "For sluttish spoils of opportunity/And daughters of the game" (4.6.55–64). Despite earlier critical claims that the condemnation is authorial, context reveals it clearly is the hypocritical attitude of the Greek leader in war.[20]

The scene in which Diomedes seduces Cressida is framed by Thersites' explicit warning to the audience: "That same Diomed's a false-hearted rogue, a most unjust knave ... Nothing but lechery! All incontinent varlets!" (5.1.85–6, 94–5), and it is overlooked by the helplessly voyeuristic Troilus, whose premonitions of jealousy become a self-fulfilling prophecy. Diomedes betrays his position of power as trustworthy "guardian" (Troilus' word), using, by turns, seductive cajoling, threats of abandonment, and bullying, until she is again left with little choice: "what would you have me do?" (5.2.24). While Troilus leaps to the conclusion that she is the one who is "false," it never seems to dawn on Cressida that he has willingly colluded in her exchange with the Greeks, and has delivered her into the hands of the very man who manoeuvres her into submission. She blames herself for the "error" of her sex, but Cressida's fate is to become another helpless victim of war, both war widow and war bride.

Judging by the frequency of Shakespeare's insertions throughout his canon, it seems that war is dramatically purposeful rather than gratuitous backdrop, when it coincides with love. The language and assumptions of war are internalized within emotional lives of citizens, even in innocent amatory experiences, and enmeshed in imagery:

> Therefore, brave conquerors, for so you are,
> That war against your own affections
> And the huge army of the world's desires.
> (1.1.8–10)

In the process of psychological internalization of conflict in war, "marital" and "martial" can become ominously interchangeable, as they do with different results in *Othello* and *Macbeth*. War can also become a metaphor for other, less savoury emotional encounters, implying sources of latent violence that seem unavoidable. Perhaps in some cases (possibly *Antony and Cleopatra*) the immediacy of war intensifies and problematizes love, but in general Shakespeare's lovers, especially the women, are likely to agree with Marlowe's character: "Accurs'd be he that first invented war!"[21]

---

20 See Harris, "Feminism and Shakespeare's Cressida ...," 65.

21 *The First Part of Tamburlaine the Great* (2.4.1), in *Marlowe: Plays and Poems*, ed. M. Ridley (London: Dent, 1955).

PART ONE

THE EMOTIONAL COSTS OF WAR

Chapter 2

"SHE SHAL BRYNGEN US THE PEES ON EVERY SYDE": THE CEREMONIAL RESTORATION OF WOMEN IN LATE MEDIEVAL CULTURE

Stephanie Downes and Stephanie Trigg*

THE CONDUCT OF medieval warfare is punctuated by powerful rituals of peace and peace-making.[1] Violent and bloody conflict rages for a certain period, and then the parties call a truce—sometimes in order to negotiate the next stage in the conflict, but ideally, to end it.[2] Such negotiations are often occasions for elaborate displays of symbolic power: formal rituals and lavish ceremonies designed to bear public witness to the chief combatants' true feeling, or to changes in feeling or policy. These occasions foster what Andrew Lynch calls a public "feeling of peace," but they also affirm the political and cultural authority of the opposing sides even as they suspend their exercise of military force.[3] When war concludes with a marriage alliance, the symbolic and practical involvement of women in securing peace is paramount. In such cases, the ceremonies associated with the making of political allegiance are grafted onto traditional wedding rituals, while public and warlike emotions of dissent and anger are displaced onto the possibility of more amicable and private feelings between the bride and groom, and the transformation of public enmity into familial amity. Throughout the medieval period the transferral of a woman from the family of her birth to that of her husband was a rite governed by well-established forms of ceremony designed to secure an unbreakable familial bond. But there

---

* **Stephanie Downes** lectures in English and Creative Writing at La Trobe University. With Andrew Lynch and Katrina O'Loughlin, she co-edited *Emotions and War: Medieval to Romantic Literature* (2015) and *Writing War in Britain and France: A History of Emotions* (2018); and with Sally Holloway and Sarah Randles, *Feeling Things: Objects and Emotions through History* (2018). **Stephanie Trigg** is Redmond Barry Distinguished Professor of English Literature at the University of Melbourne. She is author of *Congenial Souls: Reading Chaucer Medieval to Postmodern* (2002), *Shame and Honor: A Vulgar History of the Order of the Garter* (2012); and with Thomas A. Prendergast, *Affective Medievalism: Love, Abjection and Discontent* (2019), and *Thirty Myths about Chaucer* (2020).

1 We are grateful for expert research assistance from Helen Hickey and Anne McKendry. Research was supported by the Australian Research Council Centre of Excellence for the History of Emotions (project number CE110001011).

2 Andrew Lynch, "'Peace is good after war': The Narrative Seasons of English Arthurian Tradition," in *Writing War: Medieval Literary Responses to Warfare*, ed. Corinne Saunders, Françoise Le Saux, and Neil Thomas (Woodbridge: Brewer, 2004), 127–46.

3 Andrew Lynch, "'Blisse wes on londe': The Feeling of Peace in Laȝamon's *Brut*," in *Emotions and War: Medieval to Romantic Literature*, ed. Stephanie Downes, Andrew Lynch, and Katrina O'Loughlin (New York: Palgrave, 2015), 42–59.

was no recognized rite of restoration when the alliance failed or the marriage came to an end. On such occasions, the ideological work the women have performed to forge alliances is undone almost immediately. They become pawns and securities in larger political stakes, and their symbolic and/or financial value must be renegotiated. Both the historical and literary archives bear witness to numerous instances of the ritual "return" of women. But this was essentially a ceremony without a script, which sought somewhat perversely to reconfirm a bond or strike a new bargain through the act of restoration, rather than to establish one through mutual union.

In this chapter, we consider three moments from late medieval fiction and history in which a high-status woman is publicly "returned" to a male figure of authority as part of an elaborate treaty between nations or rivals. All three of our examples are fraught with unhappiness and uncertainty, but each one attempts to draw on familiar ceremonial forms designed to reconcile feuding (or potentially feuding) factions. Public rituals are problematic for historians of emotions because of the disparity between what people *do* on such occasions in contrast to how they might *feel*. Rituals and ceremonies publicly enact powerful feelings, but the demands of public discourse can produce a dissonant emotional performance from the participants.[4] We argue that this is especially pointed when individual women become the focal point of ceremonies designed to reconfirm a relationship between men. Andrew Lynch's twinned interest in both literary and historical expressions of the emotions of war helps us probe the feelings of the key participants and observers in these emotionally awkward ceremonies. Our texts draw different conclusions about the role of personal feeling in what is an otherwise unscripted public ritual; sometimes they encourage speculation about the emotions of the women at the centre of these transactions. But at all times it is clear that the most important emotional bonds are between the men who determine women's fates. All three of the restoration rituals discussed in this chapter are designed to cement social and political ties, and yet, perhaps predictably, none inaugurates the happy ending the orchestrators anticipate: the ritual moment is short-lived and thus doubly painful.

Our first example, from Geoffrey Chaucer's late fourteenth-century poem of the Trojan War, *Troilus and Criseyde*, inspires our central argument: when the besieged Trojans strike a truce with the Greeks, Criseyde is handed over from her Trojan lover Troilus to the Greek Diomede, who escorts her to her father Calchas as part of a bid to cease the fighting between the two camps. Our second example of the ceremonial restoration of a woman—also to her father—follows the collapse of Richard II's reign, just over a decade after the composition of Chaucer's poem. Isabelle de Valois, eldest daughter of the king of France, was married to Richard II in 1396. She was returned to France in 1401, after Richard's deposition and death in 1399, in an effort to prolong the peace with France which the marriage had initially secured. Our third is drawn from Thomas Malory's late fifteenth-century prose romance, *Le Morte Darthur*. Lancelot restores Queen Guenevere to her husband, King Arthur, after having rescued her from

---

4 François Berthomé and Michael Houseman, "Ritual and Emotion: Moving Relations, Patterned Effusions," *Religion and Society: Advances in Research* 1 (2010): 57–75.

being burned at the stake, and kept her with him for several months. Our reading of the emotions revealed and concealed in the ceremonial return of Arthur's queen in this final example brings late medieval history and romance together: Malory drew from chronicle accounts of royal rituals in his description of Lancelot's restoration of Guenevere to Arthur.

Like marriages, ceremonial restorations of women are primarily attempts to reconcile bonds of friendship and political affinities between men. All three of the cases discussed here exemplify the traffic in women that is a familiar feature of patriarchal culture: the return of Criseyde to her traitor father purchased a period of truce between Greek and Trojan warriors, placating both sides and offering the promise of peace to come; Henry IV hoped that by returning Isabelle to the French king, her father, he might mend the damage done to the Anglo-French peace treaty when he had forced Richard to abdicate; and the restoration of Guenevere to her husband, King Arthur, was an attempt to end the war between Lancelot and Arthur. Political stability is at stake on each occasion, while lavish ceremony and ritual are deployed to convince participants and observers of the sincerity underpinning the transactions. The passages of these women from one predominantly male group to another might proceed uninterrupted, but the narratives that surround them manage the shifting emotional dynamics of these exchanges in very different ways, depending on which participants' emotions are emphasized. It is an important feature of our argument that our examples are drawn equally from the world of historical record and of romance literature, including both poetry and prose. While it is true that our two literary examples from Chaucer and Malory are more obviously shaped and driven by the emotional lives of the protagonists, narrative accounts of Isabelle's restoration also dramatize the contrast between public acts and private feelings. A number of witnesses and commentators take a special interest in Isabelle's feelings—her sorrow and anger at her husband's death— even if her emotions are politically and historically insignificant, having little impact on the course of the Anglo-French wars. Our literary examples approach the narrative tension between participants' private emotions and the public performance of the restoration ritual in complementary ways: Chaucer probes the subtle narrative interplay between the inner feelings and outward comportment of his protagonists that is successfully "read" by just one onlooker; while Malory heightens the private drama by focusing on the public emotional responses of witnesses.

Criseyde

At the beginning of Book 5 of Chaucer's poem, the Greek prince Diomede is poised to lead Criseyde out through the gates of Troy to rejoin her father, Calchas. In this moment, Troilus can hardly sit on his horse for misery, but hides his desperate sorrow in a "ful manly" fashion (5.30).[5] Silently, he berates himself for his failure to speak against the exchange, or to halt its progress. "Whi suffre ich I? Whi nyl ich it redresse? ... Whi wol

---

[5] All quotations from *Troilus and Criseyde* are taken from *The Riverside Chaucer*, ed. Larry Benson, 3rd ed. (Boston: Mifflin, 1987), and are cited by book and line number.

I this endure?" (5.40; 5.48), he wonders. Troilus' silent agony recalls his failure in Book 4 to speak up against the proposed exchange when the idea is first mooted in the Trojan parliament. Here, too, the hero's silence, his public masking of his emotions, and his endurance of suffering are crucial: the narrator tells us that in this moment, even though he nearly died, and his face began involuntarily to change colour, he spoke not a word, "Lest men sholde his affeccioun espye," and "With mannes herte he gan his sorwes drye" (4.153–54). Criseyde has charged Troilus with secrecy about their affair. Moreover, Troilus does not disrupt the exchange for fear that Criseyde might be killed in the tumult and violence that would necessarily ensue if the terms of the treaty were not upheld (5.50–56). The Greeks want Criseyde returned to her father, and the Trojans want to recuperate the warrior Antenor, who has recently been taken prisoner; Troilus recognizes that if the exchange does not take place, violence will ensue. He fails, however, to see that his passivity will lead to new violence later in the story: Antenor himself will eventually betray Troy, and help the Greeks break the siege.[6]

When the Trojan prince Hector initially hesitates, in Book 4, to agree to the exchange, he is pressured by the Trojan people to accept the Greek terms (4.183–95). Troilus' submission to the collective will is just one of several occasions on which the narrator explains why Troilus and Criseyde do not simply run away together: the courtly imperatives of secrecy and discretion are important, but the poem also reveals seemingly insurmountable tensions between individual and public feeling. Although not technically a prisoner—"she nys no prisonere," Hector insists, when he argues against the proposed exchange (5.179)—as the daughter of a traitor, Criseyde has been given special dispensation to remain in Troy. Because the Greeks want her, she is now a valuable exchange commodity. To recuse herself—or to allow herself to be rescued—from that exchange would constitute a further act of treachery. Not only have the citizens of Troy made it clear they want her to go, they also believe that her leaving may be in the interest of mutual peace. When the women of Troy approach Criseyde in the days before the exchange takes place, they express their hope that "she/Shal bryngen us the pees on every syde" (4.691–92). Criseyde becomes a pseudo-Helen, whose restoration to the Greek camp is seen publicly by the Trojans as an opportunity to appease them.

Criseyde and Troilus' own emotional response to the exchange has occupied much of Book 4, but that drama is transmuted into subtle gestures and signs in the public ritual, and has no effect on its outward performance. Troilus berates himself, Hamlet-like, for his indecision and lack of action, but it is clear that the circumstances of their private love cannot become public; and nor can he disrupt what both the ritual and Criseyde herself represent politically in this open setting.

Yet the amorous emotions that sit beneath the formal exchange continue to flow in and around its rituals. Criseyde feels her heart bleeding with sorrow (5.17); Troilus shakes with anger (5.36) and berates himself for his inaction (5.39–49); Criseyde

---

[6] Jennifer Garrison, "Chaucer's *Troilus and Criseyde* and the Danger of Masculine Interiority," *The Chaucer Review* 49, no. 3 (2015): 333–34.

sighs—privately intones a single word, "Allas!"—and rides out slowly (5.58–61). Troilus works hard not to weep, and embraces Antenor warmly as he is delivered from the Greeks ("Antenor he kiste and made feste" [5.76–77]), but when the moment arrives for the lovers to part, Troilus looks at Criseyde "pitously" (5.79), rides up to her so close that no-one might hear them, and secretly ("sleighly" [5.83]) entreats her to remember her promise to return to him in ten days' time. When Troilus takes her "sobrely" by the hand, Criseyde begins to weep, "tenderly" (5.81–82). The accumulation of adverbs in this passage suggests a visual and highly charged emotional spectacle, and yet only Diomede seems to register what is happening. As Troilus turns his horse around, his face is pale, and he speaks neither to Diomede, nor to any of his own company (5.85–87): this is one moment where Troilus' silence is significant not just for the knowing reader, but also for Diomede, who the reader knows will replace Troilus in Criseyde's affections. Diomede has observed this scene, "As he that koude more than the crede/In swich a craft" (5.89–90), and stores up this information as he takes Criseyde's bridle. He will use this knowledge to further his own slow and careful seduction of Criseyde.

Diomede is the model reader for this scene, well able to understand the lovers' gestures, however subtle or not they may be. By extension, he is also the model reader for the romance genre and the privilege it accords to private feeling. Chaucer's poem is famously little concerned with the ins and outs of the siege; instead, it offers the reader a series of personal moments intensely experienced by its chief protagonists. Relatively few of these moments take place in public. The other great exception is when Troilus first sees and falls in love with Criseyde at the temple feast in Book 1 and similarly struggles with his body to conceal what he is feeling from his peers (1.271–80). In both scenes, Criseyde is the central symbolic object, whether she is being loved, lost, or exchanged. But the narrative significance of the exchange in Book 5 rests on Troilus, as representative of the disjunction between private feeling and public ritual, and on Diomede, as witness to his struggle, rather than on the openly grieving Criseyde, whose gender seems here to render her unable even to attempt to hide her sorrows. Troilus believes that he has lost Criseyde to her father, in a symbolic perversion of the act of marriage, but in the moment that Troilus rides away, he leaves her with his replacement and rival, Diomede, who reads the story he has entered into, interprets it correctly, and schemes how best to bend it to his will. Far from a distraction from the "real" action, the ostensibly private psychological drama that plays out within this scene of public exchange will have catastrophic effects for all of Troy.

Isabelle

Henry IV ensured that Isabelle's return to France in 1401, following the deposition and death of Richard II, was an occasion governed by high ceremony. This well-documented event generated a variety of reactions from both contemporaries and later critics: many focus on the figure of the youthful, grieving widow-queen; others criticize Henry for the enormous expense of her restoration. But all accounts of Isabelle's return to France, both eyewitness and retrospective, stress the emotional complexity of the restoration itself, the long negotiations that preceded it, and the constant interplay of public and private emotions as a drama of communal versus individual feeling.

After Richard's death, Henry hoped to marry Isabelle himself in order to keep the peace with France and retain what remained of her dowry.[7] The French emissaries made clear their vigorous opposition to the match, whether because King Charles was experiencing one of his characteristic bouts of madness, and so was unable to consent,[8] or because he considered that Richard's early death voided the original marriage (which was never consummated), subsequently entitling him to the return of both Isabelle and the full amount of her dowry.[9] The negotiations for Isabelle's return to France lasted two years, and on May 27, 1401, it was finally agreed that Isabelle would be returned to France with her jewels by the beginning of July. Jean Froissart associates her psychological state at this time with her political misfortune: Isabelle is "tourned and broken."[10] Once queen, she is subject to Fortune's turning wheel as her situation declines.

Adam Usk, who watched Isabelle on the day she waited at the Port of London to be shipped to Calais, writes that he saw her there, "dressed in black and scowling with deep hatred at King Henry, but scarcely saying a word."[11] Usk goes on to describe her departure as "the occasion of great debate among the people," who feared that "in her burning desire for revenge" she might stir up further trouble for the English once she was back in France.[12] Clearly, there were public fears about the consequences of Isabelle's feelings. Yet later accounts also emphasize this combination of Isabelle's intense grief with her anger, when it was clear her emotions were of no political threat. The Tudor chronicler, John Hayward, gives an extreme account of Isabelle's hostility towards Henry, describing how she arrived at her first meeting with her husband's successor silently weeping, "first pouring forth in a sett silence great plentie of teares," before delivering a speech intended to "reprove [the king] openly to [his] face."[13] Hayward gives the reader a direct account of the speech itself, in which Isabelle announces before the court that Henry has been foolish and appeals to his conscience to "condemne your selfe to the severest punishments which treson and parricide cann deserve." While Hayward dismisses her words as evidence of her "distempered mind"—the combined effects of her youth, sex,

---

[7] *Chronique de la Traïson et Mort de Richart Deux Roy Dengleterre*, ed. Benjamin Williams (London: Aux dépens de la Société, 1846), 263.

[8] *The Chronicle of Froissart*, trans. John Bourchier, Lord Berner (London: David Nutt, 1903), 6:400.

[9] Robert Fabyan, *The New Chronicles of England and France, reprinted from Pynson's edition of 1516*, ed. Henry Ellis (London: Rivington, 1811), 558–59; *Holinshed, Chronicles: Richard II, 1398–1400, Henry IV and Henry V*, ed. R. S. Wallace, and Alma Hansen (Oxford: Clarendon Press, 1923), 29.

[10] *The Chronicle of Froissart*, 370.

[11] *The Chronicle of Adam Usk, 1377–1421*, ed. and trans. Chris Given-Wilson (Oxford: Clarendon Press, 1997), 133.

[12] *The Chronicle of Adam Usk*, 133.

[13] John Hayward, *The Life and Raigne of King Henrie IIII*, ed. John J. Manning, Camden Fourth Series 42 (London: Royal Historical Society, 1991), 181–82.

and inexperience—he praises Henry for having the "power to governe his passions" in the face of her public attack.[14] Hayward presumably drew from and embellished earlier accounts of Isabelle's contempt for the English king such as Usk's, although his account differs in its motives for Isabelle's anger. It is rare, however, in providing an account of Isabelle's perspective, apparently in her own words: in the vast majority of sources describing the negotiation over Isabelle's return to France, and during the restoration itself, she is crucially present, but conspicuously silent.

Henry himself did not travel with Isabelle to Calais, sending Sir Thomas Percy, the Earl of Worcester, as his royal representative and spokesperson. On the day of the restoration ceremony, it was Percy who formally returned Isabelle to the French, delivering a speech which Jean Creton, author of the French metrical history of the deposition of Richard II, gives in full.[15] One important historical exception to Isabelle's silence is a document in the *Archives du Royaume*, drawn up in the days following her formal restoration to the French royal family, in which she signs her name to a statement denying recognition of Henry as sovereign and Richard's successor. In this statement, which Isabelle allegedly dictated, she claims that she had only ever recognized Henry's legitimacy as a consequence of the fear and violence to which she had been subjected in his care ("pour la paour [et] violence qui nous ont este fais").[16]

Henry spared no expense on ceremony when he returned Isabelle to her father. He appointed numerous female attendants, yeomen, squires and grooms as formal escorts: around two hundred individuals and upwards of a hundred horses. The queen and her entourage were dressed at the expense of the king, who also provided plate and furnishings for the journey. Isabelle was also given money—"Golde & siluer and mony oþer Iewelleȝ"—so she might distribute gifts to her English retinue.[17] Modern historians have compared the overall cost of the ceremony to that of Isabelle and Richard's wedding in 1396, but Isabelle was returned to France without the full complement of her dowry.[18] By using money from his own coffers to subsidize and solemnize the occasion, Henry attempted to forestall further deterioration of the relationship between the two kingdoms. Creton describes how Percy, having publicly declared Isabelle "loosed, quit, and free from all bonds of marriage, and of every other service, debt, or obligation ... with many tears, took the young queen by the arms, and delivered her with good grace to the messengers there present," receiving letters of acquittance from them in return.[19]

---

14 Hayward, *The Life and Raigne*, 182.

15 Jean Creton, "French Metrical History of the Deposition of King Richard the Second," ed. and trans. John Webb, *Archaeologia* 20 (1824), 231.

16 *Chronique* (Appendix), 277–79.

17 *The Brut or The Chronicles of England*, ed. Freidrich W. D. Brie (London: EETS by Kegan Paul, Trench, Trübner, 1906), 362.

18 Estimates are given in J. L. Kirkby, *Henry IV of England* (London: Constable, 1970), 120–22; and Harold F. Hutchison, *The Hollow Crown: A Life of Richard II* (London: Eyre & Spottiswoode, 1961), 163–64.

19 Creton, "French Metrical History," 231.

Creton also describes a ritual farewell managed by the queen: with her heart "enlightened by goodness," Isabelle brought the English ladies with her to the French tents, where they dined together and "made sore lamentation." After the meal, she distributed gifts to both the English ladies and the lords, "who wept mightily for sorrow" while Isabelle "bad them be of good cheer."[20] Creton shows how Isabelle, at thirteen, understood the ritual processes of ceremony and the emotional performances in which she was expected to participate—enough to direct them herself. Hayward frames Isabelle's political maturity in a different way: reiterating Isabelle's hatred of Henry and his supporters, he argues that she deliberately manipulated her performance of the gift-giving ritual in order to distribute her rewards "upon the ladies for favour, but upon the lordes *only for fashion*, for shee was not ether soe yong as not to perceive, nor yet soe careless as not to regard the treacheries threat they had used against King Richard."[21]

According to Hayward, Isabelle scowled and frowned openly to make her displeasure clear to all those present. At the same time, he regards her agency in these scenes with suspicion. He imagines the various contemporary reports of Isabelle's intelligence ("sharpe conceit") as the effects of pity for her condition ("pittie did raise everie thing [in her] to the highest"); and concludes that she must have "receaved instructions" about her formal behaviour on the day.[22] Usk interprets Isabelle's inability to conceal her anger in public as a sign of her youth. The critical tone of both Usk's and Hayward's accounts is not surprising, given that they each wrote with the intent to discredit Richard's kingship retrospectively. If the primary objection to Isabelle's marriage to Richard had been her youth, then evidence of her childishness in her unconcealed distaste for Henry and his supporters tended to confirm Richard's error in choosing such a young queen.

In the majority of French accounts, English tears dominate the scene of Isabelle's departure. Creton describes how, after Percy's speech, and "before the two parties separated[,] they wept most piteously." The English wept again as Isabelle left with her French escorts: "when she was forced to part with them [the English], they renewed their lamentation."[23] French witnesses and chroniclers perceived displays of weeping among the English participants as the most appropriate emotional response to the occasion. Juvenal des Ursins writes of Isabelle's own tears ("la bonne dame ausi pleuroit"), as well as those of the English men and women, who wept copiously ("pleurans a grosse larmes"), as they took their leave of her.[24] Isabelle's tears call to mind those of Criseyde, as she was returned to her father. But if ritual weeping was appropriate for Isabelle and

---

20 Creton, "French Metrical History," 232. This is the only version of Isabelle's speech during the exchange in any eyewitness account we have found.

21 Hayward, *The Life and Raigne*, 183; italics added.

22 Hayward, *The Life and Raigne*, 183.

23 Creton, "French Metrical History," 232.

24 Juvenal des Ursins, "Histoire de Charles VI, Roi de France," in *Nouvelle collection des mémoires pour servir à l'histoire de France, depuis le XIIIe siècle jusqu'à la fin du XVIIIe*, ed. M. M. Michaud (Paris, 1836), 2:420: "Et prirent les Anglois congé d'elle pleurans a grosses larmes, et la bonne dame aussi pleuroit, et plusieurs des assistans."

her English retinue, it was not, it seems, appropriate for the French in general. There are no records of French participants in the ceremony weeping: des Ursins attributes the public display of weeping to the English alone, while Fabyan goes on to observe that Isabelle "was ioyously receyued of the Frenshemen" in Calais.[25] In Paris, the French king and queen similarly met Isabelle with great joy—though they did so in stark contrast to their daughter, who continued to weep loudly ("le roy son pere, et la reyne sa mere, … la recurrent a grande joye, combien que la bonne dame pleuroit fort").[26]

The emotions each displayed at Isabelle's restoration were not shared by both parties. Instead, the emotions of each side are openly at odds, underscoring precisely the political difference between the two parties: the English wept ostensibly in lamentation for the loss of Isabelle—a ritual performance of their love for the French princess, and hence their symbolic love for France and desire for peace—while the French celebrate the return of a daughter of their kingdom. There is no cause, here, for a scene of mutual happiness, like the one that occurred at Richard and Isabelle's betrothal ceremony, five years earlier, where collective weeping signified joy:[27] in 1396, near Ardres outside Calais, eight hundred French and English knights lined up with their swords drawn to form a processional way, at the middle of which the two kings met and joined hands in token of the marriage to come, and the peace it augured. According to Froissart: "all the eyght hundred knyghtes kneled downe to the grownde and many of them wepte for joye."[28] The five hundred French knights who attended Isabelle's restoration, however, formed no part of the ceremony; instead, they lay concealed less than a league away under the command of the Duke of Burgundy, dressed and armed for battle. Creton writes that, in the event that the English changed their minds and suddenly determined to keep the queen, "every one of these might have done his duty to retain her."[29]

These accounts of Isabelle's restoration highlight a crucial contradiction between emotional feeling and ceremonial practice when a woman is returned from one party to another: such rituals attempt to mask, or strategically displace and appease, strong feelings and structural inequities. The same may be said of many public rituals, but in these cases, the awkwardness of the act and the incompatibility of each side inevitably come to the fore. While contemporary accounts often describe in minute detail the ceremonial aspects of Isabelle's restoration, those written with hindsight tend to reflect on the failure of ceremony to achieve the desired end: ceremony and ritual, however lavish or correct, ultimately have little lasting impact on the participants' emotions—let alone on history itself.

---

25 Fabyan, *The New Chronicles*, 559.

26 des Ursins, "Histoire", 420.

27 For a detailed eye-witness account of the meeting, see M. P. Meyer, M. M. Meyer, and S. Luce, "L'Entrevue de l'Ardres," *Annuaire-Bulletin de la Société de l'histoire de France* 18, no. 2 (1881): 204–24.

28 *The Chronicle of Froissart*, 227.

29 Creton, "The French Metrical History," 237.

At a distance of some centuries, Hayward wrote disparagingly of the whole affair, and both kings' efforts to solemnize the occasion and cement their alliance through this ceremony. He concludes his account with the observation that "these two kings were soe full of jealouzies on both sides that their friendship could not long indure." He pronounces: "impossible it is that old displeasures by new desertes should sodainly bee appeased."[30] Hayward is right. Any ritual that is designed to do more than celebrate a natural rite of passage or mutual joy will struggle to accomplish the emotional work of appeasement in a lasting way. Tension between private and public feeling propels many dramatic narratives. Hayward's somewhat cynical commentary on the ceremony offers his readers a moral as well as a historical lesson: he sees through or beyond the execution of the ritual, pausing on the various flaws of both the ceremony and its individual participants, to observe the deeper unresolved rivalry between Charles and Henry, as representatives of France and England. He uses the failure of Isabelle's restoration to create a "feeling of peace" as the grounds for presenting his readers with a moral conclusion. Here again, it is the unspoken feelings of the key participants—Henry, Charles, and the French and English peoples—that will be of far greater significance in determining the course of the Anglo-French wars during the fifteenth century.

Guenevere

Malory's scene of restoration is the most unusual of our three examples: there can be few precedents for a lover returning a queen to her husband. And yet the scenes of public and collective weeping he describes are nonetheless familiar. There is a narrative pause in the three-way hostilities between Lancelot, Arthur, and Gawain, as Lancelot "returns" Guenevere to Arthur in a confident procession and ceremony of his own flamboyant invention. Malory's emphasis in this passage is on ceremonial display: there is little space here for insight either into the emotional reactions of the key male participants, or of Guenevere herself; although the text carefully describes the ritual, collective weeping of Arthur and his company of knights. Individual emotions, including those of the queen herself, are strategically hidden from view.

Lancelot has rescued the queen from being burnt alive on the charges of adultery and treason after Agravain and Mordred have trapped him in the queen's chamber. He has taken the queen to his castle, Joyous Gard, and King Arthur and Gawain have laid siege to him there for fifteen weeks before battle takes place. Gawain is driven by his own enmity with Lancelot, who, in his rush to rescue the queen, has unknowingly killed Gawain's beloved younger brothers Gareth and Gaheris. During the siege, Gawain is wounded, but Lancelot consistently refuses to take up arms against King Arthur. Eventually, the Pope intervenes, and sends bulls to the Bishop of Rochester to command Arthur to take the queen back and make peace with Lancelot. Gawain agrees that the queen may safely

---

30 Hayward, *The Life and Raigne*, 183–84.

return, but he refuses to support the king's reconciliation with Lancelot. Lancelot brings Guenevere to Carlisle with an impressive procession and display of courtly grandeur, but the reconciliation is only a temporary truce, long enough to allow Lancelot's safe conduct before he must leave for France. This ritual punctuates the battle narratives and allows for the performance of long, impassioned speeches from both Lancelot and Gawain. King Arthur speaks only once, and very briefly, to reproach Lancelot. Queen Guenevere does not speak at all.

We quote the text of the Winchester Manuscript:

> So the Bysshop departed and cam to the kynge to Carlehyll, and tolde hym all how sir Launcelot answerd hym; so that made the teares falle oute at the kyngis yen. Than sir Launcelot purveyed hym an hondred knyghtes, and all well clothed in grene velvet, and their horsis trapped in the same to the heelys, and every knyght hylde a braunche of olyff in hys honde in tokenyng of pees. And the quene had foure and twenty jantillwomen folowyng her in the same wyse. And sir Launcelot had twelve coursers folowyng hym, and on every courser sate a yonge jantylman; and all they were arrayed in whyght velvet with sa<mbu>is of golde aboute their quarters, and the horse trapped in the same wyse down to the helys, wyth many owchys, isette with stonys and perelys in golde, to the numbir of a thousande. And in the same wyse was the quene arayed, and sir Launcelot in the same, of whyght clothe of golde tyssew.
>
> And right so as ye have harde, as the Freynshe booke makyth mencion, he rode with the quene frome Joyus Garde to Carlehyll. And so sir Launcelot rode thorowoute Carlehylle, and so into the castell, that all men myght beholde hem. And there was many a wepyng ien.
>
> And than sir Launcelot hymselff alyght and voyded hys horse, and toke adowne the quene, and so lad her where kyng Arthur was in hys seate; and sir Gawayne sate afore hym, and many other grete lordys.
>
> So whan sir Launcelot saw the kynge and sir Gawayne, than he lad the quene by the arme, and than he kneled downe and the quene bothe. Wyte you well, than was there many a bolde knyght wyth kynge Arthur that wepte as tendirly as they had seyne all their kynne dede afore them![31]

Lancelot invents this ceremony by drawing on components from late medieval English court culture and chronicle, especially the celebratory processions associated with weddings, coronations, and tournaments, but the emotional scene equally recalls the various chronicle accounts of profuse weeping on both sides during Isabelle's restoration. The visual pageantry of the scene recalls tournaments associated with the Order of the Garter, for example, which often featured women accompanying the Knights of the Order, all dressed in matching clothes.[32] The processions accompanying Isabelle's arrival in London and her coronation, and the Garter tournament Richard held in her honour, at which participants were required to dress in green and

---

[31] *The Works of Sir Thomas Malory*, 1196.

[32] Stephanie Trigg, "Women in Uniform: Dress and Performance in Medieval Court Culture," in *Middle English Literature: Criticism and Debate*, ed. Holly Crocker and D. Vance Smith (New York: Routledge, 2014), 180–90.

white—the queen's colours—may even be models here. When Guenevere rides out to celebrate May in Malory's text, she similarly takes ten women dressed in green, and commands each knight who comes with her to bring a squire and two yeomen with him, all "clothed all in gryne, othir in sylke othir in clothe."[33] Malory goes on to explain that the company of ten "Quenys Knyghtes" only ever bore plain white shields when they were in her service.[34]

Lancelot's choice of white and green is highly motivated. As a colour associated with purity, white symbolizes Lancelot's claim that Guenevere has remained "a true lady" to the king. The coordination of white and green suggests that Lancelot still considers himself part of the Queen's Guard. As he will repeatedly insist, he is her best and most loyal defender.

In contrast to a wedding or a formally agreed truce, in which equal attention is given to the display and demeanour of both sides, this is an uneven display. Arthur's court is not described at all, and the visual focus is on Lancelot and Guenevere's entry into Carlisle. (This recalls the emphasis on the demeanour of the English in the historical accounts of Isabelle's restoration.) In a state of war with King Arthur, Lancelot is given permission to enter the castle under a form of safe conduct, though he shows no sign of shame or embarrassment about the accusation of treason that sits over his head. His political situation may be vulnerable, and there is certainly an unanswered question about his sexual and erotic relationship with the queen. But his procession of men, women, and horses dressed sumptuously in jewels and rich textiles expresses proud defiance. This spectacular display of military and symbolic power, which includes the queen's courtly colours of white and green, constitutes a ceremonial insistence on her restoration to the place of eminence she previously enjoyed at Arthur's court. It is a highly charged emotional moment, but the only emotions we see or hear are registered in the public domain, not as private insights.

In this scene, the strength of the three main characters' emotions is measured in part by their effect on others. Thus, Arthur's bold knights are spectators to this emotional display, and they weep as tenderly as if they saw all their kin dead before them. This collective tenderness measures the affective force of the lovers' return, but it also prefigures the deaths that will ultimately ensue. For even though the queen is restored to Arthur, Gawain remains unreconciled to Lancelot, and Lancelot is argumentative and defensive in his address to the king. At the end of the scene, Lancelot departs and hostilities will soon resume.

Lancelot has orchestrated the visual and symbolic force of this ceremony to great effect, and his is the voice that is heard most insistently in the speeches that follow his arrival. Guenevere does not speak, nor does Malory's dialogue-dependant style allow for much narrative speculation about her unspoken feelings. It is clear that the emotional

---

33 *The Works of Sir Thomas Malory*, 1120.
34 *The Works of Sir Thomas Malory*, 1121.

tensions between Arthur, Lancelot, and Gawain are Malory's chief concerns. Lynch astutely characterizes Malory's distinctive "non-dramatic representation of speech."[35] It is

> not a dramatic impression, simulating what a by-stander might have heard, but rather a narration by direct means of the import of a spoken address, or, as it might be put, a continuation of the main narrative through the words of its personages, in keeping with the book's collective bent, and its sympathetic closeness to oral utterance.[36]

Lynch's emphasis on "the main narrative" and the way it is furthered through Lancelot's discourse helps us see that the feelings of the queen are of less importance than Malory's insistence, through Lancelot's vow, that Guenevere has remained "true and clean," "a true lady" to the king. Nor does King Arthur speak very much, but allows Gawain to turn the occasion from Lancelot's restoration of the queen and his defence of his actions and loyalty to the king, to a scene of continued enmity with Gawain over the death of his brothers. This will lead to the final war and the death of Arthur.

Even though the knights weep when Guenevere arrives, Lancelot's speeches "escalate" the court's emotions, as Raluca Radulescu explains, in one of the few critical commentaries on this scene.[37] None will contest Lancelot's assertion that the queen is "clean" and the dynamic shifts to Gawain's refusal to reconcile with Lancelot. Both men and women of the court weep "as they were madde" or "as people oute of mynde."[38] Radulescu suggests that the court's response indicates that "the boundaries between King Arthur's court and Malory's medieval audience have … collapsed, since it becomes evident that a clear invitation to sympathize with Lancelot and his cause is extended outside the narrative to the audience of the *Morte*."[39]

Once it is clear that reconciliation is impossible, Lancelot addresses the queen a final time, asking her to pray for him, and promising that if she is ever "hard bestad by ony false tunges,"[40] that he will quickly come and deliver her by battle. He then kisses her, brings her to the king and departs, while the court weeps again. The staging of this dramatic four-way encounter between Arthur, Lancelot, Guenevere, and Gawain is a powerful narrative turning point, propelled by the emotional discourse of Lancelot and Gawain. Its effect is indicated by the tears of the many witnesses, and the scene may well invite readerly empathy and feeling. Yet, in stark contrast to various accounts of Isabelle

---

35 Andrew Lynch, *Malory's Book of Arms: The Narrative of Combat in* Le Morte Darthur (Cambridge: Brewer, 1997), 135.

36 Lynch, *Malory's Book of Arms*, 136–37.

37 Raluca L. Radulescu, "Tears and Lies: Emotions and the Ideals of Malory's Arthurian World," in *Emotions in Medieval Arthurian Literature: Body, Mind, Voice*, ed. Frank Brandsma, Carolyne Larrington, and Corinne Saunders (Cambridge: Brewer, 2015), 105–21.

38 *The Works of Sir Thomas Malory*, 1200; 1202.

39 Radulescu, "Tears and Lies," 113.

40 *The Works of Sir Thomas Malory*, 1202.

at the time of her restoration to France, Malory shows little interest in the emotional life of Queen Guenevere. Her return triggers many of the tears and deep feeling evinced on all sides, but her own feelings are of no concern. The political enmities at work and the threat of further warfare are driven by the more consequential feelings of Lancelot and Gawain.

In his influential study, *Malory's Book of Arms*, Lynch analyzes the distinctive features of emotional performance in Malory's work. His characters' emotions are revealed through "dialogue, gesture and bodily sign," rather than through hints of an "'inner' layer of self."[41] Emotions and feelings are also structured by the "natural class system" familiar in medieval culture. As Lynch writes, "Malory's noblest knights naturally have a deeper affective life"; and "Lancelot's spectacular sorrows for Guenevere and Arthur are one of his examples here."[42] The deepest emotions are not just aristocratic; they are also those of men.

Conclusion

In the moment that a woman is ceremonially returned, it is her physical presence, including her appearance, her demeanour, and her apparel, that are of greatest value to the exchange. Such women's voices are rarely heard. When a returned woman is seen by others to express her emotions, through words or gesture, as in the case of Isabelle, whose body language was subject to endless interpretation and reinterpretation by both eyewitnesses and historians, or Criseyde, whose body was immediately subjected to Diomede's gaze, the emotions they display are rarely their own: rather, feelings are attributed to them by other participants and onlookers. Isabelle's emotions would be of no lasting consequence in the war with France: she would not take her revenge on Henry and his supporters, as various chroniclers worried; instead, she would marry her royal cousin, Charles of Orléans, and die in childbirth at the age of twenty.

The emotions of Criseyde and Guenevere, in contrast, are key drivers of plot in their respective narratives and in the larger literary traditions—Classical or Arthurian—to which each text belongs. Criseyde transfers her affections to Diomede after she is restored to her father; and Guenevere returns Lancelot's adulterous love. Yet, in the ceremonial setting, Criseyde's feelings are overshadowed by Troilus' anguish and Diomede's desire; while the intensity of Guenevere's feeling is downplayed. Women's emotions are disabled in, or absent from, medieval restoration ceremonies not because they could not be influential participants in wartime ceremony—witness the case of Queen Philippa, who, in the early stages of the Hundred Years' War, and while heavily pregnant, was reported to have pleaded publically with her husband Edward III to show mercy to the citizens of Calais—but because in such cases they *are* the ceremony. In

---

41 Lynch, *Malory's Book of Arms*, 137.
42 Lynch, *Malory's Book of Arms*, 142.

the act of restoration women are reduced—or elevated—to their status as ceremonial symbols, ideally as symbols of peace, but often in practice as symbols of more complex external relationships or internal feelings. Isabelle's tears and scowls are ultimately signs of the fracture in Anglo-French relations. As far as the participants in Criseyde's exchange are aware, she leaves the people with whom she was born and has lived with an appropriate display of sadness, though for the reader, who knows already how the story will end, she represents both Troilus' downfall and the fall of Troy. In Malory, Guenevere is restored to Arthur at the same time as she is restored to her emblematic status as his queen, although readers know that status will be short-lived. The primary social symbolism of each woman, however, is as a promise of peacetime in the midst of war.

Andrew Lynch, in his discussion of the "feeling of peace" in Laʒamon's *Brut*, gives the example of Gwendolene, the daughter of lord Corineus of Cornwall, who was betrothed to Locrin, son of Brutus and ruler of Britain. Locrin, however, refuses to marry her, having fallen passionately in love with the captive princess, Astrild; Lynch describes Corineus' fury as the "central narrative event of Locrin's reign."[43] Locrin attempts to appease his betrothed's father by pretending to banish Astrild, but when Corineus dies, he ships Gwendolene unceremoniously back to Cornwall, and marries Astrild instead. As her father's heir, Gwendolene's response is to marshal the Cornish people into action and lead them into war against Locrin, whom she soundly defeats. Gwendolene rules the land for the next fifteen years, "providing safety for all, and restoring peace to Cornwall and Logres." What ends badly for Locrin ends well for his subjects: in this example, Locrin's failure to observe due ceremony—his marriage to Gwendolene—results in a period of warfare and his own destruction, while the wronged Gwendolene herself brings a period of peace to the land. As Lynch's work on the cyclical nature of war and peace shows, the fact that the various ceremonial restorations discussed in this chapter take place during or as a prelude to war adds another layer to their emotional as well as their political complexity. And yet even the example of Gwendolene—a woman who was neither ceremonially married nor returned, but who nonetheless becomes a queen—is not entirely atypical: it is her father Corineus' righteous anger that sets his daughter's military action in motion. Again, women's emotions are estranged from the contexts and practices of war, while their ideal presence in the midst of war is tied to the promise of its conclusion.

Women sit uncertainly within the established rituals of war. The promise of peace is symbolically inscribed on the bodies of each of our three women, but narrative and history both show how the act of "restoring" a woman to a previous state or condition inevitably fails before a resolution may be reached, or a stable peace achieved. There may well be some deeper association here with women's loss of innocence and the unspoken affinities between the sexual and the political bodies of women: an anxiety

---

43 Andrew Lynch, "'Blisse wes on londe,'" 45.

that once "given" a woman may never be "restored," and so the desired effects of her restoration—to undo or reverse history—will always elude those involved. Where the restoration of women is concerned, the emotions that outlast the ritual tend to be those of individual men. Whether men's or women's emotions are experienced privately or expressed openly, it is nonetheless clear that individual emotions make history, rather than the public displays of feeling that so ostentatiously attempt to shape it in the ceremonial moment.

Chapter 3

EMOTIONS AND WAR IN CHAUCER'S *KNIGHT'S TALE*

Raluca L. Radulescu*

CHAUCER'S *KNIGHT'S TALE*, the first in the sequence of *Canterbury Tales*, speaks, to a large extent, about order and control, through what could be seen as concentric layers of prisons: from the physical prison Palamon and Arcite live in to the metaphorical prison of courtly love and Emelye's prison of her gender role. Order and control imply some fixity, and yet, as this chapter will demonstrate, it is the characters' movement (contrasting with their fixed prisoner condition), expressed through the verb "to roam," that should give us pause. The causes of this movement, I argue, are complex psychological and emotional processes triggered by prior experience (war) and current situation (confinement). This chapter thus explores the aftermath of the psychological and emotional effects of war in the behaviour of the two knight-prisoners and of Emelye in her own role as war captive.[1] It revisits previously unnoticed changes Chaucer made to the narrative he inherited from his source as well as the context of medieval romance tradition. Only by teasing out the fine articulation of emotions in this tale, properly integrated into these contexts as well as Chaucer's broader work, can we understand its novelty and effect on *The Canterbury Tales* as a whole.

The historical study of emotions has already linked war and emotion from a diachronic perspective, amply studied by Barbara Rosenwein in her pioneering work, and many other recent studies, most importantly in Andrew Lynch's edited collection *Emotions and War*.[2] Monique Scheer has demonstrated that perceptions of emotion are as deeply conditioned by historical and cultural processes as the bodies

---

* **Raluca L. Radulescu** is Professor of Medieval Literature and Director of the Centre for Arthurian Studies at Bangor University, Wales, UK. She is the author of *The Gentry Context for Malory's "Morte Darthur"* (2003) and *Romance and Its Contexts in Fifteenth-Century England: Politics, Piety and Penitence* (2013). She has co-edited eight volumes of essays; the most recent, co-edited with Margaret Connolly, are *Insular Books: Vernacular Manuscript Miscellanies in Late Medieval England* (2015) and *Editing and Interpretation of Middle English Texts* (2018).

1 The topic of trauma has only recently been granted more sustained attention in relation to medieval texts. For a nuanced introduction to the complexities of applying this modern concept to medieval experience see Donna Trembinsky, "Trauma as a Category of Analysis," in *Trauma in Medieval Society*, ed. Wendy J. Turner and Christina Lee (Leiden: Brill, 2018), 13–32. My current chapter does not attempt to approach the topic of trauma in depth, but rather trace a path for future exploration of the issues pertaining to the topic.

2 Stephanie Downes, Andrew Lynch, and Katrina O'Loughlin, *Emotions and War: Medieval to Romantic Literature* (London: Palgrave, 2015). Barbara Rosenwein, *Emotional Communities in the Early Middle Ages* (Ithaca: Cornell University Press, 2006).

who experience them.[3] The *Knight's Tale* could be seen as an exploration of emotional movement and its consequences on the fate of each character. In Palamon's case it is his "roaming" in the chamber, bordering on suicidal, which brings him the opportunity to see Emelye. In Arcite's case it is his later "roaming" in the grove which leads to the encounter with Palamon, and a pathway to win Emelye. In Emelye's case it is her "roaming" in the garden that leads to her own encounter with destiny.

To start with, in the scene depicting the first sight of the lady by two knights-prisoner in Chaucer's *Knight's Tale*, one of the most striking features is the physical manifestation of the knights' restlessness as they are placed in a confined space. Palamon, then Emelye, are seen through the very nature of their movements by the reader of the tale. Palamon is the first to be observed in his restless state:

> And Palamoun, this woful prisoner,
> As was his wone, by leve of his gayler,
> Was risen and *romed* in a chambre an heigh,
> In which he al the noble cite seigh,
> And eek the gardyn, ful of braunches grene,
> Ther as this fresshe Emelye the shene
> *Was in hire walk*, and *romed up and doun*.
> This sorweful prisoner, this Palamoun,
> Goth in the chambre *romynge to and fro*
> And to hymself compleynynge of his wo.
> That he was born, ful ofte he seyde, "alas!"
> And so bifel, by aventure or cas,
> That thurgh a window, thikke of many a barre
> Of iren greet and square as any sparre,
> He cast his eye upon Emelya,
> And therwithal he bleynte and cride, "A!"
> As though he stongen were unto the herte.[4]
> (1063-79; my emphases)

Palamon's movement is shaped by his frustration at being in a closed and controlled space, the prison. His state of mind is captured in this depiction of his "romynge to and fro" in the prison chamber; he is a trapped man, the opposite of the romance hero freely roaming in the forest, open to adventure. Now the great soldier he was once is reduced to a "woful," "sorweful prisoner" (1063, 1070). Yet when he sets eyes on Emelye and feels the sting of Cupid's arrow, he is given a new purpose. Emelye is, however, herself a war captive, yet her plight is not discussed. Chaucer's inversion of romance tropes is evident, and we shouldn't forget that his first audience would be familiar with the fate of the Amazons in the aftermath of Theseus' victory over them: the Amazons are the defeated party, who are left with no choice other than to obey their conqueror, Theseus.

---

[3] Monique Scheer, "Are Emotions a Kind of Practice (and What Is That What Makes Them Have a History)? A Bourdieuian Approach to Understanding Emotion," *History and Theory* 51 (2012): 193–220.

[4] All Chaucer quotations are from *The Riverside Chaucer*, ed. Larry Benson, 3rd ed. (Boston: Mifflin, 1987), cited parenthetically in the text by line number.

As both Hippolyta and Emelye are prisoners of war, they are also subjected to structures of control. Chaucer's romanticizing of their position cannot obscure, for a medieval audience, the very realities Chaucer's Knight, the narrator of the tale, espouses in both his life and his tale: the tragedy and trauma of war, and its aftermath, including its effects on human perceptions and emotions.

Emelye thus shares with Palamon a physical experience rooted in confinement and frustration, which may suggest, to some readers, that her pairing with him at the end of the story is somewhat justified (and not only by his sacrifice to the goddess Venus). While her sister, as the queen of the Amazons, becomes Theseus' wife, Emelye, an Amazon herself, is reduced to the role of a romance heroine observed in her "romynge up and down" in the closed and controlled space of the medieval walled garden. Yet the detail in the description of her movement shows there is more to Chaucer's innovation in this retelling of Boccaccio than adaptation to a romance framework, with the issues of destiny and human choice also considered in the process. Chaucer here emphasizes the potentialities contained in his creative reconstruction of Palamon's, Arcite's, and Emelye's movements in their respective spaces. All three characters' actions suggest at once despair at their new condition (or at least grief and fear) and openness (for good or ill) to the new adventures and chances of romance. Whether this is a healthy response to recent trauma remains a question to be answered in the following pages.

The initial scene cited above has been rehearsed in criticism, in particular how the sighting takes place "by aventure or cas" (1074), understood as the workings of fortune or the mechanism of chivalric adventure, leading to love.[5] However, a close look at the situation reveals that Palamon has engineered it (by "*his* wone .../Was risen and *romed*"); his constrained roaming in "a chambre *an heigh*" happens at his request. Now he is at the top of the prison tower, and from there he has the sight of the whole area ("al the noble cite seigh/And eek the gardyn"). He has given in to despair—since the view of the surrounding area could only bring pain—yet also opened the door to adventure: the sight of freedom is complemented by the lady roaming below and a new desire to escape. Here the spatial dimensions of the image are important: Palamon is looking down from a high place to the spaces below (city and then the garden), which are at the same time enticing but dangerous to his state of mind; as a prisoner, he cannot dream of escape without considering the likelihood of being caught and put to death.

The situation depicted here is paradoxical within the romance framework Chaucer chose for his tale and *The Canterbury Tales* as a whole. Traditionally it is the heroine who gazes down on the knight or knights who are her potential suitors—as Emelye does later, during the tournament scene—who may be engaged in battle or tournaments in order to prove their prowess in arms. The romance heroine usually *chooses* to look at her suitor; she thus manages the distance between them and uses the advantage of her location—high up and/or far away in order to stimulate his desire for great deeds or put himself in danger to save her. Emelye's situation is the complete opposite; she has no

---

5 See Susan Crane, "Medieval Romance and Feminine Difference in the *Knight's Tale*," *Studies in the Age of Chaucer* 12 (1990): 47–63.

power to manage (or even an awareness of) the space between herself and her suitors, unlike her counterpart in Chaucer's source, Boccaccio's *Teseida*, who is self-aware and behaves in a coquettish way.

Simultaneously, Palamon and his sworn brother Arcite both spy on her from their tower; due to their imprisonment, though, their view of the lady is obscured by the distance they are at and even her "brightness." Chaucer's treatment of the cousins/ sworn brothers shows a noticeable difference from his source, Boccaccio's *Teseida*. While in Boccaccio the two men continue as friends, in Chaucer they become arch-enemies. Chaucer's Arcite initially stands still and looks on, but later "roams" in the grove— thus displaying restlessness in a different location. That movement as an expression of emotion is important for an understanding of Chaucer's text is thus evident in his treatment of all three characters.[6] Arcite's "roaming" in the grove, when he is lamenting his love woes, is, I argue, another parallel, though not only between him and Palamon, as Lee Patterson has pointed out,[7] but also between him and Emelye.

Barry Windeatt, John Burrow and A. C. Spearing have explored body language and gestures in Chaucer's writing, yet the connection between movement and emotion has not been explored in this way to date.[8] V. A. Kolve interpreted the phrase "roaming up and down" to denote Emelye's movement as an expression of freedom, not of restlessness; William F. Woods suggests the same phrase is linked to "idling," a typical aristocratic "class-related activity." Finally, Peter Brown has applied medieval optical theory to the moment when Palamon and Arcite fall in love with Emelye.[9] By returning attention to

---

[6] See Alastair Minnis, *Chaucer and Pagan Antiquity* (Cambridge: Cambridge University Press, 1982). Minnis dedicates two sections of chapter 4 in his study to the three characters, though he does not examine in detail the aspects I tackle here. See also Barbara Nolan, *Chaucer and the Tradition of the Roman Antique* (Cambridge: Cambridge University Press, 1992). Nolan places the tale in the context of the *roman antique* tradition, but similarly deals primarily with *aventure* and Theseus rather than characterization in the way I do here.

[7] Lee Patterson, "The *Knight's Tale* and the Crisis of Chivalric Identity," in *Chaucer and the Subject of History*, ed. Lee Patterson (Madison: University of Wisconsin Press, 1991), esp. 205-7. Patterson's classic study does much to illuminate the ways in which Chaucer's take on the chivalric code would be interpreted in his period, but no reference is made to "roaming" or its connections with emotion and adventure.

[8] See John Burrow, *Gestures and Looks in Medieval Literature* (Cambridge: Cambridge University Press, 2002), in which he surveys some features of Chaucer's writing but does not engage with this particular tale or a typology of movement and its link to emotion and agency. Barry Windeatt, *Troilus and Criseyde* (Oxford: Oxford University Press, 1992) and A. C. Spearing, *The Medieval Poet as Voyeur* (Cambridge: Cambridge University Press, 1993) also address different emotional responses in Chaucer's work and romance, respectively, but do not tackle the issues I refer to in this chapter.

[9] See V. A. Kolve, *Chaucer and the Imagery of the Narrative* (Stanford: Stanford University Press, 1984); William F. Woods, "Up and Down, To and Fro: Spatial Relationships in the *Knight's Tale*," in *Rebels and Rivals: The Contestive Spirit in The Canterbury Tales*, ed. Susanna Greer Fein, David Raybin, and Peter C. Braeger (Kalamazoo: Medieval Institute Publications, 1991), 37-57, and William F. Woods, "'My Sweete Foo': Emelye's Role in the *Knight's Tale*," *Studies in Philology* 88, no. 3 (1991): 276-306, as well as his recent *Chaucerian Spaces: Spatial Poetics in Chaucer's Opening*

Chaucer's use of movement in contrast to his source, Boccaccio's *Teseida*, as well as examining other relevant sections of *The Canterbury Tales*, this chapter foregrounds the important but under-examined motif of roaming, linking it to anxiety, strong emotion, and traumatic event (war). It shows how movement and strong emotion form a context for Chaucer's intention to match roaming movements, not only of the two male characters, Palamon and Arcite, trapped in their respective physical and emotional prisons (not to mention the prison of human condition), but also of Emelye's roaming, indicative of her own inner emotions as well as Chaucer's interest in female movement. It focuses on the reversal of traditional male and female roles in the tower scene, and the use of roaming as a prelude to adventure, in order to address primarily Emelye's inner emotions in the initial garden scene.[10] The first part of this chapter focuses on the context in which "roaming" and its correlative, strong emotion, reveal Chaucer's treatment of Palamon's and Arcite's trajectories at the beginning of the tale, and the interpretative framework his presentation of the male characters' movement provides for Emelye's. In the second part a fresh examination of Emelye's movement reveals a new place for her among Chaucer's other female characters whose roaming has dramatic consequences in their destinies.

Physical "Roaming" and Emotional Turmoil in Chaucer and Boccaccio

In the *Knight's Tale*, movement is evident in three main spaces: the prison, the garden, and the grove/tournament. Yet movement has most often been discussed in relation to the role of the "Firste Moevere" in the story and the interplay between "aventure or cas," with characters variously assigning accidents to a providential design. Analyses of freedom have been limited to the Boethian perspective on the human condition.[11] However, there is more to physical movement in the tale than these (valuable) aspects traditionally focused on by critics. Chaucer uses movement—expressed in the rarely encountered Middle English verb "to roam" as will be shown below—as a direct correlative to physical symptoms of emotional distress.

Tales (Albany: State University of New York Press, 2008). Peter Brown, *Chaucer and the Making of Optical Space* (Berlin: Peter Lang, 2007), chap. 7.

10 I use *Sources and Analogues of the Canterbury Tales*, ed. Robert M. Correale and Mary Hamel, 2 vols. (Woodbridge: Brewer, 2002, 2005), 1, the *Knight's Tale*, and, where only summaries are available of relevant stanzas in *Sources and Analogues*, I turned to the standard edition of Giovanni Boccaccio's works in *Tutte le Opere di Giovanni Boccaccio*, ed. Vittore Branca, 10 vols. (Milan: Montadori, 1954–98), 2. The translations are taken from N. R. Havely, *Chaucer's Boccaccio: Sources for Troilus and the Knight's and Franklin's Tales* (Cambridge: Cambridge University Press, 1992). All other translations are mine.

11 See Mark Miller, *Philosophical Chaucer: Love, Sex and Agency in the Canterbury Tales* (Cambridge: Cambridge University Press, 2004), chap. 2. Character-driven analyses, on the other hand, have usually focused on the prayers of the three characters, Emelye, Arcite, and Palamon to the three deities Diana, Mars, and Venus, in particular the associations Chaucer inherited from his source between human temperament and that of the gods, and his changes to his source.

Peter Brown notes that Palamon's state of extreme emotion, discomfort, and unease, as well as Emelye's brightness, mark Chaucer's changes to the *Teseida*, and play an important role in this initial scene. Similarly, Jamie Friedman proposes a fresh examination of Emelye's interiority in the tale, but does not engage with this initial scene in relation to Emelye's movement and her encounter with destiny.[12] Here I take these discussions a lot further, to show how the movement (more specifically, "roaming") of all *three* characters (Palamon, Emelye, *and* Arcite) is indicative of the psychological effects (trauma) of war, and how the effects of this trauma are far-reaching in the economy of the story.[13]

Palamon has exposed himself to danger and left open the door to chance—or, to use Chaucer's more apposite words, "aventure or cas." Tellingly, although Emelye is in the garden at the time Palamon is looking out on the city and the garden ("Ther as this fresshe Emelye the shene/*Was in hire walk*, and *romed up and doun*" at 1068–69), the narrator does not tell us that Palamon has noticed her. Only after Palamon has been characterized a second time as the "sorweful prisoner" after his sight of the city and more "romynge to and fro," does he catch a glimpse of Emelye through the "thikke of many a barre" of a window.[14] By contrast, Arcite's movements are not described and no indication is given of his temperament or state of mind, apart from the "angwissh" and "wo" that the narrator tells us Theseus had inflicted on both cousins prior to this moment: "And in a tour, in angwissh and in wo,/This Palamon and his felawe Arcite/For everemoore; ther may no gold hem quite" (1030–32). Arcite is the one who states that they should "taak al in pacience/Oure prisoun, for it may noon other be./Fortune hath yeven us this adversitee/... We moste endure it; this is the short and playn" (1084–86, 1091). Arcite's position reflects his (wise) understanding of the advice Lady Philosophy provides in Chaucer's translation of Boethius, his *Boece*. There we learn how those in the tower of Reason are actually protected from the vagaries of fortune and should consider themselves lucky to escape the effects thereof (1. pr. 3). Arcite appears ready to engage in a Boethian debate about the conditions of the knights' imprisonment and attitude to the situation. Palamon does not seem open to the debate and instead resembles the

---

[12] See Jamie Friedman, "Between Boccaccio and Chaucer: The Limits of Female Interiority in the *Knight's Tale*," in *The Inner Life of Women in Medieval Romance Literature*, ed. Jeff Rider and Jamie Friedman (London: Palgrave, 2011), 203–22. The article focuses primarily on Emelye's prayer in the Temple of Diana.

[13] Here it is essential to remember that the way in which the effects of war and captivity were perceived and explained in medieval literature are fundamentally different from our modern understanding of the same (for more on this, see the chapters in Wendy J. Turner and Christina Lee, *Trauma in Medieval Society*). Both male and female protagonists in the *Knight's Tale* remain unaware of the consequences of their mental states on their decisions, and the male characters' reactions are much altered by Chaucer to fit genre expectations—in the sudden falling in love, the rivalry and eagerness to combat, and so on. For this reason, the application of trauma theory, as conceived in modern studies, to this text would be, to my mind, improper.

[14] As mentioned, this image is thoroughly analyzed by Brown from the perspective of the medieval science of optics; see Brown, *Chaucer and the Making*, 220ff.

fictional character of Boethius in the *Consolation* (and Chaucer's *Boece*) who anxiously frets and weeps over his condition, on the brink of despair. While both Palamon and Arcite are undoubtedly suffering from the trauma of war and imprisonment, Arcite's admonition to Palamon is all the more revealing as it conveys the unusual mental balance he maintains while in prison, at least up to this point, under such dire circumstances. In this context, he is, perhaps surprisingly, navigating the effects of war trauma in a much more serene way than we might expect, and with the wisdom displayed by medieval saints, rather than warriors, in the Middle Ages.[15]

In Boccaccio's *Teseida* neither Palemone nor Arcita are shown to spend time engaging in a Boethian debate. Within Chaucer's invented debate, however, Palamon exercises agency, not in changing his condition (escaping from prison), but in influencing, unwittingly, the course of events. He does so by roaming, at his own request, in a particular place within the prison, which in turn triggers an encounter with destiny—the sight of Emelye. When Arcite is stung by the same arrow/sight of love, or rather "roaming freedom" symbolized by Emelye, his previous disposition—calm and wise—is disturbed. The cousins' extreme emotions at the sight of Emelye—the symbol of freedom—reveal how quickly they revert to the psychology of war, that is an attitude that goes beyond the medieval romance enactment of the ideal of courtly love and the enmity resulting from violence that could result in battlefield-like slaughter displayed by two knights pursuing the same lady. This new enmity is the opposite of their previous sworn brotherhood: "And therefore, at the kynges court, my brother,/Ech man for himself, ther is noon oother" (lines 1181–82) and a sign that Chaucer's appropriation of medieval romance tropes is much more complex than critics have hitherto noticed.

The knights' world is upside down as they are *up* in the prison tower, not roaming free in search of adventures, and the lady is *down* below, in the garden, a reversal of the traditional romance, whereby ladies placed on high watch knights fighting in tournaments below. In Chaucer's source, Boccaccio's *Teseida*, it is Arcita who first wakes and seeks out Emilia, because he can hear her voice (singing love songs), and her voice is as beautiful as her appearance.[16] Boccaccio's is a radically different view of both Emilia and Arcita than Chaucer's. The sight of her eventually inflicts the pain of love in both knights, but it is her voice that literally awakes the man, here Arcita, and his senses. Boccaccio's Emilia is famously coquettish and enjoys playing with the attention she receives from the two knights, unlike Chaucer's Emelye, who remains completely oblivious of the torment her presence has caused to the knights-prisoner.[17] It becomes evident that Chaucer exploited the situation presented by Boccaccio (knights-prisoner

---

15 For an illuminating analysis of the complexities of studying trauma in the behaviour described in medieval texts (for example, St Francis of Assisi) see Trembinsky, "Trauma as a Category of Analysis" for a summary of scholarship on this topic.

16 *Sources and Analogues*, 2:147 (stanza 11). For a description of Emilia's actions in the garden see stanzas 8–10. I am not persuaded that the adverb "longingly" is implied in the original text, though the translation by Coleman and Agostinelli contains it.

17 See summary of stanzas 12–44 in *Sources and Analogues*, 2:147.

locked away, beautiful lady coquettishly singing outside) to show the characters' altered circumstances—their traumatic emotional state, with all the risks it implies.

Arcite spends the years after his release finding a way back to Athens, forging a new identity so as to be able to live near and enjoy Emelye's presence; Palamon languishes in "derknesse and horrible and strong prisoun" (1451) for another seven years. Both cousins' attitudes to love are affected by the trauma of war and imprisonment, which distort their approach to life and completely alter their prospects as initially they do not aim to escape. In other words, neither cousin remembers chivalric duty or obligations, nor do they seek revenge for the fate of their peers, going back to a soldier's career. The emotions they display in the pursuit of Emelye may, I argue, be seen to show how the trauma of both war and incarceration has altered their perception of reality and their response to stimuli.

Upon returning to Athens, Arcite's habit is to "roam" in a grove nearby, lamenting the impossibility of revealing his identity to his beloved, and having a chance, therefore, to display his love. As he roams "al his fille" (1528), his moods swing "now in the crope, now doun in the breres,/Now up, now doun, as boket in a welle" (1532-33).[18] The extreme reactions both knights display when in love also point to the confined spaces in which they express them: Palamon is captive, while Arcite, ironically freed from prison, is still a prisoner of his feelings, and of his chosen disguise. Within the framework of the story, and of *The Canterbury Tales*, the two characters are, to use Egeus' words later on, "pilgrymes, passynge to and fro" (2848) in this world. Here the "roaming" is clearly associated with "passing," that is, the condition shared by the characters with the audience of the tale, within Chaucer's whole set of tales, and outside it. The connection established by Egeus between the movement of pilgrims through life and the knights' restless roaming leads to a serious reflection on the nature of closed spaces in which these knights, who otherwise would be expected, within the romance framework, to roam freely in search of adventure, are actually trapped, and on multiple levels. Chaucer also anticipates, to some extent, his treatment of closed spaces as it appears in his *The Tale of Sir Thopas*, with Palamon's "youling and clamour" being a reflection of his feelings.[19]

Quite apart from these extreme emotions, however, Chaucer's changes to the movement associated with the two knights he inherited from his source show that he deliberately set out to present Arcite and Palamon in a different light than in Boccaccio's *Teseida*. In Boccaccio it is Pamphilus, Palemone's servant, who discovers Arcite's new identity by listening to his amorous pleas in the grove. Pamphilus then reports it all

---

[18] The effects of love on the knight protagonists in Chaucer's tale anticipate, to some extent, Chaucer's treatment of the romance genre in his famous "Tale of Sir Thopas," and the exaggerations there.

[19] The limited glimpse Chaucer allows his audience into the world of romance he mocks in "The Tale of Sir Thopas" suggests a(nother) absurd situation in which the fictional knight wanders in the enclosed fictional space of a story that goes nowhere.

to his master in prison and stirs Palemone's desire to escape and meet Arcita/now Pentheus.[20] In Chaucer Palamon escapes only "by helpyng of a freend" (1468) who remains anonymous, and no mention is made of the servant's salutary intervention. In this, Palamon shows a degree of agency and enterprise, though only after many years of emotional and physical suffering. His protracted inaction may have been the effect of torpor of the senses, an effect of the trauma of war and incarceration.

In the *Teseida* Palemone *purposefully* seeks Arcita/Penteo in the grove, though *at night*; he finds him asleep and does not want to wake him, seeing how peacefully he rests: "E' nol voleva miga risvegliare,/tanto pareva a lui che e' dormisse/soavemente" ("[Palemone] didn't want to wake him since he [Arcita] seemed to sleep so peacefully").[21] When he breaks free, Chaucer's Palamon comes upon Arcite/Philostrate (in *daylight*, and *by chance*), who is in Boccaccio's *Teseida* "roaming up and down" in the grove, lamenting his hopeless position as a lover in disguise. The contrast between the two scenes provides evidence that Chaucer deliberately presented Arcite's movement—his roaming in the grove—as an expression of his emotions. This points to a direct parallel both to Palamon's earlier "roaming up and down" in the prison chamber and Emelye's in the garden. Like Palamon and Emelye, Arcite is still a prisoner—now of his emotions—and places himself, unwittingly, in the path of change or adventure by talking openly about his condition while also expressing passionate torment in his movement. Chaucer's parallel of language shows direct links between physical and emotional/psychological imprisonment: Arcite "rometh up and down" (1515). He exercises his agency in action in the same way Palamon had done while in the prison chamber. Whereas in Boccaccio's *Teseida* no particular attention is paid to movement as a correlative to emotion and no direct implication may be observed between the location of a specific action and a character's agency, in the *Knight's Tale*, by contrast, Chaucer makes movement, its location, and the links with emotion and agency all important.

Chaucer's interest in movement therefore points to the connection he establishes between "roaming" and the inner states experienced by his characters. His descriptions of roaming and emotions also show his engagement with the romance tradition, in which male protagonists typically encounter their destiny while riding a horse or walking through an *open* space, prey to their intense emotions: love, anger, envy, despair, madness. However, while the typical knight roams freely in a landscape that offers potential adventures and opportunities to gain worship, usually in service of the beloved lady, Chaucer's Palamon and Arcite are confined to a structure already in place, a trap: their prison, their love, their human condition as pilgrims through this life on earth. In this context the verb "to roam," itself unusually frequent in the tale, functions as a pointer to both the knights', and Emelye's, multiple imprisonments and their adventure, or their encounter with destiny.

---

20 Havely, *Chaucer's Boccaccio*, 5:1–12, *Sources and Analogues*, 2:154–56.

21 Boccaccio, *Tutte le Opere*, 5:36, my translation (only a summary of this stanza is available in Havely, *Chaucer's Boccaccio*, 5:36).

Aventure as a word also features more frequently in this tale by comparison to the rest of *The Canterbury Tales*. While the presence of the word is expected, given the romance framework of the *Knight's Tale*, Barbara Nolan has pointed out that here Chaucer used *aventure* "as the mainspring of most, though not quite all, of the story's action. The word *aventure* occurs in the [*Knight's*] *Tale* eleven times, while in *The Canterbury Tales* as a whole it appears only thirty times."[22] In other words, the use of movement in the tale and its correlative, emotion, needs to also be assessed in relation to its function as a prelude to adventure in the lives of the protagonists. Motion and roaming in particular open the romance character to adventure.

The initial scenes in which Chaucer's three characters meet, are observed, are separated, and meet again are fundamentally different from Boccaccio in terms of emotion, movement and agency. Agency is located in each character, as Palamon chooses to roam to and fro at the top of the tower, Emelye chooses to roam in her garden, and Arcite ends up, later on, when free, choosing to roam in the grove. These movements do not, however, preclude the intervention of "destinee" or fate which affects human life. As Jill Mann has observed:

> The chances and changes that Boethius contemplates in the *Consolation* are chances and changes in the external world—loss of riches, family or friends. Chaucer adds to his representation of these instances of "moevable destinee" the *inner* mutations which are ceaselessly at work in every human being. It is on these inner mutations that the external occurrences work; it is from the coalescence of the two that the shape of the action is born. A spherical object placed at the top of a slope will roll to the bottom because of its own sphericity as well as because of the declivity; its own nature is "expressed" in the rolling just as much as the nature of the surrounding circumstances. So Criseyde is "expressed" in her motions towards love, even though external circumstances are needed to bring her potentialities into being.[23]

Here Mann analyzes Criseyde and chance before she moves on to examining chance in *Knight's Tale*. Although she does not touch on the idea of "bringing potentialities into being" in Palamon and Arcite, or indeed Emelye, potentialities are also brought into being in the case of our three characters, though unnoticed to date. The transformation of potential into being is a reflection of Stoic thinking on necessity and free will, with which Chaucer seems to agree, though he did not have direct knowledge of the Stoics.[24] Mann argues:

> We must be alive to [Chaucer's] use of words like "cas," "aventure" or "destinee" (and to others, such as "entencioun," "purveiaunce," "ordinaunce," "governaunce," which also belong to his exploration of Boethian problems), as signalling his reflections

---

[22] Nolan, *Chaucer and the Tradition*, 252.

[23] Jill Mann, "Chance and Destiny in *Troilus and Criseyde* and the *Knight's Tale*," in *Cambridge Chaucer Companion*, ed. Piero Boitani and Jill Mann (Cambridge: Cambridge University Press, 1986), 75–92 at 83.

[24] Mann, "Chance and Destiny," 92n12.

on the nature of the forces which work on human beings, and the extent of their own possibilities for action.[25]

To some extent the two knights resemble each other more than in Boccaccio and suffer for love in ways linked to the passions associated with their gods, Mars and Venus; in David Wallace's words, "Arcite is cruel, while Palamon is mad."[26] Steve Rigby and others see the excesses of irascibility and concupiscence in the two knights, who are both in need of a lesson to temper their passions.[27] A full examination of the passions and their associated gods is beyond the scope of the present argument, however. Instead, a limited investigation of the agency Arcite and Palamon exert in their trajectories as knights worthy of Emelye's hand shows how Chaucer brings these "potentialities" into being in the tale.

Both Boccaccio's Palemone and Chaucer's Palamon languish in prison, inactive, but consumed by jealousy. While Palemone needs his servant's report about Arcite's return to Athens to stir him to action, Chaucer's Palamon seems paralysed by his mad jealousy and only breaks out of prison after seven years. Chaucer famously emphasizes chance or *aventure* at the point of Palamon's escape: whereas Boccaccio's Palemone purposefully rides to the grove his servant has told him Arcita frequents, Palamon chances on Arcite in exactly the place where the latter takes his usual stroll. Chaucer's Arcite is the knight lover of the romance tradition, and his choice of location for his "roaming" fits in with this image. In this, Chaucer's Arcite seems to inherit some of the characteristics of Boccaccio's Arcita, who is the first to see Emilia, and appears more entitled to her than Palemone. Hence the latter is presented by Boccaccio as a perfect match for Emilia, who even shows him "a certain sympathy" on his release from prison (3:84). She recognizes him on his return to the court in disguise, when she wonders at his thin and pale appearance, and seems to reciprocate his feelings.[28] She grows even fonder of Arcita during the tournament,[29] and their wedding shows, in the *Teseida*, that the two of them are meant to be together.

---

25 Mann, "Chance and Destiny," 90–91.

26 David Wallace, *Chaucerian Polity: Absolutist Lineages and Associational Forms in England and Italy* (Stanford: Stanford University Press, 1997), 105.

27 Steve Rigby, *Wisdom and Chivalry: Chaucer's "Knight's Tale" and Medieval Political Theory* (Leiden: Brill, 2009), chap. 2, parts i and ii for a summary of criticism on these lines, and further discussion of "the passions and the parts of the soul" in Giles of Rome's *De Regimine Principum* and their reflection in the *Knight's Tale*. According to Rigby, "whilst Arcite and Palamon are each originally associated with the passions of the irascible and the concupiscible in their devotion to Mars and Venus, they also eventually achieve the characteristic virtues of these parts of the soul." Rigby, *Wisdom and Chivalry*, 109.

28 Boccaccio, *Tutte le Opere*, 4:56ff; Havely, *Chaucer's Boccaccio*, 3:57.

29 See Angela Jane Weisl, *Conquering the Realm of Femeny: Gender and Genre in Chaucer's Romance* (Woodbridge: Brewer, 1995), 59, for her comparative analysis of this section in Boccaccio and Chaucer.

On the other hand, Boccaccio's Palemone merely appears lucky. Although he did pray to Venus, as Palamon does in Chaucer's tale, Boccaccio's Emilia, in true romance fashion (understood as a validation of a lady's reward of love for her suitor's chivalric deeds), prefers a martial suitor. Emilia even advises Palemone to follow Mars rather than Cupid, which suggests that she would choose Arcita in the end.[30] Strangely, perhaps, Boccaccio's Emilia is more of the Amazon type in this respect, while at the same time being more of a courtly lady than Chaucer's heroine.

Emelye, in contrast, is silent at this stage, yearning for an opportunity to continue her life in service of Diana. Friedman analyzes in detail Emelye's prayer at Diana's temple as an indicator of the limits of Emelye's interiority; this critical approach merely reinforces the modern view that Emelye's body is ruled by men (Theseus, the Knight as narrator, the audience), just as her "breastless, resistant body with its autonomous subjectivity" is used as "an objective terrain across which men communicate, take erotic pleasure, and found and perpetuate social affiliations."[31] However, Emelye's movement earlier in the tale, in the first scene in which the two knights-prisoner see her, shows Chaucer using movement to hint at her interiority. Chaucer's original use of "roaming" to describe Emelye's positioning of herself in the world through movement, and potentially also her emotions, can only be envisaged through an examination of the presence of this word elsewhere in his work, the topic of the second part of this study. In her "roaming" movement Emelye now resembles the two male protagonists, and a Middle English audience would notice the use of the word in a context that is now used for a purpose other than fitting with the conventions of the courtly romance genre.

Emelye's Movement

The two knights' movements, emotions and agency—captured in the verb "roam"—shows them placing themselves in the path of adventure. As the analysis above shows, it is evident Chaucer envisioned an interpretative scheme for an understanding of movement in the tale. The question arising from this analysis is to what extent Emelye's own "roaming" in the initial garden scene is meant to be read in the same way, as an expression of her own emotions, and a prelude to adventure. Previous criticism has identified Emelye's prison (the garden, her condition as sister of the conquered Amazon queen Hippolyta) as the defined space in which she, like the other female characters in this tale, are controlled. There is, however, a possible suggestion here that Emelye's movement may indicate more than submissiveness to her condition.

Emelye seems, at least at first sight, to symbolize the archetypal romance heroine in her walled garden, a personification of innocent youth and freshness, even more than

---

30 Havely, *Chaucer's Boccaccio*, 8:124–25.
31 Friedman, "Between Boccaccio," 208–13 at 214.

Boccaccio's Emilia.[32] Boccaccio's Emilia is drawn to the garden by her very nature: "a ciò tirata da propria natura/non che d'amare altrui fosse costretta" (drawn to this by her own nature and not because she was obligated by love for someone else).[33] Then she becomes self-conscious once she has learned about the presence of the two knights gazing at her from the palace window. Emilia is exercising a freedom Chaucer's Emelye would never know: that of controlling the knights' passions, stirring them with her carefully contrived gestures, singing, and appearance.[34]

In her Chaucerian role Emelye is expected to instil love and passion in the hearts of young, lusty knights in the month of May, so it comes as a surprise that the effect of her sighting is fratricidal hate—and to violent extremes, as experienced by Palamon and Arcite. The images associated with Emelye transform her from an Amazon into a courtly lady—"fresshe Emelye the shene" (1068)—whose "brightness" and "freshness" dominate all other aspects of her physique. She conforms to the demands of the romance genre, although it is already clear, from her description, that something different may be going on: she is not just "in hire walk," but she "romed up and down," a movement that literally mirrors Palamon's pacing up and down in his confined space at the top of the tower.

Thus the *Knight's Tale* is the work in which Chaucer associates the verb "roam" with male as well as female characters. Yet elsewhere in Chaucer's work "roaming" is always associated with female figures.[35] "To roam" means "to walk, to wander about" (*MED* v. 1 a), but also 1 b) "to walk or pace up and down" or the more common 2 b) "to stroll."[36] "Roaming" is sometimes associated with leisurely activities such as "pleying" and "singing" (*MED* 1 a); interestingly, leisure is also defined, in chivalric language, as "a martial game" (under 2 a) when it refers to knightly pursuits, enjoyed by male romance heroes when hunting in the forest.

When depicted in their movement, female heroines are walking in a garden, orchard or by the seashore, usually involved in an activity such as "pleying" (meaning leisure of an unspecified kind) or "singing" (a more structured and reflective activity). At times "walking" or "roaming about" are associated with traumatic events when emotion is

---

32 See Weisl, *Conquering the Realm*, chap. 2, for a comparison between Boccaccio's and Chaucer's portrayals of Emilia/Emelye and the contrast between the self-conscious, flirtatious Emilia, and the unknowing Emelye. See also *Sources and Analogues*, 2:147.

33 *Sources and Analogues*, 2:145–46, from *Teseo* Book 3, stanza 8, lines 2–3.

34 Boccaccio, *Tutte le Opere*, 3:25–30 (and corresponding translation and summary in Havely, *Chaucer's Boccaccio*).

35 Akio Oizumi, *Complete Concordance to the Works of Geoffrey Chaucer* (Hildesheim: Georg Olms Verlag, 1994), and *eChaucer: Chaucer in the Twenty-First Century: Chaucer Concordance*, www.umm.maine.edu/faculty/necastro/chaucer/concordance/, and the *MED*.

36 *MED*, online version. The verb "to roam" is rarely encountered in Middle English romance, with only one example cited in the *MED* from the Auchinleck version of the poem *Arthour and Merlin*: "Þo he was cloþed, he com adoun,/Sikeende and romende vp and doun" (2372, listed under b).

displayed, as will be shown below; most importantly, at such points the link between movement and emotion also signals the outset of an unexpected adventure or dramatic change in the life of the romance protagonist.[37]

Therefore "to roam" means "to walk, to wander about" but also "to walk or pace up and down"; the last meaning may be understood, at least at a first reading, as the purpose of Emelye's garden walking where she is described "in hire walk, romynge up and down" (1069), as well as Arcite's ramble later on in the grove, when he has been enjoying freedom for a while (1515). *MED* 1 b) "to walk or pace up and down" is most evidently explored by Chaucer at the beginning of his tale and appears to be an implied reading of other types of walking. The meaning under 2 b) "to stroll" is encountered in in the *Franklin's Tale* where Dorigen "freendes ... preyde hire .../To come and *romen* hire in compaignye,/Awey to dryue hir derke fantasye" (843–45; my italics) and in the *The Man of Law's Tale*, where Custaunce "han ytake the righte way/Toward the see a furlong wey or two/To pleyen and to *romen to and fro*" (556–58; my italics). Taken out of context, these brief passages might suggest that these two female characters indeed "roam" leisurely, in the pursuit of pleasure with their friends. Looked at more closely, however, their "roaming" is actually linked to prior suffering and pain caused by separation from loved ones and the feelings of frustration resulting from a situation best described as being "trapped."

Indeed, Chaucer's use and adaptation of the association between distress, movement, and adventure, so often seen in the romance tradition from Chrétien de Troyes onwards in the trajectories of both male and female characters,[38] is evident in the *Franklin's Tale* where Dorigen's distraught state at the departure of her husband is reflected in her refusal to enjoy company in her stroll. Her choice to forsake company and instead roam in an open space by herself leads to her exposure to further distress; here the sight of the perilous rocks, which she so fears pose a danger to her husband's return, changes her response to Aurelius' advances. Dorigen's friends had pleaded with her to keep company so as to avoid "derke fantasye." In the second instance, when she chooses to "romen by the see" (896), the verb denotes a state of increasing distress that results in Dorigen's rushed request of what she assumes is impossible (the removal of the rocks). Here she may be seen to instigate the adventure itself, or rather the story whose disastrous consequences are explored in this tale, since she does want the rocks removed for the safe arrival of her husband's ship. In other words, Dorigen engineers her own destruction in subtler ways than explored to date: by choosing to roam freely close to the rocks and in the open space, without the proper company to divert her thoughts from despair, she leaves herself open to the thoughts that undermine her clear thinking. She also opens the door to change, or adventure, in a way that appears typical

---

37 Examples from romances focusing on male protagonists who experience an encounter with destiny while they roam, as a result of their intense emotions, are present in romances both in French (and Anglo Norman) and Middle English.

38 There are plenty of examples of knights or ladies in distress walking or riding in a space, their movement correlated with emotion, and functioning as a prelude to adventure, an encounter with destiny.

for the romance heroine. In this context Chaucer reminds us that here the portrayal of the landscape is indicative of the inner world of the characters.

As Kolve points out, Dorigen anxiously contemplates the sea, first in the same company of her "freendes," with whom "Hire to disporte upon the bank an heigh,/Where as she many a ship and barge seigh/Seillynge hir cours, where as hem liste go" (848–50).[39] He notes that no rocks are mentioned at this point or indeed upon Arveragus' return; emphasis is placed in the former passage on the phrase "as hem liste go," as the ships sail as their sailors and commander please. A contrast is here visible between the seashore and the garden Dorigen's friends persuade her to go back to, a garden of pleasures and of love, where the "governing mood—and mode—is *play*."[40] Kolve emphasizes freedom and inner landscapes of despair here, though "roaming" does not feature in his analysis. Dorigen is seen to be safe while on the brink of despair if she is willing to seek or at least tolerate company, but she is not so when she stubbornly contemplates the real or imaginary rocks of her fear. The shift to the garden is telling, as it is there that her thoughts will turn to a false resolution to her despair, by seeking relief (the removal of the rocks) from her potential lover, whom she scorns. The leisurely activity involved in the use of "play," and the specificity of the location—the garden—point to Chaucer's emphasis on Dorigen's foolish abandonment to fate. Play it may appear to be, but of a dangerous kind. In fact it seems that Dorigen is reckless in her choice of roaming by the seashore, and then again in her roaming in the garden.[41]

The situation in which a romance heroine allows inner turmoil to transform her plea or, indeed, leaves herself open to adventure was used by Chaucer in other instances. In *The Man of Law's Tale*, having been cast adrift at sea, princess Custaunce is shipwrecked on the coast of Northumberland and found by the constable of the castle nearby. Half-crazed by the long period of starvation and near despair, Custaunce can barely speak, and is said to have lost her mind: "she seyde she was so mazed in the see/That she forgat hir mynde, by hir trouthe" (526–27). One day after she has spent some time with the constable and his wife Hermengyld, during a period of Christian persecution in Britain which the narrator describes at some length, Custaunce, the constable, and dame Hermengyld "han ytake the righte way/Toward the see a furlong wey or two/ To pleyen and to *romen* to and fro" (556–58; my italics). It is at this point that the conversion of the old constable to Christianity takes place, once he has met a blind old Christian who recognized his wife. While at first sight the "roaming" by the sea and the conversion of the constable do not seem to push the narrative forward in any significant way, the incident is placed just before an event which will change Custaunce's life again. Immediately after the constable's conversion, the narrator tells that the devil was

---

39 V. A. Kolve, *Telling Images: Chaucer and the Imagery of the Narrative II* (Stanford: Stanford University Press, 2009), 173–74.
40 Kolve, *Telling Images*, 176 (his emphasis).
41 Gardens are notoriously unsafe spaces for romance heroines. Examples abound in romances, including the better-known abductions or rape of heroines in *Sir Orfeo* and *Sir Gowther*.

jealous of Custaunce's virtue and hence engineered the unwelcome amorous attention of a local knight. Custaunce rebuffs his lecherous advances, but the knight resolves to kill Hermengyld and place incriminating evidence (the knife) next to Custaunce, who is thus blamed for the murder. The treacherous knight's behaviour is contrasted with Custaunce's exemplary nature, as well as the constable's and his wife's; in this equation dame Hermengyld is the threatened heroine, whose association with Custaunce leaves her open to adventure or chance, and, in this case, the knight's evil deed. The apparently innocent stroll by the sea of the three characters has had a life-changing impact on their existence; not only has the constable been adopted into the Christian community (Hermengyld had already been a Christian in secret), but it may be understood that the trio of Christians attracts the devil's jealousy perhaps even more given Custaunce's implicit role in the conversion. The use of "pley" and "roaming to and fro" in this episode points to the dangers associated with female movement outside prescribed spaces, a point Chaucer exploits in various ways in *The Canterbury Tales*.

Elsewhere in Chaucer's work, roaming by the sea is similarly portrayed as dangerous, or at least as an open door to adventure or chance. In the legend of "Hypsipyle and Medea," which forms part of Chaucer's *Legend of Good Women*, Ysiphele "the shene," queen of the island of Lemnos (1467), is said to be "*romynge* on the clyves by the se" (1470; my italics). Her movement leads to her encounter with Jason and Hercules. Interestingly, the activity and its location are further emphasized twice in a short space, as Jason tells the queen's messenger that "we wery be,/And come for to pleye out of the se/Tyl that the wynd be better in oure weye" (1494–96); and "This lady [Isiphele] *rometh* by the clyf to pleye" (1497; my italics). Although she is accompanied by "hir meyne" (1498), Isiphele makes the mistake of believing Hercules' charming words about Jason and marries the latter only to be abandoned later, with their two children, when he sets sail again. She is said to be "an innocent" (1546) as well as a "fayre yonge" and "shene," attributes which may go some way towards explaining her mistake. Although not fully developed, and not a romance, Chaucer's "legend" presents Isiphele's roaming by the sea as yet another opportunity for a female character to encounter adventure or chance, with disastrous consequences. In both Isiphele's case and Dorigen's, movement is linked to an encounter with destiny following the female character's wilful decision to roam about and "pley." Roaming acts as an indicator of either extreme emotion, resulting in placing oneself in the path of destiny, or reckless abandonment to fate.

With this example in mind, Emelye's roaming "up and down" "to and fro" in the garden appears to contrast the actions of all Chaucer's romance heroines discussed above. Emelye's position is the exact opposite of Isiphele's, for Isiphele is free. Although not openly stated, it is clear that Emelye is a war prisoner along with her sister and all the Amazons, all constrained by the rules imposed on the "reign of femeny" by Theseus the conqueror.[42] With this characterization of Emelye contrasting the feisty heroine of

---

[42] Emelye has attracted attention from critics employing modern theoretical approaches, including post-colonial and feminist readings that consider Emelye's and Ypolita's roles in Theseus's political economy. Among others, see Weisl, *Conquering the Realm*, and Susan Crane, *Gender and Romance*

Middle English romance, is Chaucer's portrayal of Emelye as a passive romance heroine convincing? Or is she to be seen as the Amazonian virgin who resists the conqueror's disciplining actions, or both?[43]

As a romance heroine, she is pre-conditioned by her former state of Amazon. Emelye's roaming now appears more anxious than the image of freedom the knights project on her. All the phrases focusing on her, apart from the narrator's description in the idyllic garden setting, are particularly centred on her walking, and the very details of her appearance that would traditionally instil love in her suitors (hair, eyes, voice) do not actually seem to have a direct impact on Arcite and Palamon, who, in Chaucer's story, do not hear her singing nor seem to notice more than an overall bright appearance—goddess-like and untouchable—an almost classical encounter of the Acteon—Artemis/Diana type. Indeed, in the *Teseida*, it is Emilia's voice that literally awakes Arcita—as well as both knights' passions.

Chaucer describes Emelye's actions in the garden as "pleyynge" (1061) and "roaming"; according to the patterns just examined elsewhere in his work, here it seems he uses the verb to suggest the imminence of adventure in Emelye's life. Even more tellingly, Emelye's movement is mirrored in Palamon's before he sees her. Moreover, Palamon and Emelye are similar in that they unwittingly place themselves in the path of adventure. Chaucer clearly also intends Arcite's movement to resemble both Palamon's (in prison) and Emelye's (in the garden) in other ways. With Palamon, Arcite shares the emotional turmoil leading to "roaming," which also translates into agency in placing oneself in the path of adventure. With Emelye he shares the typical romance location of the "roaming" in a green environment (the garden and the grove), though one still threatened by the imminence of change. All three characters are thus united through an image that suggests that their status as prisoners of war makes them similar, and more prone to adventure.

Emelye, the astute medieval audience would be reminded, has also suffered the trauma of war, and thus her "roaming" in the garden cannot be read in quite as innocent a manner as modern critics have done, following changes Chaucer brought to *Teseida*. She is said to do her "observaunce" or "honour to May" (1044, 1047), then pick flowers to make a garland, and sing "hevenyssly" (1055), though the audience does not get the impression that either knight can hear her from the tower. Mark Miller argues that "[m]ore than just a fantasy of a perfect object, ... Emily, also represents a fantasy of a perfect subject and a perfect agent" insofar as it is the Knight who presents her actions arising "not only from her desires, but from her habits, what she was 'wont to do,'" so that "we have in the representation of the feminine an expression of the appeal of

---

in *Chaucer's Canterbury Tales* (Princeton: Princeton University Press, 1994), and, more recently, among others, Tory Vandeventer, "Laying Siege to Female Power: Theseus the 'Conqueror' and Hippolita the 'Asseged' in Chaucer's the *Knight's Tale*," *Essays in Medieval Studies* 23 (2006): 31–40.

43 I use the "feisty heroine" label from Helen Cooper's *English Romance in Time: Transforming Motifs from Geoffrey of Monmouth to Shakespeare* (Oxford: Oxford University Press, 2004).

normative naturalism."[44] Yet Emelye's outward appearance, from the point of view of the prisoners, denotes first movement, and, from their perspective, freedom, but also a state that may be described as restlessness: "Arcite gan espye,/Wher as this lady romed to and fro" (1112–13) and then talks about her "fresshe beauty," "Of hire that rometh in the yonder place" (1119). Emelye is active when Arcite is not, and her pathway to adventure is written in her movement, itself as expression of her inner emotions.

Emelye's later prayer to Diana, to remain a "mayden al my lyf/Ne nevere wol I be no love ne wyf" (2305–6) because she, like her goddess, loves "huntynge and venerye,/ And for *to walken* in the wodes wilde" (2308–9; my emphasis) is, I argue, a sign that her preferred action is busy-ness. Her initial walking in the garden appears as a conventional romance image of the courtly lady in the garden of love but could be read, on another level, as a reflection of her desire to be elsewhere, to "roam" and perform the "observaunce" to May in the "wodes wilde" of her chosen passion, Amazon-style hunting and "venerye." The Knight silences Emelye from this point onwards (apart from her shrieking when Arcite dies). The audience only sees her casting "a freendlich ye" (2680) on Arcite (an action which, combined with the fury sent by Pluto, to scare Arcite's horse, contributes to the latter's death). She is then shown to "schrighte" and "swownynge" (2817, 2819) at Arcite's death, and is described as "woful Emelye" (2910) at his funeral pyre. Even in her wedding to Palamon she is silent, as the Knight/Chaucer relates only Palamon's actions ("hire serveth so gentilly" at 3104). In the context of Palamon's and Arcite's own movements, and with a view to dangers presented to Chaucer's heroines when they choose to roam in gardens or remote places such as the seashore, Emelye's "roaming" displays her agency in choosing a location that exposes her to an encounter with destiny (no matter the potential dangers involved in that choice) and her (possible) anxious state of mind leading to a particular movement in the first place. It also shows that her movement is then curbed, as are her desires and emotions, through the gradual tightening of control over her as a prisoner of Theseus.

In this context the examination of Chaucer's unusually frequent use of the verb "to roam" is even more promising than initially envisaged in the first part of my chapter, in the study of the movement of the two male protagonists of the *Knight's Tale*. The analysis of male and female "roaming" in this tale suggests the interpretation of this action is both despair (or at least grief and fear) and openness (for good or for ill) to the adventures and chances of romance. Is this openness a healthy response to trauma? Or does Emelye's distress serve as a sign marking the hollowness of Hippolyta's marriage (and perhaps more generally the inability of marriage to put an end to the traumas of war, and thus potentially to answer the traumas narrated in the *Tale* itself)? Are love and marriage successful remedies for war that have been denied to Emilye to the extent that she does not even know to seek them—as a good romance heroine, as a medieval high-born lady should? Is the coda of her prayer, that if she cannot remain a virgin, she would like to marry the one who loves her best, a sign of being perhaps willing to move

---

44 Miller, *Philosophical Chaucer*, 86, 87, 88.

past an earlier identity and earlier trauma? Or are we to read it as passive (speaking of the knights' loves and not hers), or a hint of change so that she can imagine being loved and that that love might be valuable? Does her marriage at the end address any trauma at all in the work—her defeat by Theseus, the fratricidal horrors of the Theban war, Theseus' subsequent war against Creon, the strife between Palamon and Arcite, or Arcite's horrible and seemingly meaningless death? And, if so, does marriage as an end to war function the same for men and women, all scarred and roaming, or differently, when the men desire it and she seemingly does not? The richness of Chaucer's reworking of Boccaccio's tale resides in this very complex set of questions and the ambiguous, rather than straightforward, answers it proposes, as all of the above are potential interpretations that remain open to the reader's mind, startled by the restlessness of the protagonists, then the seemingly purposeful seeking of fulfilment in the tale.

This chapter thus reconsidered both Emelye's own traumas, implied in her constrained roaming, and the mirroring of these in the movements Arcite and Palamon are granted by Chaucer (in contrast to his source). By the end of the tale, Emelye has also been led into being a viewer of (and mourner for) Arcite's and Palamon's sufferings. On the one hand, this shift from her as traumatized to her as witness to trauma might represent, psychologically or ethically, improvement: a growth of affective bonds, a recognition of the power she still has to affect other lives, an understanding of her own circumstances through involvement in others' struggles. And yet it also resembles resignation to final captivity, in which her bonds are normalized through marriage, and not just her personal desires but her personal history of trauma is overwritten by male narratives of male suffering and desire.

Chapter 4

MAKING DOLE IN MALORY

Karen Cherewatuk*

ANDREW LYNCH'S WORK has been at the centre of medieval literary studies for the last quarter-century. His scholarship has embraced gender studies, medievalism, children's literature, post-colonialism, and war and peace studies. In *Malory's Book of Arms* (1997), Lynch brilliantly argues that the thematics of combat, which scholars had ignored, were in fact central to understanding Sir Thomas Malory's *Le Morte Darthur*. More recently, he has taken up the history of emotions in Arthurian texts. In attempting to honour a remarkable scholar and friend, I locate this chapter at the juncture of two areas of Andrew's expertise, linking Malory's "combat theme" with the treatment of emotion as cognitive and embodied. In particular, I turn to a common emotional experience in *Le Morte Darthur*, the grief and mourning that result from armed combat. I argue that Malory narrates scenes of death in three different ways which lead his audiences to experience different levels of emotional involvement.[1]

To describe both the subject of grief and mourning and Malory's crafting of emotional experience, I have used language associated with movement.[2] Doing so, I hope, recalls the medieval theory of feeling as motion, a movement of vital spirit in the body triggered by experience, memory, or imagination, which had both physical and psychological effects.[3] As such, the medieval idea of emotion is cognitive and embodied, and here we find parallels in contemporary theories of grief and mourning. In today's psychological discourse the terms "grief" and "mourning" are closely related, but grief generally refers to the individual's internal response to loss—shock, sorrow, anger— and mourning to externalized, public expressions, from verbalization to participation in

---

* **Karen Cherewatuk** is the Marie M. Meyer Distinguisjed Professor at St. Olaf College in Northfield, Minnesota, USA. She is the author of many articles on romance and of *Marriage, Adultery, and Inheritance in Malory's Morte Darthur* (2006). She has enjoyed the friendship and support of Andrew Lynch for a quarter-century.

1 I use the term "audiences" rather than "readers" to recognize that many fifteenth-century audiences would have experienced the *Morte* read aloud to them, as Malory indicates of his own experience in phrases such as "harde ... rede" (928.6–7). All references to Malory are to volume 1 of *Sir Thomas Malory, Le Morte Darthur*, ed. P. J. C. Field, 2 vols. (Cambridge: Brewer, 2013).

2 As Lynch explains, "To move in medieval English (as in Latin 'movere') is metaphorically 'to excite, arouse, stir up', and 'stirring' is a medieval English word also used for emotional excitation in much the same way." Andrew Lynch, " 'What cheer?': Emotion and Action in the Arthurian World," in *Emotions in Medieval Arthurian Literature: Body, Mind, Voice*, ed. Frank Brandsma, Carolyne Larrington and Corinne Saunders (Cambridge: Brewer, 2015), 47–63 at 49.

3 Corinne Saunders, "Mind, Body and Affect in English Arthurian Romance," in Brandsma, Larrington, and Saunders, *Emotions*, 31–46 at 34.

funerals. *Le Morte Darthur* depicts reactions to death that we might interpret as grief and mourning, but these are not Malory's terms. Instead he uses "greve" to indicate a general sense of injury, physical or mental,[4] and "mourn" to mean "to sorrow," "to lament" or "to complain," often in reaction to unreturned love.[5] Malory more typically acknowledges the sorrow of loss through the phrase "maken dole."[6] Malory's own vocabulary reminds us to heed Lynch's caveat against applying modern emotion terms to medieval texts.[7] Yet as I hope this chapter demonstrates, considering emotional loss in terms familiar to twenty-first-century readers allows us to appreciate the complexity of Malory's fictive characters and to speculate on how their displays of emotion affect Malory audiences, both medieval and modern.

In *Le Morte Darthur*, "making dole" is first manifested in immediate and dramatic responses to death. Dole is marked by the physical reactions of crying and swooning and followed by intense verbalization. More moderate expressions of sorrow come after initial loss, whether vocalized individually or collectively. From a modern perspective, we can distinguish these expressions as grief and mourning, or as a movement from internalized and somatic reactions to externalized and often shared demonstration of loss. Lamorak's death illustrates the distinction between them. Learning of his brother's brutal murder, Percivale "felle over his horse mane sownynge, and there he made the grettyste dole and sorow that ever made any noble knyght." Percivale then cries out, "And hit is to muche to suffir the deth of oure fadir Kynge Pellynor, and now the deth of oure good brothir Sir Lamorak!" (543.29–544.2). The knight's lack of physical control indicates overwhelming shock. Not simply a literary gesture, the swoon stops time for Percivale, allowing his mind time to absorb a new reality. Following his uncontrolled somatic reaction, he articulates his feeling as "suffering death." This phrase serves as an "emotive," defined by William M. Reddy as an articulation of an internal feeling that shapes the social reality of emotional experience.[8] Swooning suggests the depth of Percivale's feeling while repetition names and enacts his loss in speech.

In contrast to this expression of fraternal grief, the survivors at a relational distance from Lamorak's death suffer loss but do so less dramatically. From a modern perspective, Trystram, Dynadan, Gareth, and Palomydes express mourning. Their feelings remain vivid. Tristram, for example, exclaims, "hit sleyth myne harte to hyre this tale" (554.17–18). Yet as the knights repeat the story of Lamorak's murder and share memories of his prowess, they together begin to adjust to loss (553.15–554.22). These mourners are

---

4 *MED*, "greven," (v.) 1, 2, 3a.

5 *MED*, "mornen," (v.) 1a, 4.

6 *MED*, "maken dol," under "dol" (n.) 3a "to lament, to mourn." Malory typically spells "dole" with the "e."

7 Lynch, "'What cheer?,'" 48–49.

8 According to Reddy, an emotive is "an external means of influencing activated thought material that often enhances the effectiveness of internal strategies of mental control." William M. Reddy, *The Navigation of Feeling, A Framework for the History of Emotions* (Cambridge: Cambridge University Press, 2001), 322.

part of an "emotional community," to use Barbara H. Rosenwein's term, whose members share the same values and rules of emotional expression. In contrast, the Orkney faction responsible for Lamorak's violent end represent a "subordinate emotional community." Such groups demarcate the larger community's "possibilities and limitations."[9] Surely the murders and mourners of Lamorak reveal the limits of the Round Table fellowship when one faction slays a member from behind and another repeatedly voices horror and sorrow at that act. Because of Percivale's dramatic display of grief, but also because of the chivalric values shared by Lamorak's mourners and Malory's readers, audiences side with them over and against Gawayne's violent clan. Whether we interpret the repeated reports of Lamorak's death as a movement from grief to mourning—a movement from internal to externalized sorrow—or accept these displays as simply Malorian, the way these knights make dole moves audiences.

Andrew Lynch explains that Malory does not so much describe emotion as make it happen, in the same way that his characters make sorrow or joy, or as I assert, "make dole": they physically embody their feelings and verbally express them in emotives upon which they act.[10] Following Lynch's observation, in this chapter I trace examples of making dole and divide them into three narrative contexts: the field of combat, the grave, and the deathbed and funeral rite. "Grief and Anger on the Field" explores how in combat Malory limits the characters'—and thus the audiences'—experience of loss. He emphasizes the characters' movement from grief to anger instead, creating motivation for new heroic acts in the name of revenge. "Tomb Narration" explores Malory's incipient use of the emotive language that he later uses in the catastrophic death scenes. Malory encapsulates each graveside mourning as its own event, moving the internal audience from grief to mourning but limiting the external audiences' response. In contrast, at the end of *Le Morte Darthur*, Malory fully articulates the emotions by anticipating grief with a scene of leave-taking between death's victim and the survivor who responds to the loss in mourning rituals.[11] "A Great Death" explores the serial ends of the principal characters which follow one upon another, with particular focus on Gawayne's. The cumulative weight of these deaths makes sorrow and loss the lasting experience of

---

9 Barbara H. Rosenwein, *Emotional Communities in the Early Middle Ages* (Ithaca: Cornell University, 2006), 24.

10 Andrew Lynch, "Malory and Emotion," in *The New Companion to Malory*, ed. Megan G. Leitch and Cory James Rushton (Cambridge: Brewer, 2019), 180.

11 Scholars have addressed funeral rites and tombs in *Le Morte Darthur*, but given grief and mourning scant attention. For funerals, see Catherine Batt, *Malory's Morte Darthur: Remaking Arthurian Tradition* (New York: Palgrave, 2002), 174–81, and Karen Cherewatuk, "Christian Rituals in Malory: The Evidence of Funerals," in *Malory and Christianity*, ed. D. Thomas Hanks Jr. and Janet Jesmok (Kalamazoo: Medieval Institute, 2013), 77–91; for tombs, see Batt, *Remaking Arthurian Tradition*, 171–84 and Kenneth J. Tiller, "En-graving Chivalry: Tombs, Burial, and the Ideology of Knighthood in Malory's Tale of King Arthur," *Arthuriana* 14 (2004): 37–53. K. S. Whetter has recently advanced a metaphoric claim that the Winchester Manuscript, with its rubrications, functions as a "commemorative tomb to Arthurian chivalry." K. S. Whetter, *The Manuscript and Meaning of Malory's Morte Darthur* (Cambridge: Brewer, 2017), 159–98 at 163.

Le Morte Darthur. As the story becomes less focused on future good and more reflective of the past and lost loved ones, Malory audiences increasingly join with his characters in the emotional experience of making dole.

Grief and Anger on the Field: The Chastelayne

Many deaths occur in *Le Morte Darthur* with no sympathy or even interest accorded to its victims. Such is the case when, following a common romance motif of additive combats, Gareth builds his reputation by killing six thieves, two knights, then the Black Knight (230.16–22, 231.26–27, 234.1–2); or when, in battle, Sir Bowdyne slays 40,000 Saracens "and lefft none on lyve" (501.14–17). These passing deaths seem to deserve no emotional response. Only when the loss is personalized does Malory register emotion in the narrative. This generalization holds true even when the deceased are nameless and faceless enemies. King Elyas, for example, learns of the slaughter of his troops by the forces of King Mark and Sir Tristram and "made grete dole" (496.1–2). "Dole" here is individual expression, but it is often a group response, expressed chorally. When the army of the Five Kings comes upon their dead commanders, "they made such dole that they felle downe of there horsis" (103.26–27). Malory's passing references to grief and mourning typically involve embodied gestures and this set phrase.

Malory tightly controls emotional response to loss incurred in combat. On the field the *Morte*'s skilled warriors hone their grief to anger, and vengeance becomes its expression. During the Roman War when Sir Berel falls, Sir Cador laments "now carefull is myne herte that now lyeth dede my cosyn that I beste loved." Cador takes Berel's body in his arms, speaks these words, then returns to the fight, heeding Lancelot's advice: "Sir, ... meve ye nat to sore, but take your speare in youre honde" (166. 17–18, 26–27). Lancelot here warns Cador against the movement of the wrong passions. In medieval Galenic physiology, blood carrying the "vital spirits" surged toward the heart or from it, causing or prohibiting action. Sorrow or grief causes vital spirit and blood to contract in the heart, as demonstrated by the Malorian swoon, while anger causes the blood to move from the heart and out to the limbs, enabling action.[12] Lancelot hence counsels Cador to limit his grief, his "carefull [sorrowful] ... heart," and to act in vengeance. For exacting revenge instead of lamenting, Cador receives praise even from the opposing King of Lybia (166.34–35), who subsequently dies at Cador's hands. The pattern of grief followed by revenge repeats shortly thereafter, when King Arthur—believing that Kay has received a death wound—wept "for routhe at his herte," then vows "I shall revenge thy hurte" (172.9, 14–15). Cador and Arthur thus illustrate battlefield behavior attested to in texts ranging from the *Iliad* to today's war reports: the survivor of loss redirects grief, expressing it through an act of vengeance.

This redirection is grounded in Malory's combat ethos and illustrated by Gawayne's response to the death of his ward, the "chastelayne." This "chylde of Kyng Arthurs

---

[12] Corinne Saunders offers this explanation for "excessive joy and anger" and "excessive, grief, distress or fear" in "Mind, Body and Affect," 34.

chamber" manages to kill a combatant only to be chased down until "one with a swerde" slices his neck in two. At the seemingly pathetic sight of a group pursuing a youth to his brutal end Gawayne "wepte wyth all his herte and inwardly *he brente for sorow*" (184.2–7, 8–9, emphasis mine). Malory relates Gawayne's grief through the somatic marker of tears and a description of his internal feeling that elides two emotions: burning anger and sorrow. Rather than lament the loss of the child, Gawayne's anger produces future action: He kills the dauphin and sixty of his men before exacting vengeance on the one killer. Over him Gawayne vaunts, "Now, and thou haddyst ascaped withoutyn scathe, the scorne had bene *oures*!" (184.19–20, emphasis mine). The use of the plural pronoun "our" illustrates the shared emotions of men fighting on the battlefield. As Lynch explains: "Arthurian masculine 'emotional' regimes are normally distinguished by their collectivity."[13] The Winchester Manuscript, in short succession, records in the margins: "The deth of Chastelayne" at the point where the young man dies and Gawayne weeps and "The deth of Sir dolphin" when Gawayne drives the head of his spear into the enemy's heart (93r). The scribe likewise notes the acts of vengeance of Cador (83r) and of Arthur (86v). If the marginalia are authorial,[14] Malory thought noteworthy the Round Table knights' practice of battlefield revenge. If not, the marginalia illustrate a fifteenth-century reader's approval of vengeance as a response to loss.

In analyzing the chastelayne's death and Gawain's reaction, I have suggested that vengeance is a radical externalization of grief. What is absent from the narration is telling: Malory offers no lament for lost youth, no graveside speeches, no burial. The movement from grief to revenge is rapid. In fact, the entire episode of the chastelayne's end and of Gawayne's revenge is complete within one long paragraph in Field's edition; Cador's reaction to Berel's death and Arthur's revenge of Kay in two paragraphs. The three episodes are found in "King Arthur and the Emperor Lucius" and thus derive from the Alliterative *Morte Arthure*. Lest we attribute this combat reaction to this single source, I note that Malory handles grief and revenge in exactly this way in the battles of the earlier tale "King Uther and King Arthur" and in the later tournaments and single combats of the "Book of Sir Trystram." In his battle against King Ban, for example, "Kynge Lotte wepte for pité and dole that he saw so many good knyghtes take theire ende," but he then "gadred the peple togydir passynge knyghtly, and dud grete proues of armys" (26.13–14 and 19–20). After the tournament at Lonezep, Sir Palomydes comes upon men who leave off weeping to attack him as soon they recognize him as responsible for their lord's death (610.4–18). Malory's narration of death in the field thus acknowledges his characters' loss while reworking it as heroic action—to the satisfaction of survivors within the text and audiences without the narrative. The *Morte*'s skilled warriors give little time to making dole: Like Gawayne, they feel grief but leave it on the field and turn to vengeance.

---

13 Lynch, '"What cheer?,"' 56.
14 This case was first argued by P. J. C. Field, "Malory's Own Marginalia," *Medium Aevum* 70 (2001): 26–39, and recently expanded upon in Whetter, *Manuscript and Meaning*, 53–92.

Tomb Narration: Launceor & Columbe and Balyn & Balan

Turning grief to revenge is one way Malory acknowledges but limits the emotions of loss. He also does so by confining his characters' expression of dole to sites traditionally associated with death. These "tomb narrations," as I call them, are located at graves or in churches, the chapels within them, or churchyards—in other words, at the burial sites familiar to Malory's fifteenth-century audiences. Sir Gareth, for example, enters a castle and hears "muche mourning" (280.24). He finds thirty ladies at mass the next day, "grovelynge uppon dyverse toumbis, makynge grete dole and sorrow." Their expression is ritualistic, with all the women engaging in the same public display and no doubt responding to each other's emotions. Their behaviour illustrates Reddy's notion of an "emotional regime," a set of emotives and practices that express and regulate proper expression of feeling.[15] Through their embodied mourning, Gareth immediately identifies the women as widows who have lost their lords (281.13-15). Yet Gareth turns away from grief and mourning to pursue action: the rapidity of the narrative hurls him and readers into the next adventure. Likewise, the Winchester Manuscript's marginalium is not concerned with the widows, but with Gareth's revenge on their husbands' murderer: "How sir Gareth slew þe browne knyght" (144v). As with combat narrations, audiences empathize with loss but turn attention to action.

Malory's tomb narrations more typically give fuller expression to loss than this episode of the mourning widows allows. In material culture, graves and tombs are sites that merge love, loss, grief, and mourning. So too, in the textual culture that Malory creates in *Le Morte Darthur*. He achieves this effect by employing rhetoric, particularly the use of repetition, that heightens the sorrow voiced at these sites. The series of speeches attending the deaths of Launceor and Columbe, for example, is built up through the echoic language expressed by the couple and then by mourners of them. Over Launceor's corpse, Columbe keens, "A, Balyne! *too* bodyes thou haste slayne in *one* herte, and *too* hertes in *one* body, and *too* soules thou hast loste" (54.26-28, emphasis mine). With the repetitions of "one" and "two" Columbe testifies to Launceor's and her love while blaming Balyn for their deaths. She expresses her loss—making "sorrow oute of mesure" (54.26)—simultaneously with taking her life on her lover's sword. Columbe's suicide thus reflects Andrew Lynch's point that in *Le Morte Darthur* emotion *is* action:[16] In response to their double deaths, Balyn protests: "Alas! ... me repentis sore the dethe of *thys* knyght for the love of *thys* damesel, for there was muche *trw love* betwyxte *hem*" (55.3-5, emphasis mine). Balyn's words contrast the singular demonstrative "this," with which he points to each corpse, and the plural pronoun "them," which underscores the couple's "true love." In both Columbe's and Balyn's laments, deictics and repetition mark the separation and union of death.

Beyond the three actors present at the deaths—Launceor, Balyn, and Columbe—Malory brings into the scene mourners who lament and bury the dead: a dwarf who tears

---

15 Reddy, *Navigation*, 112-40.
16 Lynch, "Malory and Emotion," 178-82.

out his hair "for sorowe" and King Mark, who—repeating Balyn's phrase—made "grete sorow for the *trew love* that was *betwyxte them*," then buries the couple in a tomb "fayre and ryche" in a church (56.1–2, 22–24 italics mine, 26–27).[17] These additional mourners function as "mirror characters" who model and encourage the audiences' empathic response.[18] Their mourning shows a sharing of emotion around the grave that leads to action—specifically, the creation of the tomb. The characters' repeated expressions of grief move each other and the *Morte*'s audiences while the tomb preserves the lovers' story for the future.

Like all the monuments in the "Tale of Balyn Le Sauvage," however, Launceor and Columbe's tomb inscription functions proleptically. After the couple's burial, Merlin arrives and, echoing the phrase "true love" a third time, announces that the tomb will be the site of "the grettist bateyle betwyxte too knyghtes that ever was or ever shall be, and the *trewyst lovers*." He inscribes the names of the two knights, Lancelot and Trystram, on the tomb (56.35–57.5). Implicitly linking three couples—Launceor and Columbe, Tristram and Isolt, and Lancelot and Guenevere—Merlin's prophecy darkly anticipates the *Morte*'s theme of tragic love and the losses caused by it. Tomb narration thus simultaneously memorializes the death of these two minor characters and anticipates grief for principal characters, while keeping that emotion at a safe distance. At Launceor and Columbe's tomb, the survivors within the scene mourn the couple in the present moment while external audiences anticipate losses to the Round Table in the future.

Tomb narration in the final episode of the "Tale of Balyn" anticipates Malory's other great theme: loss of fellowship and death caused by fellow knights. This second double loss—of Balyn and his brother Balan—creates for both characters and audiences the experience of "anticipatory grief." Anticipatory grief is the feeling of sorrow experienced before impending loss.[19] When Balyn makes the decision to keep the sword-damsel's weapon, she warns of wrenching death in the future: that "ye shall sle with that swerde the beste frende that ye have and the man that ye moste love in the worlde, and that swerde shall be youre destruccion" (50.1–4). Balyn's ensuing adventures cause a chain of loss that he is powerless to halt, beginning with Launceor and Columbe's deaths and ending in unwitting fratricide. Entering upon his last adventure, Balyn travels a path toward his grave marked by predictions. A ghost-like figure, an "old hore gentylman,"

---

17 Columbe's death, like Launceor's, is recorded in the margin of the Winchester Manuscript next to the description of her monument (Columbe at 26v, Launceor at 25v). For discussion of the marginalia in "Balyn," see Thomas H. Crofts, *Malory's Contemporary Audience: The Social Reading of Romance in Late Medieval England* (Cambridge: Brewer, 2006), 61–78, and Raluca Radulescu, *Romance and its Contexts in Fifteenth-Century England: Politics, Piety, and Penance* (Cambridge: Brewer, 2013), 149–75.

18 Frank Brandsma, "Mirror Characters," in *Courtly Arts and the Art of Courtliness*, ed. Keith Busby and Christopher Kleinhenz (Cambridge: Brewer, 2006), 275–84.

19 The term "anticipatory grief" is widely used in clinical and counselling discourse. A concise description appears in D. Casarett, J. S. Kutner, and J. Abrahm, "Life after Death: A Practical Approach to Grief and Bereavement," *Annals of Internal Medicine* 134, no. 3 (2001): 208–15.

warns Balyn to turn back then disappears (70.26), and the sound of a hunting horn prompts Balyn's acknowledgement that "That blast ... is blowen for me, for I am the pryse, and yet am I not dede" (70.30–31). A damsel laments that Balyn has left behind his own shield, and he fatally responds, "what aventure shall falle to me, be it lyf or dethe, I wille take the adventure that shalle come to me" (71.24–25). The people Balyn rides past bewail his loss even before he dies; his aphoristic responses to them reveal his acceptance of death although he, unlike these premature mourners, is not aware of his role as victim and perpetrator of fratricide.

To emphasize the horror of fratricide, Malory employs the techniques we have analyzed in Launceor and Columbe's tomb narration: repetition of words and phrasing, pointed deictics, and pronominal number play. Yet here the rhetoric that elicits pathos reaches a newly dramatic height. In their contest, the disguised brothers are so evenly matched that they must halt their combat three times. When the younger brother finally identifies himself as "Balan, broder unto the good kynght Balyn," Balyn cries out "Allas! ... that ever I shold see *this day*" and falls in a swoon. Crawling pathetically "on al four feet and hands, [to] put of the helme of his broder," Balan cannot recognize Balyn's face through the blood. When Balyn wakes, he laments "O, Balan, my broder! Thow hast slayne me and I the, wherfore alle the wyde world shalle speke of *us bothe*." To this lament, Balan responds by echoing his brother's initial remark—"Allas! ... that ever I sawe *this day*" (72.25–34, emphasis mine). Close to death, they "mone eyther to other" and request, in a single voice, to be buried "in *one* pytte" since "we came bothe oute of *one* wombe." After last rights, Balyn again gestures toward their shared grave, predicting that "whan *we* are buryed in *one* tombe and the mensyon made over *us* how *two* bretheren slewe eche other, there wille never good knyght nor good man see *our* tombe but they wille pray for *our* soules." The women witnessing this scene weep "for pyte"; they function as mirror characters, as do the two dying brothers (73.14–15 and 24–27 emphasis mine, and 28). More intense than the double loss of Launceor and Columbe, this episode is rife with echoic language. Balyn and Balan use the exact aphorism about the "day of death," and three times Malory's exclamation of distress, "Allas!";[20] seven times the noun "brother," and multiple iterations of their near-identical names.[21] As in Launceor and Columbe's tomb narration, Malory chimes on singular identity and shared loss, with contrasting use of singular and plural pronouns. The rhetorical effect is powerful, one described by cognitive psychologists D. S. Miall and Keith Oatley as "foregrounded language." Foregrounded language disrupts the reader or audiences' automatic processing of language, making perception of the text more

---

20 On the aural effect of "Alas!" see Karen Cherewatuk and Joyce Coleman, "An Introduction to Aural Malory: Sessions and Round Tables," *Arthuriana* 13 (2003): 3–13.

21 "Alas" appears at 72.27, 34, and 73.3; "brother" at 71.31, 72.8, 21, 25, 30, 32, and 73.31; "Balyn" and "Balan" at 72.1, 3, 4, 5, 6, 8, 10, 21, 23, 25, 26, 27, 29, 32, 34; 73.3, 7, 16, 24, 29, 31, 32, 33; 74.4 and 75.3.

emotionally intense.[22] The same effect extends to medieval audiences hearing an orally voiced text, as would have Malory's early audiences. His use of repetition creates a sense of each brother lamenting his own life and of the two mourning each other, a particularly poignant use of anticipatory grief. Balyn and Balan in essence write their tomb inscription, repeating their story for the "wide world" and any "good man" who will stop to pray for them. They attempt to continue their memory into a future where viewers of their tomb and Malory's audiences will continue to mourn them.

Pathetically, however, the lady who completes the tomb's inscription knows only Balan's name, and not that of the "the Knyght with the Two Swerdes" whose unhappy adventures readers have been following (73.30–35). Balyn's identity is revealed by Merlin who sets the destructive sword into a marvelous floating block, so that it one day reaches Camelot and Galahad's hands. The "Tale of Balyn Le Sauvage" intersects with the Grail Quest through anticipated acts that neither the characters within the text nor Malory's audiences may yet fully understand.[23] Merlin's prophecy, however, overleaps the Grail Quest and points to the end of *Le Morte Darthur* when he predicts that Lancelot, "with thys swerd shall sle the man in the worlde that he lovith beste: that shall be Sir Gawayne" (74.12–13). Like Launceor and Columbe's tomb, this monument holds two bodies whose deaths predict future events involving principal characters. This final prophecy echoes the damsel's initial warning to Balyn (50.1–4), enfolding the chaotic narrative in mourning for lost brotherhood.

The double deaths in the "Tale of Balyn" reveal Malory's early experimentation in externalizing emotions of loss: he employs echoic language to heighten audience awareness; creates the experience of anticipatory grief through the dying person's words of leave-taking; depicts survivors reacting to loss and functioning as mirror characters; and uses inscription to fashion proleptic thematic links to the future. The surviving characters lament in a way that does not happen on the battlefield. Grief interrupts the present of the narrative, and mourning carries memory into the future. With Balyn and Balan's deaths, Malory comes close to emotional intensity of the death scenes at the end of the *Morte*—with one important difference. The tale's final "Allas!" seals away empathic responses to loss (74.35–75.2). Tomb narration creates narrative space for characters to make dole but localizes the experience at the victims' monuments.

A Great Death: Sir Gawayne

As *Le Morte Darthur* moves toward its end, Malory makes loss the focus of the narrative. All of the main characters—Sir Gawayne, King Arthur, Queen Guenevere, and Sir Lancelot—die in turn and survivors make dole, only to do so again and again.

---

22 D. S. Miall, "Anticipation and Feeling in Literary Response: A Neuropsychological Perspective," *Poetics* 23 (1995): 275–98 at 283. See also Keith Oatley, "A Taxonomy of the Emotions of Literary Response and a Theory of Identification in Fictional Narrative," *Poetics* 23 (1994): 101–17.

23 Andrew Lynch, *Malory's Book of Arms* (Cambridge: Brewer, 1997), 19–24 and Raluca Radulescu, "Spiritual Malory," in *The New Companion to Malory*, 211–26 at 212–14.

The sequence of deaths results, directly and indirectly, from the text's great themes, romantic love or betrayal by comrades. With each death in the sequence, Malory expands narration to emphasize emotion: signalling anticipatory grief, relating the moment of death, and illustrating its after-effects on mourners. In the final sweep of the *Morte*, survivors repeatedly embody loss through gestures such as falling down, fainting, sighing and sobbing, wailing, shrieking, and wringing hands. They make "dole" or "pité" through unarticulated expressions but also through specific statements and prayer requests. Contemporary therapeutic discourse sees grief and mourning as stages of loss, as in Elisabeth Kübler-Ross' well-known theory of grief,[24] or as a continuum of emotional experience. Similarly, Corinne Saunders claims that Malory's depiction of interior and exterior expressions reveal a continuum, rather than disjunction, of body and mind: "Malory's tragic tapestry is coloured by the accruing effects of love and loss, written on the bodies, minds and hearts of his characters."[25] To illustrate Malory's brilliant display of these emotions, one could turn to any of the powerfully affecting deaths of the principal characters. Here, I focus on Gawayne as his passing offers the clearest distinction between tomb narration and what I term a "great death."[26] A great death presents the character first as mourner and then as death's victim, allowing the audience to grieve with and then for that character. Inhabiting both roles, Gawayne initiates the chain of loss toward which the entire *Morte Darthur* has been tending.

Gawayne's fraternal grief, and not royal jealousy, drives the war between Arthur and Launcelot. Grief then is a cause of, not just a response to, the climactic events of the *Le Morte Darthur*. Malory's honed use of gesture and echoic language dramatically returns in Gawayne's displays of grief. Anticipating that his nephew "wyll go nygh oute of hys mynde" (886.17), Arthur inters the bodies of Gareth and Gaherys to prevent Gawayne from experiencing "overmuche" or "double" sorrow. This is all to no avail. When Gawayne hears of his double loss, he collapses into grief and "longe ... lay there *as he had ben dede*" (888.12–13, 888.1–2 and 12–13, emphasis mine).[27] His prone body mimes his brothers' corpses in a dramatic somatic reaction. Rising from his faint, Gawayne cries "Alas!" and runs to the king; together uncle and nephew weep and swoon (888.3–8). Gawayne's and Arthur's repetition of weeping and swooning demonstrates the medieval belief that

---

24 In her 1969 book *On Death and Dying*, Elisabeth Kübler-Ross famously described five stages in the process of grieving which she discovered in her work with terminally ill patients: denial, anger, bargaining, depression, and acceptance. Subsequently, Kübler-Ross clarified that patients do not necessarily move through all stages nor necessarily proceed in that order. Today this grief model is more often applied to survivors than to the dying. See Elizabeth Kübler-Ross, *On Death and Dying* (New York: Scribner, 1969) and Elizabeth Kübler-Ross and David Kessler, *On Grief and Grieving* (New York: Scribner, 2014).

25 Saunders, "Mind, Body and Affect," 46.

26 I use this phrase in a book project on which I am currently working, on grief and mourning in Malory. There I will discuss each of the *Morte*'s emotionally affecting death scenes, from Elaine of Astolat's through Lancelot's.

27 The king had the same shock reaction as Gawayne upon learning of Gareth and Gaherys's deaths (886.6).

strong sorrow causes the withdrawal of vital spirits.[28] Their identical responses also illustrate the affective pattern of responding to another's emotional display, which we know from the experience tearing up at a film or funeral in response to the reactions of those around us. In the same way, Gawayne functions as a mirror character who reflects emotions to Arthur and in turn is affected by him. Malory's audiences, meanwhile, likely respond to both kinsmen.

Gawayne, however, quickly moves from the shock of grief to battlefield response, seeking revenge in reaction to loss. Although it is the king who first expresses desire for revenge (888.21–22), Gawayne repeatedly exerts himself to enact this punishment on Lancelot. While in battlefield narration vengeance is productive, the end of the *Morte* finds Gawayne inciting war in an enraged attempt to complete this emotion script, as if violence could ease his pain. "Vengeance" echoes in Gawayne's every speech and action. He vows "frome thys day forewarde I shall never fayle Sir Launcelot untyll that one of us have slayne the othir" (888.25–27) and repeats this promise another two times in the same speech to Arthur (888.28 and 32–33). Over the next six months, he continues to voice this desire for revenge: at Joyous Garde (892.1–2 and 21–23); at court before the papal legate (901.12–14); and on Lancelot's ancestral lands (908.17), as well as before and after his single combats with Lancelot (909.24–25, 911.34–35, 912.29–30 and 914.28–29). He declares, "I woll be revenged" (888.28); he wastes French lands "thorow ... vengeance" (906.12–13); and he boasts "I shall revenge" (909.24). Even after he receives the final blow to his skull, Gawayne challenges Lancelot to "perfourme thys batayle to the utteraunce!" (914.20). Malory's employment of gesture and rhetoric is never more emotionally charged—certainly in Miall's sense of foregrounded language—than when relaying the intensity and duration of Gawayne's anger. His behaviour prompts tears in onlookers and the king who clearly prefers reconciliation. In a different context, Lynch use the phrase "exilic madness" to explain Tristram's "unstable compound of desire, anger and sorrow, tending to unceasing activity."[29] The same term could apply to Gawayne's reckless self-endangerment: his grief-induced rage overleaps the bounds of the Round Table's emotional collective and isolates him from it. In this way, Gawayne's vengeance seems a response to trauma.

In assessing trauma as a category useful to the medieval historian, Donna Trembinski notes that trauma, like emotion, is culturally situated and constructed. Employed as a category of analysis rather than as an anachronistically applied diagnosis, trauma provides "potential explanations for certain behaviors," and makes the past more understandable to contemporary interpreters. Trembinski's test-case is post-traumatic stress disorder (PTSD) as seen in Francis of Assisi's *Prima vita*.[30] To Gawayne's case

---

28 Lynch explains, "The swoon is testimony to a disordered emotional situation, yet it may also be seen as an heroic deed in itself, 'proving' the great power of an individual's feeling." Lynch, *Malory's Book of Arms*, 142.

29 Lynch, "Malory and Emotion," 186.

30 Donna Trembinski, "Trauma as a Category of Analysis," in *Trauma in Medieval Society*, ed. Wendy J. Turner and Christian Lee (Leiden: Brill, 2018), 13–32 at 21. Trembinski offers her observations as a corrective to Augustine Thompson's interpretation of PTSD in his biography of the saint.

I apply a main symptom of PTSD, "survivor's guilt," the belief that one has done wrong in surviving the sudden violent deaths of loved ones. Contemporary psychologists associate survivor's guilt not only with PTSD and the experience of war,[31] but with "complicated" or "dysfunctional" grief. Complicated grief is an emotional reaction so intense and long-lasting that the survivor cannot move past loss.[32] Gawayne had resisted Arthur's command to accompany the queen to the stake, knowing that his younger brothers could not do so (883.30–884.9). In reaction to guilt, Gawayne attempts to cope with death as he had in the field of combat after the loss of the chastelayne, by turning his grief to revenge. At every turn, however, Lancelot blocks Gawayne's path to emotional release. In depicting Gawayne's unrelieved suffering, Malory beautifully mixes embodied reactions with a range of rhetorical responses—from rich set speeches to wonderfully colloquial digs. Gawayne, for example, invokes his uncle's support for war through anaphora, addressing Arthur with titles of increasing familiarity and kinship: "My kynge, my lorde, and myne uncle" (888.23–24). In contrast, he harasses Lancelot with a soldier's plain speech: "Leve thy babelynge and com off and lat us ease oure hartis!" (910.16–17).[33] In medieval terms, the heart is the seat of emotion and is associated especially with "blood emotions like anger and impetuosity."[34] While attempting to "ease" his heart on the field, Gawayne remains frozen in a backward-looking present with Lancelot barring future action.

As Gawayne moves into his second role—that of death's victim—his confrontation with his own end moves him past anger. Following the chronicle tradition, Gawayne falls during the landing at Dover against Mordred. When Arthur finds him in a boat, "liynge more than halff dede" (917.29–30), the king displays the familiar reaction to the shock of grief:

> And there the kynge made greate sorow oute of mesure, and toke Sir Gawayne in hys armys, and *thryse* he there *sowned*. And than whan he was waked, Kyng Arthur seyde, "*Alas*! Sir Gawayne, my syster-son, here now thou lyghest, the man in the worlde that I loved moste. And now ys my joy gone!"
>
> (917.31–918.1, italics mine)

---

[31] *Diagnostic and Statistical Manual of Mental Illness-V* (DSM–V), published in 2013, accessed through the American Psychiatric Association, www.psychiatry.org/patients-families/ptsd/what-is-ptsd (October 1, 2018).

[32] DSM–V defines "Persistent Complex Bereavement Disorder" (PCBD) as a "severe and persistent grief and mourning reaction" in "Other Specified Trauma- and Stressor-Related Disorder" (October 1, 2018).

[33] I have cited only Gawayne's part of the debate. Raluca Radulescu analyzes "Gawain's vehement rebuttal" and Lancelot's "polished political speeches" in "Tears and Lies: Emotions and the Ideals of Malory's Arthurian World," in *Emotions in Medieval Arthurian Literature*, 105–21 at 109.

[34] The heart has been associated with the seat of emotions at least since Galen. For the quotation, see Damien Bouquet and Piroska Nagy, *Medieval Sensibilities: A History of Emotions in the Middle Ages*, trans. Robert Shaw (Cambridge: Polity, 2018), 160.

The king's exclamation—"now ys my joy gone!"— repeats Gawayne's exact words upon learning of Gareth's and Gaherys' deaths (887.35). Malory's echo underscores the transfer of the role of mourner from nephew to uncle. But rather than then seek vengeance as had Gawayne, the king stays with his nephew, voicing his "lost joy" three times more (917.35–918.1, 918.3 twice, and 918.4). Arthur thus initiates a powerful scene of Gawayne's deathbed leave-taking, as the king tenderly ensures that the sacraments are given to his dying nephew (918.21, 919. 21). Central to this scene of leave-taking are Gawayne's two confessions, the first spoken to Arthur and the second written to Lancelot. By confirming the loss to come, these doubled confessions create anticipatory grief for Arthur; as important, they redeem Gawayne for Malory's audiences.

Insisting on civil war from which no principal character could emerge emotionally intact, Gawayne is hardly an admirable hero at this point. His deathbed leave-taking rebalances his character. At court Lancelot had charged Gawayne with being "orgulous sette" or "proudly fixed" (902.26). Since the head is the traditional seat of pride, Gawayne's "old wound" reminds audiences of this fault. Yet Gawayne's wound also functions as a visible metaphor for grief, in which past hurts inflicted by Lancelot and his kin enabled and strengthened new ones, in factional competition that has led to the bleeding out of the Round Table. Pride has left Gawayne in grief and injured his king, for which Gawayne now confesses: "And thorow me and *my pryde* ye have all thys shame and disease." Gawayne acknowledges twice that he caused the war "thorow ... wylfulnes" (918.10–11, 918.7) and laments not having reached agreement with Lancelot. He ends his oral confession to Arthur seeking "paupir, penne, and inke" with which to write to Lancelot (918.16–20).

Gawayne's double confession before death—spoken to Arthur, written to Lancelot— underscores a shift of emotion, from pride to humility and from outrage to apology, ending with concern for the future beyond his own life. In his written confession to Lancelot, Gawayne refers five times to his "wounde" and "the strooke that ye [Lancelot] gaff me of olde" as the cause of his end (918. 27, 29, 35 twice, and 919.14). He accepts responsibility—"I, Sir Gawayne, Knyght of the Table Rounde, soughte my dethe," through "myne owne sekynge" (918. 30–31)—but subtly hints at Lancelot's culpability. According to Lynch, Gawayne's letter "is a striking instance of the mixture of bodily, emotional and cognitive information centred in the cultural practice, and the technology, of writing and reading, as evidenced in the *Morte* itself."[35] One detail of the mixing of body, cognition and emotion stands out, the ambiguous phrasing of the letter's valediction: "And the date of thys lettir was wrytten but too owrys and an halff afore my dethe, wrytten with myne owne honde and *subscrybed with parte of my harte blood*" (919.15–17, emphasis mine).[36] It is not surprising that a warrior whose strength is tied to the sun would be

---

35 Lynch, "Malory and Emotion," 181.

36 Foreknowledge of death is quite typical in traditional society and a marker of the medieval sense of a "good death." See Philip Ariès, *The Hour of Our Death*, trans. Helen Weaver, 1st ed. (New York: Knopf, 1981), 310, and Paul Binski, *Medieval Death: Ritual and Representation* (Ithaca: Cornell University, 1996), 33–36.

able to predict that his death would occur at noon (919.23). Startling is the emotional and physical cost of writing the epistle: Gawayne signs it—for that is the meaning of "subscriben"—with "harte-blood." This is lifeblood, the blood carrying the vital spirit, thought to be essential for survival.[37] Malory shows us Gawayne spending his last bit of his blood, of his strength and life, to make amends with Lancelot and to influence him to return to England to save the king.

Before the Winchester Malory breaks off, the last surviving marginalium points to Gawayne's leave-taking, calling attention to the epistle itself: "How Sir Gawyn wrote a letter to Sir Launcelot at the tyme of his deþe" (fol. 477r). Like Balyn, Gawayne seeks prayers at his grave, twice requesting that Lancelot "se my tumbe" (918.33–34, 919.17–18). Gawayne's end completes the prophecy of Balyn's tomb inscription, for Lancelot has slain "the man in the worlde that he lovith beste: that shall be Sir Gawayne" (74.12–13). Yet while tomb inscription predicts the future in a detached prophetic voice, the motif of the deathbed epistle gives the dying a powerful personal voice that reaches out from the grave to effect emotional alliances. In the case of the Fair Maid of Ascolat (829.19–27), Elaine uses her letter to move mourning away from family members who love her to the court who has so far ignored her. She calls upon "ladyes" to recognize the legitimacy of her emotions (829.13) and to mourn her as someone who deserved a place among them. In effect, Elaine crafts of the Round Table a community of mourners.[38] As Elaine's deathbed leaving-taking shows, the immediacy of grief depends upon pre-existing emotional attachment—it seems natural that Sir Bernarde makes "grete dole" for his daughter (828.18), or Gawayne for his brothers, and Arthur for his nephew. Mourning, however, is not always an obvious consequence of human relations. Given Gawayne's outrageous behaviour, audiences might question whether Lancelot is even willing to grieve for Gawayne. Gawayne's epistle, however, effectively voices his apology to Lancelot and serves as an interpellation to act as a mourner rather than as a victor, potentially repairing the emotional bond between the still-living Arthur and Lancelot. When Gawayne finishes the letter, nephew and uncle are moved to make dole—to weep and swoon together in anticipatory grief—for the third and final display before the moment of death. The affective pull of Gawayne's epistle connects Arthur's present loss at the deathbed to the time when it arrives in Lancelot's hands and acts upon its request. Writing the letter allows Gawayne movement past anger to acceptance of the death of his brother and of his own death; he sidesteps the vicious cycle of revenge and dies believing himself reconciled to Lancelot and hopeful that Arthur might be saved.

At the point of Gawayne's death, the Winchester Manuscript's visual presentation reinforces the experience of loss. The scribe's use of red ink for personal names reminds readers of the manuscript of the ballet of blood which these characters have danced. As Whetter explains about folio 477r, the page that marks Gawayne's letter, "Since the

---

[37] *MED*, "subscriben" (v.) b; "herte-blod" (n.) a and b.
[38] Other deathbed epistles that shift emotional alliance and create mourning communities include those of King Harmaunce (555.19–20), and of Perceval's sister (768.21–23).

only names appearing ... are the repeated triad of Launcelot, Gawayne, and Arthur, Winchester's rubrication visually foregrounds the personal ties between these three men."[39] When Arthur buries Gawayne "in a chapell within Dover Castell" (919.24–25), Malory expands that triad into a community of mourners. Entering the narrative in his own voice, he comments: "And there yet all men may se the skulle of hym, and the same wounde is sene" (919.25–26). Gawayne's immediate audience at the deathbed had been Arthur, with readers simultaneously "hearing" Gawayne's oral confession and "reading" the written one. Modern readers might consider this textual experience as eavesdropping on an intimate scene yet, in late medieval practice, the deathbed itself was a public space where relatives and friends aided the dying in the final hours and were thus reminded of their own mortality. Malory's testimony, his indication of the historicity of Gawayne's death and the skull's still visible wound, transfers the emotional experience of death at the deathbed from the text's past to the present moment of the audiences' experience. This sense of the continuity of mourning stretching from Arthur's time to the audiences' own is reinforced through the paratatic chronologic markers at the start of clauses: "*And than* he wepte and Kynge Arthur both, and sowned ... *And whan* they were awaked bothe ... *And so* at the owre of no one. ... *And there yet* all men may se ...." (919.19–25, emphasis mine). At Gawayne's deathbed and burial, echoic language draws Arthur, author, and audiences into a mourning circle.

Absent from that circle is Lancelot, the recipient of Gawayne's "dolefull lettir" (930.13–14, 18). For the remainder of *Le Morte Darthur*, through all the great deaths, Lancelot serves—in Lynch's words—as "the register of emotion."[40] Reacting to Lancelot's grief-filled response to the epistle, Bors counsels the battlefield restraint that Lancelot had once offered Cador: "Now leve youre complayntes ... and firste revenge you of the dethe of Sir Gawayne" ... and "revenge my lorde Arthur and my lady Quene Gwenyvere" (930.28–31). At Dover, however, Lancelot learns that the time for vengeance has passed: it has come to rest with Gawayne, Mordred, Arthur, and the "hondred thousande" dead at Baram Downe (931.9). When townspeople lead Lancelot to Gawayne's grave, he immediately honours his comrade's request for prayer: "Than Sir Lancelot kneled downe by the tumbe and wepte, and prayed hartely for hys soule" (931.18–20). Unlike the emotionally limited episodes of tomb narration, the unfolding scene of Gawayne's burial demonstrates the way mourning leads to acceptance of loss. His original interment, occurring in the midst of war, had been brief. Now, in the absence of Arthur, Lancelot takes on the role of chief mourner and arranges a full funeral. From the distribution of the poor-dole to establishing masses of remembrance, Lancelot follows church rituals that comfort survivors by ensuring that prayer and penance continue to

---

39 Whetter, *Manuscript and Meaning*, 181.

40 Lynch, *Malory's Book of Arms*, 156. Catherine Batt also astutely notes that "Lancelot enacts all modes of participation in death rituals. He is mourner, penitent survivor making restitution, officiating priest, memento mori, and, finally, the corpse itself." Batt, *Remaking Arthurian Tradition*, 175.

be offered for the loved one.[41] Malory's medieval Christian audiences would recognize that these rites create hope for reunion with the deceased in a world beyond time. When the formal public mourning for Gawayne ends, Lancelot enters private prayer. He "lay too nyghtes uppon hys tumbe in prayers and in dolefull wepynge" (931.32–33). As do the widows Gareth comes upon, Lancelot uses his body to release pain in ritual performance, essentially miming tomb sculpture in his grief for Gawayne. This action anticipates Lancelot's grovelling on the tomb of King Arthur and Queen Guenevere, and like that powerful scene is inscrutable because of its very privacy. Lancelot voices no thoughts. His body, however, focuses the sympathy of Malory's audiences, stirring our past private memories of loss. Lancelot's mourning reminds us that despite acceptance, grief never really ends.

All the funerary details, from Gawayne's shrift to Lancelot's prayers on Gawayne's tomb, are Malory's additions to the narrative. They reveal an author centrally concerned with the experience of grief and mourning. The sense of tragedy emanating from Malory's great deaths lies in the dwindling numbers of the Round Table, whose survivors focus less and less on future good and more and more on the past and lost loved ones. No longer willing to leave grief on the field or seal it in a tomb, Malory fills the central narrative with heavily repetitive, richly echoic and interconnected experiences of making dole: beginning at Gawayne's deathbed and moving onto Arthur and Mordred's stylized circle of slaughter, Guenevere's longed-for passing, and Lancelot's own beatific end. For each character, the figure of the mourner and the deceased collapse into one as Malory builds toward tragedy over time through echoing episodes. Arthur's ambiguous disappearance complicates the grief reaction. Again breaking into the narrative, Malory calls attention to other writers' responses to Arthur's loss (928.5–28, especially 5–8, 15, and 22); he seems to indicate that their claims for the king's return might be, to use Kübler-Ross' term, a form of denial. The lasting impression of the great deaths nonetheless justifies Caxton extending the title of Malory's final tale to his whole book (940.17–20). His exquisite rendering of these deaths remains in audiences' memories because, unlike any character within the text, readers outside the *Morte* experience all of them. As *Le Morte Darthur* moves toward its apocalyptic end, Malory makes his audiences into mourners. The dole made in the final sweep of *Le Morte Darthur* is what its audiences never forget.

---

[41] For a full description of funeral ritual in Malory, see Cherewatuk, "Christian Rituals in Malory," 81–84. The term "poor-dole" refers to the donation—ranging from a meal to a monetary gift—to the poor men and women who were hired to recite prayers (921.20–25).

PART TWO

VOICING CONLFICT

Chapter 5

THE HERO "REMEMBERS": THE VERB *GEMUNAN* IN *BEOWULF* AND *THE BATTLE OF MALDON*[1]

Ad Putter*

THE ANIMUS BEHIND this chapter is a dissatisfaction with interpretations of medieval texts that present them as exemplifying or critiquing "codes" of behaviour. Below are two examples of the kind of criticism I have in mind; they will take us immediately to the two poems I would like to focus on, *Beowulf* and *The Battle of Maldon*:

> The fundamental ethical code of the poem [*Beowulf*] is unmistakably secular: it is the warrior code of the aristocracy, celebrating bravery, loyalty and generosity ...[2]

> *The Battle of Maldon* is often viewed as a celebration of the heroic code, but it can also be viewed as a tragedy stemming from the failure of some adherents to that code, when put to the test. The possibility of such failure is foreseen in the poem by the retainer Offa:

>> Swa him Offa on dæg ær asæde
>> on þam meþelstede, þa he gemot hæfde,
>> þæt þær modelice manega spræcon
>> þe eft æt þearfe þolian noldon.
>> (*Battle of Maldon*, 198–201)

(So had Offa told them earlier that day in the meeting place, when he held council, that there were many who spoke vauntingly who at the time of need would be unwilling to hold out.)[3]

---

* **Ad Putter** is Fellow of the British Academy and Professor of Medieval English at the University of Bristol, where he co-directs the Centre for Medieval Studies. He has published widely on medieval literature in a range of languages. His books include *Sir Gawain and the Green Knight and French Arthurian Romance* (1995) and *An Introduction to the Gawain Poet* (1996). With Elizabeth Archibald, he co-edited *The Cambridge Companion to Arthurian Literature* (2009) and, with Myra Stokes, *The Works of the Gawain Poet* (Penguin, 2014). His latest book, *North Sea Crossings: The Literary Heritage of Anglo-Dutch Relation (1066–1688)*, co-authored with Sjoerd Levelt, is forthcoming with Bodleian Library Publishing.

1 I would like to thank Myra Stokes and Daniel Donoghue for reading an earlier draft of this version and for suggesting various improvements. I would also like to thank the editors, Anne Scott and Claire McIlroy, and the anonymous reader, who made some excellent suggestions.

2 Edward B. Irving Jr., "Christian and Pagan Elements," in *A Beowulf Handbook*, ed. Robert E. Bjork and John D. Niles (Lincoln: University of Nebraska Press, 1997), 175–92 at 175.

3 Hugh Magennis, *Images of Community in Old English Poetry* (Cambridge: Cambridge University Press, 1996), 198–99.

The quotations are from Edward Irving and Hugh Magennis respectively. Other commentators have said similar things, but I cite Irving and Magennis because they are excellent critics of Old English poetry, and what they say is always worth taking notice of.

The language of "codes" seems to me problematic for two main reasons. The first is that it attributes to the poem the outsiders' perspective that we have of it. We see behavioural "codes" in literature—the "chivalric code," the "code of courtly love," the "heroic code," and so on—whenever the behaviour in question no longer seems natural and self-explanatory to us. But just as we do not generally imagine our own behaviour to be code-driven, so medieval writers, too, do not normally explain their characters' behaviour with reference to codes. What Andrew Lynch says about Malory's *Le Morte Darthur* is true of other medieval texts: "The text assumes an audience consensus about ... things which no longer obtain. *The once explicit has become a more distant code*" (emphasis mine).[4]

My second issue with the word "code" is that, in Patrick Wormald's words, "it turns social ethic into legal prescription."[5] The "warrior code" implies the existence of some collection of rules: the retainer must be brave; he must make good his boasts; if his lord dies on the battlefield, he must avenge him rather than flee from the battle, and so on. According to Hugh Magennis, Offa in *The Battle of Maldon* predicts that some warriors will fail to adhere to this "code." What the poet says is something rather different: he makes no mention of failure to observe a code or general precept in this passage or anywhere else in the poem; instead he recalls words spoken at a particular time ("earlier that day") and on a particular occasion (the council meeting). While it is possible to formulate the poet's outlook as a set of generic ethical principles—heroes fulfil their vows; it is wrong to repay gifts with cowardice—the lines in question recall the concrete social situation, the *gemot* ("meeting") *on þam meþelstede* ("at the place of assembly"), as the setting where commitments to action are made and where socially accepted behaviour is ratified. By contrast, "code" suggests that the cultural values and beliefs implicit in these interactions led a generalized existence independent of such face-to-face communications: the word belongs to a pervasively literate world with written laws and rules that have been abstracted from the particularities of specific social situations.

Such is not the world of *Beowulf* and *The Battle of Maldon*, however. While the real world of early medieval England clearly had social spheres permeated by literacy and codified precepts (think of the Old English laws and penitentials), the heroic world

---

[4] Andrew Lynch, *Malory's Book of Arms: The Narrative of Combat in "Le Morte Darthur"* (Cambridge: Brewer, 1997), 137. See also Jill Mann's objections to the "code of courtly love": "My objection to the term 'courtly love' is that it puts an unnecessary and alienating distance between modern reader and medieval text." Jill Mann, "Falling in Love in the Middle Ages," in *Traditions and Innovations in the Study of Medieval English Literature: The Influence of Derek Brewer*, ed. Charlotte Brewer and Barry Windeatt (Cambridge: Brewer, 2013), 88–110 at 88.

[5] Patrick Wormald, "Anglo-Saxon Society and its Literature," in *The Cambridge Companion to Old English Literature*, ed. Malcolm Godden and Michael Lapidge (Cambridge: Cambridge University Press, 1986), 1–22 at 4.

did not. It had scope for exemplification and didacticism—*Swa sceal geong guma gode gewyrcean* ("So must a young man perform good deeds," 20)[6]—but general precepts tend to be bodied forth by a specific person rather than being drawn from a "code of conduct." I would like to argue in this chapter that it is actually the absence of a "code" of heroic behaviour that explains the importance that *Beowulf* and *The Battle of Maldon* attach to "remembering," and that helps to account for some of the peculiar ways in which *gemunan*, the Old English equivalent of modern English "remember," is used in both poems.

Let us begin with *The Battle of Maldon*.[7] The poem retells the historical events of a Viking raid on the Essex coast, which according to the Anglo-Saxon Chronicle took place in the year 991. The raid ended in defeat for the East-Saxon army led by Byrhtnoth, ealdorman of Essex, but the poet manages to present defeat as courageous achievement, and nostalgically invokes the old world of heroic epic to carry this off.[8] The Vikings win, at least partly because they are cunning (*ongunnon lytegian*, "they began to resort to guile," l. 86), persuading Byrhtnoth to surrender his strategic advantage by allowing them free passage across the water. Magnanimous to a fault, Byrhtnoth agrees to this and is killed in battle. The defending army's resistance is weakened when some of Byrhtnoth's retainers flee, one of them on Byrhtnoth's horse, thereby leading others to think that their own leader is on the run. The soldiers who fight on are killed, but again the poet snatches triumph from the jaws of defeat. Though heavily outnumbered, Byrhtnoth's remaining retainers prefer to die with their lord rather than incur shame by abandoning the battlefield: they lose their lives because they value their honour more. The poet could not change the outcome of history by claiming victory for the English against the Vikings, but he could claim a moral victory by redefining the terms of success and failure—which he does by praising those who remained steadfast in battle and, conversely, by naming and shaming those who did not.

What makes some men heroes and others cowards? In answering this question, it is natural for us to think abstractly of the values of the "heroic code" (loyalty, bravery, steadfastness) and easy to pass over the remarkable emphasis the poet places on the need to "remember." In the various critical discussions of the qualities that make up the epic hero,[9] I have never seen memory mentioned, but it certainly matters in *The Battle of Maldon*. The poem makes a pointed contrast between those who remember and those

---

[6] Quotations are from *Klaeber's Beowulf*, ed. R. D. Fulk, Robert E. Bjork, and John D. Niles (Toronto: University of Toronto Press, 2008). All translations from this and subsequent Old English passages are my own.

[7] Citations are from *The Battle of Maldon*, ed. D. G. Scragg (Manchester: Manchester University Press, 1981).

[8] Renée Trilling, *The Aesthetics of Nostalgia: Historical Representation in Old English Verse* (Toronto: University of Toronto Press, 2009), 125–74.

[9] The most comprehensive discussion is Dean A. Miller, *The Epic Hero* (Baltimore: Johns Hopkins University Press, 2000).

who do not. Compare the description of the cowards as they flee the battleground with the rousing words spoken by Ælfwine:

> Godwine and Godwig, guþe ne gymdon,
> ac wendon fram þam wige and þone wudu sohton,
> flugon on þæt fæsten and hyra feore burgon,
> and manna ma þonne hit ænig mæð wære,
> gyf hi þa geearnunga ealle gemundon
> þe he him to duguþe gedon hæfde.
> (192–97)

(Godwine and Godwig did not care about warfare, but fled from the battle and ran off to the forest, fled into that place of safety and rescued their lives, and many more men did so than was at all reasonable if they had remembered all the favours that he [Byrhtnoth] had bestowed on them for their benefit.)

> Ælfwine þa cwæð (he on ellen spræc:)
> "Gemunaþ þa mæla þe we oft æt meodo spræcon,
> þonne we on bence beot ahofon,
> hæleð on healle, ymbe heard gewinn:
> nu mæg cunnian hwa cene sy..."
> (211–15)

(Then Ælfwine said, he spoke bravely: "Remember the times when we often spoke at mead, when on the benches we made boasts about tough fighting, heroes in the hall. Now it may be known who really is bold...")

The heroes of this poem "remember"; the cowards "forget."

To understand what *gemunan* has to do with heroic action in Old English epic poetry, we need to begin by ridding ourselves of the idea that it primarily looks inwards and denotes a mental activity. In grammars of present-day English, the verb "remember" is usually classified as a "verb of cognition" or a "verb of mental process,"[10] along with "understand," "forget," "know" and other verbs that modern grammarians claim "have less to do with an overt action since they involve mental or cognitive processes."[11] But this cannot be said of the Old English examples of *gemunan* cited above. When Ælfwine urges his comrades to "remember" the boasts they made, he is asking them not merely to bring to mind past events, but above all to act in accordance with these memories. Vows have been made by "heroes in the hall" and these must be fulfilled in a place where it is harder to be a hero: *hæleð on healle* must now become *hæleð æt hilde*. This form of

---

[10] For example see Thomas E. Payne, *Understanding English: A Linguistic Introduction* (Cambridge: Cambridge University Press, 2011), 148, and Randolph Quirk and Sidney Greenbaum, *A University Grammar of English* (London: Longman, 1973), 12.19, 362.

[11] See https://www.tesol-direct.com/tesol-resources/english-grammar-guide/verbs/, and cf. Thomas E. Payne, *Understanding English: A Linguistic Introduction* (Cambridge: Cambridge University Press, 2011), 148.

"remembering" *is* about "overt action," and more specifically about action that makes present behaviour consistent with past behaviour.

In the passage describing the cowards' flight from battle, the performative sense of remembering is even clearer. For the poet's problem with Godwine, Godwig and their ilk is not that they have no mental recollection of the gifts they have received from Byrhtnoth—whether or not they are oblivious or painfully conscious of these gifts as they run away is quite irrelevant. His problem with them is that they do not do what someone mindful of these gifts ought to do. Gifts received impose obligations, and it is the fact that gifts are here reciprocated with betrayal, even with theft (Godric flees on Byrhtnoth's own horse), that prompts the poet to talk about a failure of "moral memory."[12]

There is no such disconnect between past and present for the heroes of the poem. No sooner has Ælfwine asked his friends to "remember" their boasts than he steps out to put his words into action:

>   Þa he forð eode,   fæhðe gemunde,
>   þæt he mid orde   anne geræhte,
>   flotan on þam folce,   þæt se on foldan læg
>   forwegen mid his wæpne ...
>   (225–28)

(Then he went forth, remembered the feud, so that he wounded a sailor from that horde with his spear-point in such a way that the latter lay dead on the ground, killed by his weapon.)

The repetition of the verb *gemunan*, immediately after it has been used in Aelfwine's adjuration, shows that he is a man of his word, and the syntactical context again makes it plain that it is here primarily a verb of action. *Gemunde* is grammatically parallel with *forð eode*, and the result clause that follows it ("such that he wounded a sailor") is dependent on it. Obviously, Æfwine does not kill someone by an act of mental cognition. He does by avenging the death of his leader and lord in the context of the feud (< OE *fæhðu*). Byrhtnoth has been killed by some unnamed Viking—it is significant that no single individual is identified as the killer and that no Viking leader is named—and so it is right that some unnamed Viking must die in return.[13] "Remembering" certainly

---

[12] I owe the phrase to Georg Simmel's thought-provoking description of gratitude as "as it were, the moral memory of mankind." Georg Simmel, "Faithfulness and Gratitude," in *The Sociology of Georg Simmel*, ed. Kurt H. Wolff (Glencoe: Free Press, 1950), 377–95 at 388.

[13] The point is made by Rosemary Woolf in "The Ideal of Men Dying with Their Lord in the *Germania* and in *The Battle of Maldon*," *Anglo-Saxon England* 5 (1976): 63–81 at 76. Since the idea that warriors were supposed to die with their lord has often been taken as one of the conventions of the "heroic code," Woolf's larger argument (that there was no such rule) and her conclusion "Liberated from the view that it illustrates a central tenet of the heroic code *The Battle of Maldon* becomes more moving" (81) is also worth noting. On the *Maldon* poet's deliberately impersonal presentation of the Vikings as "a vague inimical force," see also Fred C. Robinson, "Some Aspects of the Maldon Poet's Artistry," in *The Tomb of Beowulf and Other Essays on Old English* (Oxford: Blackwell, 1993), 122–37 at 135.

involves reference to the past, but above all it means acting in order to bring the present into alignment with the past.

These observations about the way in which *gemunan* is used in *The Battle of Maldon* can, I hope, help us with some difficult passages in *Beowulf*, to which I now turn. I begin with the Finnsburgh episode. The use of the verb *gemunan* in this passage has already attracted some attention, and it will be interesting to see how it has been dealt with. The narrative context of the episode is as follows. A band of Danish warriors, led by Hnæf, receive hospitality from King Finn in Frisia. Finn has married Hildeburh, Hnæf's sister, apparently in an attempt to settle an earlier feud, and the two have had a son. While staying as a guest in Finn's household, the Danes are treacherously attacked, and both Hnæf and Hildeburh's son are killed. The visiting Danes cannot be defeated, however, and a standoff ensues. The unsailable winter seas oblige the Danes, under their new leader Hengest, to spend the winter with Finn. Peace is sworn on both sides, and an uneasy winter passes:

>   ... Hengest ða gyt
>   wælfagne winter   wunode mid Finne;
>   he unhlitme   eard gemunde
>   þeah þe ne meahte   on mere drifan
>   hringedstefnan –   holm storme weol
>   won wið winde;   winter yþe beleac
>   isgebinde—oþ ðæt oþer com
>   gear in geardas,   swa nu gyt deð,
>   þa ðe syngales   sele bewitiað,
>   wuldortorhtan weder.   Ða wæs winter scacen,
>   fæger foldan bearm.   Fundode wrecca
>   gist of geardum;   he to gyrnwræce
>   swiðor þohte   þonne to sælade,
>   gif he torngemot   þurhteon mihte
>   þæt he Eotena bearn   inne gemunde.
>   (1127–41)

(Hengest then stayed on for a slaughter-stained winter with Finn. Eagerly, he remembered his homeland, though he could not sail his ring-prowed ship on the sea. The ocean surged with storms, battling with strong winds. Winter locked the waves in icy bonds, until another year came to human habitations, as it still does, the times of wonderful bright weather observing, as always, their due season. Then winter departed, the earth's bosom was fair. The exile was eager to go, the stranger, away from these lands. He thought of revenge for injury more than of sea-travel, if he might bring about a hostile encounter so that he might remember the sons of enemies in the bottom of his heart.)[14]

---

14 Because it is immaterial to my argument whether "Eotena" refers to "Jutes" or is a poeticism (literally "giants") for the Frisians, I have side-stepped this issue in my translation. For discussion, see Andy Orchard, *A Critical Companion to Beowulf* (Cambridge: Brewer, 2003), 112. More relevant to my argument is the crux "inne," which, to mention but a few possibilities, could be a preposition dependent on *þæt* (understood as relative pronoun referring back to *torngemot*) or perhaps mean "in the hall." See Bruce Mitchell, "Two Syntactical notes on *Beowulf*," *Neophilologus* 52 (1968), 292–99, and Scott Gwara, *Heroic Identity in the World of Beowulf* (Leiden: Brill, 2008), 171–72. The emendation to *irne* ("with iron," i.e., with the sword) has not found favour with

The wonder of *Beowulf* is that the poem is profoundly insightful about the human heart without psychologizing its characters. The natural instinct of someone in a strange land where terrible things have happened is to want to go home, and so it is with Hengest (*eard gemunde*). But by the time winter gives way to glorious springtime and circumstances finally make sea-travel possible, Hengest's priorities have changed, and what he now "remembers" more powerfully than his homeland is the enemy. The connection between the coming of spring and the impulse to revenge explains the poet's choice of words when Hengest predictably takes up the sword offered to him by a companion who wants revenge: Hengest *ne forwyrnde worold-rædenne* ("did not resist the prompting of the world," 1142).[15] After a *wælfagne* winter, that is, a winter in which the slaughter that has occurred has been Hengest's only psychological reality, revenge has the same inevitability as the coming of spring, and promises a sense of relief comparable to that of the springtime sun.

In the glossary to Klaeber's *Beowulf*, *gemunan* is simply glossed as "remember, think of." In this passage, however, *gemunde* is used twice, and the difference between the two tells the psychological story. The first *gemunde* is elegaic. Hengest yearns for home, and he visits it in mind as he is prevented from doing so in body. In this instance, *gemunan* can comfortably be glossed as a verb of mental process ("remember, think of"), but only because the action which the Old English verb normally invites is thwarted. Here, as in other elegiac passages in Old English verse,[16] the senses where *gemunan* and its cognates occur are confined to mental processes because people confront histories that cannot be retrieved: looking inwards and being unable to move history forwards are two sides of the same coin. In the second *gemunde*, which is forward-looking, the semantic restriction placed on the verb by context are lifted with a vengeance. Hengest has unfinished business with his enemies and means to conclude that business. The verb here is no longer simply cognitive but behavioural. To "remember the sons of enemies" is not just to have memories but to *act* on them by settling old scores, to hold enemies to account for acts of violence that lie unavenged.

I am aware of an attempt to construe the second *gemunan*, too, as a verb of cognition, but this attempt seems unconvincing. Scott Gwara tries to make "mental" sense of *inne gemunde* by offering the following translation of lines 1140–41: "if he might engineer

---

recent editors, including those responsible for the fourth revised Klaeber edition, but Klaeber's reasons for adopting it in the editions over which he himself presided remain cogent: "Trautmann's emendation ... greatly improves the sense; it also fits in admirably with the immediately following mention of the bestowal of the sword": Friedrich Klaeber, ed., *Beowulf and the Fight at Finnsburgh*, 3rd ed. (Boston: Heath, 1941), n. to 1141.

15 For a different interpretation of the word "worold-rædenne" (as "leadership") see *Klaeber's Beowulf*, n. to 1242–44.

16 Cf. *The Wanderer*, 34, *gemon he selesecgas ond sincþege* ("he remembers hall-companions and treasure-giving"), and 50–51: *Sorg bið geniwad,/þonne maga gemynd mod geondhweorfeð* ("Grief is renewed when the mind is consumed by the memory of kinsmen").

an angry meeting, that he might remind the sons of the giants within [the hall]."[17] Gwara suggests that Hengest is scheming to arrange a meeting in which he will remind the Frisians of the hostilities and so goad the Frisians into breaking the truce. This is implausible for a number of reasons. The first is that, as the poet knows, it is not the Frisians who would be touchy about being reminded of the slaughter that has occurred, but the Danes. It is they who have lost their lord in a treacherous attack—which is why the terms of the truce specifically stipulate that the Frisians should not mention the war (see 1101–6). The second problem is that the sense Gwara posits, "to remind (someone)," stretches the normal sense, as he himself acknowledges in a note:

> Orchard suggests *gemunan* "remember" can also mean "call to mind" (*Critical Companion*, 186), but this sense would require justification if it meant "to call to (someone else's) mind." Yet Orchard's reading of the verb would solve multiple problems in this passage!

The "multiple problems in this passage" can be solved more satisfactorily by abandoning the modern assumption that "remembering" primarily denotes involves a mental process.

As I have argued, *The Battle of Maldon* challenges this assumption, and *Beowulf* is even clearer on this point. Here, for instance, is how Eofor avenges Hæthcyn's death on the Swedish war-leader Ongentheow:

> guðhelm toglad, gomela Scylfing
> hreas hildeblāc; hond gemunde
> fæhðo genoge, feorhsweng ne ofteah.
> (2487–89)

(The battle-helm split, the old Scylfing fell battle-pale; the hand remembered plenty of hostilities: it did not hold back the deadly blow.)

To the extent that "the hand" is a metonym for the person, Ongentheow's memory of the past is not irrelevant, but the poet's formulation makes the verb action-focused. The hand that "remembers the feud" is the hand that strikes the fatal blow. Since hands have no minds, the cognitive sense of *gemunan* is clearly not the one the poet wished to emphasize at this point.

I have so far treated the question of "remembering" and its meaning in Old English as a glossarial problem, but the difference of meaning may be symptomatic of larger cultural and historical differences. "Remembering" in Old English is not like "remembering" in modern English, first, because Anglo-Saxon literature was less "inward"-looking than our own, and second, because the role of memory in Anglo-Saxon culture is not like that of memory today.

The first consideration takes us away from the theme of memory, and I can only deal with it sketchily here. I would argue that the semantic difference between Old

---

[17] Gwara, *Heroic Identity*, 170. Gwara's later observations about Old Icelandic *muna* in the context of taking revenge (171) are more pertinent to the sense of the word in this passage.

English *gemunan*, with its behavioural emphasis, and modern English "remember," which looks inwards rather than outwards, forms part of a larger story, at once literary-historical and linguistic, of meaning retreating from the visible and public sphere to a private and interior domain. In scholarship on semantic change the process is known as "subjectification."[18] For instance, "feel" (< OE *felan*) used to mean "touch"; the perceptual "inner" sense only developed slowly from late Old English onwards.[19] Similarly, "to notice something" used to mean "to give public notice of (a thing)" (*OED*, sense 1), and "to notice someone" used to mean "to openly acknowledge someone," "to treat a person favourably" (*OED* sense 4). These senses are now obsolete, while the sense "to become aware of someone" (*OED*, sense 3) thrives in the modern world, which sharply distinguishes between inner and outer domains, and puts greater value on the former. A good summary of the modern outlook is the pronouncement by Dwight Bolinger and Donald Sears:

> This is the sense in which we must take the term *reality*, for it includes both what is viewable within and what can be seen by anyone. In fact, the inner view is more important for most of the things adults talk about. Utterances about what is going on at the moment, like *Now I get up, now I walk to the window, now I look out*, are exceptional; more usual are *Last night I got up because I couldn't sleep* ... where we look inward on our memories or plans. Whatever it is that represents these past or future events or imagined events in our minds is the main part, if not the whole, of reality as we grasp it.[20]

For *Beowulf* and *The Battle of Maldon* this is simply untrue: the utterances in these poems deal largely with "what can be seen by anyone," and so we need to adopt these texts' "outer view" if we are to understand what they mean when they speak of people "remembering" things.

Although *OED* does not register it, the verbs "love" and "hate" have undergone comparable semantic shifts, respectively from "supporting/showing favour to (a person)" to "having affectionate feelings for someone," and from "engaging in hostilities with someone" to "harbouring feelings of hostility." When in *Beowulf* 2460–66 it is said of Hrethel that he cannot hate (*hatian*) his son, the poet means that he is unable to persecute him, not that he cannot stop loving him (in the modern sense of "love").[21] That is why *hatian* takes the behavioural complement *laðum dædum* ("with hostile deeds"). Scholarship on the history of private life and on the cultural differences between honour-and-shame cultures and guilt cultures provide relevant contexts for these broad

---

18 Elizabeth Closs Traugott, "On the Rise of Epistemic Meanings in English: An Example of Subjectification in Semantic Change," *Language* 65 (1989): 31–55.

19 Traugott, "Epistemic Meanings," 34.

20 Dwight Bolinger and Donald A. Sears, *Aspects of Language*, 3rd ed. (New York: Harcourt Brace Jovanovich, 1981), 110.

21 The word *hatian* was indeed glossed as "persecute" by C. L. Wrenn in his edition of *Beowulf*, rev. W. F. Bolton (Exeter: University of Exeter Press, 1997).

semantic trends that have gradually tilted our sense of reality and semantics towards "the inner view."[22]

The second reason why "remembering" in Anglo-Saxon times cannot have been what it is today has to do with the way memory operates in oral or semi-oral cultures. Anglo-Saxon society had a mixed economy with "both 'oral' and 'literate' ways of knowing."[23] In matters of war, it was predominantly oral, largely trusting to human memories to transmit its cultural tradition. Now, in non-literate cultures the past exists only insofar as it is remembered, and what makes the memorial transmission of history possible is that such cultures by necessity remember history selectively, according to the needs of the present. What is remembered, moreover, is not the kind of abstract and objective knowledge that writing allows cultures to store up, but rather what has been heard or seen in face-to-face encounters with others:

> The transmission of the verbal elements of culture by oral means can be visualized as a long chain of interlocking conversations between members of the group. Thus all beliefs and values, all forms of knowledge, are communicated between individuals in face-to-face contact ... There can be no reference to "dictionary definitions," nor can words accumulate the successive layers of historically validated meanings which they acquire in a literate culture. Instead, the meaning of each word is ratified in a succession of concrete situations. ... What the individual remembers tends to be what is of critical importance in his experience of the main social relationships ... and whatever parts of it have ceased to be of contemporary relevance are likely to be eliminated by the process of forgetting.

I cite here the work of two social anthropologists, Jack Goody and Ian Watt, based on their study of present-day non-literate societies,[24] and in applying this to early medieval England some caveats are in order. English society of the early eight century (the likely age of *Beowulf*[25]), let alone the late tenth (the age of *The Battle of Maldon*), did possess writing and, indeed, written codes (the earliest Old English law codes are attributed to Æthelbert of Kent, ca. 600[26]). The poets of *Beowulf* and *The Battle of Maldon* were

---

22 See, for instance, *A History of Private Life, II: Revelations of the Medieval World*, ed. Georges Duby, trans. Arthur Goldhammer (Cambridge, MA: Belknap Press, 1993) and on the characteristics of honour-and-shame cultures see Lynch, *Malory's Book of Arms*, especially chap. 1, and further references therein.

23 Katherine O'Brien O'Keeffe, "Orality and Literacy: The Case of Anglo-Saxon England," in *Medieval Oral Literature*, ed. Karl Reichl (Berlin: De Gruyter, 2012), 121–140 at 122.

24 Jack Goody and Ian Watt, "The Social Consequences of Literacy," in *Literacy in Traditional Societies*, ed. Jack Goody (Cambridge: Cambridge University Press, 1968), 27–68 at 29–30.

25 After a revisionist phase in which critics dared to defy common sense by assigning the poem a date of composition as close as possible to the date of copying (ca. 1000), scholarship has reverted to the date (early eighth century) proposed long ago by Klaeber. For the reasons why, see the editorial introduction and the essays collected in *The Dating of Beowulf: A Reassessment*, ed. Leonard Neidorf (Cambridge: Brewer, 2014).

26 For text and discussion see "The Laws of Æthelbert of Kent: A Student Edition," ed. Lisi Oliver, *Old English Newsletter* (2018), available at www.oenewsletter.org/OEN/print.php/essays/oliver38_1/Array.

presumably literate themselves. Literacy, however, was largely restricted to a clerical elite, even after King Alfred's attempts to reform the education of laymen,[27] and the fact that a poet is highly literate does not necessarily mean that he has lost touch with the traditions of oral poetics with which he grew up. The two cultures, literate and oral, can co-exist and interact with each other.[28] As Tom Shippey writes, "literate people can live in illiterate societies, just as illiterates can live in our own. ... I can now say that many of the problems of *Beowulf* dissolve if one accepts it as the work of a literate man in a pre-literate society—one might say, a sort of Caedmon in reverse."[29]

With these qualifications in mind, anthropological insights into how pre-literate cultures remember can, I think, illuminate how *gemunan* works in *Beowulf* and in *The Battle of Maldon*. To begin with, it explains the uncomplicated way in which the *Beowulf* asserts that there are people who "remember all." In a pervasively literate society where the sum of human knowledge continues to accumulate in writing (or in bytes), no-one who claims to remember *everything* will be taken seriously. "Remembering all" is certainly said colloquially today (typically with the pronoun "it" as object), but everyone knows it is a hyperbolic way of saying that something made a big impression on a person. By contrast, when Hrothgar uses the phrase to extol Beowulf's pre-eminence, its point is precisely the opposite, to indicate that no hyperbole is intended:

> Þæt, la, mæg secgan   se þe soð ond riht
> fremeð on folce,   feor eal gemon,
> eald eðelweard   þæt ðes eorl wære
> geboren betera.
>   (1700–1704)

(Lo! He who does what is true and right among his people, who remembers everything from far back, the old guardian of the homeland, may well say that this warrior was born the better man!)

Hrothgar gives Beowulf his just place in history by comparing him with other men of great promise (including Heremod, who did not live up to this promise). What makes it possible for someone to survey the past completely is that this past is shaped by the horizons of the present. The *eald eðelweard* who *eal gemon* does not remember people from the past in their historical moment but remembers the exemplary figures that set the current standards of greatness. "Structural amnesia" is an inescapable part of this present- and future-directed remembering.[30] Similarly, when Beowulf predicts

---

27 Patrick Wormald, "The Uses of Literacy in Anglo-Saxon England and its Neighbours," *Transactions of the Royal Historical Society* 27 (1977): 95–114.

28 Daniel Donoghue, *How the Anglo-Saxons Read Their Poems* (Philadelphia: University of Pennsylvania Press, 2018), chap. 2.

29 T. A. Shippey, *Beowulf* (London: Arnold, 1978), 59.

30 See Goody and Watt, "Consequences," 33. For an application of the concept to medieval literature see Jan-Dirk Müller, "Medieval German Literature: Literacy, Orality and Semi-Orality," in *Medieval Oral Literature*, ed. Karl Reichl (Berlin: De Gruyter, 2012), 295–334.

that Freawaru's marriage will fail to end the ancient feud between the Danes and the Heathobards, he imagines the resentful words of an older Danish warrior who will reignite the vendetta. This Dane is someone *ðe eall geman* ("who remembered all," 2042). Again, *eall* means "all that matters for the present purposes," which in this case is the *garcwealm gumena* (2043), the "spear-death of men" who are as yet unavenged. The old warrior was there when it happened, and it is the transmission of traumatic memories across generations that keeps the feud alive.

The final example of the "all-remembering" man is Beowulf himself. Just before the fight with the dragon, which Beowulf senses might be his last, he recalls the campaigns of his youth: *ic þæt eall gemon* (2427). Nothing is forgotten, because the past that Beowulf remembers is brought into being by the challenges of the present: he faced many dangers before and he will now do so again, even though this time he may not survive.

The key characteristic of *gemunan*, and its ultimate value, is that memory creates what Goody and Watt call "homeostasis":

> The social function of memory—and of forgetting—can thus be seen as the final stage of what may be called the homeostatic organization of the cultural tradition in a non-literate society. The language is developed in intimate association with the experience of the community, and it is learned by the individual in face-to-face contact with the other members. What continues to be of social relevance is stored in the memory while the rest is usually forgotten: and language—primarily vocabulary—is the effective medium of this crucial process of social digestion and elimination which may be regarded as analogous to the homeostatic organization of the human body by which it attempts to maintain its present condition of life.[31]

When in *The Battle of Maldon* the cowards are said not to "remember" the past, the poet recognizes the threat that memory failure poses to the "homeostatic organization of the cultural tradition." The cowards have not in their actions carried forward the socially relevant past into the present, and so have violated the chain of "interlocking communications"—gifts given to them, vows made by them—on which the transmission and survival of oral cultures depend.

The contrast in *The Battle of Maldon* between the heroes who maintain cultural homeostasis and the anti-heroes who do not is also present in *Beowulf*. Beowulf remembers "everything" in the past that is relevant to his behaviour in the present. He makes his vows in the hall, on the evening before his fight with Grendel, and when he stands up to face the monster at night he "remembers" his words by putting them into action:

>   Gemunde þa se goda,   mæg Higelaces,
>   æfenspræce;   uplang astod
>   ond him fæste wiðfeng ...
>   (758-60)

---

31 Goody and Watt, "Consequences," 30–31.

(The noble man, Higelac's kinsman, remembered his speech that evening; he stood upright and seized Grendel firmly.)

Goody and Watt emphasize "face-to-face contacts" as channels for the transmission of social values, and this is consonant with the *Beowulf* poet's focus. What motivates Beowulf is not a general principle, a "dictionary definition" of courage, but specific words uttered that evening in the presence of Hrothgar's retinue. In *The Battle of Maldon*, Ælfwine's battle-cry—*Gemunaþ þa mæla þe we oft æt meodo spræcon,/þonne we on bence beot ahofon,/hæleð on healle*—has the same specificity, as later on in *Beowulf* do Wiglaf's words, when he urges his companions to come to Beowulf's rescue:

> Ic ðæt mæl geman   þær we medu þegun
> þonne we geheton   ussum hlaforde
> in biorsele   ðe us ðas beagas geaf
> þæt we him ða guðgetawa   gyldan woldon
> gif him þyslicu   þearf gelumpe,
> helmas ond heard sweord ...
> (2633–8)

(I remember the time when, enjoying mead in the beer-hall, we vowed to our lord, he who gave us treasure, that we would repay him for this war-gear, helmets and hard sword, if the need should ever arise.)

By contrast with the "collective remembering" that unites the remaining warriors in *The Battle of Maldon*, these lines from *Beowulf* isolate the "I" who remembers from the "we" that made the vows, and Wiglaf's sense of betrayal is located in this isolation. They all pledged their futures to Beowulf, but Wiglaf alone "remembers" it in the proper performative sense of the verb.

In the examples we have just discussed, the things that are remembered and forgotten are not the values of a "heroic code" but the implicatures of words spoken in face-to-face interactions. Other things that warriors remember in *Beowulf* as in *The Battle of Maldon* are hostilities that require retaliation and "gifts" that require counter-gifts. In the passage above, Wiglaf's re-description of Beowulf as "he who gave us treasure" serves as a pointed reminder of the social obligations they have incurred as recipients of this treasure. To repay (*gyldan*) the gifts they have received, the "war-gear," helmets and hard sword, they must put these weapons to use. In fighting Grendel, Beowulf, too, remembers more than just his pledges in the hall:

> Þær him aglæca   ætgræpe wearð;
> hwæþre he gemunde   mægenes strenge,
> gimfæste gife,   ðe him god sealde ...
> (1269–71)

(There the monster took hold of him; but he [Beowulf] remembered the power of his strength, the jewel of a gift that God had given him.)

Beowulf "remembers" his strength, not arrogantly but morally, that is, with gratitude for this gift that God has given him,[32] and again the proper way of "remembering" this gift is by using it against the donor's enemy. The language of the feud is modelled on that of giving and counter-giving.[33] An act of hostility against one's lord or kinsman is a "gift" that is not to be forgotten but to be honoured and emulated by giving an even finer gift in return. That is the spirit in which Beowulf takes vengeance for the death of Hygelac's son, Heardred: *Se ðæs leod-hryres lean gemunde/uferan dogrum* ... ("He remembered the gift of the prince's death on a later day," 2391–2). The word *lean* here is often glossed as "retribution,"[34] but the logic is grimmer: Beowulf remembers the killing of Heardred as a "gift" that obliges him to proffer a counter-gift in appreciation of this earlier act of "generosity."

Whenever Beowulf "remembers," *gemunan* is primarily a behavioural verb. Of course, consciousness of the past is relevant to the course of action he takes, but whether Beowulf "remembers" it in any mental sense is not the poet's chief concern. Beowulf is therefore never presented like Hamlet, as someone who "remembers" the duty to revenge before executing it. In *Beowulf*, the execution of vengeance *is* the act of remembrance, and what we call "history" (for example, the fact that Heardred was killed) only enters the frame as the orientation for decisive action.

In the case of *gemunan*, the feedback loop between present and past is most strikingly shown in the war of words between Beowulf and Unferth about an incident from Beowulf's "history," the swimming contest with Breca. Unferth and Beowulf represent this episode from Beowulf's youth very differently. According to Unferth, Beowulf acted recklessly and foolishly, and was shown up by Breca who won the contest. According to Beowulf, it was an act of youthful derring-do; it required huge strength, but after slaying numerous sea-monsters, he came ashore and triumphed. The episode raises various questions. Why does the poem offer us these "trips down memory-lane," and how do we know that Beowulf is the one who has represented the past correctly?

The clue to the first of these questions is that in oral cultures remembered history is, to paraphrase Goody and Watt, a "charter for the present."[35] Their story of the foundation myth of Gonja illustrates the point well:

> The state of Gonja in northern Ghana is divided into a number of divisional chiefdoms. ... When asked to explain their system the Gonja recount how the founder of the state, Ndewura Jakpa, came down from the Niger Bend. ... When the details of this story were first recorded at the turn of the present century ... Jakpa was said to have begotten seven sons, this corresponding to the number of divisions whose heads were eligible for the

---

[32] See above, n. 12.

[33] The point has been well made by William Ian Miller in his study of feuding in Icelandic sagas: "The Icelanders did have a model of the feud ... The model takes over the entire vocabulary of gift-exchange and inverts it." William Ian Miller, *Bloodtaking and Peacemaking: Feud, Law and Society in Saga Iceland* (Chicago: University of Chicago Press, 1990), 182.

[34] See for example, *Beowulf: A Student Edition*, ed. George Jack (Oxford: Clarendon Press, 1994).

[35] Goody and Watt, "Consequences," 33.

supreme office by virtue of their descent from the founder of the particular chiefdom. But at the same time as the British had arrived, two of the seven divisions disappeared ... Sixty years later, when the myths of state were again recorded, Jakpa was credited with only five sons and no mention was made of the founders of the two divisions which had since disappeared from the political map.[36]

Is it history that shapes the present or is it the present that retroactively shapes history? When history is transmitted in living memories, it is impossible to say.

The history of Beowulf's boyhood similarly circulates in two versions, Beowulf's and Unferth's, and putting their differences in the context of the conflicting versions of Jakpa's life story helps us to see that the disparities between these versions are not significant as matters of biographical record but because the versions offer alternative "charters for the present." If Unferth is right, Beowulf is a braggart and the Danes would be foolish to believe that he can defeat Grendel (see Unferth's closing words: ll. 525–28). However, if Beowulf is right, he is the man who has killed many monsters before and can do so again. When Hrothgar hears Beowulf's side of the story, its significance for the here and now is clearly picked out. What Hrothgar concludes from it is that it bodes well for the fight to come: *gehyrde on Beowulfe ... fæstrædne geþoht* ("he heard from Beowulf firm resolve," 608–9).

The feedback loop between past and present also settles the second question: how do we know which memory is right? It is ultimately by killing Grendel that Beowulf proves his account of the past to have been right and Unferth's wrong.[37] Interestingly, the poet brings this point home in the language of memory and forgetfulness. After Beowulf's fight with Grendel, Unferth "forgets" what he said in opposition to Beowulf. Just before Beowulf dives into the mere to fight Grendel's mother, Unferth gives Beowulf his sword Hrunting, and the poet writes:

> Huru ne gemunde   mago Ecglafes,
> eafoþes cræftig,   þæt he ær gespræc,
> wine druncen ... (1465–67)

(Indeed, he did not remember, Ecglaf's kinsman, powerful in strength, what he had said before, drunk with wine ...)

If this were a scene from a modern novel, like *The Great Gatsby*, we might think the author was talking about alcohol-induced amnesia. However, the right comparison is not with *The Great Gatsby* but with *The Battle of Maldon*, where the deserters are said not to "remember" Byrhtnoth's gifts. In *Beowulf*, as in *The Battle of* Maldon, we are not

---

36 Goody and Watt, "Consequences," 33.

37 As Peter Baker has emphasized, there is no suggestion in the poem that Beowulf wins the battle of words with Unferth because he presents a more faithful account, but his conclusion that Beowulf wins the day because he is a better rhetorician does not follow. What vindicates him and what makes Unferth eat his words is the hero's victory over Grendel. Peter Baker, "Beowulf the Orator," *Journal of English Linguistics* 21 (1988): 3–23.

dealing with a comment about someone's mental awareness or lack of it, but about actions in the present that belie earlier ones.

It is time to sum up my main findings. As we have seen, the verb *gemunan* in *The Battle of Maldon* and *Beowulf* is not used in the restricted sense of "having a mental recollection of the past." The verb focuses on performance of duty and on behaviour, and is used with reference to actions that bring past and present into alignment: actions such as fulfilling vows and repaying gifts, whether in the context of the gift economy or the feud, which uses the same discourse of gift and counter-gift. This difference of emphasis between "remembering" in present-day English and heroic *gemunan* may, as I have suggested, be part of a larger story of semantic change towards "subjectification," which in turn reflects broad differences between modern cultures that privilege the "inner view" of reality and earlier ones that took the "outer view" and between literate and non-literate societies (or in the case of Anglo-Saxon England, societies with restricted literacy). In oral and semi-oral cultures, knowledge and ethical values cannot be stored in writing or condensed in abstract "codes" of behaviour. Rather, they are transmitted in face-to-face encounters and never abstracted from specific social settings—which is why such settings are always vividly present when moral imperatives are remembered in *Beowulf* and *The Battle of Maldon* (*gemunaþ þa mæla þe we oft æt meodo spræcon*). In such cultures, moreover, the function of memory is not to record the past but to create "cultural homeostasis." This involves carrying forward from the past what is critical to the present (which is what "remembering all" in *Beowulf* means) and acting in a way that makes this present consistent with the past. The heroes of *Beowulf* and *The Battle of Maldon* are, as it were, agents of cultural homeostasis. Even in his last battle Beowulf "remembers himself" by going out to fight the dragon; Unferth, on the other hand, capitulates: he cannot stand by his earlier words; in the poet's revealing phrase, he fails to "remember" them.

The semantic and cultural differences between Old English "remembering" and modern English should not be exaggerated, however, and the Old English epics may yet have something to teach us about the ways in which we ourselves operate in oral modes. As Daniel Donoghue has recently argued, the "great divide" between orality and literacy is a false division. As he points out, highly literate Anglo-Saxon poets could without difficulty access the thought-world of an oral tradition.[38] Conversely, even in today's pervasively literate society, we continue to transmit a great deal of cultural knowledge by oral transmission and reliance on memory. It is significant in this regard that Goody and Watt's insights into the "homeostatic" function of memory in pre-literate cultures were not just based on their anthropological fieldwork; their inspiration, as they acknowledge,[39] was the classic study of remembering by the psychologist Frederic

---

38 See n. 24 above.
39 Goody and Watt, "Consequences," 30.

Bartlett, who, in a series of controlled experiments with volunteers, demonstrated the way human memories tend to reconfigure the past in line with present concerns.[40] Homeostasis is at work in the brains of literates, not just in the remembering of Anglo-Saxon epic heroes.

The senses and functions of Old English *gemunan* are therefore not discontinuous with the semantics and pragmatics of the equivalent verb "to remember" in Present-Day English. As I said at the start of this chapter, "remember" and "forget" have usually been understood by linguists as "cognitive" or "mental-process" verbs, but it is relevant to this chapter to note that this classification has recently been called into question.[41] Looking at actual conversations rather than idealized sentences, Hongyin Tao concludes that in spoken English, at least, "remember" is not just a cognitive verb but is "in the process of becoming a discourse particle indicating epistemic stance [which] can be used as a meta-linguistic device regulating interaction."[42] So in the following examples from Tao's data the primary function of "remember" is to "regulate interaction" by attempting to bring the addressee round to the speaker's position:

> (5) SE: In fact, there will be a new section on–a new little section within this chapter on that. The chapter is becoming two chapters. **Remember?**
>
> BU: Uh-huh. But we're worried now about what's existing here.
>
> SE: Okay. Yeah. I'll just rearrange it.
>
> (6) GU: **Remember**, we did something earlier. We have a similar sentence. And we kind of softened it a bit. I think we made an (Inaudible).
>
> Jack, do you **remember?** (Sound momentarily lost due to static.)

The Old English data should be of interest to linguists who, like Tao, think that we have overlooked the pragmatic functions of the verb, though, by the same token, they suggest that what modern "remembering" according to Tao is "in the process of becoming" is in some respects what OE *gemunan* always already was. Certainly, my own recent experiences of the verb—for instance, "HP: Did you **remember** to put the bins out?"—have taught me that it often concerns actions. HP's question means "did you *do* what you are supposed to do?"[43] As in the case of the Old English examples,

---

40 Frederic C. Bartlett, *Remembering: A Study in Experimental and Social Psychology* (Cambridge: Cambridge University Press, 1930).

41 See Cecilia E. Ford, Barbara A. Fox, and Sandra A. Thompson, "Social Interaction and Grammar," in *The New Psychology*, ed. Michael Tomasello, 2 vols (New York: Taylor and Francis, 2014), 2, 119–44 at 121–2.

42 Hongyin Tao, "A Usage-Based Approach to Argument Structure: 'Remember' and 'Forget' in Spoken English," *International Journal of Corpus Linguistics* 8 (2003): 75–95 at 86.

43 *OED* has this sense under "remember" *v.*1, sense 4.c: "not to forget, to bear in mind, to do something."

the salient background to "remembering" here is the shared knowledge of a duty to which the addressee has committed himself in the past (in a face-to-face encounter, not in writing), and in this case, I admit, a history of "forgetting," that is, dereliction of duty, on the part of the addressee. We should have no difficulty tuning into Old English usages of *gemunan*, because the "outer view" of the equivalent verb in modern English is still with us today. In short, there is still much we can discover in Old English poetry about ourselves.

Chapter 6

THE HARD PARTING: CONFLICTING CODES OF *FIN'AMORS* AND CHRISTIAN DUTY IN THE OLD FRENCH *CHANSONS DE CROISADE*

Helen Dell*

THIS CHAPTER IS founded on a question: in considering the Crusades, what kinds of knowledge can we hope to glean from reading or listening to songs, especially love songs?[1] In particular, can a song give us an indication of public sentiment towards the Crusades? This is the first question Linda M. Paterson and Stefano Asperti bring to their comprehensive online project on troubadour and trouvère crusade songs, Troubadours, Trouvères, and the Crusades: "What did the secular public in the Middle Ages think of the Crusades?"[2]

> As if in answer, William Jackson, in *Ardent Complaints and Equivocal Piety*, asserted (previously) that the crusade poetry of the German-speaking laity of the later 12th and 13th centuries, is at base a poetry of inner struggle, misgivings, and disenchantment about the Crusades, and, in a few cases, outright rejection of that undertaking.[3]

I am not assuming that one can answer a question about the trouvères and troubadours by reference to the *Minnesänger* (their German counterparts). I am suggesting that in medieval song, or in any song, *what* is said can never be separated

---

* **Helen Dell** is an Honorary Research Fellow in the School of Culture and Communication at the University of Melbourne. Her core research is in the field of trouvère song. Her PhD was published as *Desire by Gender and Genre in Trouvère Song* (2008). More recently she co-edited, and contributed the chapter "Dying for Love in Trouvère Song" to, *Singing Death: Reflections on Music and Mortality*, ed. Helen Dell and Helen Hickey (London: Routledge, 2016). She is also the author of a chapter, "Handmade Women: The Manufacture of Femininity in the *Chansons de Femme*," in *Female-Voice Song in the Middle Ages*, ed. Lisa Colton and Anna Grau Schmidt, forthcoming (2021). She also works in the area of medievalism, usually in relation to music.

1 In this chapter I have confined myself mainly to a consideration of the *chansons de croisade* in the trouvère corpus.

2 Paterson and Asperti's comprehensive online project provides the songs with translations (which I have used throughout), all relevant details, and whatever historical knowledge there is of the trouvère or troubadour, sometimes sketchy and uncertain, in relation to the Crusades. The numbers for trouvère songs used by Paterson, Stefano, Harvey, Radaelli, and Barberi refer to the Raynaud/Spanke system: Professor Linda M. Paterson, Professor Asperti Stefano, Professor Ruth Harvey, Dr Anna Radaelli, and Dr Luca Barberi, "Troubadours, Trouvères and the Crusades": www2.warwick.ac.uk/fac/arts/modernlanguages/research/french/crusades/

3 William E. Jackson, *Ardent Complaints and Equivocal Piety*: *The Portrayal of the Crusader in Medieval German Poetry* (Lanham: University Press of America, 2003), 3.

out from *how* and in what generic context it is sung. Two things concern me about Jackson's statement. The first is what appears to be an assumption about the sincerity of the speakers, conveyed in particular by the words "*inner* struggle," in this case the lyric "I" of 12th- and 13th-century *Minnesänger* lyric. Such an assumption, along with its implication that the emotions are already present within the author/composer, waiting to be expressed, would be mistaken if applied to troubadour or trouvère song. As Matilda Bruckner wrote, the "red herring of troubadour criticism [is] the question of sincerity as understood in the context of a lyric tradition which claims to equate and represent lived experience."[4] The same is true of trouvère song. The masculine lover of *chanson* (*canso* for the troubadours), the high-status song of *fin'amors*—fine, pure, refined Love—claims sincerity. That is the appropriate sentiment for a *fin'amant*, but it cannot be translated into sincerity on the part of the author/composer.

In this context of the sincerity topos, Brooke Heidenreich Findley compares two troubadour songs. The first is by Bernart de Ventadorn: "Chantars no pot gaire valer." This is the first stanza:

> Chantars no pot gaire valer,
> si dins dal cor no mou lo chans;
> ni chans no pot dal cor mover,
> si no i es fin'amors coraus.
> Per so es mos chantars cabaus
> qu'en joi d'amor ai et enten
> la boch' e.ls olhs e.l cor e.l sen.

(Singing cannot be worth anything if the song does not spring from within the heart, nor can the song spring from the heart if refined, heartfelt love is not there. That is why my singing is superior, since I consecrate to love's joy my mouth, my eyes, my heart and my understanding.)[5]

As Findley notes, however, "writing a generation later, Arnaut de Mareuil claims that it is impossible to differentiate a true song from a false one, thus making Bernart's standard of poetic value impossible to apply."[6] This is stanza one of Arnaut's "D'aisso sai grat als autres trobadors":

> D'aisso sai grat als autres trobadors
> qu'en sas chansos pliu chascus et afia
> que sa domna es la genser que sia,
> si tot s'es fals, lot digz lau e mercei,
> qu'entre lurs gaps passa seguts mos vers,
> qu'uns non conois ni no so ten a mal
> c'atressi ere chascus, sia plazers.

---

[4] Matilda Tomaryn Bruckner, "Fictions of the Female Voice: The Women Troubadours," *Speculum* 67, no. 4 (1992): 865–91 at 866.

[5] Brooke Heidenreich Findley, "Reading Sincerity at the Intersection of Troubadour/Trobairitz Poetry: Two Poetic Debates," *Romance Quarterly* 53, no. 4 (Fall, 2006): 287–303 at 288.

[6] Findley, "Reading Sincerity," 288.

(For this I am grateful to other troubadours, for each one swears and affirms in his songs that his Lady is the noblest who exists, and it is all false, for which I praise and thank them, for between their boasts my truth/verse [vers] passes safely, so that no one understands or thinks badly of it, for everyone thinks I'm just fooling.)[7]

Findley's comparison makes it clear that the sentiments of a *canso* author (insofar as they can be said to exist in a pre-linguistic state) are impossible to detect. We cannot regard their declarations as expressive or representative of inner feeling. Sincerity and its opposite, falsehood, are certainly preoccupations for authors but in what sense do they occupy them? That is much harder to answer. All we can say for sure is that they are motifs to be worked, played with, re-arranged and rung the changes on, in a display of poetic, musical, and rhetorical skill.[8] The same is true of the *chansons de croisade*.

The second, related aspect of Jackson's statement that concerns me is that word "about" in "about the Crusades." Can we expect a song to be precisely *about* anything? Bernard Guenée, allowing a kind of threshold between literature and history, spoke of "the imprecise and doubtful fringes where history and literature mingle."[9] Linda Paterson, in the "Introduction" to her recent book *Singing the Crusades*, assumes separability when she states that "[s]ince the focus of interest in this book is what the lyric poets say about the Crusades, questions of genre are secondary."[10] I do not believe that questions of genre can ever be secondary. We cannot simply reach in to the supposedly concrete historical reality conveyed in a song, extractable from its generic, even its poetic dress; the two are not separable in this way. As Stefano Asperti contends, propaganda in the troubadour crusade songs "is constructed by way of the formal aspects of the text."[11] Paterson excludes from her study crusade songs which are "of little historical value," a distinction which raises related problems.[12] Some of these are excluded because they are "judged to be essentially literary exploitation of crusading locations or ideas."[13] But all crusade songs involve literary exploitation which, as I argue, cannot be disengaged from the history embedded in them. History is itself a form of literature—many and changing

---

7 Findley, "Reading Sincerity," 288–89.

8 Findley, "Reading Sincerity," 288–89.

9 Bernard Guenée, *Histoire et culture historique dans l'Occident médiéval* (Paris: Aubier-Montaigne, 1980), 350.

10 Linda Paterson, Luca Barbieri, Ruth Harvey, Anna Radelli, and Marjolaine Ragain, *Singing the Crusades: French and Occitan Lyric Responses to the Crusading Movements, 1137–1336* (Cambridge: Brewer, 2018), 7.

11 Stefano Asperti, "Testi poetici volgari di propaganda politica," in *Propaganda del basso medioevo, Atti del XXXVIII Convegno storico internazionale, Todi, 14–17 ottobre 2001* (Spoleto: Centro Italiana di Studi sull'Alto Medioevo, 2002), 533–59 at 558. See also Marco Grimaldi's comment: "In general, according to Asperti, in the troubadour *sirventes* with political or topical content ... the expressive function is more important than the persuasive one." Marco Grimaldi, "Il sirventese di Peire de la Caravana," *Cultura Neolatina* 73 (2013): 25–72 at 69.

12 Paterson, *Singing*, 7.

13 Paterson, *Singing*, 8.

forms of literature, each with its own generic constraints—rather than a transparent window onto the world of events of the past, history "as it was," in Ranke's phrase.[14]

How Songs Work: I

So how can songs inform us? There are many aspects to this question of the interaction between the what—what it is *about*—and the how and where of a song. First, songs work within the constraints imposed by register, genre, and form, both poetic and musical form (all of which involve gender) although they also play with these constraints, indicating an awareness of their presence from outside the world of the song, as it were, as in "D'aisso sai grat als autres trobadors."[15] They may not say much about generic expectations but they know how to use and confuse them. Part of the play in troubadour and trouvère song relies on a conflation (encouraged by authors and performers) between the author and the persona of the lover in love lyric which has had readers and listeners bamboozled from the first and led to all kinds of wild biographical speculations.[16]

Following Lance St. John Butler, in *Registering the Difference: Reading Literature through Register*, I find it useful to think of register as what organizes language and music to make a song sound as it does. Genre is the product which results from its sounding that way. For instance, as he argues,

> [E]very register hints at, sounds like, belongs to a genre; it is impossible to imagine the one without the other. [Edward] Gibbon sounds as he does (register) because he is writing classical history (genre) in the eighteenth century.[17]

---

[14] Linda Paterson mentions an important distinction between the troubadour and trouvère repertoires: "the development of the Old French crusade lyric in the direction of the love song" while the Old Occitan crusade songs have taken rather different, more anecdotal paths, for instance, "celebration of an imminent crusade." Paterson, *Singing*, 10–11. I have focused on the Old French corpus in which the play of literature and history may be differently slanted from that of the Old Occitan, which might perhaps provide more grist for a historical reading, although the same problems of genre and register would still intrude to complicate the message.

[15] I ask the reader's tolerance for this rather lengthy section on genre and register but as these matters have been somewhat contested within the community of trouvère criticism I believe a brisk summary of some relevant theories is necessary. On this topic, see, for instance, Joan Tasker Grimbert, "Songs by Women and Women's Songs: How Useful is the Concept of Register?," in *The Court Reconvenes* [Selected Proceedings of the Ninth Triennial Congress of the ICLS], ed. Barbara Altmann and Carroll Carleton (Cambridge: Brewer, 2003), 117–24 at 122. See also Elizabeth Aubrey, "Reconsidering 'High Style' and 'Low Style' in Medieval Song," *Journal of Music Theory* 52, no. 1, Essays in Honor of Sarah Fuller (Spring, 2008): 75–122.

[16] As Elizabeth Poe remarks, "[t]he major source for the stories told in the *vidas* and *razos* [different types of alleged author biographies] is of course the troubadour poems." Elizabeth W. Poe, "The *vidas* and *razos*," in *A Handbook of the Troubadours*, ed. F. R. P Akehurst and Judith M. Davis (Berkeley: University of California Press, ca. 1995), 185–98 at 189.

[17] Lance St. John Butler, *Registering the Difference: Reading Literature through Register* (Manchester: Manchester University Press), 126.

Jeff Rider's account of genre also emphasizes its character of differentiation:

> Like a phoneme, a genre may be defined "only by those of its characteristics that have differentiating value," as a bundle of distinctive traits defined in opposition to other such bundles, thus receiving its value from its place within a generic system of opposition.[18]

This is the case even when a song flouts its own generic requirements. As Todorov remarked:

> The fact that a work "disobeys" its genre does not mean that the genre does not exist ... because, in order to exist as such, the transgression requires a law—precisely the one that is to be violated.[19]

Any attempt to escape genre results only in the creation of a new (anti)genre.

Paterson acknowledges this circularity when she argues that the troubadour Sordel's *Lai al comte mon segnor voill pregar* "can be seen as a kind of an anti-crusading song" created within a game of generic subversion. Fooling with genre is part of the game:

> If parody is "a composition in which the characteristic turns of thought and phrase of an author are mimicked and made to appear ridiculous, especially by applying them to ludicrously inappropriate subjects," then *Lai al comte mon segnor voill pregar* might be termed a parody of courtly love clichés and crusading exhortations mixed with elements of political satire. However, the tone is above all ludic, with the troubadour burlesque tradition being taken to extremes.[20]

Parody is bound to its generic constraints just as securely as the genre it parodies and we can never be sure of the effect of this intergeneric play on any outside information offered to the listener.

According to Mikhail Bakhtin, we can only speak from within a particular genre. In "The problem of speech genres" he wrote: "Speech genres organize our speech in almost the same way as grammatical (syntactical) forms do. We learn to cast our speech in generic forms."[21] I take Bakhtin's speech genres to be the same as Butler's registers. Both conceive our speech and its meaning effects as organized by opposition. What *it* (whatever we are talking about) *is*, is predicated on what it is not. That is the approach I follow here.

---

18 Jeff Rider, "Genre, Antigenre, Intergenre," in *Intergenres: Intergeneric Perspectives on Medieval French Literature*, ed. Sara Sturm-Maddox and Donald Maddox, Special issue of *L' Esprit Créateur* 23.4 (1993): 18–26 at 18. The quotation within Rider's is from Oswald Ducrot and TzvstenTodorov, *The Encyclopedic Dictionary of the Science of Language* (Baltimore: Johns Hopkins University Press, 1983).

19 Tzvetan Todorov, "The Origin of Genres," in *Modern Genre Theory*, ed. David Duff (Harlow: Longman, 2000), 193–209 at 196.

20 Linda Paterson, "Lyric Responses to the Crusades. Parody and Dissent," in *International Courtly Literature Society*, ed. Margarida Madureira, Carlos Clamote Carreto, and Ana Paiva Morais (Paris: Classiques Garnier, 2016). *Parodies courtoises, parodies de la courtoisie*, ed. Margarida Madureira, Carlos Clamote Carreto, and Ana Paiva Morais (Paris: Classiques Garnier, 2016), 525–32 at 528 and 532. The inner quotation is from *The Shorter Oxford English Dictionary*, ed. Charles T. Onions, 3rd ed. (Oxford: Clarendon Press, 1964).

21 Mikhail Bakhtin, "The Problem of Speech Genres," in *Modern Genre Theory*, 90.

What we hear in the songs, for instance Bernart's claim of superiority to all other lover/singers due to his greater sincerity, is a playing with opposition, the contrast—to his benefit—between himself and all the others; Arnaut's song plays with it in a different, more explosive way, indicating that awareness of genre that I spoke of earlier. Each song adds its own twist to an intertextual conversation in which all previous *cansos* are implicated. Opposition occurs at every level: intertextual (between songs) as well as intergeneric (between genres), often within a song (intratextual), where two voices or two personae, two choices, attitudes or emotions are pitted one against another. The *chansons de croisade* communicate to the reader or listener through the kinds of oppositions set up within a song and between different songs and genres. In particular they communicate comparative value, again at every level.

These conversations within and between literary/musical genres are not closed. They also open out into the world beyond, but whatever from that world makes its way into a song, even a song in the interests of outside causes (crusade or anti-crusade propaganda for instance) is subjected to the pressures of genre and suffers mutation in the process. *Chanson* itself, of course, also undergoes mutation by the incorporation of new elements; no genre is impervious to change, but these mutations themselves will then become genericized; new oppositions will be set up. Generic evolution occurs as a series of these interchanges.

So with reference to my concern with genre, register, voice, and gender, some relevant questions are: Where does the song fit within the system of genres? Who is speaking in the song? What kinds of sentiments would we expect from such a genre, such a speaker? What is the comparative value of these different utterances? How does the crusade reference function within the song and what is its effect?

Within the hierarchy of genres the pure *chanson* stands alone, as its unmarked status indicates. The addition of "de" and a qualifier (as in *chanson de croisade*) marks it, rendering it inferior. Furthermore, the "of" of the *chanson de* ... is often also a "for." The song has a purpose. Dante, in *De vulgari eloquentia*, said of the Italian *canzone*, which he saw as the equivalent of the *canso* and the *chanson*, that it produced, "by itself and without aid that for which it was made."[22] Thus it is nobler than the *ballate* (dance-songs), "which," said Dante, "need the presence of dancers for whom they are produced."[23] The *chanson* needed no external aid or exterior justification for its existence. The only thing it was made for was its own glory. The *canzone* was characterized, Dante continued, by "gravity of thought, magnificence of poetic line, exaltedness of construction and excellence of vocabulary."[24] It should include only the "noblest words."[25] Johannes de Grocheio named *chanson* the *cantus coronatus*, the crown of

---

22 Dante Alighieri, *De Vulgari Eloquentia*, in Marianne Shapiro, *De Vulgari Eloquentia: Dante's Book of Exile* (Lincoln: University of Nebraska Press, 1990), 73.
23 Shapiro, *De Vulgari*, 73.
24 Shapiro, *De Vulgari*, 74.
25 Shapiro, *De Vulgari*, 79.

monophonic secular song.[26] In comparison with the forms related to dance, for instance, these qualities were expressed in generally longer lines, more exalted language, and more intricate rhyme schemes.

The speaker, the lyric "I" of *chanson* is nearly always a man, which renders his utterances superior to those of a woman. His words carry more weight—that is a given.[27] He is, generically speaking, high-born, and speaks a refined language contrasted with the crude utterances of the peasantry, sometimes heard in *pastourelle*. These are the oppositions, explicit and implicit, defining *chanson* in relation to other genres.

How Songs Work: II

While one cannot answer with any certainty the question of what a song can say *about* the world external to it (for instance the Crusades), it is possible to ask the question in a different way. We can ask, not how a song *in*forms us of its world, but how it *per*forms it, that is, to ask again the question of how a song works, but differently slanted from those questions of genre etcetera, which I raised earlier, although related to them. We can ask how a song can stage responses to the Crusades, within and through its generic constraints and opportunities.

Many songs in twelfth- and thirteenth-century courtly European repertoires combine themes of *fin'amors* with references to the Crusades. They are generic hybrids and like all such offspring they favour sometimes one parent and sometimes the other.[28] My primary focus in this chapter is with those favouring *chanson*. Those songs that favour the crusade over the *fin'amors* elements contain strong elements of the older

---

26 Christopher Page, "Johannes de Grocheio on Secular Music: A Corrected Text and a New Translation," *Plainsong and Medieval Music* 2, no. 1 (1993): 17–41 at 23. Christopher Page argues that "in some important respects Grocheio's distinction between *cantus* and *cantilena* corresponds to our distinction between the High Style and the Lower Styles." See also Christopher Page, *Voices and Instruments of the Middle Ages: Instrumental Practice and Songs in France 1100–1300* (London: Dent, 1987), 67–68. Page's useful typology outlines important poetic and musical distinctions between the "High" and "Lower" styles. See Page, *Voices*, 12–16. Although these distinctions between styles are not clear cut, as Elizabeth Aubrey argues, the contrastive aspect of genre in the trouvère song system cannot be ignored. See Aubrey, "Reconsidering," 118.

27 For an account of how masculine superiority is established in trouvère song see Helen Dell, *Desire by Gender and Genre in Trouvère Song* (Woodbridge: Brewer, 2008), chap. 2. For an account of how women found a way to write themselves into *canso* and *chanson* as author/subjects, see Bruckner, "Fictions." See also Helen Dell, *Desire by Gender*, chap. 7, and Doris Earnshaw, *The Female Voice in Medieval Romance Lyric* (New York: Lang, 1988), in particular chap. 5.

28 As Paul Zumthor noted, the *chansons de croisade* "can be divided into two groups, one of which is a subcategory of love lyric, while the other has strong religious overtones." Paul Zumthor, *Toward a Medieval Poetics*, trans. Philip Bennett (Minneapolis: University of Minnesota Press, 1992 (1972)), 63. See also Zumthor, *Medieval Poetics*, 205 for the question raised by D. A. Trotter, citing Peter Hölzle: "'crusade lyrics' are those songs in which crusades to the Holy Land play a significant part, a definition which does, of course, beg the question of what constitutes a significant part." D. A. Trotter, *Medieval French Literature and the Crusades (1100–1300)* (Geneva: Librairie Droz, 1988), 173.

troubadour *sirventes*, creating a different hybrid from the type which favours *fin'amors*. The *sirventes* is overall a song of exhortation and denunciation. And, as *chanson* is the song valued only for itself, any other purpose introduced must, I think, devalorize it in comparison, as the *ballate* are devalorized in Dante's view. That is its situation generically speaking although it is not the references themselves (which can have an enriching effect) but the *sirventes* tone with its weight of purpose which effects the devalorization. That purpose of exhortation also alters the song's staging in a variety of ways, rearranging its topoi and its position relative to its audience. It heightens the emphasis on the "you" who is exhorted and directs attention away from the lyric "I," also introducing strong ethical and religious messages foreign to *chanson*. In this case one could say that, rather than expressing an emotion, it produces one. It could be called an emotive in William Reddy's sense:

> Emotives are similar to performatives (and differ from constatives) in that emotives do things to the world. Emotives are themselves instruments for directly changing, building, hiding, intensifying emotions, instruments that may be more or less successful.[29]

These elements are familiar from other forms of crusade literature, for instance sermons, on which they draw.[30] In Conon de Béthune's "Ahï! Amors, com dure departie" (RS 1125), only the first stanza is wholly devoted to the Lady:

> Ahï! Amors, com dure departie
> me convenra faire de la millor
> ki onques fust amee ne servie!
> Diex me ramaint a li par sa douçour,
> si voirement ke m'en part a dolor.
> Las! k'ai je dit? Ja ne m'en part je mie!
> Se li cors va servir Nostre Signor,
> li cuers remaint del tot en sa baillie.

(Ah, Love, how hard it will be for me to part from the best Lady who was ever loved and served! May God in his sweetness bring me back to her, as truly as I leave her in sorrow. Alas! What have I said? I am not leaving her at all! If my body goes off to serve our Lord, my heart remains entirely in her service.)[31]

In "Ahï! Amours" the Lady is dealt with somewhat perfunctorily in comparison to God in terms of the space she is given; she is almost a foreign body in the song. She

---

29 William M. Reddy, *The Navigation of Feeling: A Framework for the History of Emotion* (Cambridge: Cambridge University Press, 2001), 105.

30 For examples see Christoph T. Maier, *Crusade Propaganda and Ideology: Model Sermons for the Preaching of the Cross* (Cambridge: Cambridge University Press, 2000). See also Penny J. Cole, *The Preaching of the Crusades to the Holy Land, 1095–1270* (Cambridge, MA: Medieval Academy of America, 1991).

31 All *chanson de croisade* translations are by Linda Paterson, taken from the Old French section of the website mentioned above: Paterson, "Troubadours, Trouvères and the Crusades."

frames it, however, given pride of place in the opening stanza and a brief but telling allusion in the envoi at the end:

> Lais! je m'en voix plorant des eulz del front
> lai ou Deus veult amendeir mon coraige;
> et saichiés bien c'a la millor dou mont
> penserai plux ke ne fais a voiaige.

(Alas, I leave with tears in my eyes to the place where God desires to purify my heart; and be well aware that I shall think more about the best lady in the world than of the crusade.)

The guts of "Ahï! Amours" are devoted to exhortation. The second stanza ushers in God and what is owed to Him in earnest; the Lady is briefly introduced again, as the last in a list of prizes gained by fighting for God (although last could be considered the place of honour):

> Por li m'en vois sospirant en Surie,
> car je ne doi faillir mon Creator;
> ki li faura a cest besoig d'aïe,
> saiciés ke il li faura a grignor,
> et saicent bien li grant et li menor
> ke la doit on faire chevallerie
> ou on conquiert Paradis et honor
> et pris et los et l'amor de s'amie.

(Sighing for her I set out for Syria, since I must not fail my Creator. If anyone should fail Him in this hour of need, be aware that He will fail him in a greater; and may great and small know well that a man ought to perform knightly feats in the place where one wins paradise and honour, reputation, and praise, and the love of one's beloved.)

There is something of a tussle for generic supremacy in "Ahï! Amours." Conon seems himself to have been uncertain where the emphasis should lie but I think God and the *sirventes* tradition are the overall winners. D. A. Trotter has suggested that "[t]o determine whether the poem ['Ahï! Amours'] is a love-song first and propaganda second, or vice versa, is impossible and perhaps pointless."[32] I think it is possible and, for my purposes, useful, to determine the difference on the basis of which element appears integral to the song overall and which looks like an interpolation, although this must always remain a matter of interpretation.

In its *sirventes* voice Conon's song offers us many of the tropes common to the genres of exhortation employed to whip up enthusiasm for the Crusades: God is owed feudal service by the Christian vassal; those who accept the call will be honoured; those who refuse it will be shamed; God suffered and died on the cross for us; He is now under siege and needs our help in return; He will reward those who die fighting on his behalf with "the precious kingdom," that is, heaven; He will punish those who forsake Him in his hour of need; they will go to hell.

---

32 Trotter, *Medieval French Literature*, 181.

Thibaut de Champagne uses all these tropes in another *sirventes*-like *chanson de croisade*, "Seignor, sachiez, qui or ne s'an ira" (RS 6). Here are stanzas one and four:

> Seignor, sachiez, qui or ne s'an ira
> en cele terre ou Diex fu mors et vis
> et qui la croiz d'outremer ne penra
> a painnes mais ira en paradis.
> Qui a en soi pitié ne remembrance,
> au Haut Seignor doit querre sa vanjance
> et delivrer sa terre et son païs.

(Lords, know this: whoever will not now go to that land where God died and rose again, and whoever will not take the cross to Outremer will find it hard ever to go to heaven. Whoever has pity and good remembrance in his heart must seek to avenge the Highest Lord and liberate His land and His country.)

> Diex se laissa por nos en croiz pener
> et nos dira au jor ou tuit vanront:
> "Vos qui ma croiz m'aidastes a porter,
> vos en irez là ou mi angle sont:
> là me verroiz et ma mere Marie;
> et vos par cui je n'oi onques aïe
> descendrez tuit en anfer le parfont."

(God allowed himself to suffer pain upon the cross and will say to us on the day when all come together: "You who helped me carry my cross, you will go to where my angels are; and you from whom I had no help will all descend into the depths of hell.")

The only Lady mentioned in this song is the Virgin Mary who is invoked in the envoi:

> Douce Dame, roïne coronee
> priez por nos, vierge bone eüree,
> et puis aprés ne nos puet mescheoir.

(Sweet Lady, crowned queen, pray for us, blessed Virgin, and then no harm can befall us.)

These same tropes figure in other trouvère *chansons de croisade*, in varying degrees, often but not always in tandem with *fin'amors* motifs. In *chansons de croisade* where the *chanson* element of *fin'amors* is more prominent, it is the duty to God which is more perfunctorily dealt with. In such songs the lover's response to God's call is not wholehearted—to bring the heart back into play, as in the first stanza of "Ahï! Amours"—but rather pragmatically undertaken for earthly glory and eternal reward and as a prophylactic against the reverse. In those *chansons de croisade* which favour *chanson* over *sirventes* the typical arrangement is to contrast the pain of leaving the beloved with the duty of fighting for God and perhaps receiving the martyr's crown.[33] This particular

---

33 Other contrasts are also possible. For instance, Raoul de Soissons? (RS 1204) insists that the pains he experienced in the Holy Land are nothing compared to those inflicted by his beloved on his return.

opposition, and the conflict which it engenders in the lover, is a frequent theme, adding an intensifying twist to the usual scenario of the Lady's hardheartedness and inaccessibility; producing God as a third persona offers the opportunity to stage more, and more complicated, contrasts.

What emerges in this opposition is a distinction between what the lover/crusader owes to the Lady and what is owed to God. This is most tellingly evoked in the contrast between the heart and the body. Stanza four of "Aler m'estuet la u je trairai paine" by the Chatelain d'Arras (RS 140) employs the heart/body topos:

> Ha Dex, dame, cis mos me rent la vie;
> biaus sire Diex, com il est precïeus!
> Sans cuer m'en vois el regne de Surie:
> od vos remaint, c'est ses plus dous chateus.
> Dame vaillans, comment vivra cors seus?
> Se le vostre ai od moi en compaignie,
> adés iere plus joiaus et plus preus:
> del vostre cuer serai chevalereus.

(Oh God, lady, these words bring me back to life; good Lord God, how precious they are! I go off to the kingdom of Syria without a heart: it remains with you, it is its sweetest gain. Worthy lady, how will my body survive alone? If I have yours (your heart) for company, I shall be constantly more joyful and fight better: thanks to your heart I shall be bold in battle.)

The body *must* leave to fight God's war but the heart remains at home with the beloved Lady, or, as here, the lover begs for hers to accompany him. "Li departirs de la douce contree" (RS 499) by Chardon de Croisilles also uses the heart/body trope. These are the first three stanzas:

> Li departirs de la douce contree
> ou la bele est m'a mis en grant tristor;
> lessier m'estuet la riens qu'ai plus amee
> por Damledieu servir, mon criator,
> et neporquant tot remaing a Amor,
> car tot li lez mon cuer et ma pensee:
> se mes cors va servir Nostre Seignor
> por ce n'ai pas fine amor oubliee.
>
> Amors, ci a trop dure desevree
> quant il m'estuet partir de la meillor
> qui onques fust ne qui jamés soit nee;
> tote a en li et biauté et valor,
> nus ne s'en doit merveillier se j'en plor;
> quant mes cors va fere sa destinee,
> et mes fins cuers s'est ja mis el retor,
> qui sanz fauser pense a ma dame et bee.
>
> Dame, en qui est et ma mort et ma vie,
> dolens me part de vos plus que ne di;
> mon cuer avez pieça en vo baillie:
> retenez le, ou vos m'avez traï.
> Dex, ou irai? ferai je noise ou cri,

> quant il m'estuet fere la departie
> de mon fin cuer et lessier a celi
> qui ainc du sien ne me lessa partie?

(Departure from the sweet land where lives the beautiful one has put me into great sadness; I am constrained to leave the one I have loved the most in order to serve the Lord God my creator, and yet I belong completely to Love, since I leave it all my heart and my thoughts: if my body goes to serve Our Lord, I have not forgotten true love on this account.

Love, this is too hard a parting, when I am forced to leave the best Lady who ever existed or who was ever born; in her is all beauty and worth, and none should marvel if I weep at this; when my body goes to fulfil its destiny, see how my noble heart has already begun its return journey, musing and longing after my Lady.

Lady, in whom is my death and my life, I depart from you more grief-stricken than I say; henceforth you have my heart in your power: keep it, or you have betrayed me. God, where shall I go? Shall I utter loud laments or cries when I am constrained to divide myself from my noble heart and leave it with the one who has never left me part of hers?)

The Crusades allow the *chanson* to stage different forms of presence, absence, and distance—being *here*, being *there*, not being *here*, not being *there*, as applied to subject and object. These sites of *here* and *there* are given substance and made feelingly accessible; the separating space itself is staged along with the longing stretching across it, as in Jaufre Rudel's famous *canso*, "Lanquan li jorn son lonc en may," where the words "*amor de lonh*" (love from afar) are interpolated into the second line of each stanza.[34] Also staged are different forms of subjective division and alienation, even mutilation (the heart torn from the body). That is to say, different formulations of what are already *chanson*'s primary concerns are introduced.

The heart/body trope in Chardon's song stages the emotional contrast between the duty owed to God and that owed to the Lady: as an obedient vassal the lover offers his fighting body to God as his feudal lord, while his heart is given over *completely* to Love and the Lady. One would have to conclude that his heart isn't in the Crusades. Yet staying at home is clearly no bed of roses either. He leaves his heart in the keeping of one "who has never left me part of hers." The Lady does not become an angel of compassion in opposition to the cruelty of God's decree. But her cruelty is of a different order; it is capricious while God, harsh though his decrees, can be relied upon. Reciprocity is guaranteed with God whilst the Lady is beyond any such equitable arrangement. She is uncontainable within the economy of exchange in which dealings with God are placed. There is between her and the lover no possibility of a relation.

Hugues de Berzé's "S'onques nuns hons por dure departie" (RS 1126) spells out the difficulty of responding to the competing claims of God and the Lady:

> Mult a croissiés amorous a contendre
> d'aler a Dieu ou de remanoir ci,

---

34 *Songs of the Troubadours and Trouvères: An Anthology of Poems and Melodies*, ed. Samuel N. Rosenberg, Margaret Switten, and Gerard Le Vot (New York: Garland, 1998), 56–57.

> car nesuns hom, puis k'Amors l'a saisi,
> ne devroit ja si grief fais entreprendre:
> on ne puet pas servir a tant seignor;
> proec qe fins cuers qi bet a haute honor
> ne se poroit de tel chose deffendre,
> por ce, dame, ne m'en devés reprendre.

(A crusader in love must well ponder whether to go towards God or to remain here, for no-one, once Love has taken hold of him, ought ever to assume such a heavy burden: one cannot serve more than one lord; but since a noble heart that aspires to high honour cannot avoid doing this, you ought not, my Lady, to blame me for it.)

It is not a question here of competing loves. Love is rarely spoken of as owed to God although gratitude is sometimes mentioned or implied.[35] What are, in the main, called forth in relation to God in the songs are obligation and self-interest.[36] It appears that love in *chanson* is so indelibly associated with the Lady that it resists application as a motive for crusading or as incited by God, especially when He appears as the agent of separation. The *chanson/chanson de croisade* blend creates an environment which allows the incorporation of these incommensurate elements together within one song.

God's demand is backed up with a lot of firepower. As presented, it is certainly very much in the lover/crusader's short- and long-term interests to respond with alacrity. As in other forms of crusade propaganda, crusading is a business proposition, for instance, in Gilbert de Tournai's Sermon 1: "[N]ow the Lord offers a very good business for his kingdom, when he gives the heavenly kingdom to crusaders for a short pilgrimage."[37] It's a bargain!

Love for the Lady is a different matter; it is unconditional. She has a different kind of firepower from God, the power of her mastery over the lover's desire. No degree of bad behaviour on her part is sufficient to loosen the hold she has over the hapless lover. His immeasurable desire makes of the Lady herself something immeasurable and uncontainable. She cannot be captured within the sphere of the spatial and temporal

---

35 See for instance Huon de Saint-Quentin's "Jerusalem se plaint et li païs" (RS 1576), stanza 1, which hovers between gratitude and self-interest. Maistres Renas speaks of "the good people who love and fear God" (RS 886), stanza 8.

36 There are exceptions, for instance in the anonymous dialogue "Douce dame, cui j'ain en bone foi" (RS 1659) where the lover exclaims: "But no-one can do too much for the Lord God: when I remember that He died for me, I have so much compassion and faith in Him that nothing I leave behind could hurt me," to which his exemplary beloved responds that, despite her anguish he is free to go, "since this pleases God and you." Though little used in the repertoire, the model of love for God or Christ as a motive was at hand in crusade propaganda. For instance, James of Vitry (ca. 1160/70–1240), who preached the Albigensian and the Fifth Crusades, used it in the first of his model crusade sermons, speaking of those who "after they have taken the sign of the salutary cross out of the love of Christ and out of devotion, exert themselves on land and at sea." Maier, *Crusade Propaganda*, 89.

37 Maier, *Crusade Propaganda*, 189. Gilbert of Tournai (ca. 1200–1277) wrote three popular model sermons.

present, never here and now, within the circle of the song, whereas God, in this setting, is in the same, very practical sphere of a business operation or a feudal obligation. The Lady does not speak but remains silent, an absent "presence." Like the God whom Augustine questions in the *Confessions*, she appears both to contain space and fill it to overflowing:

> Do heaven and earth, then, contain the whole of you, since you fill them? Or, when once you have filled them, is some part of you left over because they are too small to hold you? ... Or is it that you have no need to be contained in anything, because you contain all things in yourself and fill them by reason of the very fact that you contain them?[38]

These questions would be more appropriately asked of the Lady of *chanson* in her mystical incommensurability than of God.[39] She is far more like Augustine's God than is the God of *chanson de croisade*.

A different and conflicting complication brought about by reference to the Crusades in trouvère *chanson* is an alteration in the tense of desire. The desire for the Lady in *chanson* is usually couched as a desire for her acknowledgement or acceptance in the future. Crusade elements turn the *chanson* into a song of parting (a *chanson de departie*), inflecting desire with the pain of loss rather than the suffering of privation. Sometimes the implication is allowed of more having been granted by the Lady in the past, on the basis that this joyous situation is now about to cease. Suffering being the key component of the lover's state in *chanson*, this implication is permissible since the more he has been given, the more he has to lose. Such is the case in the Chatelain de Couci's "A vous amant, plus k'a nul'autre gent" (R679):

> Beaus sire Diex, k'iert il del consirrer,
> del grant soulas et de la compaignie
> et des samblanz ke me soloit moustrer
> cele ki m'ert dame, compaigne, amie?
> Et quant recort sa simple courtoisie
> et les dols mos ke suet a moi parler,
> coment me puet li cuers el cors durer?
> quant ne s'em part, certes molt est mauvais.

(Good Lord God, what will become of the kind thoughts, the great solace, the companionship and loving looks which the one who was my Lady, companion, friend, used to bestow on me? And when I call to mind her simple courtesy and the sweet words with which she is accustomed to speak to me, how can my heart remain within my body? If it does not part from there it is assuredly most wretched.)

---

38 Augustine, *Saint Augustine of Hippo, 354–430. The Confessions of Saint Augustine*, trans. and intro. R. S. Pine-Coffin (London: Penguin, 1961), 23.

39 But it is not enough to suggest that *chanson* is simply a way of talking about mystical love for God. As Sarah Kay, citing Jean-Charles Huchet, notes: "all of the theories of the origin of the lyric necessitate a displacement from the putative model (e.g., the love lyric is *like* mystical writing but *different* from it)." Sarah Kay, *Courtly Contradictions* (Palo Alto: Stanford University Press, 2001), 210. The difference is very evident in the *chansons de croisade*.

In trouvère song, "amie," like its masculine equivalent "ami" in *chanson de femme*, usually has the implication of sweetheart or lover rather than friend. This beloved, as Lady, companion *and* sweetheart/lover, is a good deal more intimately known than the usual distant and unattainable Lady of *chanson*. Their love is rendered mutual by these descriptors, disturbing the foundational disposition of *chanson* by allowing a relation between lover and beloved. The past tense of gratified love—not necessarily sexual—breaks with the eternal "perhaps" of future-oriented desire in *chanson* with its accompanying gyrations between hope and despair. Narrative elements—an assumed place and time in which the two have been together—are given more definite form by this inversion of tense. These elements create an atmosphere of greater materiality in the song. A more coherent scene swims into view.

"Amie" is unusual in *chanson* also because it is associated with "lower style" genres, in particular, like the masculine "ami," in the *chansons de femme*. The woman's voice provides another contrast in the trouvère song system, as Matilda Bruckner (citing Doris Earnshaw) has written:

> [C]ultures—like that of the medieval courtly world—"coopt" [women's songs] and use the persona of the female voice as a contrast, the voice of the other inscribed within its own polyphonic system. The dominant male voice responds to its complement, the female voice, and recognizes itself by the difference.[40]

This feminine voice, so reassuringly inferior to the man's in its language and its sentiments, allowed less restrained and dutiful responses towards the Crusades to find an outlet.[41] Because less nobility and refinement were expected of her she could say outright what was generally expressed in the masculine voice suitable to *chanson* only as a distinct lack of enthusiasm for crusading. This anonymous *chanson de croisade/chanson de femme* is a good example, "Jherusalem, grant damage me fais," (RS 191) stanza 1:[42]

> Jherusalem, grant damage me fais
> qui m'as tolu ce que je pluz amoie!
> Sachiez de voir: ne vos amerai maiz
> quar c'est la rienz dont j'ai pluz male joie!
> Et bien sovent en souspir et pantais,
> si qu'a bien pou que vers Deu ne m'irais,
> qui m'a osté de grant joie ou j'estoie.

(Jerusalem, you do me great harm in robbing me of the one I loved most in the world! Be assured I shall nevermore love you, for he is the creature who brings me the saddest joy.

---

40 Bruckner, "Fictions," 872.

41 The *chansons de femme* are usually anonymous but their role, insofar as they maintain the superiority of the dominant masculine voice by contrast, suggests masculine authorship.

42 Jehan de Neuvile has been mooted by some (including Linda Paterson) as a possible author.

And time and time again I sigh in anguish so that I am on the point of railing at God, who has withdrawn me from the great joy in which I used to live.)[43]

It is usually here, in the woman's voice, that a rebellious note is found. God's plight, besieged in the holy city, does not concern her. Her only concern is with the danger to her lover and his unjustifiable removal from her presence. Rebelliousness is expected of her—of *la femme*, that is, not *la dame* of *chanson*, whose desires are unknowable since her speech is not heard. But in "A vous amant, plus qu'a nulle autre gent," the rebellious, almost blasphemous note is spoken by the man:[44]

> Ne me vaut pas Diex por noient doner
> tos les deduis k'ai eüs ens ma vie,
> ains les me fait c(h)ierement comperer,
> s'ai grant paour chis loiers ne m'ochie;
> merchi Amors, s'ainc Diex fist vilonie,
> ke vilains fait boine amor desevrer:
> ne je ne puis l'amor de moi oster
> et si m'estuet ke jou ma dame lais.

(Not for nothing has God wished to grant me all the delights I have had in my life; instead he makes me pay dearly for them, to the point where I fear that this price will be my death. Have pity, Love, if God ever acted basely, it is a cruel thing to sunder good love: but I cannot free myself of love, and yet I am obliged to leave my Lady.)

Love (or the god of love) is apparently being invoked here against God. The lover's accusation is made cautiously in the conditional, as if to say: "If it were possible to speak of God acting basely (which, of course, I would not presume to do) then this act of separating me from my Lady could be called a base act," but, nonetheless, it is an instance of an unusual registral infiltration of the rebellious note from the "lower style" *chanson de femme* to the *chanson de croisade* in *chanson* mode. The alteration in tense is another deviation which references the woman's voice in *chanson de femme*. It is usually the woman who mourns a lost love (as in the *chansons de délaissée*), sometimes on account of her own misbehaviour, sometimes that of her *ami*, sometimes because the demands of feudal lords (including God) carry her lover away.

Tentative Conclusions

What can be said about the *chansons de croisade* is that the Crusades, by the emotional intensification which they offered to the *chanson* through the inclusion of the "separation motif" and its various accompanying disruptions,[45] extended the range of the genre, as in

---

43 See also RS 1656B: *Lasse, pour quoy [Mestre de Rodes!]* and Guiot de Dijon's "Chanterai por mon corage" (RS 21), another *chanson de femme/chanson de croisade*, where she interrogates the Almighty: "Oh God, why did You do this? If the one desires the other, why have You separated us?"
44 To be fair, the lyric subject of "Jerusalem, grant damage me fais" also stops short of blasphemy.
45 Trotter, *Medieval French Literature*, 183.

"A vous amant." Separation is a poignant and powerful theme in love song. The Crusades, by situating the lover in an impasse between God and the Lady, obligation and Love, raise the stakes in *chanson*. To have two supreme figures, God and the Lady, in opposition but very differently positioned in relation (or non-relation) to the lover and his desire, was obviously a gift to the genre in the complexities it offered. Crusade references also allowed the staging of situations which disturbed the usual tenor of the lover's plaint, giving his discourse a flavour of regret and (in "A vous amant") rebelliousness, usually confined to the woman's voice in *chanson de femme*. The crusade element also allowed in *chanson* the staging of different and incommensurate planes of space, time and desire, a different and more complex distribution of personae and a web of conflicting demands for the lover/crusader. Perhaps also, the very materiality of the threat as an actual event, an actual obligation, gave vividness to conventional *chanson* motifs.

The question of what the *chanson de croisade* in *chanson* mode might have offered to the Crusades effort—or taken from it—is much harder to answer. In my opinion, as I have argued above, the generic and registral conventions in which the songs were framed makes it impossible for us to answer directly the question posed by Linda M. Paterson and Stefano Asperti, quoted in my first paragraph: "What did the secular public in the Middle Ages think of the Crusades?" A trouvère love song could only be composed within the particular conventions of genre and register in which it fell. Even in flouting them, as Todorov argued, it remained caught within them. A song cannot tell us what authors *thought* or *felt* about the Crusades. It can only tell us what they *did* with them.

One could, however, turn the question around as I did above. Instead of asking questions about emotions expressed in the *chansons de croisade* one could ask instead about emotions *produced* by the song.[46] It could be said that the added complexity and the sense of present danger and poignant loss which the inclusion of crusade references offered to conventional *chanson* motifs might have their effects on the listener or even on the author/composer. While such references mutated as a result of their inclusion in a song, they nonetheless allowed into the fiction the intrusion of serious events demanding an emotional response. As William Reddy suggests, an emotion could also arise or coalesce for the speaker in the act of saying it as in the following passage taken from a biography of Bertrand Russell by Ronald W. Clark:

---

46 There is a significant body of research linking music to emotional effects. See, for instance, work conducted by so-called "emotivists": "It is also a pervasive belief that music can, at times, actually produce emotion in listeners. The distinction between perception and production is related to the distinction between cognitivism and emotivism proposed by philosophers in their analysis of emotion in music (e.g. Kivy 1989). Whereas 'emotivists' hold that music elicits real emotional responses in listeners, 'cognitivists' argue that music simply expresses or represents emotions ... Our purpose in this chapter is to provide a formalization of the processes whereby music produces emotional effects in the listener that go beyond the cognitive inference of what the music can be said to express." Klaus R. Scherer and Marcel R. Zentner, "Emotional Effects of Music: Production Rules," in *Music and Emotion: Theory and Research*, ed. Patrick N. Juslin and John A. Sloboda (Oxford: Oxford University Press, 2001), 361–92 at 361.

It was late before the two guests left and Russell was alone with Lady Ottoline. They sat talking over the fire until four in the morning. Russell, recording the event a few days later, wrote, "I did not know I loved you till I heard myself telling you so—for one instant I thought 'Good God, what have I said?' *and then I knew it was the truth.*"[47]

Song lyrics are deeply influential, presented, as they are, in a beautiful and moving form. Both singers and listeners may be affected by a song.[48] The performance and circulation of crusade songs might therefore, in Reddy's term, "do things to the world" by evoking in their audiences (and perhaps their authors) an intensity and urgency about the Crusades or providing an acceptable articulation for anxieties already existing in a less coherent form.

---

47 Ronald W. Clark, *The Life of Bertrand Russell* (New York: Knopf, 1976), 176. See also William Reddy, "Emotional Liberty: Politics and History in the Anthropology of Emotions," *Cultural Anthropology* 14 (1999): 256–88 at 269, my emphasis.

48 Singers too may weep as they sing, as Kathleen Ferrier once did, according to the Gramophone Records obituary for her: "It was at Edinburgh, in 1947, that she sang Mahler's *Das Lied van der Erde*. At the final repetitions of the word 'Ewig' [forever], her eyes filled with tears, her voice faltered into silence. In the artistes' room she was full of contrition to Bruno Walter that she had failed at the end. 'My dear Miss Ferrier,' he said, 'if we had been all as great artists as you, we should all have wept—orchestra, audience, myself—we should all have wept.' ": www.gramophone.co.uk/features/focus/ferrier-remembered-in-her-gramophone-obituary

Chapter 7

CHRIST VERSUS LUCIFER IN *PIERS PLOWMAN*

Anne M. Scott*

THE TWENTIETH PASSUS of the Middle English narrative poem, *Piers Plowman* (eighteenth in the B-text), narrates the final days of Christ's life, his entry into Jerusalem, his trial, crucifixion, death, descent into hell and liberation of the souls held captive by Lucifer. Much of the story is based on the Gospel narrative and early Christian apocrypha; the scenes described are familiar to readers who encounter these texts in the course of their religious devotions or as writings of scholarly interest. This passus presents the reader with dramatized conflict and highlights Langland's method of making theological truths concrete by presenting them through images that can be grasped even by a non-theologian. The foundation doctrine underlying these scenes is that God became man in the Incarnation; this apparently simple statement is explored, developed, and explained throughout the poem. The other doctrine is of sin and salvation. Humankind sins, God saves, and these truths are dramatized in the conflict that is the harrowing of hell. Langland shows, through poetry, how sin itself is greater than humanity; he portrays the intrinsically metaphysical nature of sin in the anthropomorphically dramatized person of Lucifer. Grace is greater than both sin and humanity, and grace enters the world through the divine and human person of Jesus Christ. Christ, the human embodiment of God's love, embraces the conflict with sin; love goes to war with evil.

Imagery in *Piers Plowman*

As a thinker, Langland understands the theology of the Trinity with great subtlety. As a poet and teacher, he presents the concept of three persons in one God in imagery that makes it unmistakably clear that Jesus Christ is both a divine and a human person. This hypostatic union of two natures in Christ is the cornerstone of the conflict between Christ and Lucifer as Langland presents it in the twentieth Passus, where Lucifer complains that God, concealed within human nature, had managed to beguile Lucifer, the father of guile.[1] To witness Christ vanquishing Lucifer and his cohorts of devils is to witness

---

* **Anne M. Scott** is an Honorary Research Fellow in English and Literary Studies at The University of Western Australia. She studied under Andrew Lynch who she greatly admires as scholar, mentor, and friend. She has published a monograph on *Piers Plowman*, seven essay collections, and several articles on late Middle English literature. She was, for ten years, Editor of *Parergon*, Journal of the Australian and New Zealand Association for Medieval and Early Modern Studies.

1 There is a significant body of text and commentary on the "guiler beguiled" literature, assembled and interpreted in C. William Marx, *The Devil's Rights and the Redemption in the Literature of Medieval England* (Cambridge: Brewer, 1995).

how the power of God overcomes sin, evil, and death. Yet this statement, derived from traditional Christian teaching, is an abstraction in itself. Langland's gift to his readers is a poem that reinterprets doctrinal abstractions in vivid and sensuous images. These become the material presented to Wille, the poem's protagonist, as he journeys through life in a quest for truth, salvation, and, simply, the best way to live.

Readers of *Piers Plowman* owe much to Mary Clement Davlin who wrote with keen sensitivity to the words of *Piers Plowman*. Her book, *A Game of Heuene*, is a stylistic study of word play in the B-version of *Piers Plowman*.[2] Like other notorious "shifting, unstable" elements of style in *Piers Plowman*, its word play is enigmatic and demands of the reader intense attention and what Davlin calls "play of mind." Davlin argues that such demands are a way of involving the reader in the text as "a game of heuene" (a game of heaven, Langland's phrase for language (B.9.102)). Twenty years later Davlin brought out a work designed to lead non-specialist readers into the mystery of *Piers Plowman*. She called this book *A Journey into Love: Meditating with the Medieval Poem "Piers Plowman."*[3] In this small volume, she selects sections of the poem which she calls straightforward yet invitingly complex, and gives commentaries intended to guide the reader towards an appreciation of how reading *Piers Plowman* can help a modern reader connect the human with the divine in daily life.

This chapter is offered as a further meditation on that connection. I will not revisit here the discussions about Langland's understanding of the divine and human natures of Christ and whether Langland's views are "Pelagian" or "Augustinian." Those arguments have been widely aired and rehearsed, one of the most satisfying treatments for this reader being in David Aers' work.[4] What I want to do here is to examine the poetic presentation of Langland's Christology, particularly in the imagery Langland uses to describe the Incarnation, and demonstrate how the poetry signals the overcoming of sin and darkness by the risen Christ's transcendent light. Aers has stated that both Langland's Christology and his "profound engagement with the consequences of sin" have been neglected in modern literary criticism.[5] Following Davlin's delight in wordplay, and Aers' theological insights, I select for close reading Passus C.20 (B.18), the crucifixion and the harrowing of hell, because it encapsulates Langland's representation of the humanity and divinity of Christ and dramatizes the metaphysical nature and effect of sin in the clash between Christ and Lucifer.[6]

---

[2] Mary Clement Davlin, *A Game of Heuene* (Woodbridge: Brewer, 1989).

[3] Mary Clement Davlin, *A Journey into Love: Meditating with the Medieval Poem "Piers Plowman"* (Los Angeles: Marymount Institute, 2008).

[4] See particularly David Aers, *Salvation and Sin: Augustine, Langland and Fourteenth-Century Theology* (Notre Dame, IN: University of Notre Dame Press, 2009), 83–131.

[5] Aers, *Salvation and Sin*, 88.

[6] The term "passus," the Latin word for a step, is used for each section of the poem. All references, unless otherwise stated, are taken from the C-text, in *Piers Plowman*, ed. Derek Pearsall (Exeter: University of Exeter Press, 2008; repr. University of Liverpool Press, 2014).

Piers Plowman deals with a huge canvas of meta-history that underlies the medieval understanding of the Incarnation, from the fall of the angels and the fall of humankind to the resurrection of Christ.[7] While this can be read as a very spiritual poem, as Davlin's approach demonstrates, it is also a poem which concentrates squarely on human nature, that of the Dreamer, Wille, and the incarnate Christ. Wille is assiduous in his search for the spiritual, "how Y may saue my soule?" (C.1.80), while fully conscious of and living in his body in the here and now. In addressing the many enigmas which confront him in his journey through the poem he teases out the implications of what it means to be truly human while understanding the human being's capacity to live spiritually in the image of God, as "a god by the gospel" (C.1.86).

Langland and the Three Persons of God

Langland has a view of God as personal; portraying God as Trinity, three persons in one God, leads him to develop a sense of the divinity united with the humanity of Christ which sits at the heart of his response to Wille's question about salvation. In Passus C.18 the dreamer encounters Abraham who is presented as prefiguring the crucifixion in his willingness to sacrifice his son, Isaac, and Langland attributes to him a prophetic role in looking forward to the Incarnation. The poem presents Abraham as the representative of Faith, having experience of God only as a transcendent being, but looking forward to the Incarnation as a historical event when Christ as human will take on "the fende" in combat for souls. In this presentation of Abraham, the poem unrolls Salvation History, a temporal concept. The biblical Abraham had an experience of encountering the three persons of God, as recounted in Genesis 18:1–15, yet although Abraham has had this encounter with the Trinity, in Langland's work he speaks with an understanding that he must wait for justice until the second person of the Trinity has become a human being.

In this context Abraham shows the dreamer the vision of the souls in his bosom:

> "Hit is a preciouse present," quod he, "ac the pouke hit hath atached,
> And me therwith,"quod the weye; "may no wed vs quyte
> Ne noen bern be oure borw ne bryngen vs out of that daunger—
> Fro the poukes pondefold no maynprise may vs feche—
> Til he come that Y carpe of, Crist is his name ...."
>
> (C.18.277–81)

("It is a precious gift," he said, "but the devil has laid claim to it, and myself, as well. No pledge can pay for our release, nor can any man be our surety nor bring us out of that peril—no bail can release us from the devil's pound—until he comes of whom I speak, Christ is his name ....")[8]

---

7 The fall of the angels is referenced in Passus C.1.102–121 and is referenced intermittently until Passus C.20.

8 Rendering into modern English is the author's own throughout.

While Abraham is represented at a late stage in the poem as having had an encounter with the Trinitarian God, the human and divine natures of the second person of the Trinity, characterized as Love, are poetically imagined early on in the poem at the start of Wille's journey. In Passus 1 the allegorical teacher Holy Church, teaching Wille about the Incarnation, conceptualizes the second person of the Trinity as "Love" and speaks to Wille of his powerful longing to take on flesh and blood and to share the human condition (C.1.148–152). Here Wille is taught how "Love" was too heavy to be contained in heaven, and this desire to share human nature compelled him to descend to earth and become human.[9] This audacious image does many things. It confirms the willingness of God the Son to become human; it equates the Incarnation with divine love; and it acts as reversal of what is normally assumed to be the upward yearning of humanity to be united with God, by asserting boldly that God as Love yearned to become human. Further, it grasps the unimaginable magnitude of the "kenosis" (Philippians 2:7), the emptying himself of his status as divine which the second person of the Trinity undertook by becoming man.[10]

Towards the end of the poem, in the imagined encounter between Christ and Lucifer at the harrowing of hell, this love-longing for humanity is reiterated in the metaphor of drinking the new wine, the "must," of resurrected and redeemed humanity:

> For Y that am lord of lyf, loue is my drynke,
> And for that drynke today Y deyede, as hit semede ...
> Y fauht so me fursteth yut for mannes soule sake: *Sicio.*
> May no pyement ne pomade ne preciouse drynkes
> Moiste me to the fulle ne my furste slokke
> Til the ventage valle in the vale of Iosophat
> And Y drynke riht rype must, *resureccio mortuorum.*
> (C.20.403–4; 408–12)

(For I who am lord of life, love is my drink, and for that drink, to all appearances I died today. ... I fought in such a way that I thirst still for the sake of humankind: *I thirst.* No honey drink nor apple juice nor costly drinks can fully hydrate me nor slake my thirst until the grape-harvest falls in the Valley of Jehosaphat, and I drink the ripe new wine, *the resurrection of the dead.*)

In these two images at the start and the end of the poem, Langland suggests that the divine nature of God as Love (1 John:4, 8) has the attributes of a human emotion which is heavy with desire for the beloved—for humanity, and a major force in the defence of humanity against the destructive power of sin.

---

9 The B-text uses the metaphor: to eat his fill of the earth (B.1.154). References to the B-text are taken from A. V. C. Schmidt, ed. *Piers Plowman: A Parallel-Text Edition of the A, B, C and Z Versions* (London: Longman, 1995).

10 For a study on "kenosis" see Nicholas Watson, "Conceptions of the Word," in *New Medieval Literatures I*, ed. Wendy Scase, Rita Copeland, and David Lawton (Oxford: Clarendon Press, 1997), 85–124. For "kenosis" as it underlies *Piers Plowman*, see Anne M. Scott, *Piers Plowman and the Poor* (Dublin: Four Courts, 2004), 216–23.

The Incarnation

Before his vision of Abraham in Passus C.18 Wille is shown by his guide, *Liberum Arbitrium* (Free Will), a fruitful tree in the middle of a garden, a tree called "Trewe-loue" (true love), planted by the Trinity, and propped by three posts, each of which represents a member of the Trinity. Wille asks to taste the fruit, and *Liberum arbitrium* calls upon Elde (Age) to shake down some fruit. The shaking of the tree, in itself a reference to the Genesis story of the Fall of Humankind, is developed in a metaphor which portrays the devil running off with the fruit that fell: Abraham, Moses, and all the just who died before Christ. While this is an allegorical scene, this image will be picked up again in Passus 20, when Christ descends into hell to redeem the souls of the just who died before his crucifixion, a moment when time and eternity converge. A similar convergence occurs at this point in the poem, as the narrative shifts into historical mode, describing the Annunciation (C.18.123–34). This, as Derek Pearsall remarks, is "the moment of the intersection of the timeless with time."[11] Images tumble over each other. The moment of the Incarnation comes in the gentle words of the Holy Spirit expressed through the mouth of the Angel Gabriel, and the powerful image of Jesus as a hawk swooping down from the heavens and coming to rest on his perch within the Virgin's womb: "Jesus, a iustices sone, moste iouken in here chaumbre" (C.18.125). This moment when love swoops down from heaven towards earth is reminiscent of the image mentioned above from Passus 1, when love was too heavy to be contained in heaven, and the fullness of God's love is echoed by the expression: *plentitudo temporis* (C.18.126).

This, Langland says, is *plenitudo temporis*, the fullness of time, and the poetry now moves to prefigure the conflict between Christ and Lucifer as a joust; the second person of the Trinity is compared to a knight and the promise is given that he will joust to determine who should lay claim to this fruit, these precious souls, Christ or the devil. "That Iesus sholde iouste ther-fore and by iugement of armes|Who sholde fecche this fruyt, the fende or Jesus suluen" (C.18.128–29). As a fulfilment of this promise, in Passus 20, the moment of the crucifixion is described as the time of reckoning for the fruit belonging to Piers the Ploughman, "Pers fruyt the Plouhman" (C.20.18), to be reclaimed. Now death is going to be brought down, thoroughly "forbite" (C.20.34), bitten down to nothing. The biting of the original fruit which brought sin and death into the world in the Genesis story (Genesis:3) is counteracted by this "forbiting" in which Jesus jousts, not with a lance, but with his cross. Significantly, in the harrowing of hell, both the Devil and Christ make much of the original sin, the eating of "the appul," the devil using it as a reason to claim humankind as his own, Christ using it as a call on his mercy.

The imagery of knightly combat is, as many scholars have discussed, a significant thread in the discourse of the poem.[12] Knights were themselves ambivalent figures,

---

[11] Pearsall, *Piers Plowman*, 301n123.

[12] See Pearsall, 322n11, 323n21; Lawrence Warner, "Jesus the Jouster: The Christ-Knight and Medieval Theories of Atonement in *Piers Plowman* and the 'Round Table' Sermons," *The Yearbook of Langland Studies* 10 (1996): 129–43; Emily Steiner, *Reading Piers Plowman* (Cambridge: Cambridge

being committed to acts of war and violence while being at the same time regarded as protectors of the church and of the vulnerable.[13] Thus, the image of Christ as a knightly jouster is a complex one and Christ's action in the poem draws on this ambivalence, his knightliness being identified by his coat of arms, *humana natura*, and his valour in jousting with the universal enemy of human nature, death. But specifically, the poem at this point prepares the reader for jousts between Christ and "the fende" (devil), Christ being clothed in *humana natura*, as a young tyro on his way to being dubbed, his deity concealed, and Christ "the lord of lyf and of liht" (the lord of life and of light, C.20.59) being pitted against death and the darkness of sin (C.20.104–5).

The full humanity of Christ is portrayed dramatically at the opening of Passus 20, when Christ enters Jerusalem on an ass, and is subsequently crucified and dies. Langland enhances the simple Gospel narrative of Palm Sunday by foreshadowing Christ's divinity; he portrays Christ as a knight going to get his spurs—God the Son about to do his Father's business. The dreamer who envisions the whole scene further identifies this knightly character as one resembling the Samaritan, a significant Son-of-God figure who has been developed in Passus 16. Additionally, he comes in the likeness of Piers the Ploughman, who, throughout the poem, signifies humanity, but has Christ-like qualities. The account of Christ's passion and death follows Scripture closely and succinctly, stressing that Jesus dies in full control of his death when all is *consummatum*, so that, while yielding to death as a human being, in apparent defeat he is *consummatus Deus* (the consummate Godhead). The function of the second person of the Trinity, Christ, is to win back humankind from the power of sin, evil, and death. In the combat against these three, personified in the poem by "the fende," or "the pouke" (the devil), the weapon used by Christ is love, and the climactic expression of that love is the death of Jesus on the cross, when he bleeds his life away, but in bleeding, gives sight to the blind Longinus (C.20.80–94), causes the earth to quake and the sun to grow dark, and opens the graves of the dead who await the resurrection (C.20.60–69). From this point onward the dominant images in the passus are of light conquering darkness, life conquering death, justice overcoming guile and the humanity of Christ being the subtle weapon that wins mankind for the Divinity.

The Humanity of the Second Person of the Trinity

For Langland, the humanity of Jesus is the overriding factor in the story of salvation. He goes beyond the empathetic imaginings of a writer like Margery Kempe, who fixes imaginatively on the human Jesus as a person with whom she can develop a human love relationship. In *Piers Plowman* the mechanics of how salvation has been achieved is portrayed in graphic imagery. At the opening of Passus 20 Jesus was shown entering

---

University Press, 2013), 78–79; R. A. Waldron, "Langland's Originality: The Christ-Knight and the Harrowing of Hell," in *Medieval English Religious and Ethical Literature: Essays in Honour of G. H. Russell*, ed. Gregory Kratzmann and James Simpson (Cambridge: Brewer, 1986), 66–81.

[13] Nigel Saul, *Chivalry* (Cambridge, MA: Harvard University Press, 2011), 197–218.

Jerusalem as a young knight on his way to being dubbed. In the course of the Passion narrative, he jousted as a knight and yielded his life in apparent defeat. But the image of Longinus kneeling before the cross (C.20.89–94) is one of homage to a victor, and this victor, in the harrowing of hell which forms the final section of the passus, is shown as victorious over death and sin.

Whereas in several earlier passūs, sin has been examined as a debilitating moral condition, at this point Langland deals with sin both as a cosmic force of evil, typified by the metaphysical activities of the devil, and as a human act, made concrete in the Genesis narrative of the fall of Adam and Eve. The image through which the poem presents the conquest of sin is of Christ's encounter with Lucifer in the harrowing of hell. In keeping with tradition handed down through apocryphal gospels, particularly the *Gospel of Nicodemus*, and through patristic and early medieval commentaries and writings, *Piers Plowman* presents sin and evil as conditions of Hell, a physical place ruled by the devil, a place of punishment for sin.[14] Unlike many medieval texts which mention the devil, particularly those such as *Handlyng Synne* which employ the use of exempla, there is no sense here of the devil being a near and present danger to human beings in their daily lives.[15] Satan, Belial, Gobelin, and Lucifer are all players in the drama of the harrowing of hell, and Christ's encounter with them is on the metaphysical plane.

A prelude to the drama of Christ's traditional descent into hell comes in the meeting of the Four Daughters of God: Truth, Righteousness, Mercy, and Peace, whose verbal debate establishes the polemic of man's first sin and the devil's rights over mankind (C.20.115–270). The four daughters' debate and the dramatic preparations of the devils for a final encounter with the risen Christ sift out conflicting arguments about sin and damnation, with overt allusions to the learning of the Fathers and the scholars.[16] The logic of these scenes is based on the biblical narrative of sin, the disobedience of the first human beings whose punishment for sin was expulsion from Paradise and subsequent death (Genesis: 3). Mercy proposes an argument of hope for those in hell, when the lord of life and of light will overcome the lord of darkness. Truth counters this, basing her arguments on the biblical account of the Fall. Righteousness (Justice) is said to be the eldest of the four daughters and her words propose the justice of explicit punishment for explicit sin. Countering her, Peace talks of the importance of experience, and recognizes that the sufferings of the just in hell align them with the deity: God became man in order to experience the pains and joys of human life; he became Adam's kind. And Adam's kind must experience pain: it is the fabric of life. Joy and pain must both exist and God wants to experience both. The dominant line of argument put forward by Mercy and Peace is

---

14 For an explication of *The Gospel of Nicodemus* see Marx, 47–64. For the edited text, see *The Gospel of Nicodemus: Gesta Salvatoris*, ed. H. C. Kim (Toronto: Pontifical Institute of Mediaeval Studies, 1973).

15 Robert Mannyng, *Handlyng Synne*, ed. Idelle Sullens (Binghampton: Medieval and Renaissance Texts and Studies, 1983).

16 For an overview of the patristic and scholastic sources for these debates see Marx, *The Devil's Rights*, passim.

that by the Incarnation, God the Son became kin with humanity whom he had created and permitted to sin so that he could the better experience both the sorrow of wrong and happiness of good.

> Forthy God of his goodnesse the furste gome Adam
> Sette hym in solace furste and in souereyne merthe
> And sethe he soffrede hym to synne, sorwe to fele,
> To wyte what wele was ther-thorwe, kyndeliche to knowe hit.
> And aftur, god auntred hymsulue and toek Adames kynde
> To wyte what he had soffred in thre sundry places,
> Bothe in heuene and in erthe—and now to helle he thenketh,
> To wyte what al wo is, that woet of alle ioye:
> *Omnia probate; quod bonum est tenete.*
>
> (C.20.227–34)

(Therefore God, of his goodness, placed the first man Adam in peace and sovereign joy, and then allowed him to sin, so that he would experience sorrow, so that through this he would understand what happiness was, learning it by experiencing it. And after this, God himself ventured forth and took on the nature of Adam in order to understand what he had suffered in three different places, in heaven and on earth; and now he intends to go into hell, so that he who understands the joy of everything can learn what misery is: *Experience everything, and hold on to what is good.*)

The devil, who is given anthropomorphic form in the characters of Satan, Gobelin, and Lucifer, echoing the interpretations voiced by Righteousness, takes literally God's edict that having sinned, all humankind is condemned to death and banished from Paradise, and concludes that banishment from Paradise means being committed to hell, with no hope of ever being released (C.20, 300–311). This is a dark, unmerciful state of affairs, a pre-Incarnation dialectic, drawing on human logic to interpret the Scriptural narrative, but ignorant of the divine mercy about to be transmitted through the mediation of God the Son. Langland is insistent on the difference between pre- and post-Incarnation theology, and the opposition here expressed is between the strict justice attributed to an anthropomorphic God who expelled the first parents from Paradise, and the mercy attributed to the incarnate second person of the Trinity.

All this is the prelude to the magnificent declaration by Christ of his kinship with humanity, as the risen Christ erupts into the gloom of the underworld. The conflict now dramatized is between Christ and sin as Langland constructs a scene which dramatizes the power of sin and evil. The devils in their stronghold seem powerful; they are determined to preserve the darkness of their realm, "And y shal lette this lorde and his liht stoppe." (C.20.283), and rather comically prepare their war engines, boiling brimstone, crossbows, brazen guns, millstones, and other missiles. Yet this physical arsenal is wide of the mark, because what they fear most is the light of Christ, which they know will blind and therefore overwhelm them. Even before Christ's arrival, the imagery anticipates his conquest. The advance of the Lord is announced by a special light reminiscent of the light at the raising of Lazarus (C.20.275). Satan speaks for all the hosts of hell: he is most afraid of being blinded by brightness. Lucifer, once the light-bearer, now cannot bear the light which threatens to blind him and all the devils. The preparations for battle involve stopping up every last chink to keep out the damaging light (C.20.279–86).

The sound of Christ's arrival, heralded by the cry "*Atollite portas* ..." reflects the office of Tenebrae, the liturgical re-enactment of Christ's descent into hell, and anticipates the end of the passus, when Wille awakens from his sleep and goes with his wife Kit, and his daughter Calote, to church on Easter Day (C.20.471–75). This clash in the harrowing of hell is an endorsement of the power of God in the three persons of the Trinity, and particularly the role of God the Son. It is a dramatized exposition of the Creed: "He descended into hell; the third day he rose again from the dead. He ascended into heaven and sitteth at the right hand of God the Father Almighty." Liturgy and poetic drama here run in parallel.

The crux of the conflict between Lucifer and Christ is that the devil has been surprised into recognizing the man Jesus as God. The God that Lucifer recognized was the anthropomorphic God of the Genesis story, a God of strict justice who demands punishment for sin. Until it was too late, Lucifer did not recognize Jesus as being God incarnate, who went about in human form teaching people to love one another:

> For the body, whiles hit on bones yede, aboute was hit euere
> To lere men to be lele and vch man to louye other;
> The which lyf and lawe, be hit longe y-vysed,
> Hit shal vndo vs deueles and down bryngen vs all.
> (C.20.337–40)

(For while that body went about in flesh and bone, it was always intent on teaching people to be faithful, and each person to love the other; and if this way of life and fidelity to this law is put into practice for too long, it will be the undoing of us devils and bring us all down.)

Lucifer makes a forlorn attempt at logic: God is the Lord of Truth and he said the human race would be damned if Adam and Eve ate the apple. "That Adam and Eue and alle his issue|Sholde deye with doel and here dwelle euere,|Yf that they touched a tre or toek therof an appul" (C.20.303–5). But using imagery of light against darkness, the poem shows Lucifer as vanquished; blinded by the light that comes with the risen Christ, and defeated by the loss of the souls who flood out of hell in the river of light brought by Christ: "Lucifer loke ne myhte, so liht hym ablende,|And tho that oure lord louede forth with that liht flowen" (C.20.368–69).

The final analysis of Christ's saving power stresses the kinship of Christ with humanity. Jesus demonstrates that he is a God who hungers and thirsts for the human beings whose nature he shares, who has fought hard for them, and whom he loves. The contrast is drawn by Christ between the bitter brew that Lucifer has made and the full "must" that he will drink at the wine harvest. He contrasts Lucifer's deep bowl from which he will drink death with his own thirst that will last until the resurrection of the dead in the valley of Jehoshaphat. Lucifer is brewing a drink of death, whereas the drink of Christ is love. Love is repeatedly imaged as the factor that overcomes sin.[17] Thus,

---

[17] For an analysis of this passage see Elizabeth Salter, *Piers Plowman: An Introduction* (Oxford: Blackwell, 1962), 49–52.

Christ shows himself one with humanity and expresses his love for his blood brothers and his oneness with mankind:

> The bitternesse that thow hast browe, now brouk hit thysulue;
> That art doctor of deth, drynke that thow madest!
> For y that am lord of lyf, loue is my drynke,
> And for that drynke today Y deyede, as hit semede.
> Y fauht so me fursteth yut for mannes soule sake: *Sicio*.
> (C.20.401–405)

(You are the doctor of death, by the drink that you made. For I who am lord of life, love is my drink, and for that drink, to all appearances I died today ... I fought in such a way that I thirst still for the sake of humankind: *I thirst*.)

The emotion of the redemption speech is palpable. This is a God who experiences human needs and human emotions, who has fought in a joust; who in dying is victorious. Human emotions are expressed and, in the debate with Lucifer, seem to constrain the divine nature. God cannot act in any other way because he has become human:

> Ac to be merciable to man thenne my kynde asketh,
> For we beth brethren of o bloed, ac nat in baptisme alle.
> (C.20.437–38)

(But to be merciful to humankind at that time is what my nature demands, for we are brethren of one blood, even though all are not one in baptism.)

Conclusion

While the poem presents God as Trinitarian throughout, Langland makes it quite clear that Christ is God, attributing to him roles traditionally associated with the Father and the Holy Spirit. Traditionally the Holy Spirit is imaged as the one who comes to the Virgin at the Annunciation, yet Langland clearly images Jesus as the hawk, alighting within the Virgin's chamber, rather than the traditional image of the Holy Spirit coming in the form of a dove. And in the imaging of Jesus as vanquishing Lucifer in hell, Jesus is God the judge, a role more often assigned to God the Father. "'Ac for the lesynge that thow low, Lucifer, til Eue|Thow shal abye bittere!' quod god, and bonde hym with chaynes." In these images, Langland portrays the oneness of the Triune God. It is God who overcomes the power of sin because the Son of God is kin with the sinners, and he cannot endure to see his kin destroyed. Lucifer's view is of strict punishment for disobedience to God's command, but the great speech of Christ (C.20.370–449) is an apologia for God's mercy. And the mercy is born of God sharing human nature.

This finally brings me back to my indebtedness to Davlin's meditative approach to the reading of *Piers Plowman* and the reason why I embarked on this topic in a volume whose theme is war and conflict. Several chapters in this volume examine the impact of war on human emotion, the grief occasioned by loss, the anxiety of separation, the violence done to loving relationships. Langland deals head-on with love and war, pitting love itself as the conquering force against evil. The Four Daughters of God debate in the well-known terms of arid logic based on traditional theological and philosophical tenets. But Langland, interested in human beings and their everyday lives, presents Christ's joust as a war that is, in the end, not a war. Christ vanquishes Lucifer by undermining him in human form, going about as a warm human being doing good to other human beings. This is translated into the final resolution of conflict where the light of love erupts to dispel evil's darkness.

Love, yearning, hunger, thirst, oneness: these are the metaphors that express the otherwise inexpressible wonder that the Divinity has become humanity. Langland has understood the essential human impact of the conflicts that underlie the human condition. His poem does not deny the effects of sin and suffering in human life, nor does it present an over-optimistic view. The final passus (C.22) envisions the corruption of the Church and the onslaught of Antichrist at the end of time when all earthly institutions will fail. Yet the poem ends with the figure of Conscience striding out to seek Piers the Plowman (C.22.380–86), bolstered by the confident knowledge that since sin and death have been vanquished by the incarnate Christ, they will have no power to destroy the individual human being whose human life Christ has shared.

Chapter 8

BREATHING IN PEACE AND WAR: MALORY'S *LE MORTE DARTHUR*

Corinne Saunders*

ANDREW LYNCH'S ESSAY "What cheer?" probes the ways that medieval Arthurian writing complicates contemporary reductive notions of emotion as facilitative. Emotions promote the political and ethical project of King Arthur, but are also multi-faceted and sometimes conflicting: "the Arthurian world ... gives us a compelling narrative of the problems that arise when a more developed and intense 'emotional literacy' supplants a narrowly instrumental and goal-oriented reading of events."[1] Lynch's exploration of "cheer" demonstrates too the differences between past and present understandings of emotions, and the underpinning of medieval conceptions by the idea of the "stirring" and movement of the passions. Central to Lynch's work is his interest in the politics of emotions, and their relation to arms and warfare. He draws attention to the special status of Sir Thomas Malory's *Le Morte Darthur*, his "book of arms," as "a record of the (sur)'passing' and the wonderful; ... it deals with the most deeply felt of things, providing their fitting written correlative."[2] This chapter takes up these emphases to explore the role of breath in Malory's *Le Morte Darthur*: its emotional literacy, the movement of the passions and spirits, the "deeply felt" in peace and war.

Rarely attended to, yet essential to being and consciousness, breathing is unique in its combination of voluntary and involuntary elements, and in connecting interior and exterior, mental and physical states.[3] The medieval thought-world, with its integration of mind, body, and affect, privileges the role of breath in embodied experience and the

---

* **Corinne Saunders** is Professor of English and Co-Director of the Institute for Medical Humanities, Durham University, UK. Her books include *Magic and the Supernatural in Medieval English Romance* (2010) and the co-edited volumes *Emotions in Medieval Arthurian Literature: Body, Mind, Voice* (2015) and *Romance Rewritten: The Evolution and Reception of Middle English Romance* (2018).

1 Andrew Lynch, "'What cheer?': Emotion and Action in the Arthurian World," in *Emotions in Medieval Arthurian Literature*, 47–53 at 63.

2 Andrew Lynch, *Malory's Book of Arms: The Narrative of Combat in "Le Morte Darthur,"* Arthurian Studies 39 (Cambridge: Brewer, 1997), 134.

3 The collaborative *Life of Breath* project (https://lifeofbreath.org/), funded by the Wellcome Trust and based at Durham University, takes up these mysterious yet crucial aspects of experience, proposing that breathing and breathlessness can only be understood fully through the insights of cultural, historical, and phenomenological sources, and that perspectives derived from the arts and humanities can illuminate and improve medical understanding. Research for this chapter has been funded by Wellcome Trust Awards WT098455, WT108720, WT103339/Z/13/Z, and WT209513/Z/17/Z. I am grateful to my colleagues for their insights.

centrality of breathing to being in the world. Breath shapes portrayals of battle and peace, knightly prowess, and emotional experience. It is intimately connected with the spiritual, and with the bodily spirits. Being "well-breathed"—the ability both to exert and control breath to the utmost—is an essential quality of great knighthood, while its inverse, breathlessness, manifest in swoons, sobs, and sighs, makes visible emotional life, denoting feeling from love to loss to spiritual ecstasy. Breath literally and metaphorically animates a community of knights in war and in peace. In both, the extremes of breath are Malory's typical focus. Breath connects the two faces of medieval romance—the pursuit of war, arms and chivalry, and the life of the emotions—the intersecting subjects that have been of primary importance in the work of Andrew Lynch.

The Virtue of Life

Central to medieval medicine was the humoral theory of the Greek physician Hippocrates (460–370 BC), refined by Galen (129–ca. 216 AD): both physical and mental health required the balance of the humours. Mind and body formed a continuum, a model directly contrary to post-Cartesian dualism. Aristotle placed rational, intellective being as a property of the soul but situated the senses and cognitive faculties in the heart, an idea that persisted in popular and literary culture well beyond the early modern period. Breathing was governed by the heart, itself the source of heat causing the blood to pulse and flow, and the dilating of the lungs which drew in air; breath cooled the heart through the bellows-like action of the lungs. Aristotle's theories were complicated by the emphasis of Alexandrian medicine on the brain as the centre of cognition and the senses, which underpinned medieval psychology. This new focus on the brain was complemented by the concept of the "spirits" elaborated by Galen and his followers, central to Arabic medicine, in particular, the works of Avicenna, and dominant in medical thought across the Middle Ages. *Pneuma* (air), "the life breath of the cosmos," was understood to be taken into the body and transformed into three kinds in the three principal organs: in the liver, the "natural spirits," carried through the veins and governing generation, growth, nutrition, and digestion; in the heart, the "vital spirits," formed of air mixed with blood and transported through the arteries, heating and animating the body, and governing breathing; in the brain, the "animal spirits," sent through the nerves and controlling sensation, movement, and thought.[4]

The Christian West inherited these theories through the dissemination of Latin translations of Arabic and Greek medical texts in the early twelfth century, in particular

---

[4] Roy Porter, *The Greatest Benefit to Mankind: A Medical History of Humanity from Antiquity to the Present* (London: HarperCollins, 1997), 76–77. On *pneuma* in classical and early Christian thought, see G. Verbeke, *L'Évolution de la doctrine du "pneuma" du stoïcisme à S. Augustin, étude philosophique* (Paris: Desclée de Brouwer, 1945), and on classical thought, Philip van der Eijk, *Medicine and Philosophy in Classical Antiquity: Doctors and Philosophers on Nature, Soul, Health and Disease* (Cambridge: Cambridge University Press, 2005), 119–35. On medieval psychology, see my discussion in Corinne Saunders, "Mind, Body and Affect in Medieval English Arthurian Romance," in *Emotions in Medieval Arthurian Literature*, 31–46 at 31–35.

the works of Constantine of Africa and Avicenna; Galenic works entered the university curriculum in the thirteenth century, and strongly influenced, for example, Aquinas and Albertus Magnus.[5] The classical descriptive model of the lungs is explicated in Isidore of Seville's widely disseminated *Etymologies*: "pulmo," the lung, is so-named in Greek

> because it is a fan for the heart, in which the pneuma, that is, the breath, resides, through which the lungs are both put in motion and kept in motion—from this also the lungs are so named ... The lungs are the engine of the body.[6]

Works such as John Trevisa's translation of Bartholomaeus Anglicus' *De proprietatibus rerum* rendered physiological and psychological theories accessible beyond university circles from the later fourteenth century onwards. John, translating Bartholomaeus, draws directly on Constantine to describe the centrality of the vital spirits (the "virtue of life"):

> Aftir þe vertu of kynde folewiþ þe vertu of lif þat ȝeueþ lif to þe body and haþ place in þe herte. Out of þe herte comeþ lif to al þe limes. ... Þis vertu of lif openiþ þe herte by worchinge of þe longen and draweþ in aier to the hert and sendiþ forþ from þe herte to oþir limes by smale weyes. And by help of þe vertu þat closith and riueþ and openith þe herte þis vertu worchiþ and makeþ breþinge in a beest. And by breþinge þe brest meueþ continualliche, but sinewis and brawnes beþ first imeued. Þis blast, breþ, and onde [breath/spirit] is nedeful to slake þe kindeliche hete, and to foode of þe spirit of lif, and also to þe gendringe of þe spirit þat hatte *animalis* þat ȝeueþ felinge and meuynge ... . Perforc noþing is more nedeful to kepe and to saue þe lif þan breþ, wel disposid and ordeyned in alle pointis. All þis seiþ Constantinus in *Pantegni*.[7]

Breath both cools the heart and generates the vital spirits, which in turn create the animal spirits. Breath is the root of being.

Physiological theory was complemented by theological notions of *pneuma*. St Paul takes up both the classical idea of *pneuma* and the Hebrew concept of *ruach*, the breath of God. The Spirit of divinity and life is external to the individual, moving within the cosmos, but also inspiring and inspired, moving the souls of men and women and breathing the new life of the Spirit into them. Augustine employs the concept of *spiritus* (*pneuma*)

---

5 Constantine's *Pantegni theorica*, translating parts of the tenth-century Galenic medical encyclopaedia of "Haly Abbas" (Ali ibn al-'Abbas al-Majusi), and a translation of the treatise on the Galenic theory of humours and spirits by the ninth-century physician "Johannitius" (Hunayn ibn Ishaq), were foundation texts in the *Articella*, the collection of six medical works forming the basis of Western medical theory. On medieval medicine see Faye Getz, *Medicine in the English Middle Ages* (Princeton: Princeton University Press, 1998), Carole Rawcliffe, *Medicine and Society in Later Medieval England* (Stroud: Sutton, 1995), and Nancy G. Siraisi, *Medieval and Early Renaissance Medicine: An Introduction to Knowledge and Practice* (Chicago: Chicago University Press, 1990).

6 Isidore of Seville, *The Etymologies of Isidore of Seville*, trans. Stephen A. Barney, W. J. Lewis, J. A. Beach, Oliver Berghof, with Muriel Hall (Cambridge: Cambridge University Press, 2006), 9.i.124.

7 John Trevisa, *On the Properties of Things*, ed. M. C. Seymour (Oxford: Oxford University Press, 1975) 3.15, vol. 1, 104–5; for the Latin, see Bartholomaeus Anglicus, *De rerum proprietatibus* (1601; Frankfurt: Minerva, 1964).

to explore both the immaterial quality of the divine and the life force.[8] The centrality of breath to the medical model of the vital spirits lent such notions a new materiality, while distinctions between soul and air not made by Galen were also required: Isidore of Seville emphasizes that soul is generated in the womb before air is breathed in (XI.i.7). *Pneuma* was most typically viewed within a physiological framework as "the instrument of the soul."[9] Yet the terminology and concepts of the "vital spirits" and *pneuma/spiritus* (Holy Spirit) inevitably overlap, giving breath a special status as the animating force. The heat associated in medical theory with the heart also created a physiological rationale for the prevalent imagery of fire connected with the Holy Spirit. Divine *pneuma/spiritus* is understood as both air and fire, corresponding readily to physiological concepts of *pneuma* as breath and vital spark of life.

All these aspects of breath underpin medieval theories of the emotions. Emotions were understood to occur through the movements of the vital spirits and natural heat, produced in the heart and travelling through the arteries. They could be caused by direct sensory experience or by imagination and memory, but always had both physical and mental consequences. In extreme joy or anger, the vital spirits and accompanying heat moved out of the heart to other parts of the body: the heat might be visible in blushing or even frenzy. In extreme grief, distress, or fear, by contrast, the vital spirits and heat withdrew from the arteries into the heart. Such withdrawal of spirit was synonymous with withdrawal of breath, and might cause unconsciousness or even death. Thus the swoon signals great sorrow, shock, or similarly overwhelming emotion, while the sigh functions to purge and cool the overburdened or overheated heart. Ultimately, excessive sighing could be dangerous, causing the heart to dry out and wither. The Middle English terms for sigh and swoon are closely related, and may even be spelt identically.[10] Such ideas are discussed by Arnoldus de Villa Nova and Gilbertus Anglicus whose works, like that of Bartholomaeus, were available in later medieval intellectual circles. *De proprietatibus rerum* was one of the earliest books printed by Caxton in Cologne; John Trevisa's translation was printed by Wynkyn de Worde in 1496.[11]

Writers such as Chaucer and Gower, both well versed in natural philosophy and medicine, engage in striking detail with conceptions of breath and vital spirits. But what

---

8 See Verbeke, *L'Evolution de la doctrine du "pneuma,"* 489–508.

9 Gerald J. Grudzen, *Medical Theory About the Body and the Soul in the Middle Ages: The First Western Medical Curriculum at Monte Cassino* (Lewiston: Mellen, 2007), 63–64, 200–201.

10 Middle English "swough" (sigh) can also mean a forceful motion or impetus, deriving from Old English "swōgan," to resound, sound, rush, or roar; "swoun" (swoon) derives from Old English "geswogen," in a faint/overcome, also ultimately from "-swōgan" ("āswōgan," to overcome); see *OED*, sigh, *n.* 1, sigh *v.* 1a., 2a., 3b.; swoon, *n.* 1a., 1b; swoon *v.* 1a, 2; *MED*, swŏugh, *n.* 1, 2.

11 On Caxton's and de Worde's prints, see Norman F. Blake, *William Caxton and English Literary Culture* (London: Hambledon, 1991) and *William Caxton: A Bibliographical Guide* (New York: Garland, 1985), and Lotte Hellinga, *William Caxton and Early Printing in England* (London: British Library, 2010).

of Malory, a century later, whose *Le Morte Darthur* is most often seen as dependent on the accretion of action, and as resisting psychological interiority? Yet it is feeling, above all, that brings to life the key moments in the narrative, in peace and war—feeling evoked in the reader by the movement of plot, from its dramatic opening to the great tragedy of the death books, by the extraordinary feats of Malory's knights, the sublimity of divine vision, the threat of villainy and treachery, and the so frequently disastrous narratives of love woven through the book. Emotion, writes Lynch, "forms the prelude, the accompaniment and the response to the narrative's praiseworthy actions"—and, we might add, to its blameworthy ones, its joys and its losses.[12] Feeling is repeatedly signalled by affective terms—cheer, dole, marvel, mourning—to which meaning accrues in the course of the narrative, and such terms are typically accompanied by physical affects, many of them connected to breath—tears, swoons, laughter, sickness, changes in colour.[13] In deeply spiritual states, breath changes—to the tears of sinfulness, the reduced ventilation of sleep and vision, or the withdrawal of breath in swoon. Breath is not only integral to emotional movement, however: it also signals the crucial physical qualities of knighthood, and, thus, functions to connect exterior and interior, mind, body, and affect. If breath is central to passion, it also fuels exertion. In the *Morte*, the enacting of chivalry finds a counterpoint in the movement of the passions: the "active" body is always shadowed by the "passive" body. The play of breath shifts in emphasis and colour within individual episodes and from one part of the work to the next, animating the narrative and illuminating the relationship between chivalry and emotion. Breath is a constant across time, a quality that is not learned but innate: Malory's characters breathe through the book.

In translating, adapting, and reshaping his sources, Malory consistently points up breath, both as a quality demonstrating prowess and marking identity, and as a crucial indicator of embodied emotion. The four main divisions of the narrative map different, but related, aspects of breath in peace and war, to weave a complex tapestry of prowess and passion. The first five books establish the integral part played by breath in war and its centrality to knightly identity; while being "well-breathed" wins battles, it also, in the tale of Balan and Balin, leads to tragedy. Breath is crucial too to emotional experience and its articulation, most of all in Malory's greatest knights. The dialogue between public play and private passion is pointed up in the central section of the *Morte*, in particular, the books of Sir Tristram with their repeated encounters of arms, balanced by the love affairs of its protagonists. Battle moves into a new sphere in the Grail Quest, where the conflict is between demonic and divine, and breath inspires not prowess but vision. In the last books of the *Morte*, all these aspects of breath come together to shape the tragic denouement of the work, most of all in the unique intersection of chivalry and feeling in its central figure, Sir Lancelot.

---

[12] Lynch, *Malory's Book of Arms*, 134.

[13] See also my discussion of Malory's *Morte* in "Mind, Body and Affect in English Arthurian Romance," 42–46.

The Breath of War

From the opening books onwards, Malory weaves a tapestry of breath and breathlessness. The affects of emotion are complemented by the physicality of chivalric existence: to be a knight is also to exercise the breath, and the best knights are the most "well-breathed." To be "well-breathed" is to "to excite the respiratory organs," to be well-exercised, an adverbial use of "to breathe" (*OED v.* 14a), yet in the *Morte* the phrase seems to convey the sense of possessing the best breath—superior strength and vital spirits—and the best control of breath. Malory uses the term only of his greatest knights—Sir Lancelot, Sir Tristram, Sir Lamorak. Life and death are delineated by breath and its loss: we repeatedly hear of breath leaving the body, and of the swoons preceding death. The withdrawal of spirits into the heart is suggested by phrases such as "youre harte faylyth you"; to die is to be "full colde at the harte-roote."[14] Shocks presage swoons that render individuals "as [they] had bene dede" (6.34, 358). "Heaviness" conveys the weight of the spirits on the heart—often the affect of melancholy.[15] Emotions are typically enhanced by Malory through an emphasis on embodied response, to which the play of breath that accompanies the movement of the spirits is central.

The opening books of the *Morte* are coloured by the frenzied exhalation of breath in battle, which reaches its height in the narrative of Arthur's war against the Emperor Lucius. Here, unlike in other parts of the work, accounts of combat do not explicitly mention breath but instead repeatedly instance the quality gained through being well-breathed, "freshness" in battle: Malory echoes a term sometimes used in his source, the Alliterative *Morte Arthure*, but much heightens its use.[16] Thus Bors and Gawain "freyshly folowed on the Romaynes," "sir Borce and sir Berel were formeste in the frunte and freyshly faught," and Idres, "a freysh knyght," urges them on (5.6, 209); though in the Alliterative *Morte* the knights ask "freshly" (eagerly) after their friends, none of these uses occurs in the poem (see 1426–42). Bors' urging, "lette us set on hem freyshly, and the worshyp shall be oures" (5.7, 214), is similarly not in Sir Cador's comparable speech in the Alliterative *Morte* (1708–23). Malory's depiction of the battle between Sir Gawain and Sir Priamus points up breath: they fight each other "so freysshly" that flaming fire

---

[14] *The Works of Sir Thomas Malory*, 10.57, 696; 10.59, 699; 20.1, 1162. References to Malory are to this edition, cited by Caxton's book and chapter numbers, and page numbers. The phrase "your heart faileth you" translates "li cuers vous faut!," *Le Roman de Tristan en Prose*, ed. Philippe Ménard, 9 vols., Textes Littéraires Français (Geneva: Librairie Droz, 1987–97), 5.73, 149. References to the *Prose Tristan* from the "Folie Tristan" onwards are to this edition, cited as *PT*, by volume and page number. The phrase "full colde at the harte-roote" is not in the Stanzaic *Morte*, Malory's source for this passage. When sources are not mentioned, Malory is translating directly.

[15] On the physiological understanding of the heart in Malory, as well as its role in perception, see also Lynch, *Malory's Book of Arms*, 145–46.

[16] See for example line 1495, Alliterative *Morte Arthure*, in *King Arthur's Death: The Middle English "Stanzaic Morte Arthur" and "Alliterative Morte Arthure,"* ed. Larry D. Benson, Exeter Medieval English Texts and Studies (Exeter: Exeter University Press, 1986), 113–238. References to the Alliterative *Morte Arthure* (*AMA*) are to this edition, cited by line number.

flows from their helmets (5.10, 229–30; *AMA* "stoutly," 2553). Freshness implies both exertion and control of breath.

Full-scale warfare does not occur again until the end of the *Morte*, but throughout the breath that affords such "freshness" is crucial to the enactment of prowess: individual battles depend both on knights "getting them wind" (48) and being well-breathed, a combination of physical strength and skill. The emotion that fuels such chivalric achievement is not only focused on victory. Early on in the narrative, Sir Griflet's attacker regrets wounding him, and acts to "[get] hym wynde" by loosening his helmet; the phrase is repeated (1.23, 48). Malory changes the emphasis from "pour le vent recueillir" ("to let air in"; *Merlin* 1, 183, *L-G* 8, 24), and specifies that Griflet's "myghty herte" (1.23, 48) causes his opponent's heaviness of spirit: strength of vital spirits inspires feeling in his enemy and leads to his recovery.[17] In the tale of Sir Gareth, by contrast, breath underscores chivalric challenge. Gareth's opponent, the Red Knight, who has the strength of seven men, is summoned by the blowing of the "grettyst" horn ever seen (7.15, 20), and the subsequent battle is punctuated by the play of breath. They encounter with such force that both are "astoned," knocked from their horses, to fight on foot "tyll at the laste they lacked wynde bothe, and than they stoode waggyng, stagerynge, pantynge, blowynge, and bledyng, that all that behelde them for the moste party wepte for pyté" (7.16–17, 322–23). Breath provides a physical marker of the greatest achievement.

In the books of Sir Tristram, although they are punctuated by many wounds and swoons, the breath of battle-play often remains more light-hearted. Tristram, like

---

[17] For this part of the narrative, Malory draws on the Post-Vulgate Cycle, first identified through the Huth manuscript (British Museum Add. 38117), which contains versions of the Vulgate *Estoire del Saint Graal* and *Merlin*, and a much-reworked *Suite du Merlin* (which begins with Arthur's coronation). Sections missing from the Huth manuscript are found in Cambridge Add. 7071, which contains the same works. The work of Fanni Bogdanow has identified further continuations of the Post-Vulgate Suite: see Bogdanow, *The Romance of the Grail: A Study of the Structure and Genesis of a Thirteenth-Century Arthurian Prose Romance* (Manchester: Manchester University Press, 1966). A complete translation of the whole is found in Norris J. Lacy, ed., *Lancelot-Grail: The Old French Arthurian Vulgate and Post-Vulgate in Translation*, vols. 8 and 9, *The Post Vulgate Merlin Continuation*, trans. Martha Asher (Cambridge: Brewer, 2010, originally New York: Garland, 1992–96); the editors assume this would have been preceded by versions of the *Estoire del Saint Graal* and *Merlin* comparable to those in the Vulgate (vols. 1 and 2 of this translation). The translation of the *Suite* is keyed to the edition of the Huth manuscript by Gaston Paris and Jacob Ulrich, *Merlin: Roman en Prose du XIIIᵉ Siècle*, Société des Anciens Textes Français 23, 2 vols. (Paris: Société des Anciens Textes Français, 1886); references to the French are therefore to this (cited as *Merlin*, by volume and page number), supplemented by the more recent edition of the *Suite* proper by Gilles Roussineau, *La Suite du Roman de Merlin*, Textes Littéraires Français, 2 vols. (Geneva: Librairie Droz, 1996), which draws on other manuscript evidence, and by Vinaver's notes; translations are from Lacy, ed., *Lancelot-Grail* 8 and 9 (cited as *L-G*, by volume and page number). The French source for this description is more general: "il estoit trop hardis," *Merlin* 1, 183, "he was very bold," *L-G* 8, 24; see *The Works of Sir Thomas Malory*, 1300n48. Lynch cites John Trevisa's description of the "vertue and complexioun of the herte" as demonstrated "be grete breth and blowynge; by swift puls and þicke," as well as strength, wrath, hardiness, and rashness, and by "largenes of brest," *On the Properties of Things*, ed. M. C. Seymour, 5.36, vol. 1, 241 (Lynch, *Malory's Book of Arms*, 146).

Lancelot, is specially marked by the quality of breath, "ever more well-wynded and bygger" than Morholt (8.7, 382).[18] In the tournament of Lonazep, Lancelot praises Tristram in just such terms, "ye may se he dothe all knyghtly, for he hath strengthe and wynde inowe" (10.74, 748). Neither reference to breath occurs in the French.[19] The phrase again signals the crucial combination of vigour that enables exertion and the ability to control that exertion. Strength of breath is also associated with Tristram's special excellence in hunting, as the originator of "all the syses and mesures of all blowyng wyth an horne" (10.52, 682), a quality repeated in a series of passages original to Malory, drawing on the English tradition of Tristram as founder of the art of venery.[20] Tristram's companionship with Lamorak is pointed up by Lamorak's similar qualities of breath, again not described in the French: "In all my lyff mette I never with such a knyght that was so bygge and so well-brethed" (9.11, 483); equality in breath leads to reconciliation.[21] Tristram's lament for Lamorak, a passage apparently original to Malory, emphasizes this quality: "I dare say he was the clennyst-myghted man and the beste-wynded of his ayge that was on lyve" (10.58, 698). At the end of the books of Sir Tristram, it is in part Palomides' admiration for Tristram's qualities of breath that leads to their reconciliation and his christening: "now I dare say I felte never man of youre myght nothir so well-brethed but yf hit were sir Launcelot du Laake, wherefore I requyre you, my lorde, forgyff me ..." (12.14, 844). Neither this battle nor Palomides' conversion are recounted in the French. Breath, like blood, is part of "the basic currency of fights," and recognition of breath in battle corresponds to what Andrew Lynch has called "moment[s] of vision, in which the action is assessed from a point of vantage within the text."[22] Breath betokens honour as well as physical prowess.

To be well-breathed in these instances is to be victorious in battle, or to be reconciled through mutual admiration. Those "moments of vision," "the celebration of prowess," can also point up tragedy.[23] In the tale of Balin and Balan, the ominous forces of destiny

---

[18] References to the *Prose Tristan* prior to the "Folie Tristan" are from Renée L. Curtis, *Le Roman de Tristan en prose*, 3 vols., Arthurian Studies 12–14 (vol. 1: Munich: M. Hueber, 1963; vol. 2: Leiden: Brill, 1976; vol. 3: Cambridge: Brewer, 1985, vols. 1 and 2 repr. Brewer, 1985), cited as *RT* by volume, section and page number, and, where appropriate, from Curtis' abridged translation, *The Romance of Tristan: The Thirteenth-Century Old French "Prose Tristan,"* World's Classics (Oxford: Oxford University Press, 1994), cited by page number. In the French source for this passage, Tristan "plus estoit vistes et legiers," *RT* 1.302, 153.

[19] Cf. "Il moustre bien k'il est boins cevaliers et preus et de grant pooir," *PT* 5.240, 327.

[20] See also 8.3, 375, 10.6, 571, 10.52, 682, and *The Works of Sir Thomas Malory*, 1456n375, 1485n571, 1510n682.

[21] In the *Prose Tristan*, Tristan wonders whether Lamorat is Arthur or Lancelot, "por la grant bonté qu'il a en li trovee et por la grant proesce," and comments on his excellence "la bonté que je voi en toi," *RT* 3.785, 787, 96–97.

[22] Lynch, *Malory's Book of Arms*, 60, 54.

[23] Lynch, *Malory's Book of Arms*, 54–55.

combine with the breath of battle, which moves between action and affect. While the promise of adventure to Balin "reysed his herte" (2.2, 63), a reference to the movement of the vital spirit outwards, the "unhappy" nature of the tale, in which Balin's choices and actions conspire against him at every turn, is repeatedly played out in breath. Balin's wounding of King Pellam, the "Dolorous Stroke" that causes the king to swoon, removes his own vital powers: he falls, unable to move. Misfortune—ultimately the failure of power over the breath and the loss of breath from the body—is eerily marked by the external "breath" of the horn Balin hears, "That blast … is blowen for me, for I am the pryse, and yet am I not dede" (2.17, 88). Malory frames Balan's response to the ominous announcement that he must joust with an unknown knight, in terms of the vital spirits: "though my hors be wery my hert is not wery. I wold be fayne ther my deth shold be" (2.17, 88).[24]

The battle between Balin and Balan, one of the most extended of the entire work, demonstrates acutely the intersection of different aspects of breath in battle, and the interconnection of physical strength and depth of emotion. Here exertion tragically overcomes the control of breath. The brothers fight so fiercely that they "lay bothe in a swoun," and yet they continue "tyl theyr brethes faylled" (2.18, 89); the emphasis is shifted by Malory from "catching the breath" to its loss.[25] In Malory's narrative, the absence of breath—in swoon and utter exhaustion—signals the intensity of knightly commitment even while heightening the tragedy that the brothers, equal in prowess, should fight each other to death. Their prowess is in part indicated by their ability to regain breath even now: "Soo they went unto bataille ageyne, and wounded everyche other dolefully, and thenne they brethed oftymes, and so wente unto bataille that alle the place thereas they fought was blood reed" (2.18, 89); the French makes no reference to breath. Despite their great wounds, enough to be "the death of the mightiest giant in the world," they return to battle, but recovery is impossible. Breath, like blood, "is marvellous but also fearful … to contemplate."[26] When Balan's identity is revealed, Balin's swoon is of a different kind, reflecting the agony of recognition. It is the breath of lament, the "mone" of the knights, and the weeping of the ladies and gentlewomen who discover them, that colours the conclusion, speaking its "grettist pité" (2.18–19, 90–92). The intense drama of the tale is played out in breath.

---

24 In the French, by contrast, Balin asserts, "je ne sui ne si lassés ne si travilliés …," "I am neither tired nor toil-worn," though now, on hearing a damsel's warning, fear, "qui onques mais ne pot en son cuer entrer," "which had never before been able to enter his heart," keeps him company, *Merlin* 2, 46–47, *L-G* 8, 105.

25 "les estuet il reposer ou il voelent ou non, car mau gret eus lor convient il lour alainnes reprendre," "they had to rest, like it or not, for they had to catch their breath," *Merlin* 2, 51, *L-G* 8, 108; Malory perhaps draws on this description a few lines later.

26 Lynch, *Malory's Book of Arms*, 71.

Play and Passion

Breath both enables battle and inspires great deeds through the affective movement of the vital spirits. The physical qualities of knighthood are balanced by the potential to be profoundly affected by emotion and to inspire feeling in others. Great prowess, again and again, is accompanied by great love, and in both, breath plays an essential part. Malory adds details of feeling in his depictions of the literally inspiring effects of love: seeing Isode's laughter and "good chere" at Tristram's prowess occasions "suche a rejoysynge" in Palomides that he strikes down all he encounters (10.70, 737); Gareth's heart is "lyght and joly" when he looks on his lady in battle (7.17, 323).[27] The breath of the court, and particularly of ladies, responds to war and battle in weeping, laughter, and swoons. Guinevere swoons at Arthur's departure to Rome; Isode's love for Tristram is reflected in the movement of her vital spirits, withdrawing into the heart to cause tears and faintness, affecting the wits and rushing out in anger. Again embodied affect is heightened by Malory: she "wepe[s] so hertely for the dyspyte of sir Palomydes that well-nyghe there she sowned" (10.76, 751), is "well-nyghe oute of her mynde for sorow" at Tristram's battle with Lancelot (10.76, 752; not in the French), and is so angry at Palomides' deceit that "she chaunged than her coloures" on seeing him (10.77, 755); Malory adds the swoons and the change in colour, as well as the reference to near-madness.[28] Joy and laughter recur, but the movement of breath is most frequently evoked through the withdrawal of spirits into the heart in sorrow, the effects on the body heard in the sound of "great dole" or seen in the swoon. The affects of grief are conveyed through images of death that signal the absence of the vital, animating spirits: "hit sleyth myne harte" (10.58, 699, not in the French), says Tristram on hearing the account of Lamorak's death. In men as in women, breath signals the truth of feeling: the swoon conveys the most profound emotion.[29] Inaction, paradoxically, reflects the extreme action of the vital spirits, the rush of breath into the heart that removes consciousness.

The movement of breath in the passions of Tristram, Palomides, Isode, Lamorak and Morgause forms a counterpoint to the exertion of breath in battle. Sir Palomides offers the most extreme example, repeatedly discovered weeping and crying on account of his love, and sitting "as he had slepe," "in suche a study" that he fails to hear the instruction

---

[27] In the French, seeing her laughter and beauty, "sa force li croist et double," *PT*, 5.202, 285.

[28] In the French Iseut is "so angered and so upset at Palomides' spite that she might have died from grief," "ele estoit tant irie et tant courecie durement c'a poi que ele ne moroit de doeil," *PT* 5.247, 334; similarly, at Tristan's battle with Palomides, she is "tant dolente et tant courecie," *PT* 5.248, 335; on seeing Palomides, "ele n'a oeil dont el puisse regarder Palamidés sans felonnie," *PT* 5.255, 343.

[29] Raluca L. Radulescu contrasts the "noble reaction" of "swooning and shedding of tears" to the dangers of "excessive feeling" in "'Oute of mesure': Violence and Knighthood in Malory's *Morte Darthur*," in *Re-Viewing Le Morte Darthur: Texts and Contexts, Characters and Themes*, ed. K. S. Whetter and Raluca L. Radelescu, Arthurian Studies 60 (Cambridge: Brewer, 2005), 119–31 at 126.

to take up his harness: "he slepe or ellys he was madde," Governal reports to Tristan (Malory's addition, 8.31, 424).[30] Sorrow is also manifest in the frenzied movement of breath outwards, comparable to madness, again Malory's additions: "he was nyghehonde araged oute of hys wytte," "romynge and cryynge as a man oute of hys mynde" (9.35–36, 535–36 [Caxton "rorynge"]).[31] In Palomides's anger and sorrow at the reprimand he receives for concealing his identity in the tournament of Lonezep, he "wayled and wepte oute of mesure," "wacch[ing]" all night, and is discovered with the marks of tears on his cheeks. While Malory abbreviates overall, he again heightens the manifestation of emotion (10.78, 758).[32] Most striking is the moment when Palomides catches sight of his reflection in a well and sees "how he was discolowred and defaded, a nothynge lyke as he was" (10.86, 779).[33] An extended account in the French is encapsulated in the description of Palomides as "hevyar ... day be day" (10.86, 779)—more and more melancholy, as the spirits press on his heart, causing the loss of colour and animation. Though here and elsewhere Malory reduces the descriptions of Palomides's illness and pain, his narrative points up the embodied experience of the withdrawal of the spirits in extreme emotion. At the same time, Palomides remains "well-breathed," one of the greatest knights of prowess, both enemy of and companion to Tristram, their successive battles ultimately resolved in friendship. The crucial ability to balance exertion and control of breath is shadowed by the overpowering affects of desire—yet it is also passion that literally inspires and enables Palomides.

The extreme play of breath in jousting and tournaments finds its inverse too in the heightened passions of Tristram and Lancelot, which reach their height in episodes of madness. Malory considerably adapts as well as abbreviates the narrative of Tristram's madness, again conveyed through the dramatic movements of breath. The traumatic revelation of Tristram's marriage to Isode les Blanches Mains occasions grief so great that he swoons, falling from his horse and making such sorrow for three days and nights that he is "allmoste oute of hys mynde" (9.18, 495). While the French similarly places much emphasis on Tristan's grief (weeping, wailing, sighing, and near-madness), the swoon for three days and nights, which leads directly into his madness, is apparently Malory's invention.[34] His response is precisely mirrored in Isode's as she falls in shock "to the earth" at the revelation and lies sick in bed, "makynge the grettyste dole that ever

---

30 In the French, Palomides "pensoit si durement que a poines savoit il ou il estoit"; Governal "cuide bien qu'il se dorme," but here, himself wakes Palomides from his deep thought, *RT* 2.508, 112–13.

31 Cf. French "durement iriés," *PT* 2.195, 351; "il plouroit mout tenrement et a chief de piece jete un souspir grant et lonc et de parfont cuer," *PT* 2.196, 353.

32 In the French, "il em pleure mout tenrement et en cel plourer s'endort dusc' a l'endemain," *PT* 5.272, 358.

33 Malory's balanced, alliterative prose heightens the effect of the French, "Pale se vit et maigre si merveilleusement qu'il se merveille a soi meïsmes que sa force estoit devenue," *PT* 6.22, 95.

34 Malory enhances the French: "il chiet arrieres toz envers," "he fell down backwards," *RT* 3.857, 158, trans. Curtis, 218.

ony erthly woman made" (9.18, 495); Malory places the descriptions of the lovers' grief within a few lines of each other, whereas the extended account of Iseut's suicidal despair occurs later in the French.[35] The verbal patterning with its repeated articulations of high affect, the breathing of grief so great that it causes unconsciousness, runs through the narrative in the manner of a musical motif.

Breath is differently evoked in Malory's detailed account of the discovery that the sick man rescued from the forest is Tristram himself. His identity is revealed not by his face but his "savoure," recognized by the queen's brachet (9.21, 501). In Malory's most extended addition to the French *Tristan* romance, he recounts Tristram's recognition of Isode, "he knew her well inowe, and than he turned away hys vysage and wepte" (9.21, 501), and offers a strikingly realistic description of the dog's response, whining, licking, "quest[ing]," "she smelled at hys feete and at hys hondis and on all the partyes of hys body that she myght com to" (9.21, 501–2)—a poignant evocation of the *pneuma* that surrounds the individual, though sensed only by animals.

The extreme affects of passion are similarly manifest in Lancelot when he is deceived into sleeping for a second time with Elaine of Corbenic.[36] He responds with a sudden withdrawal of spirits, first falling into a swoon and then into madness. Like Isode, Guinevere weeps in response "as she were wood," falling "in a dede sowne" (9.9, 808, not in the French). Lancelot's awakening in the presence of the Grail combines "miracle" with the realism of breathing, "he groned and syghed, and complayned hym sore of hys woodnes" (12.4, 824, not in the French). The physicality of deeds of arms is balanced by the bodiliness of feeling: the best of knights both fight and love to the utmost. The exertions of battle are rivalled by those of love and both are animated by and reflected in breath. The peculiar combination of exertion and control that defines battle-play, however, has no place in the overwhelming play of the individual passions.

Battles of the Spirit

In the "Tale of the Sankgreal," battle is fought on a different plane, between the forces of good and evil and over the human soul. Divine *pneuma* becomes visible, the veil between celestial and earthly is lifted. Malory enhances the sensory quality of the Grail to emphasize the emanation of spiritual presence from it and its power over human breath. In the events leading up to the Grail Quest, mortally wounded, Percival and Ector are healed by the passing of the Grail, "wyth all maner of swetnesse and savoure";

---

35 In the Prose *Tristan*, Iseut is not present when Tristan challenges Kahedin, and wishes to "escuser et raconter li la verité de ceste chose," "justify herself and tell him [Tristan] the truth about the whole matter"; her swoon occurs later as a result of a maiden's news that Tristan is certainly dead, *RT* 3.840, 143, trans. Curtis, 206; for Iseut's despair, see *RT* 3.876–940, 177–235, trans. Curtis, 234–69.

36 This and the subsequent episodes leading up to the Grail Quest draw on a section of the *Prose Tristan* borrowed from the *Prose Lancelot*: references are to *PT* and *L-G* 5: pt. 5 and 6.

its "savour" is experienced by Lancelot at Pelles's castle (9.14, 816, 11.2, 793).[37] The Grail appears in the court at Pentecost, the occasion of the descent of the Holy Spirit, accompanied by a great wind and "good odoures" as well as thunder, lightning, and marvellous sustenance: its "blast" takes from all "breth to speke" (13.7, 865); in the French, there is no reference to breath.[38] Images of air and flame recur, as when Gawain and Ector see a hand carrying a clearly burning candle, representing "the Holy Goste" (16.4, 948).[39] In the Quest, the workings of the Holy Spirit are embodied and felt.

The Quest makes visible and tangible the spirit world of the air not normally seen; the movements of its demonic and angelic occupants who battle over the soul are marked too by winds, cloud, and smoke. Percival's temptress arrives in a black ship "saylyng in the see as all the wynde of the worlde had dryven it," her pavilion collapses in "a smooke and a blak clowde," and she disappears into the burning water "with the wynde, rorynge and yellynge" (14.8–10, 915–19).[40] The winds of the devil are balanced by the mysterious winds of providence that guide the ships in which the Grail knights sail: they arrive at the ship of Faith when "the wynde arose and drove hem thorow the see into a mervayles place" and are driven on "a grete pace" (17.2, 984, 17.7, 995); Malory heightens the sense of marvel from the French.[41] On the Grail ship, Lancelot is sustained only by air, experiencing sweetness and fulfilment, "he was susteyned with the grace of the Holy Goste" (17.13, 1011). Embodied vision reaches its height at the Castle of Corbenic: divine *pneuma* is made manifest when at the consecration the knights see Christ emanating from the Grail. In the face of such presence, however, human breath, and the "dedly fleysh" cannot ultimately be sustained: Galahad begins "to tremble ryght harde," and in response to his prayer his soul is carried into heaven (17.22, 1034). This

---

37 In the French, Lancelot experiences "les boines odours," *PT* 6.32, 119, "sweet scents," *L-G* 5, 101, but in the episode of Percival and Hector, only brightness and wonder are described, *PT* 6.65, 182–83, *L-G* 6, 417.

38 Malory's "Tale of the Sankgreal" closely follows the Vulgate *Queste del Saint Graal*, but abbreviates the detail, in particular, the allegorical explanations, while heightening sympathy for Lancelot. References are to the edition of Albert Pauphilet, *La Queste del Saint Graal: Roman du XIIIe Siècle* (Paris: Honoré Champion, 1965), cited as *Queste*, by page number; to which *L-G* 6: *The Quest for the Holy Grail*, trans. E. Jane Burns, is keyed. See also the more recent edition of Fanni Bogdanow, with a modern French translation by Anne Berrie, *La Quête du Saint-Graal: Roman en Prose du XIIIe Siècle*, Lettres Gothiques (Paris: Librairie Générale Française, 2006). The Grail brings with it "si bones odors come se totes les espices terriennes i fussent espandues," "a delicious fragrance, as if every earthly spice had been strewn there"; all are rendered silent "come bestes mues," "like mute beasts" (*Queste* 15, *L-G* 6, 12).

39 The French emphasizes the burning of charity, set afire by the Holy Spirit, *Queste* 160, *L-G* 6, 99.

40 Cf. French, "une si grant tempeste," "a great whirlwind"; "une fumee et une nublece," "smoke and fog"; "si bruiant," "making a loud racket," *Queste* 110, *L-G* 6, 68–69.

41 Cf. French, "Et maintenant començe la nef a aler grant aleure parmi la mer, car li venz se feroit enz granz," "Then the ship began to sail swiftly out to sea, propelled by a strong wind," *Queste* 199–200, *L-G* 6, 123; "et li venz se fu feruz ou voile, qui tost les ot esloigniez de la roche," "the wind caught the sail and carried them away from the cliff," *Queste* 229, *L-G* 6, 141.

quest requires sacrifices far beyond those of secular prowess. The world of the Grail is one not of peace but of profound conflict against the forces of the flesh, as well as between the angelic and the demonic.

The affects of that conflict are most dramatically written on the body and breath of Lancelot. Repeatedly, his vital spirits withdraw into the heart, effecting a swooning or trance-like state in response to the divine *pneuma*. Thus, unable to enter the chapel he comes upon, he is "hevy and dysmayed" (13.17, 894): the emphasis on heaviness of the spirits is original to Malory.[42] The effect is to reduce breath so that, lying "half wakyng and half slepynge," he sees the Grail but has no power to move (13.18.894)—affects that he interprets as the result of his "olde synne": "I had no power to stirre nother speke whan the holy bloode appered before me" (13.19, 896, not in the French).[43] Only within a swoon does Lancelot achieve the vision of the Grail. At the Castle of Corbenic, he sees into the Grail chamber, but on trying to enter is struck to the ground by a fiery breath (17.16, 1015–16). The vital spirits are so overcome that they withdraw completely, removing breath and consciousness. Whereas in the *Queste*, Lancelot is aware of people moving his body, here his swoon is absolute: he lies "stylle as a dede man" for twenty-four nights. Yet this is also a visionary state in which "grete mervayles" are seen "opynly" (17.16, 1016–17). By contrast to the French, which stresses the defilement of his sight by sin, the words of Malory's Lancelot characterize the swoon as a space of revelation, "there where no synner may be" (cf. *Queste* 258; *L-G* 6, 157). The swoon is a positive rewriting of the earlier sinful sleep, an extreme movement of breath that opens onto spiritual revelation. The Grail books end with this redemptive vision onto the sublime, but also with the finality of loss of breath in the deaths of Perceval, Galahad, and many of the knights, and with Galahad's prayer that Lancelot remember "thys unsyker worlde" (17.23, 1036; not in the French)—looking forward ominously to the death books that follow.

The Heaviest Tidings

As the final books of the *Morte* return to the unstable earthly world, all these aspects of breath come together. The later books engage in part with the question of how, in battles against Lancelot, the principle of might is right can be enacted, when Lancelot, identified much earlier by Sir Tarquin as "the byggyst man that ever I mette withall, and the beste-brethed" (6.8, 266; not in the French), is necessarily the best of all earthly knights.[44]

---

[42] Cf. French, "tant dolenz," "with great sadness," *Queste* 58, *L-G* 6, 37.

[43] Cf. French, "en tel point que il ne dormoit bien ne ne veilloit bien," "ausi come entransés," "in that dreamy state between waking and sleep," "in a trance-like state," *Queste* 58, *L-G* 6, 38; here, Lancelot laments the misfortune resulting from "mes pechiez et ma mauvese vie," "my sins and wicked life," blaming the devil for his blindness, *Queste* 61, *L-G* 6, 40.

[44] In the Prose *Lancelot*, Tericam simply describes Lancelot as "li mieldres chevaliers que je onques trouvasse, puis que primes portai escu," "the best knight I've met since first I bore a shield," *Lancelot: roman en prose du XIIIe siécle*, ed. Alexandre Micha, 9 vols., Textes Littéraires Français (Geneva: Librairie Droz, 1978–83), 5.lxxxv.41, 29, *L-G* 5.v, 197.

When he searches Urry's wounds, an episode original to Malory, divine *pneuma* speaks through his hands, but in his love for the queen divinity of spirit is separated from physical strength of breath and disorder occurs. Most of all breath is connected in these books with passion and loss, written on the body in extreme ways.

The death of Elaine of Astolat makes visible the profound connection between breath and feeling, mind, body, and affect. In an extended account not present in the French, Elaine's response to Lancelot's rejection of her love is characterized by high affect manifest in the extreme movements of breath: shrill shrieks and swoons, wasting away through the withdrawal of the spirits, and finally, death.[45] Breath is central to her perception of being:

> Why sholde I leve such thoughtes? Am I nat an erthely woman? And all the whyle the brethe ys in my body I may complayne me, for my belyve ys that I do no offence, though I love an erthely man, unto God, for He fourmed me thereto, and all maner of good love comyth of God. And othir than good love loved I never sir Launcelot du Lake.
>
> (18.19, 1093)

Breath signifies life and feeling, but also the ability to speak, interpret, and exercise intellect. The notion of love that is natural, arising from the "harte selff" (18.20, 1097; not in the French), is one of Malory's great subjects, and it is the playing out of such affect cognitively and physically that shapes the pattern of the narrative. At its extremes, it is all consuming: Isode too dies swooning on the corpse of Sir Tristram (19.11, 1150; not in the French). Yet however destructive love may be, feeling not demonstrated in affect is condemned: Morgan, for example, "kepte hir countenaunce" at her lover Accolon's death, denying the "sembelaunte of dole" (4.14, 150).[46] Such inhibition of the vital spirits denotes the illicit and the malign; unnaturalness and conscious manipulation of feeling are invariably seen negatively by Malory.

The final books of the *Morte*, as Raluca Radulescu remarks, are characterized by "extreme passions": being "oute of mesure" "gradually becomes the dominant mode of the entire narrative"; " 'oute of mesure' becomes the unique measure of extreme anger and sorrow, as the two main dimensions of doom."[47] Lack of measure in feeling fuels the inexorable downward spiral of violence and warfare. The overwhelming emphasis of the denouement, however, is not on battle but on the breathing out of sorrow. These are

---

45 References to the *Mort Artu* are from the edition of Jean Frappier, *La Mort le Roi Artu*, Textes Littéraires Français (Geneva: Droz, 1964), cited by page number; which is keyed to *L-G* 7: *The Death of Arthur*, trans. Norris J. Lacy.

46 In the French, Morgan adopts "la bele chiere," "cheerful manner" to conceal her grief, treating the message as a joke, *Merlin* 2, 217, *L-G* 8, 201.

47 Radulescu, "Oute of mesure," 126, 130, and see further her discussion of public tears, "Tears and Lies: Emotions and the Ideals of Malory's Arthurian World," *Emotions in Medieval Arthurian Literature*, 105–21. In relation to the last books, Lynch argues that "a change occurs in the valuation of affective reactions and gestures generally, which could be said … to re-evaluate the 'feminine' status of certain affective gestures outside the realm of male combat"; he notes too the reduction of descriptions of battle within these books, *Malory's Book of Arms*, 155.

desolate books, their depictions of deep grief heightened through Malory's use of the Stanzaic *Morte*: Gawain's and Arthur's "criyng and wepyng," and swoons at the deaths of Gareth and Gaheris (20.10, 1185); Arthur's tears at Lancelot's "curtesy"and the return of Guinevere, which causes "many a wepyng ien" (20.13–14, 1192–96; Malory's account is much extended).[48] Most of all, Malory elaborates not the war within the fellowship but the emotions occasioned by it, and especially Lancelot's grief and its affects. His awareness of his conflicted being is memorably depicted in his searching of Urry's wounds, which causes him to weep "as he had bene a chylde that had bene beatyn" (19.12, 1152–53). His offer of penance following the deaths of Gareth and Gaheris is so moving that "all the knyghtes and ladyes that were there wepte as they were madde, and the tearys fell on kynge Arthur hys chekis" (20.17, 1200); his lament, he "syghed, and therewith the tearys felle on hys chekys, and than he seyde …" is echoed in "sobbyng and wepyng for pure dole" at his departure (20.17, 1201–2).[49] The weight of the spirits on the heart is evoked by his "hevynes" (20.17, 1203; not in sources). Lancelot's attempt to effect a treaty, "for better ys pees than allwayes warre" (20.19, 1212), a line original to Malory, is especially memorable, provoking Arthur's tears; Gawain's insistence on revenge provokes tears of regret in the damsel who brings the offer and "many a wepyng yghe"; Lancelot's tears "ran downe by hys chekys" (20.20, 1213–14).[50] The repetitions of these images of the moving of the spirits underscores Lancelot's profound feeling, and casts Gawain's persistence in revenge in firmly negative terms despite the grief caused by the death of his brothers.

Now the strength that raised questions about Lancelot's might in battle is portrayed in terms of virtue, as he holds his ground against Gawain during the period that his strength increases: he "kepte hys myght and hys brethe duryng three owrys"; Gawain seems "a fyende and none earthely man" (20.21, 1217). The emphasis on retaining the quality of breath, rather than catching breath, is Malory's own.[51] It is as if physical breath and *pneuma* once again coincide in Lancelot. When the scene is repeated, an episode

---

48 References to the Stanzaic *Morte Arthur* are from Benson, ed., *King Arthur's Death*, 1–111, cited by line number as *SMA*. Arthur's words in Malory, "Alas, alas, that ever yet thys warre began!," 20.13, 1192, echo those in the Stanzaic *Morte* at Lancelot's departure, 2442–43; at the return of the Queen, "weeping stood there many a knight," *SMA* 2379.

49 Lancelot's offer of penance is not in the French *Mort*; the Stanzaic *Morte* places Arthur's lament, "'Alas!' With sighing sore, 'That ever yet this war began!'" here, 2442–43; Lancelot's lament is elaborated from French in which he laments "si basset," "softly," so that only Bors hears, *Mort* 162, *L-G* 7, 85, but his "si grant duel et merveillex" inspires "pitié" in the onlookers, "he began to grieve so terribly that no one could see him without being moved to pity," *Mort* 163, *L-G* 7, 86; Malory also draws on *SMA* "dole and weeping sore," 2458.

50 The episode is elaborated from the Stanzaic *Morte*, which also does not include the details of tears, though the maiden's heart is "drery," 2701.

51 In the French, by contrast, at noon Lancelot "fu il auques reposez et ot reprise sa force et s'aleinne," "he was able to rest a little and regain his strength and breath," *Mort* 200, *L-G* 7, 103; in the Stanzaic *Morte*, he awaits his "venture" and "endure[s]" many blows, 2811–12.

not in the French *Mort*, Lancelot again "wythhylde hys corayge and hys wynde" until the period of Gawain's increasing "wynde" and superhuman strength is past (20.22, 1220); the references to breath are not in the Stanzaic *Morte*. The balance of exertion and control exemplified by Lancelot finds its opposite in Gawain's lack of measure, despite his superhuman strength. Being well-breathed signals not only physical but moral virtue—paradoxically, in the knight whose own passion is the ultimate cause of the fall of the kingdom. By contrast to Lancelot, who retains breath, Gawain repeatedly falls and swoons, struck on his old wound—a prescient image of his death, when he is discovered lying in a great boat, "liynge more than halff dede." While in the sources Gawain is already dead, here Arthur's grief and the emotive drama are heightened by his "thryse" swooning as he clasps Gawain in his arms to bid him farewell while the breath leaves his body (21.2, 1230).[52]

With the death of Gawain, the book returns briefly to the ethos of the Grail Quest, as Arthur experiences a vision "nat slepynge nor thorowly waykynge" (21.3, 1233), a phrase unique to Malory that echoes descriptions of vision in the Quest—but within the very different context of civil war. Despite the fact that Gawain's visitation to warn against the battle is allowed by God's "speciall grace" (21.3, 1234; not in sources), the truce is shattered when a soldier draws his sword to kill an adder. The still, restorative breath of sleep, with its opening onto the divine *pneuma*, is replaced by the breath of battle, a return to much earlier in the book: "than they blewe beamys, trumpettis, and hornys, and shoutted grymly; and so bothe ostis dressed hem togydirs" (21.4, 1235); Malory's account is based on the Stanzaic *Morte* and further abbreviated, but the noise of battle is his addition, and he heightens too the intimate connection between breath, the bodily spirits, and emotion. Arthur's prowess is demonstrated by his ability to sustain his vital spirits, "at all tymes he faynted never," until he is dealt his death blow and "felle in a swoughe to the erthe, and there he sowned oftyntymys"; lifted by the dying Lucan, both swoon (21.4, 1236–37).[53] The emphasis of both Arthur and the ladies who arrive by barge is on the cold of the body as the spirits withdraw into the heart: "I have takyn colde"; "Alas, thys wounde on youre hede hath caught overmuch coulde!" (21.5, 1239–40); while the dialogue is drawn from the Stanzaic *Morte*, neither English nor French sources include this affect of the vital spirits. Now, breath causes not the noise of battle but the weeping and shrieking of the ladies, and the weeping and wailing of Bedivere, who swoons on Arthur's tomb (21.6, 1241).[54] The news of the battle of Barham Down is "the hevyest tydyngis that ever cam to [Launcelot's] harte," and he lies

---

52 In the Stanzaic *Morte*, Gawain is already dead, and Arthur's heart "An hundreth times ... nigh brast," 3135; in the French, Arthur "en pleure, et fet grant duel, et se pasme seur lui souvent et menu," "wept and lamented loudly and fainted repeatedly over the body," *Mort* 221, *L-G* 7, 114.

53 The description draws on the Stanzaic *Morte*, "three times he swooned there," 3399; but the graphic account of Lucan's death is original to Malory.

54 In the Stanzaic *Morte*, Bedivere falls to the ground in grief, 3549; in the *Mort Artu* Girflet "se pasme desus la tombe," "fainted upon the tomb," *Mort* 251, *L-G* 7, 129.

two nights on Gawain's tomb "in dolefull wepynge" (21.8, 1250–51); his lament on the tomb is Malory's addition.[55]

Swoons, the most extreme expression of grief, are repeated: Guinevere swoons three times at seeing Lancelot; both lament "as they had be stungyn wyth sperys, and many tymes they swouned"; Lancelot departs, weeping (21.9–10, 1251–54): while the details are drawn from the Stanzaic *Morte*, the physicality and the number of swoons are heightened. It is indeed a hard-hearted reader who does not feel the affective weight. Arriving at the hermitage and hearing Bedivere's story, Lancelot's heart "almost braste for sorowe" (21.10, 1254), a detail drawn from the Stanzaic *Morte*. Yet the breath of lament is also a turning towards heavenly things. In the account of Guinevere's death and Lancelot's grief, original to Malory despite his mention of the French book, tears are in part restrained: on seeing Guinevere's face, "he wepte not gretelye, but syghed" (21.11, 1256). Recollection of his part in the fall of the kingdom, however, causes Lancelot's vital spirits to withdraw: "[the memory] sanke so to myn herte that I myght not susteyne myself" (21.11, 1256); he swoons on Guinevere's coffin.

In this desolate, post-war world, as in the Grail Quest, affect is also consciously written on the body in actions of penance and abstinence: Lancelot's vital spirits gradually withdraw as he fasts: "he seekened more and more and dryed and dwyned awaye" (21.12, 1257; details are much heightened from those in the Stanzaic *Morte*, 3832–35). Lament and privation are countered in death, however, both by the bishop's laughter and vision of Lancelot in heaven, and by the affects of holiness, elaborated by Malory: "he laye as he had smyled, and the swettest savour aboute hym that ever they felte" (21.12, 1258).[56] Breath is transformed from grief to joy, and once again, the divine *pneuma* is made manifest. In death, the vital spirits have moved out of the heart, to be positively seen and felt through joyfulness of expression and sweetness of smell, and to coincide with heavenly breath. Malory depicts the affects of the deepest grief at the end of the book: "wepynge and wryngyng of handes, and the grettest dole they made that ever made men" (21.12, 1258).[57] Yet grief is combined with profoundly positive spiritual affect, the wonder of sanctity and redemption, as the perspective shifts from earthly ruin to celestial joy, from the breath of earthly life to that of the spirit.

In Malory's great canvas of peace and war, breath is a constant. From the establishment of the kingdom in the battle against Rome, won by Arthur's well-breathed knights, to the marking of individual prowess through excellence of breath, breath is integral to prowess. Breath articulates and makes visible emotion, in joy, but most of all in laments,

---

55 In the French, Lancelot is "moult corrouciez," "very distraught," *Mort* 252, *L-G* 7, 130; and the Stanzaic *Morte* asks, "What wonder though his heart were sore?," 3575.

56 The description elaborates on the Stanzaic *Morte*, "Red and fair of flesh and blood," 3888, a line echoed in the description of Guinevere's body, 3956.

57 The description is heightened from the Stanzaic *Morte*, "There was none but his handes wrang" (3916), perhaps drawing on the *Mort Artu*, "oïssiez entor le cors si grant duel et si grant noise qu'a peinnes i oïst on Dieu tonnant," "around the body you could have heard such grieving and sobbing that scarcely could one have heard God's thunder," 262, *L-G* 7, 135.

sighs, and swoons. The movements of breath mark the greatness both in love and war of Malory's protagonists—Lancelot, Tristram, Lamorak, Palomides. Passion and prowess prove to be intimately connected. The sphere of conflict shifts as romantic feeling finds a counterpart in spiritual vision, and the bodily spirits are rewritten as divine *pneuma*. In the Grail Quest, the spiritual is seen and felt in the movements of the air and the embodied experience of vision, through tears, sleep, and swoon—an experience that illuminates the deepest internal conflicts even as it redeems. As the final events of *Le Morte Darthur* unfold, the breath of war returns, but is shot through with that of lament and loss, imaged again and again in tears, sighs, and swoons, but also, finally, with the breath of sanctity. Malory's great book of arms is also a book of breath.

Chapter 9

GIVING AND GAINING VOICE IN CIVIL WAR: ALAIN CHARTIER'S *QUADRILOGUE INVECTIF* IN FIFTEENTH-CENTURY ENGLAND[1]

James Simpson*

THE THREAT AND reality of civil war haunts the entirety of the fifteenth century in England. In this chapter I sketch the way in which powerful works of literature rehearse that fear of future civil war; represent the reality of civil war as it happens; and imagine political solutions from within the experience of civil war. The substance of my argument focuses, however, on two independent translations of the same remarkable text by Alain Chartier, *Le Quadrilogue Invectif* (1422), each made most probably in the late 1460s.[2]

Fifteenth-century English literary and para-literary works rehearse the tragedy of civil war, either as pre-civil war admonition, or as literary expression of grief for the peculiar pain of civil war as it happens, or as inventive political theory designed to avoid the terrible predicament of civil war. The *Le Quadrilogue Invectif* translations certainly express the pain of civil war as it is happening; and they are, indeed, in part political theory. The aspect of these translations on which I focus here, however, is their dramatic performativity. They model the way voices and texts, and especially *this* set of voices and *this* text, can gain traction in the muddled and fractured discursive conditions that civil war necessarily produces. The English translations do so by directly applying the catastrophic French experience of civil division in the 1420s to the no less violently divided situation of England in the 1460s.

I

In the works of Thomas Malory, the Arthurian kingdom is haunted by the fate of Balan, the hero and victim of the second narrative in the very first sequence of stories of this

---

* **James Simpson** is Donald P. and Katherine B. Loker Professor of English at Harvard University. He is the author of *Reform and Cultural Revolution*, being volume 2 in the *Oxford English Literary History* (2002); *Burning to Read: English Fundamentalism and its Reformation Opponents* (2007); *Under the Hammer: Iconoclasm in the Anglo-American Tradition* (2010); and *Permanent Revolution: The Reformation and the Illiberal Roots of Liberalism* (2019).

1 I dedicate this chapter to my much-admired friend Andrew Lynch, an excellent scholar, ever-generous colleague, and deeply wise soul.

2 *Fifteenth-century English Translations of Alain Chartier's "Le Traité d'Esperance" and "Le Quadrilogue Invectif,"* ed. M. S. Blayney, Early English Text Society, o.s. 270, 281, 2 vols. (Oxford: Oxford University Press, 1974, 1980).

long work. In a story of unmitigated disaster and consistently malign chance,[3] Balan unwittingly kills his own brother Balyn. Not only are their names nearly indistinguishable, but after their fight so too are their very faces unrecognizable: Balan lifts the visor of his moribund brother, but he "myght not knowe hym by the vysage, it was so ful hewen and bledde."[4]

Civil war produces the horror of disfiguring essential sources of recognition. English military policy in the fifteenth century is frequently focused on avoiding this terrible eventuality. Fifteenth-century English literary writing is frequently focused on expressing the horror of that eventuality.

One standard way of avoiding civil war was to make external war.[5] A speech made on behalf of Edward IV to the Commons in 1472 makes this point concisely. The speech is made after 18 years of civil war, in which two English kings have been deposed, one of whom has been murdered. In 1472 Edward IV, who had returned from his deposition in 1470, is now secure as king, but only, the speaker insists, so long as he declares war on France. No-one has escaped the trouble of recent history, the speaker begins, but now the problem is "rotely taken awey and extincte, so that there can be lefte no colowr or shadowe ... in any mannys mynde but that our Soverayn Lord is in dede ... sole and undoubted Kyng." No sooner does he make this affirmation, however, than he qualifies its confidence: there is many a "perilous wounde left unheled," and the kingdom is full of "the multitude of riotous people." Considering the inveterate nature and extensiveness of this violence, the speaker concedes that the "rigour of the lawe" should not be applied, since it would result in the decimation of the population, and render the realm vulnerable to foreign attack by the Scots, Danes, and French. No, the only solution is to set the riotous and idle multitude, under the leadership of the king, the lords, and the "Gentils," to the work of "werre outward," in which many "gentilmen, as well yonger brothers as other, myght there be worshipfully rewarded." War will best serve for "pacifieng of the londe inwards," since,

> be it well remembred, how that it is nat wele possible, nor hath ben seen since the Conquest, that justice, peax, and prosperite hath contenued any while in this lande in any Kings dayes but in suche as have made werre outward.[6]

Awareness of the intimate relation between "werre outward" and the "pacifieng of the londe inwards" also shapes literary texts across the fifteenth century in England. This is true from the beginning of the century, as we can see in the Alliterative *Morte*

---

3 For which see Jill Mann, "'Taking the Adventure': Malory and the *Suite du Merlin*," in *Aspects of Malory*, ed. Toshiyuki Takamiya and Derek Brewer, Arthurian Studies 1 (Cambridge: Brewer, 1981), 71–91.

4 Sir Thomas Malory, *Le Morte Darthur*, ed. Stephen H. A. Shepherd (New York: Norton, 2004), 60.

5 For many examples of which, see Catherine Nall, *Reading and War in Fifteenth-Century England: From Lydgate to Malory* (Cambridge: Brewer, 2012), 139–58.

6 *Literae Cantuarienses*, ed. J. Brigstocke Sheppard, Rolls Series, 3 vols. (London: Her Majesty's Stationery Office, 1889), 3:274–85 at 282.

Arthure, probably composed around 1400, but copied between 1420 and 1440 by Robert Thornton, a member of the minor Yorkshire gentry.[7] If there are historical resonances in this representation, they would seem to be designed to evoke the continental victories—"war outward"—of that Arthurian enthusiast, Edward III.[8] But just as the poet draws on textual sources from different periods of English military history,[9] so too does he insist that victory in external war can be the very thing that prompts civil war.

For, from the moment that Arthur is about to be crowned emperor in Rome, he plunges into civil war, reminiscent of the period 1369 forwards. By 1372–1373 most of the gains of French territory made by 1360 had been lost again, and were not regained before the end of Richard II's reign (and not before England had suffered a minor civil war in 1387, by the Lords Appellant against the reigning king, Richard II).[10] In the Alliterative *Morte*, Arthur dies not at the hands of a foreign enemy, but rather by the hand of his nephew Mordred, whom Arthur also kills.[11] The poem's basic matter, all ultimately derived from Geoffrey of Monmouth's *Historia Regum Britanniae* (ca. 1138), is here finally disallowed a propagandistic use. Instead, the work brings to the fore the dynastic fragilities inherent in feudal polities—fragilities frequently represented in Geoffrey's own narrative. As Lee Patterson has said, the Galfridian material "never lost its capacity to call into question the very purpose for which it was designed."[12] If narratives in the *Historia Regum Britanniae* are framed by imperial conquest, their substance is frequently characterized instead by civil war.

Lydgate's *Troy Book* (1412–1420) might also present itself as a narrative of foreign war, but is ultimately no less about civil implosion. As the situation within Troy degrades under the pressure of external war, the city is finally lost as a result of internecine division within Troy itself. In Book 4, the space for rational, prudential conciliar argument gives way to the sinister manipulation of aristocratic lords capable of waging civil war against their king. Antenor and Aeneas both forestall Priam's plot to assassinate them by appearing in council surrounded by henchmen. They out-manoeuvre Priam in swaying

---

7 For information on Robert Thornton, see John J. Thompson, *Robert Thornton and the London Thornton Manuscript* (Woodbridge: Brewer, 1987), 2–5.

8 For the evidence, see William Matthews, *The Tragedy of Arthur: A Study of the Alliterative "Morte Arthure"* (Berkeley: University of California Press, 1960), 184–87. This does not invalidate an early fifteenth-century date for the poem, for which see Larry D. Benson, "The Date of the Alliterative Morte Arthure," in *Medieval Studies in Honour of Lillian Herlands Hornstein*, ed. Jess Bessinger and Robert R. Raymo (New York: New York University Press, 1976), 19–40.

9 For the many sources, both Latin and vernacular, of this poem, see *Morte Arthure: A Critical Edition*, ed. Mary Hamel, Garland Medieval Texts 9 (New York: Garland, 1984), 34–53.

10 For the military history of these years, see Maurice. H. Keen, *England in the Later Middle Ages: A Political History* (London: Methuen, 1973), 251–90.

11 *A Critical Edition*, ed. Hamel, lines 4227–53.

12 Lee Patterson, "The Romance of History and the Alliterative *Morte Arthure*," in *Negotiating the Past, The Historical Understanding of Medieval Literature* (Madison: University of Wisconsin Press, 1987), 203.

the popular decision, and so seal the destruction of the city, which then happens very quickly (4.4440–5098).

Troy falls, then, not primarily through military weakness: the crucial events happen not on the battlefield but in the council-chamber. Civil implosion is a much more significant factor than military action in the overall destruction of the city. And civil implosion also overtakes the Greeks, who fall victim to assassination by apparent allies on their return home. Book 5, which recounts the return of the victorious Greeks, contains by far the most savage and internecine narratives of the whole work.

Lydgate's *Siege of Thebes* (?1423) is more directly about the horror of civil war, which produces military invasion from outside. The text, which is proximately dependent on the twelfth-century *Roman de Thebes*, recounts the story of Thebes from its foundation by Amphion until its destruction by Theseus. After narrating the story of Oedipus, we turn to the fraternal strife between Polynices and Etiocles, both competing for governance of Thebes. The main action of the story concerns the Argive mission, under Adrastus, to enforce a proper exchange of power in Thebes. This mission ends with the destruction of the entire Argive force, as well as of the two warring brothers, before the city itself is utterly destroyed by Theseus. Foreign invasion is rendered possible, not to say simple, by internal division.

Lydgate's story is told by the monk Lydgate on a fictionalized extension of *The Canterbury Tales*, now heading back to London. The back-to-London tale ends narratively precisely where the tale of Chaucer's Knight had begun on the first story out from London, with the destruction of Thebes by Theseus. So in this extended version of *The Canterbury Tales*, events that happen *earlier* than those of the *Knight's Tale* are recounted *after* it. One effect of this is to provide an unsettling reminder that the events of the *Knight's Tale* are but a reflex of the larger destructive, fratricidal patterns that dominate and destroy Thebes.[13] Whereas, however, the fratricidal tendencies of the *Knight's Tale* can be contained by the governance of Theseus and his arena, the same is not true of Lydgate's fifteenth-century prequel: *before* the "civil war" of the *Knight's Tale*, Thebes has already been destroyed by external war, itself prompted by fratricidal hatred and a civil war entirely out of control.

The dating of this text is uncertain, but in my view it was written *after* the death of Henry V in August 1422, precisely by way of warning of the dangers of civil war between Henry V's surviving brothers.[14] The most likely date of composition is when the kingdom of England was divided in an uneasy balance between Henry V's two brothers, John, Duke of Bedford (Regent in France) and Humphrey, Duke of Gloucester (Protector in England while Bedford was in France). The fragility of the situation is evident in the most explicitly apologetic piece of Lydgate's career, *The Title and Pedigree of Henry VI*, translated from a French original under Richard Beauchamp,

---

[13] For which see James Simpson, "'Dysemol daies and Fatal houres': Lydgate's *Destruction of Thebes* and Chaucer's *Knight's Tale*," in *The Long Fifteenth Century: Essays in Honour of Douglas Gray*, ed. Helen Cooper and Sally Mapstone (Oxford: Oxford University Press, 1997), 15–33.

[14] For the date, see Simpson, "'Dysemol daies,'" 16n2.

Earl of Warwick's patronage in 1426. Warwick was acting Regent in France, while the Duke of Bedford was back in England trying to keep his brother and uncle (Cardinal Beaufort) from civil war.[15]

English policy makers and literary writers in the earlier fifteenth century were, then, conscious of the spectre and the reality of civil war as a possibility for England. Because they understood the intimate relation of foreign and civil war, they were also conscious, as we shall see, of the terrible reality of civil war in France between Armagnacs and Burgundians, which had rendered the English victory of 1415 possible. By mid-century, the grim, dialectical logic of foreign and civil war that had so badly weakened France between 1407 and 1429 was to play itself out in England. The lands gained in France by Henry V's conquests had all been lost by 1453; the first battle of the civil war known as the Wars of the Roses occurred in 1455, a period of violent internal fracture that was to last until 1485. This period of civil war produced two sets of texts, by Chief Justice John Fortescue (?1395–?1477) and Thomas Malory (d. 1471), both produced in periods of enforced exile or of imprisonment as a result of civil war activity.

Fortescue was appointed Chief Justice of the King's Bench in 1442. In March 1461, after the Battle of Towton and the defeat of Henry VI's forces, he fled to Scotland to join Henry VI, Margaret and Prince Edward in Edinburgh; later that year he was named in an act of attainder passed against those who had resisted Edward IV. He remained in Scotland until 1463, writing tracts in defence of the Lancastrian legitimacy. In 1463 he accompanied Margaret and Edward to France. In the Scottish period Fortescue wrote *De titulo Edwardi Comitis Marchiae*; "Of the Title of the House of York"; and *Defensio juris domus Lancastriae* (short, polemically driven works designed to bolster shaky Lancastrian claims to the throne, and destroy equally fragile Yorkist claims),[16] and the much more substantial *De natura legis Naturae*. This text is also designed to contribute to the resolution of civil war, but takes the occasion of a feeble king and profound civil strife to formulate a remarkable vernacular account of proto-constitutionalist governance.

Thus Part I of the *De natura legis Naturae* takes a very much broader view of the succession question, by situating it within the terms of the law of Nature itself, which Fortescue defines as "nothing else than the participation of eternal law in a rational creature."[17] In this discussion Fortescue first develops his distinction of polities: the

---

15 For the unsteadiness of this apparently triumphalist attempt to eulogize Henry VI as king of both France and England, see Lee Patterson, "Making Identities in Fifteenth-Century England: Henry V and John Lydgate," in *New Historical Literary Study: Essays on Reproducing Texts, Representing History*, ed. Jeffrey N. Cox and Larry J. Reynolds (Princeton: Princeton University Press, 1993), 69–107 at 92–93.

16 For which see P. E. Gill, "Politics and Propaganda in Fifteenth Century England: The Polemical Writings of Sir John Fortescue," *Speculum* 46 (1971): 333–47, and James Simpson, "Pecock and Fortescue," in *A Companion to Middle English Prose*, ed. A. S. G. Edwards (Woodbridge: Boydell & Brewer, 2004), 271–88 and further references.

17 *De natura legis Naturae*, in John Fortescue, *The Works of Sir John Fortescue*, ed. Lord Clermont (London, 1869), 1.5, 194.

regal, the political, and a third, mixed category, the *dominium regale et politicum*.[18] This political theory stands at the centre of the two works for which Fortescue is best known: the *De laudibus legum Anglie* (1468–1471) written in Latin, and the vernacular *On the Governance of England* (ca. 1471, also known as the *Monarchia*), which was possibly written for Edward IV (once Fortescue had definitively recognized Edward IV as king in 1471).[19] The Latin text is written as a dialogue between Fortescue as Henry VI's Chancellor in exile, and Henry VI's son Prince Edward.

Civil war (and a feeble king) was, then, the occasion for fresh conciliar, if not proto-constitutionalist political theory, fictionalized in the form of a dialogue between counsellor and the next putative king. It was also the broadest motivation for the entire corpus of Malory's *Works*, otherwise known as *Le Morte Darthur* (completed 1469–1470).[20] Malory's works are divided generically from within. The entire set consistently underlines the instabilities within chivalric society that lead to civil war. Arthur's victory over Roman imperial might in the *Lucius* sequence turns out to be a transitory moment of glory in the larger scheme of Malory's work, in which Malory is much more pressingly concerned with civil war. It has been persuasively suggested that the presentation of Arthur in the *Lucius* sequence is designed to recall the victories of Henry V in France between 1415 and 1420;[21] if that is true, then the historical memory of Malory's whole book reveals those continental victories to have been a delusive distraction from the internal threats to fifteenth-century English society.[22]

The very structure of the *Works* points to "war inward," and away from external war. External war dominates the *Lucius* sequence. Before we return to wars conducted outside English territory in the final book, we read romances. The effect of these intervening romances (i.e. Lancelot, Gareth, Tristram, the Holy Grail, Lancelot and Guinevere), before the deferred fall of Arthur in the final book, profoundly modifies the significance of that fall.[23] In the Alliterative *Morte*, Arthur's fall occurs principally

---

[18] See in particular, *De natura legis Naturae*, 1.16. For a larger account of the relation of this treatise to the succession question, see Veikko Litzen, *A War of Roses and Lilies: The Theme of Succession in Sir John Fortescue's Works*, Annales Academiae Scientiarum Fennicae, 173 (Helsinki: Suomalainen Tiedeakatemia, 1971), 29–39.

[19] For the argument that Edward IV was the intended recipient, see John Fortescue, *The governance of England: otherwise called the difference between an absolute and a limited monarchy*, rev. ed., ed. Charles Plummer (Oxford: Clarendon Press, 1885), 94.

[20] For Malory's text in its various historical contexts, see Andrew Lynch, "Malory's *Morte Darthur* and History," in *A Companion to Arthurian Literature*, ed. Helen Fulton (Oxford: Blackwell, 2009), 297–311.

[21] For a summary of the evidence see *The Works of Sir Thomas Malory*, 3:1367–68.

[22] I am unpersuaded by Catherine Nall's argument that Malory has a clear policy of promoting external war as the solution to civil war. Nall, *Reading*, 139–58.

[23] For the relation of Malory's romances to his tragic narratives, see James Simpson, *Reform and Cultural Revolution, 1350–1547*, being volume 2 of *The Oxford English Literary History* (Oxford: Oxford University Press, 2002), chap. 6.

because Arthur is wholly focused on his imperial mission. In Malory's overall structure, by contrast, the intervening romances are decisive, since they generate irresolvable civil tensions between warring aristocratic groups, over which the king has no power.

Lancelot is the king of France; recognizing defeat, his distribution of lands constitutes a remarkably detailed map of south-western France in the fifteenth century, including areas fought over by the English in 1453.[24] Lancelot's leave-taking is certainly nostalgic for those continental claims, but equally a recognition of their futility. In any case, Lancelot's leave-taking, despite its catalogue of foreign conquests, is represented as much more an act of *civil* fragmentation, provoked ultimately by Lancelot's adulterous relationship with the queen, and immediately by Gawain's relentless pursuit of Lancelot for having accidentally murdered his brother. From the perspective of the end of Malory's book, the apparent triumphalism of Arthur's imperial conquest turns out to look like a distraction, a victory whose simplicities are revealed by the infinitely more dangerous business of managing magnates internally. External war can defer, but not finally extinguish the ever-present dangers of civil war.

II

Alain Chartier (ca. 1385–1433) wrote the *Quadrilogue Invectif* (1422) from his position as secretary to the disenfranchised Dauphin (to whom admiring reference is made in the *Quadrilogue*),[25] after the Treaty of Troyes (1420). France had been subject to civil war between Burgundian and Armagnac parties since the assassination of the king's brother, Louis d'Orleans, in 1407 at the instance of John the Fearless, leader of the Burgundian party (himself to be assassinated in 1419). Internal division rendered France vulnerable to English incursion, so facilitating English victory at Agincourt (1415) and the disenfranchisement of the French prince by the Treaty of Troyes in 1420. The Dauphin Charles was of course later to become Charles VII of France in 1429, but in 1422 that was far in the future. The *Quadrilogue*, written in 1422, was written in the context, then, of vicious and debilitating civil war within France.

Political theory and historical fiction are, as we have seen from the English examples so far considered, two possible ways of gaining voice in a civil war context. Another is drama, which gains voice by giving voice. This is what the *Quadrilogue* does: its procedure is fundamentally dramatic, allowing different voices of a polity painfully broken from within ("Le Peuple" and "Le Chevalier," translated as "The People" and "The Knight" in both English translations), before a third voice ("Le Clergié"/"Clergy") intervenes.[26] All these three voices are overseen, both prompted and stopped, by a fourth voice, that of

---

24 *The Works of Sir Thomas Malory*, 3:1205. This passage is not in Malory's source; see the same edition, 3:1640–42.

25 *Fifteenth-century English Translations*, 149, line 11.

26 Reference to the French text will be made to the following edition: *Le Quadrilogue Invectif*, ed. Florence Bouchet (Paris: Champion, 2011).

"France" (translated as such by R, and by U as "The Land"). And all these four voices are presented, as if passively, by a fifth voice, "Acteur" (or Author).

Two fifteenth-century English translations of Alain Chartier's *Le Quadrilogue Invectif* exist, one surviving in five manuscripts (edited as R [Rawlinson MS A.338]), and one in a single manuscript (edited as U [University College Oxford MS 85]).[27] Both are entirely competent, generally lucid translations, even if each pursues a different strategy as translation: R is more expansive, determined as the translator is to transmit the sense of the original. U is more dense.[28] It is entirely possible that John Fortescue himself was the author of one of these translations.[29]

Some brief synopsis of the *Quadrilogue* is necessary. The text begins in the voice of the author, lamenting the fall of kingdoms (e.g. Thebes). He reports on the English glorying in their victory, and compares himself to the speaker of Isaiah, such that, he says, "myn herte is troubled with fere and myn yien wex derk with teeris" (141.2–21).[30] He wakes and sees in his imagination the parlous state of France, and falls back to sleep. In this second sleep he sees France herself ("Land" in U), whose splendid garment, with representations of previous victories, political discourse and the state of the land itself, is badly torn (145–46). She is surrounded by the three speakers listed above (People, Knight and Clergy).

The Land ("France" in R) begins the quadrilogue with vehement upbraiding of the speakers around her: they are worse than the external enemies of France (153): France will be destroyed, she says to them all, "to your perpetuall schame and malediccion" (165).

---

27 For a list of the manuscripts, see *Fifteenth-century English Translations*, 1:ix. For the ownership and English reception of these manuscripts, see Catherine Nall, "William Worcester Reads Alain Chartier: *Le Quadrilogue invectif* and its English Readers," in *Chartier in Europe*, ed. Emma Cayley and Ashby Kinch (Cambridge: Brewer, 2008), 135–47.

28 For brief characterizations of the translation policies of the R and U manuscripts, see *Fifteenth-century English Translations*, 2:46–7.

29 Fortescue, as we have seen, was in France between 1463 and 1471, as Chancellor in exile in the retinue of Henry VI. One of the works he wrote towards the end of that period was the Latin *De laudibus legum Anglie* (1468–71), which is cast in the form of a dialogue between Fortescue as Chancellor, and Henry VI's son Prince Edward. Fortescue's situation in the 1460s is, then, exactly parallel to that of Chartier in the 1420s: both are in exile, in a country subject to civil war, and both have sided with the legitimate king and or his heir. A fragment of a translation of a work by Chartier, *Le Traité de l'Esperance*, was attributed to Fortescue by the librarian of the Cotton library; the person who made that translation was also responsible for translations of Chartier's *Le Quadrilogue Invectif*, and his *Dialogus familiaris amici et sodalis*. The attribution is, however, far from certain. For a careful discussion of this plausible attribution, see *Fifteenth-century English Translations*, 2:26–31. See also Julia Boffey, "The Early Reception of Chartier's Works in England and Scotland," in Cayley and Kinch, *Chartier in Europe*, 105–16 at 110–11.

30 All citations from the text itself are drawn from *Fifteenth-century English Translations*, volume 1, and will be made, from the edition of the U manuscript by page and line number in the body of the text.

The Author introduces the speech of the People (a singular voice), who complains persuasively that he has been exhausted by the exploitation of the nobles, who have engaged less in war than private robbery of the people themselves. He labours, only to feed cowards (i.e. military nobles) who themselves menace him: "They lifen by me, and I dye for theim" (167:8-9). He has become an exile in his own house (169). The people need to be heard; the nobles and the clergy cannot make well-grounded policy without taking them into account (173).

The Knight responds, vigorously and aggressively: it's your fault, he declares to the People: you are unable to sustain the pressure of wartime, and you are given to sedition (175). Our foreign enemies have been emboldened by your fickleness (181). Nobles have suffered just as much as you, by being exiled from their territories (181); the soldier's life is full of hardship, and we have had to mortgage our lands (181). Your complaints are just making things worse (183:15). We should stop complaining and think differently—for example, by promoting non-aristocrats, "som out of every estate and degree, and namely of the servauntes, which should lerne to exercise the deedes of armes" (185:18-20). People and Knight accuse each other once more each (195-207).

At this point the Author introduces Clergy, who attempts to resolve the dispute. We need wisdom, money, and "obeissance" (by which Clergy means military discipline, but discipline based on true loyalty). He explicates these three needs in what is the longest speech in the text (211-41).

The Knight replies that the prince needs better counsellors (245). Each party wishes to say more, but is silenced by Land (i.e. France): you should each take more blame than you give (245). The Author is ordered by Land, from within the dream, to record the debate. He wakes and writes the text we have just read (247).

Certainly Chartier's laments about the state of France riven by civil war in the early fifteenth century would have been fit (and available) matter for English intellectuals, such as Fortescue, in the later fifteenth century, when England was suffering exactly the same condition as France in the 1420s. Chartier's 1422 France makes the point with regard to the "happe" of the English that Fortune will not "alleweyes ... be to theim propice," which must have struck English ears in the late 1460s forcefully; the *Quadrilogue* would have been saturated with historical irony for later fifteenth-century English readers. It must have been even more painful than it was for earlier fifteenth-century French readers, given the text's own emphasis on English military superiority in the earlier fifteenth century. That emphasis easily survives the changes that U in particular makes to diminish the specificity of reference to France (e.g. by labelling the speaker "Land").[31]

Other scholars have analyzed changes in the English translations that reflect the different historical circumstances of England, in its period of civil war, from the circumstances of France forty years earlier.[32] In this discussion I will not add to the

---

[31] For U's diminution of references to France, see *Fifteenth-century English Translations*, 46-48.
[32] See Nall, *Reading*, 48-74.

historical specificity of these texts; instead I analyze their rhetorical strategy, by which they reveal how poly-vocal, divided invective can be turned into the constructive voice of the Nation, how the act of giving voice to speakers serves ultimately to gain voice for a national counsellor. Such a discussion applies as directly to the French original as to the English translations.

The rhetoric of invective is common in the Hundred Years War. It is, however, routinely directed against the other side.[33] What is remarkable about the *Quadrilogue* is that the invective is internal to a given society. It will be clear, too, from the bald synopsis above that the invective is extremely direct and forceful: Land attacks all, and People and Knight attack each other. Clergy also makes forceful critique of, for example, faithlessness "in alle maner of estates" (215:10), and private profiteering (223), even if he makes them without direct attack on those present. The only person who makes no critique at all is the outermost voice, that of Author.

The effect of these internal critiques—internal to a given society, internal to the *Quadrilogue* itself—is, apparently, counter-productive. The Author begins the text with a profoundly affective complaint about the division of France, whom he sees "in myn imaginacion" (143:8). Within his vision proper, his first imagined vision of France focuses on the torn, internal fabric of France's garment. The garment is "tissued and assembled" (145:20) of three main materials: military victories; "lettres and carectes and figures of dyvers sciences which clarifien the understandynge and redressen in rightwissenesse the operacions of the men" (145:26–28); and the physical land itself. Each woven representation is badly torn, through "violent handes broken and brosid and defouled" (147:10). The middle (textual) part is no longer coherently legible, "nor the lettres fourmed nor sett in thaire ordre" (147:12), such that hardly any "sentence" is perceptible.

Into this state of *discursive* incoherence, Chartier introduces ... discursive incoherence. Speakers (Land, Knight and People), as I have said, attack each other with unrestrained verbal force, using what little physical energy they have left to do so. On the face of it, the internally torn texture of discursive support for France is only exacerbated by this very text: the voices of this text both angrily attack each other, and speak past each other. Chartier seems only to be giving voice away, as it were.

The Author emphasizes the affective state of the speakers in the links between their speeches: each is exhausted and overwrought, yet ready for more verbal attack. Thus after her first, caustic salvo, Land is weeping and "felt herself by them [i.e. by Knight, People and Clergy] iniuried and disknowen" (165:21). People is next to speak: he, too, has only such energy remaining to speak, all physical forces having been depleted by the circumstances of exploitation he so forcefully explicates. He is "so fer ateint with importable doloure and care that in him was left no vertu sauf oonlie the vois and the crie" (165:23–5). Once finished, Author comments only on People's affective state of

---

33 For which see Ardis Butterfield, *The Familiar Enemy: Chaucer, Language and the Nation in the Hundred Years War* (Oxford: Oxford University Press, 2009), 112–14.

near-total depletion: the representative of the People is "as he that full soore is engraived with sorowe," who only "with grete payn might speke a woorde more" (175:10–11).

The *Quadrilogue* is a dangerous game: People complains acutely that "the policie of this lande is like to the furious man which in a woodnesse [madness] biteth and renteth his othir membres" (173:9–10). It is easily possible to see the text as giving vent to precisely those self-destructive tendencies of inwardly turned invective. The text appears, it might be said, as has been said about psychoanalysis, to be the disease of which it purports to be the cure.[34] The Knight himself makes this point about the danger of loose and plaintive invective. Societies implode, he argues, most frequently "in theim that sittith [set] forth thaire complaintes and murmure" (183:15). "To miche [too much] speche," he later concludes, "in charge or accusacion of othir is nat laudable" (187:19–20).

The Knight's very critique of complaint serves, however, only to produce more. The representative of the People, earlier exhausted, now jumps vigorously to defence of his own verbal attack, "full of impacience for to here repreve his defautes" (195:17–18). The phenomenon of injustice is, he argues, top down. Misuse of goods by nobles in times of plenty served as a bad model for ordinary people. What the Knight calls seditious murmur was instead the warning of the people. Through excess comes "murmure, of murmure rumore, of rumore division, of division desolacion and slaunder" (197:33–199:1). People justifies his complaint in the name of giving warning, but the text itself seems at this stage to be replicating the very process that People so astutely sketches (i.e. complaint leading to further desolation and slander). The Knight responds by pointing, provocatively, precisely to the offensive and provocative rhetorical posture of the People: you may be afraid to speak your mind, he insults People, but your "language, egre and bytinge" is "allwey reddy by detraccion to renne upon him that is thy better" (201:23–24).

What sense can we make of this apparently reverse direction of the *Quadrilogue*? Is the text only giving voice away to others, without profit, and without gaining a voice for itself?

The French text of the *Quadrilogue* proper begins with a rhetorical cue: "Incipit quarilogium invectivum et comicum ad morum Gallicorum correctionem."[35] Scholars disagree about the sense of *comicum*;[36] the French *Quadrilogue*'s latest editor takes it to mean "theatrical."[37] I take it to mean "comic" in the classical sense of "having a happy ending." The ending of the *Quadrilogue* itself cannot be described as fully resolved, or happy in the way of, say the *Divina Commedia* of Dante. It does, however, point in

---

34 Karl Kraus (1874–1936): "Psychoanalysis is that mental illness for which it regards itself as therapy." The quotation is cited liberally; I have been unable to locate its precise source.

35 *Le Quadrilogue Invectif*, 8.

36 The English texts are flummoxed by this word, producing the nonsensical "comitum" instead of "comicum" (142–43).

37 *Le Quadrilogue Invectif*, 89.

that direction, and it predicts a future for the *written* text of the quadrilogue that is not actualized by the debate recorded in the text. France/Land orders the Author to write the text down, so that it has an ongoing, therapeutic effect, "so that yche man maye therynne knowe his owne defautes by exaumple of othir, and because that thei shall reede thaim, may put out the erroure of that is in thaire hertes" (247:6-8). The text is, to use a formulation by Julian of Norwich about her own ostensibly completed text, "begunne" but "not yet performed, as to my sight."[38]

The text, then, predicts from within itself a longer life than the fictional time of its performance. But how will that constructive effect occur from a text that appears to move in reverse from the achievement of a constructive, synergetic voice? Like many works of late medieval literature the *Quadrilogue* works by a homeopathic procedure, therapeutically supplying more of the pathogen so as to provoke a cure.[39] Clergy articulates something very close to this therapeutic approach at the text's cardinal turning point (when Clergy begins to speak (207)). He says that no-one can recover from a long sickness without "accesse and merveilous mutacions and paynes" (209:23); that moment has not yet arrived: we must wait until the "contagious infeccion" has "finallye endid his cours" (209:26-7). The *Quadrilogue*, then, is what might be called a "not yet" text: it registers its own incapacity to cure a wounded present, but creates the reading conditions that are conducive to such cure in the future.[40]

This is what makes the *Quadrilogue* not only a performance text, but also a properly performative text, insofar as it changes its own status across its course (moving from passive record to active instrument), and predicts a changed event in the world of its readership. It aims to make things happen in the world. It does this by supplying the energies for a synergistic, "comic" movement, counter to its own most obvious movement. Its most obvious movement is in the direction of invective-driven fragmentation. The very process of fragmenting voices, however, paradoxically initiates its counter movement, as articulated by the penultimate speech of the Knight, who says that truth has the property of bouncing back, precisely under pressure: "the more that it is defouled, so miche more it is exaltid and releevid" (207:8-9). By giving voices to others, the text paradoxically gains voice for itself.

The key turning point comes as Clergy speaks. Clergy, it should be stated immediately, by no means promotes an otherworldly solution to the very worldly issues debated in the quadrilogue. On the contrary, Clergy directly addresses the material and ethical needs in order to regain national strength out of civil war and military defeat: money, wisdom, and military discipline are what France needs, by his account. His examples

---

38 *A Revelation of Love*, in *The Writings of Julian of Norwich*, ed. Nicholas Watson and Jacqueline Jenkins (University Park: Pennsylvania State University Press, 2006), chap. 86, 379.

39 Other late medieval English examples would include Chaucer's *Book of the Duchess* and Gower's *Confessio Amantis*.

40 For which concept, see James Simpson, "Not Yet: Chaucer and Anagogy," Biennial Lecture of the New Chaucer Society, *Studies in the Age of Chaucer* 37 (2015): 31-54.

are drawn as much from classical as from biblical literature, and the biblical examples are military leaders (e.g. 217).[41] The form of his arguments is different from that of the People and Knighthood, since he does not attack single figures, and takes a broader perspective, embracing all players. But his very solutions are proposed from the material supplied by the invectives of both People and Knighthood. Like the People, he castigates private enrichment in time of war (cf. 167 and 223); like the Knight, he recommends the remarkable idea that military promotions should be made from all classes (cf. 185 and 235). Clergy, that is, repurposes matter drawn from invective to communal and constructive ends.

The dramatic "personne" of Clergy (cf. R, 140:30), however, comes from within the fiction, and does not drive it. The driver is, rather, the least visible, least apparently agential, outermost presence of the text, who mediates its engagement with the world beyond it. That figure is "Author." For it is, after all, from the Author's imagination that the figure of France appears. That single figure of the nation transforms the entire direction and force of the quadrilogue, since the other figures (People, Knight and Clergy) are implicitly prompted to speak not by affiliation to the private interests and formations so often attacked by every speaker, but rather by affective and rational commitment to something that looks very like the Nation.

The last point made by the Knight in this text is that France needs good counsellors, who serve not appetite but reason; in the loyalty of good counsellors lies "the suerte of the prince and the salvacion of the publique well, and there aught we to seeke the roote of alle oure difficultees and the solucion of oure debates" (245:9–11). Chartier finally points discreetly to himself as the lowest profile figure of the entire quadrilogue (not even counted, indeed, as one of the four speakers).[42] He is the brilliant dramaturge who has imagined a play in times of civil war whose textual effects will extend long after the imagined oral performance is over. Chartier ends by asking his readers not to do what I have just done: not to praise the ingenuity of the work itself ("the glorye of the operacion" [247:26]), since the work is made "through compassion of publique neede than by presumpcion of understandinge, and for the profite by good exhortacion more than for any repreef" (247:28–30). Even in its final, elegant word, the text moves beyond self-destructive invective and towards synergy. It registers that the voices of estates have been given in order that a parliamentary, national voice be gained.

---

41 For the function of biblical reference in the *Quadrilogue*, see Florence Bouchet, " 'Vox Dei, vox poetae': The Bible in the *Quadrilogue invectif*," in Cayley and Kinch, *Chartier in Europe*, 31–44.

42 For the importance of the theme of counsel in the *Quadrilogue*, see also Nall, "William Worcester Reads," 146.

PART THREE

THE IMPACT OF WAR

Chapter 10

ORIENTAL DESPOTISM AND THE RECEPTION OF ROMANCE

John M. Ganim*

FROM THE TWELFTH century onward, romance is imbricated in and by the discourse of the Crusades, and a case can be made that its flowering depends on a certain compensation for the erosion of crusader territory. After the fall of Constantinople, crusading rhetoric and crusade motifs reemerge, this time embedded in new forms inspired by the rediscovery of Greek prose romances. A host of new romances and romance epics emerge in several European languages which send their heroes off to battle a disturbingly refashioned infidel.[1] The Ottoman Empire presents a different challenge to the political ideology of crusade narratives, due to its imagined resemblance to an absolutist sovereignty also emerging in Western Europe at the same time, one that threatened the political existence of the knightly class.

Because the following pages cite the prejudices and projections of these romance texts themselves, let me state my argument at the outset. To be sure, the Ottoman Empire was not by any definition of political economy an absolutist state. It adapted the forms and flexibility of successful empires in the region over many centuries past, although it introduced military and financial innovations. While its leaders were demonized in both the romances discussed below and in alarmed responses to Ottoman victories, this itself was not unusual either, and within a very short time, frequent and subtle cultural and political interchanges began to occur. In late medieval chivalric romances, however, a distinctive discourse can be identified. The Ottoman Empire is imagined as an absolutist state, which in fact was a projection on to this formidable adversary of a formation which was emerging not in the East, but in the tendencies towards centralized authority that marked the formerly feudal European states. This projection was an historical irony, since the rise of absolutism in the West fundamentally transformed the feudal culture that gave rise to chivalric romance and to the images of heroism and identity it

---

* **John M. Ganim** is Distinguished Professor of English at the University of California, Riverside. He is the author of *Style and Consciousness in Middle English Narrative* (1983), *Chaucerian Theatricality* (1990), *Medievalism and Orientalism* (2005), translated into Arabic in 2012 by the Kalima Foundation, and *Cosmopolitanism and the Middle Ages* (2013).

1 By now the notion that romance was appreciated as much for its topicality as for its escapism is widely accepted. This is especially so in the fifteenth century, a point made persuasively by Helen Cooper, "Romance After 1400," in *The Cambridge History of Medieval English Literature*, ed. David Wallace (Cambridge: Cambridge University Press, 1999), 690–719. Romance "acquires a new significance in promising to preserve the old values of high chivalry and orthodox piety against the dangers of theological and political innovation" (690).

embodied. At the same time, the ceremony and imagery of absolutist courts themselves, Henry VIII is a striking example, adapted the trappings both of Arthurian romance (though emphasizing the Imperial Arthur) and, occasionally, Ottoman style. The fiction of polar opposition constructed by the romances discussed below is belied by a wealth of evidence of mutual borrowings, adaptations, and influences, political, military, and aesthetic.[2]

At the conclusion of *Le Morte Darthur*, after the utter devastation of the realm and of the Round Table, Malory tells us that his sources differ as to the fate of the surviving knights. Some versions, he says, state that they never left England, but that he prefers another ending:

> Than Syr Bors de Ganys, syr Ector de Maris, syr Gahalantyne, syr Galyhud, syr Galyhodyn, syr Blamour, syr Bleoberys, syr Wyllyars le Valyaunt, syr Clarrus of Cleremounte, al these knyghtes drewe them to theyr contreyes. Howbeit kyng Constantyn wold have had them wyth hym, but they wold not abyde in this royame. And there they al lyved in their cuntreyes as holy men. And somme Englysshe bookes maken mencyon that they wente never oute of Englond after the deth of syr Launcelot but that was but favour of makers. For the Frensshe book maketh mencyon and is auctorysed that syr Bors, syr Ector, syr Blamour, and syr Bleoberis wente into the Holy Lande, thereas Jesu Cryst was quycke and deed. And anone as they had stablysshed theyr londes, for, the book saith, so syr Launcelot commaunded them for to do or ever he passyd oute of thys world, there these foure knyghtes dyd many batayles upon the myscreantes, or Turkes. And there they dyed upon a Good Fryday for Goddes sake.[3]

(1259.34–1260.15)

A century before, a penitential crusade would not have been a surprising endeavor for English nobles, and we have records of even some of Chaucer's acquaintances embarking on armed pilgrimages. Philippe de Mézières, the French soldier and diplomat, had pressed the European nobility to take up the cross again and recover the Holy Land. The Battle of Nicopolis in 1396, another failed attempt to staunch the advance of the Ottomans, was the last large scale Crusade. More crucially, the passage reflects a changed awareness of the nature of the generalized Saracen enemy (often treated with some grace in *Le Morte Darthur* itself), for it is now, and will be for centuries to come, the much more specific "miscreant Turk." And the historical frame of reference is not the loss of Jerusalem in 1187, but the fall of Constantinople in 1453.

I want to suggest, however, that this odd passage, however conventional in its sentiments regarding the ideals of European knighthood, even after the trials of the Hundred Years' War and the Wars of the Roses, reveals a shift in the significance of crusading narratives. Scholarship has not ignored this passage, nor its context. The place of the "Saracens" in Malory has been well studied over the past decade, often debating exactly what a Saracen might be exactly. Mary Hamel, for instance, noted that Sir

---

[2] See, for instance, Lisa Jardine and Jerry Brotton, *Global Interests: Renaissance Art Between East and West* (Ithaca: Cornell University Press, 2000) and, for a later overview, Lisa Jardine, *Captives* (New York: Pantheon, 2002).

[3] See *The Works of Sir Thomas Malory*.

Priamus, a noble opponent who is christened and is welcomed into Arthur's fellowship, was not actually Arab nor Turk, but Hebrew and Greek, and that Malory had softened the contours of Saracen violence that appeared in his inspiration, the Middle English *Sir Ferumbras*. Hamel suggests that the lobbying efforts of the Byzantine emperor in various Western European courts may have been an inspiration.[4] Donald L. Hoffman argued that Malory's "Saracens" were, as is often in medieval literature, a stand-in for otherness, with a notable prejudice against those from the South, with the reconquest of Spain, rather than the Crusades or Ottoman expansion as the primary current event. Hoffman shifts our attention to Palomides, the Saracen Knight in the Tristram sections of Malory. Despite his nobility and knightly zeal, or perhaps because of his wholehearted embrace of courtly love, he remains other, even after his baptism and inclusion in Camelot. The following Grail books replace a landscape peopled with occasional Saracen enemies with one filled with demonic adversaries. For an analogue, Hoffman points towards the debate between Frederick II and Pope Gregory IX concerning Frederick's proposed relocation of Muslim subjects from Sicily to mainland Italy, suggesting a wider shift from a restrained tolerance to outright phobia.[5] Meg Rowland finds the passage so anomalous that she rehearses evidence that it might have been Caxton's interpolation, reflecting Caxton's own zeal on the issue, reflected in many other books he printed.[6] For Peter Goodrich, Malory's elegiac view of chivalry, shifting from history into fantasy, is mirrored in the Orientalizing of his Saracen characters, whatever information he might have received from relatives with first-hand knowledge, as P. J. C. Field surmised.[7]

Malory's passage elegiacally inverts the origin of the Grail Quest itself. Grail romances start appearing within a few years after the loss of Jerusalem in the early thirteenth century, and Helen Adolf long ago plausibly suggested that the Grail Quest was in some sense a transfer or redirection of the crusading ideal.[8] I want to argue that this new enemy represents a threat on a social and political as well as military and theological level to the knighthood to which Arthur's remnant belongs. The polity represented by the "miscreant Turk" is Empire, not merely a kingdom. To predict my larger argument,

---

4 Mary Hamel, "The 'Christening' of Sir Priamus in the Alliterative *Morte Arthure*," *Viator* 13 (1982): 295–308.

5 Donald L. Hoffman, "Assimilating Saracens: The Aliens in Malory's *Morte Darthur*," *Arthuriana* 16, no. 4 (2006): 43–64.

6 Meg Roland, "Arthur and the Turks," *Arthuriana* 16, no. 4 (2006): 29–42.

7 Peter H. Goodrich, "Saracens and Islamic Alterity in Malory's *Le Morte Darthur*," *Arthuriana* 16, no. 4 (2006): 10–28. See also Dorsey Armstrong, "Postcolonial Palomides: Malory's Saracen Knight and the Unmaking of Arthurian Community," *Exemplaria* 18, no. 1 (2006): 175–203. For earlier engagements between English literature and the "Orient," see Carol Falvo Heffernan, *The Orient in Chaucer and Medieval Romance* (Woodbridge: Boydell & Brewer, 2003) and the classic account by Dorothee Metlitzki, *The Matter of Araby in Medieval England* (New Haven: Yale University Press, 1977), though neither considers the Ottoman Empire more than briefly.

8 Helen Adolf, *Visio Pacis, Holy City and Grail: An Attempt at an Inner History of the Grail Legend* (College Park: Pennsylvania State University Press, 1960).

the Ottoman Empire represents a new form of sovereignty and incomprehensible networks of allegiances. Moreover, it is a sovereignty and system that Europe itself is changing into. The rise of absolutism, mirrored in the Ottoman Empire, is undermining the role and function of chivalry and feudalism, even if it borrows the trappings and symbols of the old order.

The concept of "Empire" was one first used by French sources to describe the Ottoman state, and there was no analogous terminology used in early Ottoman records. Nevertheless, Ottoman rulers, largely for strategic purposes, adapted titles that suggested world-historical rule. From the Sufi missions that may have followed or may have preceded their earliest conquests, their majesty was accorded a certain sense of divine right. In an effort to impress the Mongol bands that threatened their Eastern flanks and which they had initially held off in support of the Seljuks, they employed titles that echoed those of Mongol rulers. After the Battle of Ankara in 1402, the Ottomans turn their attention to the Balkans, and as they do, employ Byzantine titles and traditions. Finally, established as the chief Islamic state after the conquest of Constantinople, they deploy both Roman imperial claims and the Arabic word sultan. Combined with the institutionalization of a professional army, the Ottomans predicted the structures of absolutism *avant la lettre*. It differed substantially from its later Western counterparts, of course, not least of all because the land of the Empire was legally the property of the Porte rather than of a hereditary aristocracy. What the Europeans saw was the fusion of energies that fuelled the first conquests of the Ottomans, its *ghazi* zealotry and its military discipline, which stood as a reproach to the failures of their own crusades. But the difference, at least from their perspective, was that this fusion was now embedded in a state. The long history of the association of the Ottoman Empire with despotism, and with what Marx and Engels called "the Asiatic mode of production," begins almost immediately.[9]

The reception and revival of the Crusades after the fall of Constantinople was almost immediate. William Caxton's *The History of Godefrey of Boloyne and of the Conquest of Iherusalem* (STC 13175) appeared in 1481 and his translation of the story of Fierabras from the French was printed in 1484 as *The History and Lyf of the Noble and Crysten Prince Charles the Grete* (STC 5013). Indeed, many of Caxton's books are romances

---

9 For overviews of this vast literature, see, for instance, Michael Curtis, *Orientalism and Islam: European Thinkers on Oriental Despotism in the Middle East and India* (Cambridge: Cambridge University Press, 2009); Thomas Kaiser, "The Evil Empire? The Debate on Turkish Despotism in Eighteenth-Century Political Culture," *Journal of Modern History* 72 (2000): 6–34; Richard Koebner, "Despot and Despotism: Vicissitudes of a Political Term," *Journal of the Warburg and Courtauld Institute* 14 (1951): 275–302. Barbara Fuchs and Emily Weissbourd, ed. *Representing Imperial Rivalry in the Early Modern Mediterranean* (Toronto: University of Toronto Press, 2013) contains several helpful chapters on the merging of admiration and identification, on the one hand, and revulsion and distance on the other, between Ottoman and European empires: see especially Larry D. Silver, "Europe's Turkish Nemesis," 58–79 on visual representations, and Carina L. Johnson, "Imperial Succession and Mirrors of Tyranny in the Houses of Hapsburg and Osman," 80–100 on political projection.

and *chansons de geste* of Charlemagne, who more or less represents a form of imperial kingship for Europeans. In the little-known Franco-Italian *chanson de geste, Macario*, an unjust accusation against Charlemagne's Byzantine wife starts the chain of events, largely because Charlemagne himself does not defend her.[10] The narrative begins by the collapse of the marriage alliance and Constantinople itself seems almost preferable to the internecine treachery of feudal France. Luke Sunderland has tracked a number of Venetian and Franco-Italian romances in which Charlemagne comes off badly.[11] Charlemagne is represented as a central authority trampling on the privileges of local magnates. Charlemagne in such narratives becomes the double of the imperial Byzantine court he ostensibly is opposing. The romance epic returns to the matter of Charlemagne, or at least what an earlier generation of comparativists called epic degeneration, deploying an underlying narrative politics of empire against empire, however much the plot may tell us of individual adventure. The most popular English medieval heroes to survive into Renaissance retellings, such as Bevis of Hampton and Guy of Warwick, do so partly on the basis of their travels to the East.

The transformation of the Crusades as a symbol is expressed in genre. Dorothy Metlitzki and Geraldine Heng have demonstrated how the romance genre not only represented the Crusades and the Arabic world, the genre itself was shaped by their challenges. Fifteenth-century romances that deal explicitly with the Ottoman threat tend to return to older models for understanding the new challenge. *The Sege off Melayne* revives the cast of characters from the *Song of Roland* to defend Milan against an Arab sultan, giving heroic roles to warrior bishops. Similarly, *Capystranus*, a historical romance based on the actual siege of Belgrade by the Turks, valorizes its title character, giving him, an actual friar who preached a crusade, a messianic role.[12] At a turning point in the siege, his appeal to God results in armies of dead warriors coming back to life and rejoining the battle. Lee Manion notes how *Capystranus* is unusual in imagining a "non-knightly crusader army," despite its traditional portrayal of the savagery of the Turks and Saracens (169–170).[13]

For centuries, medieval romance had employed familiar motifs such as crusading rhetoric or other forms of spiritual and martial traditions, many of them deriving from

---

10 See Rima Devereaux, *Constantinople and the West in Medieval French Literature: Renewal and Utopia*, Gallica 25 (Cambridge: Boydell & Brewer, 2012).

11 Luke Sunderland, *Rebel Barons: Resisting Royal Power in Medieval Culture* (Oxford: Oxford University Press, 2017).

12 Anastasija Ropa, "Imagining the 1456 Siege of Belgrade in *Capystranus*," *The Hungarian Historical Review* 4, no. 2 (2015): 255–82.

13 Lee Manion, *Narrating the Crusades: Loss and Recovery in Medieval and Early Modern English Literature* (Cambridge: Cambridge University Press, 2014). Manion tracks the transition from late medieval romance to Early Modern drama, and reminds us that the later English romances seem more concerned with Spain, Italy, and Eastern Europe than with the recovery of Jerusalem. See also the important article by Rebecca Wilcox, "Romancing the East: Greeks and Saracens in Guy of Warwick," in *Pulp Fictions of Medieval England: Essays in Popular Romance*, ed. Nicola McDonald (Manchester: Manchester University Press, 2004): 217–40.

Charlemagne romances, resulting in the defeat or conversion of non-believers. After the fall of Constantinople and the rise of the Ottoman Empire, these stereotypical responses become both focused and troubled. Diane Vincent has argued, for instance, that Christian-Pagan debates in recyclings of Charlemagne romances were actually oriented towards internal, insular conflicts, such as the Lollard controversies.[14]

Where earlier romances created such enduring forms as the quest romance, with its ineffable goal of personal perfection, and with its individual knightly protagonist, the encounter with the newly threatening Ottoman Empire required a new generic fusion. The romance epic, from the continuations of *Amadis of Gaul* to Tarquato Tasso to Spenser, invariably finds its heroes slouching towards Constantinople or its refraction in a historical past, sometimes in triumph and sometimes in confusion. Often the hero finds himself in disguise, as a double agent or as a temporarily deranged renegade. In this fusion, and confusion, the crisis of chivalric values becomes explicit. The narrative no longer is a matter of individual perfection, but an imagined clash of civilizations, whose formal expression is the epic. Yet except for the essential difference of religious confession, the clash is between increasingly indistinguishable political entities.

The focus on Constantinople can be tracked in one of the most widespread and influential chivalric romance cycles, *Amadis of Gaul*, which begins in a Spanish original dating from the early fourteenth century but is added to through the early sixteenth century, and is translated into French, English, and other European languages.[15] Don Quixote tosses his romances on a bonfire, but then pulls out the first four books (of twelve) of *Amadis of Gaul*, because they are the best of their kind. Our interest is in the books that Don Quixote consigned to the bonfire, in which the setting moves from Great Britain ("Gaul" might in fact be Wales and the Amadis cycle circles around Arthurian origins) to Constantinople. Consistency of time and place is not one of the concerns of the cycle, but Constantinople becomes the geographic centre of its latter books and of its many sequels. That city becomes the capital of an empire of magic, as Geraldine Heng puts it, and while Amadis's own life may stretch all the way back to Arthurian Roman days, the focus of many of the battles in the cycle involve defending Constantinople from pagans or Saracens.[16] By the fifteenth century, when the cycle is circulating widely, those menacing pagans or Saracens were identified with the "Turks" who already threatened the city and its empire. The magical Constantinople of *Amadis of Gaul* is figured as the source of romance and chivalry, so its defeat presages the extinction of both. As a result, the battles in *Amadis of Gaul*, long, detailed even in the early British books, become horrendous and gruesome in the later books. The future of European Christian

---

[14] Diane Vincent, "Reading a Christian-Saracen Debate in Fifteenth-Century Middle English Charlemagne Romance: The Case of the *Turpines* Story," in *The Exploitations of Medieval Romance*, ed. Laura Ashe, Ivana Dvordjević, and Judith Weiss (Woodbridge: Brewer, 2010), 90–107.

[15] See John J. O'Connor, *Amadis de Gaule and its Influence on Elizabethan Literature* (New Brunswick: Rutgers University Press, 1970).

[16] Geraldine Heng, *Empire of Magic: Medieval Romance and the Politics of Cultural Fantasy* (New York: Columbia University Press, 2003).

civilization is at stake, defended by Amadis and his descendants. Books 5 and 6 witness the Turkish attacks on Constantinople, with gory and elaborate land and sea battles. In one of the later books, a pagan Russian king, with his many vassal kings, actually takes the city, but it is regained by Christian forces. While the specific adventures of knightly prowess in *Amadis* are typical of chivalric romance, of which it is the last great encyclopedia and compendium, its world view is that of an epic in the continuations, in which a final battle, or series of final battles if that is possible, may be the last stand of Christian civilization as we know it. *Amadis of Gaul* becomes the source and model for the continental and insular national romances.

One of the most widely cited sequels of the Amadis cycle is Garcí Rodriguez Ordóñez de Montalvo's *Las Sergas de Esplandían*, printed in 1510:

> On the right hand of the Indies, there is an island called California, very close to the side of the Terrestrial Paradise, and it was peopled by black women, without any man among them, for they lived in the fashion of Amazons.[17]

These women feed their male children and captured males to griffins. Eventually, Califia finds her way to Europe, and takes part in both the attack and defence of Constantinople. Califia is claimed as an inspiration for present-day gender rebels, but she also becomes domesticated as a founding figure of California in public art and popular culture, and her name has become commercialized by a large dairy corporation. Even in Montalvo, she changes valences. She meets a Muslim warrior and joins him in the siege of Constantinople. When the city holds out, she unleashes her lethal griffins, but they are unable to distinguish between Muslim and Christian warriors, resulting in general mayhem. Leading her own forces, she attacks without the griffins. Eventually, she is entranced with Esplandian, and changes sides. He rejects her as unnatural and pagan, but she ends up converting to Christianity and marrying his son, resettling in California to found a dynasty.

Ariosto, Tasso, Camoens, and others write as poets of the nation in a Vergilian mode, and when their heroes fight against the Saracen, it is as the agent of nation against the minions of Empire, but such a pattern becomes increasingly difficult to manage as their plots develop and braid. Think how often, in Spenser's *Faerie Queene*, knights fight against their allegorical opposites, only to enact the pitfalls of their protagonists shortly before or after their battle. The many adventures of aristocratic individual characters are eventually gathered, almost in a bibliographic sense, into a national synthesis with the future authority of the Faerie Queene herself established at its end, ushering in a new era in which the sphere of these knights will be limited and directed from above.

The drama of the same period, largely after the fall of Constantinople, offers a spectrum of representations, which, while often reverting to earlier simplistic

---

17 Garci Rodríguez de Montalvo, *Sergas de Esplandián*, ed. Carlos Sainz de la Maza, Clásicos Castalia (Madrid: Editorial Castalia, 2003); I am citing the Little translation, Garci Rodríguez de Montalvo, *The Labors of the Very Brave Knight Esplandián*, trans. William Thomas Little (Binghamton: Center for Medieval and Early Renaissance Studies, 1992).

stereotypes, reflect recognition of a new reality. When, in the St George sword plays of the fifteenth century and after, St George confronts the Turkish Knight, the battle takes place on English soil, and St George is an emblem of Englishness. He is always played with a red crusading cross on a white tunic. The Turkish Knight recalls both the archaic past—the dying and reborn god of the Old Religion—and the future; the relentless professionalized military force of the new imperial order, of which both the Turkish Knight and his Christian vanquisher will be agents. The tradition of the sword dance (itself traceable to Turkish analogues) is adapted to a new paradigm of nation versus Empire. Indeed, in the waning days of the Ottoman Empire, pressures from the creditor nations of Western Europe forced the Ottoman state to define itself increasingly in terms of the post-Westphalian nation state, with disastrous consequences for such policies as the relocation of ethnic and religious populations.

In his arresting account of the Turk in English folk plays, placed against the long history of ignorance of actual Turkish experience, David Lawton notes that the "English cult of St George is a crusader cult. St George, who is to be the patron of English national identity, enters English consciousness at much the same time, and in the same context, as the Turk." I would suggest that Lawton's typology (the Seljuk Dynasty, the Saracen armies of the sultan and ultimately the Ottoman Empire) is also a progression.[18] The most fully developed exegesis of St George is, of course, the narrative of the *Faerie Queene*, and at least one of the many implications of that work is that knightly virtue deriving from feudalism will ultimately be incorporated into the service of the sovereign herself, and of the nation and state that she rules. Lawton observes the many paradoxical ways in which the Turkish Knight in folk dramas becomes oddly domesticated, becoming part of regional identities and sometimes of deeply Christian festivals, such as Christmas, and as he also reminds us, both St George and St Nicholas first originally appeared in what is now Turkey. "The drama," writes Lawton "marks the appearance in the later medieval period of a kind of festive Turk, who enacts the role of enemy but is also potentially a double, mirroring the Western Christian." The adversary, originally a generalized Saracen, now becomes a more specific, though still ambiguous, Turk.

But 1453, as Lawton recognizes, changes the equation, more or less eliminating the hope for a world Christian empire. The Ottoman Empire, a true empire by any political measure, appears to be a monolithic state, at the moment when the feudal west is being reconfigured into the absolutist state. The psychology of projection that Lawton so convincingly describes as a dialectic between otherness and identity, seems increasingly to be understood in political terms. The Ottoman Empire, under Western eyes, seems to loom as an absolute state, which it is not, while the regalia of the Christian feudal west increasingly disguises and often abets a radical centralization of power that dissolves both the knightly class and the hope for a universal Christianity.

---

[18] David Lawton, "History and Legend: The Exile and the Turk," in *Postcolonial Moves: Medieval through Modern*, ed. Patricia Ingham and Michelle Warren (New York: Palgrave Macmillan, 2003), 173–94.

Medieval romances of the thirteenth and fourteenth centuries are copied and printed in the fifteenth century. Romances with crusading and Orientalizing themes, often originally French, are especially popular and may have provided reassurance to a newly shaken faith in the superiority and historical mission of the West. In the late fifteenth and early sixteenth centuries, these plots and characters are retranslated and reworked in the evolving genre of the romance epic, which takes the romance of individual adventure and places it in the service of nation and empire. A brief survey of these romance plots makes clear how easily their themes could be adapted or read in a new light.

Since I began with a reference to Caxton's publication of Malory and the possibility that Caxton himself may have interjected his enthusiasm for a new crusade against the Turk into his edition, we could do worse than to describe some of Caxton's publications as evidence of this revival of crusading chivalry in a new and immediate context. *Godefrey of Boloyne* recounts the First Crusade by way of William of Tyre's history, though chronicle and romance qualities are indistinguishable. The construction of the Church of the Holy Sepulchre is recounted, to underline the significance of its loss to the Turks. The apocalyptic jeremiads of Peter the Hermit are answered by the rise of Godfrey. The holy lance, which becomes a crucial symbol in Grail legends, is discovered, resulting in a turn in Christian fortunes. In a vain attempt to repel the superior technology of the Christian war engine, the Turks turn to "ii old wytches" and "iii maydens, for to helpe to make theyr charme," but the Christian artillery tears them apart and their souls go off to hell. When the Christian army enters the city, the phantoms of dead soldiers join them. These details, found in Caxton's source, are shaped as to imagine a disciplined and unified Christian force against a desperate defender, strikingly resembling the actual experience of the last defenders of Constantinople. Interestingly, when Tasso rehearses the First Crusade in his *Gerusalemme liberata* (1581), the knight who exhibits the most typical medieval chivalric behaviour, Rinaldo, must be ultimately rendered subservient to Godfrey's overall strategy and give up individual adventure for the greater good of the unified and organized force.

Caxton prints a version of the thirteenth century *Fierabras* as part of his *The Lyf of the Noble and Crysten Prynce, Charles the Grete*. Caxton's version includes the typical theme of conversion to Christianity as an aspect of the hero's innate nobility, but it also represents the Christian and Saracen worlds as mirrors of each other. The Saracen Fierabras challenges Charles' champions, but the result is dispute and disagreement among them. Roland is especially embittered, violently so, towards Charles. Oliver, not yet recovered from wounds suffered in previous battles, takes up Fierabras' challenge, but is momentarily disarmed. Fierabras offers to spare Oliver if he will convert to Islam, and offer him his sister in marriage. Oliver, however, grabs Fierabras' sword, magically named "baptesme," and wounds Fierabras grievously. Fierabras now himself seeks conversion, but to Christianity, and the two warriors treat each other solicitously. Oliver borrows Fierabras' armor, but in a twist is captured by an invading Saracen army. A second section of the romance opens with the conversion of Fierabras, but then moves to his sister, Floripas, who joins the captured French warriors and Fierabras himself.

In a third section, Charles has returned with an army and rescued everyone. He offers to spare Balan, the Saracen king and father of Fierabras and Floripas, if he converts, but Balan responds contemptuously, spitting into the baptismal font. Floripas, who has rejected her father, herself converts, motivated by her love for Guy of Burgundy.

If the medieval romances of the East acquired new currency and popularity in the fifteenth century, partly by contrasting the feudal fantasy of adventure with the forbidding and total despotism of the Saracen polity, early humanism took what we might consider to be a compromised and paradoxical position. For the early humanists, the proximity of Constantinople to the presumed site of ancient Troy was too much to ignore. Medieval origin myths had proposed that Western European civilization was founded by Aeneas and one Brutus, refugees from the fall of Troy. Thus, European nations were fundamentally Trojan. The fall of Constantinople was imagined as a historical irony, even historical revenge, and a disarmingly positive light was shone on the Ottoman conquerors at times. While eyewitness accounts were available and published, neo-Latin humanist accounts often viewed the battle through the perspective of the *Iliad* and the *Aeneid*. In some accounts, the Greek leaders were described as if they were Priam, and non-existent Cassandra figures were thrown into the narrative, supposedly violated on the altar area of the Hagia Sophia as a delayed vengeance for what the Greeks did to the Trojans.[19] It is possible that Mehmet the Conqueror himself may have encouraged a Trojan identification. Prophetic books, such as the *Visions of Daniel*, also played a role in emphasizing the fulfillment of eschatological predictions. Meanwhile, various caliphs are modelled as apocalyptic figures, who may convert to Christianity and unify the world; conversely, Constantine, the last Byzantine emperor, may, like Arthur, return. In contrast, Aeneas Sylvius compares the sultan to the most reviled Eastern enemies of classical civilization, Xerxes and Darius. It was easy enough to update these tyrannical and totalizing states of the ancient world to describe the Ottoman threat, despite the enmity between the Ottomans and contemporary Persian rulers. The revision of national and cultural identities had been part and parcel of the medieval engagement with Islam and the East, despite an overall tone of demonization. As Thomas H. Crofts and Robert Allen Rouse have pointed out, however, the romances that situate purportedly English heroes in alien territory unsettle fixed notions of identity between East and West.[20] Romances such as *Richard Coer de Lyon*, *Guy of*

---

[19] For an account, see Marios Philippides and Walter K. Hanak, *The Siege and the Fall of Constantinople in 1453: Historiography, Topography, and Military Studies* (Farnham: Ashgate, 2011), 193–296. Nancy Bisaha, *Creating East and West Renaissance Humanists and the Ottoman Turks* (Philadelphia: University of Pennsylvania Press, 2004), emphasizes the crisis in older models of *translatio imperii* occasioned by the fall of Constantinople and provides an account of how Italian writers of the *cinquecento* revise earlier Charlemagne romances.

[20] Thomas Crofts and Robert Allen Rouse, "For King and Country: Reading Nationalism in Popular English Romance," in *A Companion to Medieval Popular Romance*, ed. Raluca L. Radulescu and Cory James Rushton (Cambridge: Brewer, 2009), 79–95.

Warwick and *Bevis of Hampton*, all popular throughout the fifteenth century, not only face off English protagonists against Saracen antagonists, they sometimes reverse and complicate national allegiances, though there is usually a reconsolidation at the end of the narratives. Such romance motifs are put to new uses in the fifteenth and sixteenth centuries, and scholars such as Jennifer Goodman and Barbara Fuchs have analyzed the ways in which the accounts of exploration and discovery are shaped by the psychology of romance. Fuchs argues persuasively that dramatic representations are especially complex, in that pirates and piracy represent an arena uncontrolled by the Jacobean state. In general, however, these romance motifs, like their protagonists, are now in the service of Empire and royal authority.[21]

The reality of diplomatic and economic exchange, as Jonathan Burton and others have argued, begins to influence the representation of the "Turk" on the Elizabethan stage. Burton argues that instead of a blanket category of "otherness," representations of Islam, and especially of the Ottomans, was a negotiated "traffic," reflecting the many complicated connections between a reformed England and an Ottoman diplomatic strategy sophisticated in manipulating both alliances and symbols.[22] Calls to take back the Holy Land rang hollow when the entire Eastern Mediterranean was under Ottoman control. As Protestants, the English could be called the "new Turkes" by their continental opponents. By the 1580s, Elizabeth was exchanging letters with Murad III. Even earlier, the Tudor and the Ottoman courts exchanged diplomatic gifts displaying their common splendor.

Over the past decade, there has been an explosion of rich scholarship on the encounter between the Ottomans and Europe, with special attention to Elizabethan drama and with a focus on religious difference, which is how Early Modern Europeans understood this alterity.[23] I am suggesting here that tracing the experience of the medieval chivalric subject of romance in the face of a threatening political order is also worth emphasizing, and that the romance epic—the early modern revision of medieval romance—is the result of that realization. Underpinning my argument are the debates about sovereignty and subjectivity that have concerned political philosophy over the

---

21 Jennifer R. Goodman, *Chivalry and Exploration, 1298–1630* (Woodbridge: Boydell, 1998), and Barbara Fuchs, *Mimesis and Empire: The New World, Islam, and European Identities* (Cambridge: Cambridge University Press, 2001), who emphasizes Mediterranean as well as New World encounters.

22 Jonathan Burton, *Traffic and Turning: Islam and English Drama* (Newark: Delaware University Press, 2005).

23 See Matthew Birchwood and Matthew Dimmock, ed. *Cultural Encounters Between East and West, 1453–1699* (Cambridge: Cambridge Scholars, 2005); Matthew Dimmock, "The Tudor Experience of Islam," in *A Companion to Tudor Literature*, ed. Kent Cartwright (Chichester: Wiley, 2010), 49–62; Samuel C. Chew, *The Crescent and the Rose: Islam and England* (Oxford: Oxford University Press, 1937) remains important; Gerald MacLean, ed. *Re-Orienting the Renaissance* (Basingstoke: Palgrave, 2005); Gerald Maclean and Nabil Matar, *Britain and the Islamic World, 1588–1713* (New York: Oxford University Press, 2011).

past few decades, from Perry Anderson's *Lineages of the Absolutist State* to Agamben's *Homo Sacer* and his debate with Carl Schmitt's Political Theology, and to Kathleen Davis' *Periodization and Sovereignty*, on how early modern jurists deployed feudal legal thought.[24] In the romance epics which develop over the next centuries, Malory's shell-shocked knights will be moving not only into the holy landscape of a crusading past, but into the hypermodern setting of the absolutist future which, as its first step, will limit their agency as hereditary aristocrats and the possibility of "establishing their lands," despite what the French book saith.

---

24 See Perry Anderson, *Lineages of the Absolutist State* (London: Verso, 1979); for an important exploration of sovereignty at the end of the Middle Ages, see Kathleen Davis, *Periodization and Sovereignty: How Ideas of Feudalism and Secularization Govern the Politics of Time* (Philadelphia: University of Pennsylvania Press, 2012). Both discuss Jean Bodin, who described the Ottoman State as more arbitrarily tyrannical than contemporary European states, but whose cosmopolitanism offered a positive alternative. For an extended discussion of Bodin and Hugo Grotius and the early articulation of political theology as "romance," using Fulke Greville's poetry as a fulcrum, see Benedict Scott Robinson, *Islam and Early Modern English Literature: The Politics of Romance from Spenser to Milton* (New York: Palgrave Macmillan, 2007), 104–15. "Oriental Despotism" as a commonplace in political thought is not used until the seventeenth century, but its origins are earlier. An extremely helpful contextualization of Bodin can be found in Noah Malcolm, "Positive Views of Islam and Ottoman Rule in the Sixteenth Century," in *The Renaissance and the Ottoman World*, ed. Anna Contadini and Claire Norton (Farnham: Ashgate, 2013), 197–217. For a pioneering exploration of the relation between absolutism and medieval literature, see David Wallace, *Chaucerian Polity: Absolutist Lineages and Associational Forms in England and Italy* (Stanford: Stanford University Press, 1997).

Chapter 11

BELON, PALISSY, RONSARD, AND THE WAR FOR THE FORESTS OF FRANCE

Susan Broomhall*

WELL BEYOND THEIR role as a basic resource for fuel, housing, and shipbuilding, early modern French forests provided pasture for livestock during the year and supplied food provisions of their own with the fauna that inhabited them. Forests supported a diverse range of occupations that were dependent upon their resources and were also sources of pleasure, not least the game hunting enjoyed by the aristocratic elite. Scholars have recognized the enormous range of forests' impact and influence in early modern French economic and social culture.[1] The relationship between forests and contemporary religious experiences has perhaps seen less study to date. Yet, when conflict between Huguenots and Catholics erupted into war during the mid-1560s, forests numbered among the casualties, in both concrete and ideological ways. France's forests supplied the firepower for numerous technologies of war, were destroyed by crossfire, and were enlisted as a financial resource to fuel partisan politics. But additionally, in a range of genres, contemporary French scholars and poets, Catholic and Huguenot, reflected upon the role of forests in making and shaping religious conflicts, and upon the spiritual responsibility to manage arboreal resources responsibly. In practice, these authors produced very different visions of the capacity for forests to participate in the religious politics of sixteenth-century France.

The role of natural resources and environment in early modern worldviews has occupied scholars from a range of disciplines, including geography, philosophy, anthropology, and archaeology. Emerging conceptualizations offer ways to read landscape as "a dense and complex system of signs" as well as through its involvement in economic and social processes.[2] As Alexandra Walsham suggests, landscapes

---

* **Susan Broomhall** is Professor of History at The University of Western Australia. Her research explores women and gender; emotions; environment, science, technologies, and knowledge practices; material culture; cultural contact and global encounters; and the heritage of the early modern world.

1 The most comprehensive and the foundational study remains Michel Devèze, *La vie de la forêt française au XVIe siècle*, 2 vols. (Paris: S.E.V.P.E.N., 1961). For research on forests in periods earlier and later, see G. Geneau de Sainte Gertrude, *La législation forestière sous l'ancien régime* (Nancy: Berger-Levrault, 1945); Roland Bechmann, *Des arbres et des hommes: La forêt au moyen-âge* (Paris: Flammarion, 1984); Kieko Matteson, *Forests in Revolutionary France: Conservation, Community, and Conflict, 1669–1848* (Cambridge: Cambridge University Press, 2015).

2 Alexandra Walsham, *The Reformation of the Landscape: Religion, Identity, and Memory in Early Modern Britain and Ireland* (New York: Oxford University Press, 2011), 6.

form "a porous surface upon which each generation inscribes its own values and preoccupations ... a surface onto which cultures project their deepest concerns and recurring obsessions."[3] The sacralization of the landscape in the early modern era has been a focus of Walsham's recent study in which she persuasively argues that Protestant and Catholic communities in Britain and Ireland found new ways to interpret the landscape in spiritual terms after the Reformation. The meanings of particular environments were renewed as places of reflection, while other landscapes found new meanings when effects of nature, such as weather and atmospheric anomalies, were read through new interpretive lenses as signs of God's providence. This led to conceptualizations of nature that permeated not only faith practices but also natural knowledge disciplines that were practised by Protestant thinkers. More recently, Peter C. Mancall considers how early modern understandings of nature and ecological sensibilities also shifted in the light of interactions with new societies across the Atlantic basin.[4] These works encourage us to look anew at the complex relationships between faith behaviours and the environments, natural and constructed, in which they were practised.

The geographer Paul Arnould outlines a range of lenses through which forests can be considered, including their ecosystem, their geosystem (analyzing the spatiality and chronology of forest units), their politicosystem of laws, customs, and decrees, and their sociosystem of economic stakes and competition for forests resources. Additional to these is a critical psychosystem, which Arnould defines as the forest "perceived, represented, idealized, symbolized, imagined, dreamed," as "objects of myth and legend, the product of changing modes and discourses."[5] These insights suggest that we might interpret forests through the multiple ways by which they were both participant and object in the faith politics of sixteenth-century France, as an idea and a lived reality, and how the spiritual components of forest politics shaped contemporary discourses and conceptualizations. This chapter analyzes three different ways in which faith entered the forest in the years preceding and during the French Wars of Religion, in the works of authors operating in different generic, spiritual, and professional contexts. As their authors considered the nature of time, profit, and the politics of place and memory in relation to the forest, these texts articulate divergent meanings and practices of productivity, reproductivity, and sustainability that were founded in particular faith positions.

---

3 Walsham, *Reformation*, 6.

4 Peter C. Mancall, *Nature and Culture in the Early Modern Atlantic* (Philadelphia: University of Pennsylvania Press, 2018).

5 See the Special Issue "Les forêts entre nature et société," especially the editor's introduction: Paul Arnould, "Introduction. Forêts: entre nature et société," *Bulletin de l'Association de géographes français* 78 (2001–2002): 107–9 at 109: "perçu, représenté, idéalisé, symbolisé, imaginé, rêvé ... objets de mythes, de légendes, de faits de mode et de discours."

Pierre Belon: Productivity and the Call for Forest Exploitation

In the years leading up to the French religious wars, the idea that the forests of France could constitute a productive resource if well managed emerged in the work of Pierre Belon. The Catholic natural philosopher from Le Mans represented one of the first published voices of concern for the future of France's forests. Belon had commenced his unconventional education as an apothecary, but he later studied botany under Valerius Cordus in Wittemburg and medicine in Paris. Although he was part of the French delegation sent to foster an alliance with the German Lutheran princes, he later found support for his scientific studies with Cardinal François de Tournon, no friend to the growing Huguenot movement in France.[6] Belon had already published research about silviculture in 1553, with his Latin work *De arboribus coniferis resiniferis, aliis quoque nonullis sempiterna fronde virentibus*.[7] However, it was his vernacular *Les remonstrances sur le default du labour & culture des plantes, & de a cognoissance d'icelles*, published in 1558, that argued strongly for the development of France's natural arboreal resources, in order to produce a profit that was both economic and intellectual.[8] Belon suggests that the text serves two purposes: to provide "the teaching of a new knowledge to lettered men" on the one hand, and "revenue to villagers" on the other. It would do so by offering tailored learning, for the former, "the knowledge of trees" and for the other, more practically, "how to cultivate them."[9]

Profits were, repeatedly, the terms in which this knowledge was extolled. Reading his book, one would "without expenditure, render an inestimable profit."[10] After all, Belon himself acknowledged that "never had a man who cultivated or had lands worked, if it were not in the hope of profit."[11] However, Belon had a broad sense of the beneficiaries of forest labour, and of the long-term nature of its outcomes. In chapter 5 of his work he argues that "the worker whose labour is not saleable, must be supported, since the

---

[6] See multiple editions of Paul Delaunay, "L'aventure existence de Pierre Belon," *Revue du Seizième Siècle* 9 (1922): 251–68; 10 (1923): 1–34, 125–47; 11 (1924): 30–48, 222–32; 12 (1925): 78–97, 256–82.

[7] Pierre Belon, *De arboribus coniferis resiniferis, aliis quoque nonullis sempiterna fronde virentibus* (Paris: Guillaume Cavellat, 1553).

[8] Pierre Belon, *Les remonstrances sur le default du labour & culture des plantes, & de la cognoissance d'icelles* (Paris: Gilles Corrozet, 1558). Belon's work has been discussed by Henry Heller, *Labour, Science, and Technology in France, 1500-1620* (Cambridge: Cambridge University Press, 1996), 75–79 and Danièle Duport, "Le beau paysage selon Pierre Belon du Mans," *Bulletin de l'Association d'étude sur l'humanisme, la réforme et la renaissance* 53 (2001): 57–75 at 66–75.

[9] Belon, *Les remonstrances*, fol. 5r: "l'vne pour l'enseignemēt d'vn nouueau sçauoir aux hōmes lettrez: l'autre annoncera reueu aux villageois, pour l'vsage, l'vn en illustrant la cognoissance des arbres, l'autre en enseignāt à les cultiuer."

[10] Belon, *Les remonstrances*, fol. 5r: "sans despence, rendront proffit inestimable."

[11] Belon, *Les remonstrances*, fol. 8v: "Oncques ne s'est trouué homme qui ait cultiué ou faict remuer terre, sinon en esperance de proffit."

work cannot be purchased except by republics and lords."[12] He likened this labour to that of painters, poets, sculptors, and the like, whose work, as much a public as a private commodity, required support for its development.[13] Belon explained that his text was not simply for the present, but for the future, "for the mission of this work is not for a year, or for one individual, but for the long term and for the whole world."[14]

Forests, in Belon's view, were resources that should be "tamed" to human needs. His detailed discussion of the preparation of soils and conditions for arboreal achievement is premised on the need to control and discipline trees to human desires, just like animals. However, this "taming" requires sensitivity to the particular conditions of specific species and their requirements.[15] Belon recognizes that "neither men, nor the earth or beasts too could suffer pain longer than the laws of nature had ordained it."[16] Trees need to have time to rest and recover to prosper, and thus people require patience when managing them. The diligent gardener invests for the future by re-planting each year.

France's leaders, the lords of great estates, had a particular role to play in future-proofing via investments in forest resources. The commitment of the kingdom's leading men to the foreign fields of the Italian Wars that had preoccupied them over the first half of the sixteenth century ought to be no excuse not to attend to this important task.[17] What these travels might bring to France, however, were new tree stocks that might adapt to French soils and prosper. Belon even included an extensive list of managed horticultural sites elsewhere in Europe, to which French lords might look for inspiration.[18] Here, Belon may have intended to push back against the kinds of aesthetic justifications offered in contemporary royal ordinances protecting woods and forests, such as that of Henri II in February 1552. The preamble of that ordinance, for the purchase of the wood of the Abbey of Lys, voiced the value of landscape as a resource for aristocratic pleasure. The preamble extolled the forest of Bière as "one of the most ancient of our realm, in which at present we make our home for part of the year, for the beauty of the place and the pleasure of hunting."[19]

---

12 Belon, *Les remonstrances*, fol. 10r: "L'ouurier duquel la besogne n'est vendible, doibt estre supporté, puis qu'elle ne peult estre achetée, sinon des republiques & seigneurs."

13 Belon, *Les remonstrances*, fol. 12r.

14 Belon, *Les remonstrances*, fol. 33v: "Car l'entreprinse de cest ouurage, est, non pour la durée d'vne année, ou pour vn particulier, mais pour longueur de temps, & pour tout le monde vniuersel."

15 Belon, *Les remonstrances*, chap. 9: "Discours approuuants l'apprivoisement des arbres sauuages."

16 Belon, *Les remonstrances*, fol. 21v: "ne les hommes ne la terre, & les bestes aussi, ne peuuent plus souffrir de peine, que ce que les loix de nature leur a ordonné."

17 Belon, *Les remonstrances*, fols. 31v–32r.

18 Belon, *Les remonstrances*, chap. 20.

19 Archives nationales (AN) X1A 8618, fol. 33v cited in Devèze, *La vie*, 2:194: "une des plus anciennes de nostre royaume, où de present faisons une partie de l'an nostre demeure, pour la beauté du lieu et plaisir de la chasse."

In Belon's work, the unexploited productive capacity of the forests of France was a clear loss to the realm, a loss that was both intellectual and economic. For a further author, Bernard Palissy, whose work followed in the next decade, productivity could only be of *real* value if it was combined with a management plan for sustainability that was undertaken within a clearly articulated spiritual framework.

Bernard Palissy: Sustainability As the Spiritualization of Forest Exploitation

Bernard Palissy, a self-taught Protestant natural philosopher, produced a series of texts during the worst days of the century's violent religious wars. In these he sought to reveal his understanding of the value of nature, because, he claimed, his close contemplation of both the natural world and of God had revealed it to him. Productive nature, Palissy reasoned, was part of God's plan:

> God did not create these things to leave them idle, thus each does its duty, according to the command given to it from God. The Stars and Planets are not idle, the sea travels from one side and the other, and is working to produce profitable things, the land is similarly never idle.[20]

Palissy is therefore interpreted by scholars as "highly utilitarian," an advocate with an agenda for well ordered society stressing "the conscientious use of science and technology for the improvement of agriculture, forest conservation and landscape gardening."[21] These were certainly part of the claims made in his publication, but his observations and recommendations were nuanced as explicitly spiritual acts, part of the Calvinist faith that defined the peregrinations of his life, exile, and eventual death in imprisonment in Paris in 1590.[22]

---

20 Bernard Palissy, *Œuvres complètes*, ed. Keith Cameron, Jean Céard, Marie-Madeleine Fragonard, Marie-Dominique Legrand, Frank Lestringant, and Gilbert Shrenk (Paris: Honoré Champion, 2010); Bernard Palissy, *Recepte veritable par laquelle tous les hommes de la France pourront apprendre à multiplier et augmenter leurs thresors* (La Rochelle: Barthélemy Berton, 1563), 132: "Dieu ne crea pas ces choses pour les laisser oisifves, ains chacune fait son devoir, selon le commandement qui luy est donné de Dieu. Les Astres et Planetes ne sont pas oisifves, la mer se pourmeine d'un costé et d'autre, et se travaille à produire choses profitables, la terre semblablement n'est jamais oisifve: ce qui se consomme naturellement en elle, elle le renouvelle, et le reforme derechef, si ce n'est en une sorte, elle le refait en une autre."

21 Louisa Mackenzie, *The Poetry of Place: Lyric, Landscape, and Ideology in Renaissance France* (Toronto: University of Toronto Press, 2011), 141; Jitse M. van der Meer, "European Calvinists and the Study of Nature: Some Historical Patterns and Problems," in *Calvinism and the Making of the European Mind*, ed. Gijsbert van den Brink and Harro Höpfl (Leiden: Brill, 2014), 103–30 at 112.

22 For biographical studies, see Louis Audiat, *Bernard Palissy, étude sur sa vie et ses travaux* (Paris: Didier, 1868); Ernest Dupuy, *Bernard Palissy: l'homme, l'artiste, le savant, l'écrivain* (Paris: Société francaise d'imprimerie et de libraire, 1902; repr. Geneva: Slatkine Reprints, 1970). On the impact of his faith on his ideas about nature, see Leonard N. Amico, *Bernard Palissy: In Search of Earthly Paradise* (Paris: Flammarion, 1996); Susan Broomhall, "Feeling Divine Nature: Natural History, Emotions and Bernard Palissy's Knowledge Practice," in *Natural History in Early Modern*

Palissy's occupations included, variously, glass painter, land surveyor, preacher, author, and self-taught potter. He became a favoured artist of the royal court when his unique ceramic style captured the interest and patronage of first the *connétable* Anne de Montmorency and then the queen mother, Catherine de Médicis. Although his epistemology did not conform to the conventions of contemporary natural philosophy taught in the universities, Palissy may have been exposed to ideas about botany and literature of his time. Henry Heller suggests that he may have been at the periphery of the circle of Jacques Gohory, another client of the queen, who celebrated her patronage of botanical studies in his treatise on the newly introduced plant, tobacco.[23] In this period, Gohory was well connected to the leading literary lights of the court, cultivated a botanical garden, and held a *Lycium Philosophal* in his house at Saint-Marcel near Paris.[24]

In his *Recepte veritable*, published 1563, Palissy, like Belon, critiqued the lack of engagement and responsibility taken by the nobility for improving the state of French agriculture, and of their forests. And, like Belon, he looked to Italy for exemplary aristocratic practice:

> I praise greatly an Italian duke, who, some days after his wife had given birth to a daughter, reflected to himself that wood gave a revenue which grew while sleeping; therefore, he ordered his servants to plant on his lands a hundred thousand feet with trees, saying thus that the said trees would be worth twenty sols each before his daughter was ready to marry, and so the said trees would be worth a hundred thousand *livres*, which was the dowry he planned to give his daughter. That was a praiseworthy prudence, would that there were several in France who did the same. There are many here who love to hunt and frequent the woods; but they take what they find there without worrying about the future.[25]

This lack of foresight in managing forest resources in a sustainable way was a key concern for Palissy. As he argued,

> there is no treasure in the world so precious nor which should be held in such great esteem, as the little branches of trees and plants ... I value them more highly than mines of gold and silver. And when I think of the value of the very smallest branches or thorns,

---

France: The Poetics of an Epistemic Genre, ed. Raphaële Garrod and Paul J. Smith (Leiden: Brill, 2018), 46–69.

23 Jacques Gohory, *Instruction sur l'herbe petum ditte en France l'herbe de la Royne ou Medicée* (Paris: Galiot du Pré, 1572) and Heller, *Labour*, 113–14.

24 Heller, *Labour*, 113.

25 Palissy, *Œuvres complètes*, 195: "Je louë grandement un Duc Italian, qui quelques jours apres que sa femme fut accouchee d'une fille, il philosopha en soy-mesme, que le bois estoit un revenue qui venoit en dormant: parquoy, il commanda à ses serviteurs de planter en ses terres le nombre de cent milles pieds d'arbres, disant ainsi, que lesdits arbres pourroyent valoir chacun vingt sous auparavant que sa fille fust bonne à marier: et ainsi, lesdits arbres vaudroyent cent milles livres, qui estoit le prix qu'il pretendoit donner à sa fille. Voila une prudence grandement louable: à la miene volonté, qu'il y en eust plusieurs en France, qui fissent le semblable. Il y en a plusieurs qui aiment le plaisir de la chasse, et la frequentation des bois: mais cependant ils prenent ce qu'ils trouvent sans se soucier de l'advenir."

I am amazed at the great ignorance of men who seem these days only to study how to break, cut, and destroy the beautiful forests that their predecessors had so preciously guarded. I would not find it wrong if they cut the forests down, provided they afterwards replanted some of it but they do not think at all of times to come, not realizing at all the great harm they are doing to their children in the future.[26]

For Palissy, therefore, it was not simply that forests could be managed as a greater productive resource for his contemporaries, but that this should occur only within a sustainable framework:

I find it a very strange thing that many lords do not require their subjects to sow some part of their land with acorns, other parts with chestnuts, and others with filberts, which would be a public good, and a revenue that increases while sleeping.[27]

Indeed, as the pedagogue of his dialogue insisted in dramatic terms, the end of wood would signal the end of the realm as an economic entity and a biome:

I once wanted to a make a list of the arts that would cease if there was no more wood, but when I had written a large number of them, I could see no end to my writing, and having considered all, I found that there was not a single one which could be undertaken without wood: and when there was no more wood, all navigation and all fisheries would have to cease, and even the birds and several species of animals, which nourish themselves upon fruits, would have to migrate to another kingdom, and that neither oxen, cows nor other bovine animals would be useful in a land where there was no wood.[28]

Clearly Palissy's plans involved human control over forest and other natural resources, in a psychosystem that was firmly Calvinist. The rustic grottos that Palissy imagined disciplined the non-human world so that people could understand the message that the potter called upon nature to convey—that God's design was not to be ignored nor his creation squandered. He discusses biblical phrases (taken from the Book of Wisdom,

---

26 Palissy, *Œuvres complètes*, 195: "qu'il n'y a thresor au monde si precieux, ni qui deust estre en si grande estime, que les petites gittes des arbres et plantes ... Je les ay en plus grande estime, que non pas les minieres d'or et d'argent. Et quand je considere la valeur des plus moindres gittes des arbres ou espines, je suis tout esmerveillé de la grande ignorance des hommes, lesquels il semble qu'aujourd'huy ils ne s'estudient qu'à romper, couper, et deschirer les belles forests que leurs predecesseurs avoyent si precieusement gardees. Je ne trouveray pas mauvais qu'ils coupassent les forests, pourveu qu'ils en plantassent apres quelque partie: mais ils ne se soucient aucunement du temps à venir, ne considerans point le grand dommage qu'ils font à leurs enfans à l'advenir."

27 Palissy, *Œuvres complètes*, 195: "Je trouve une chose fort estrange, que beaucoup de Seigneurs ne contraignent leurs sujets de semer quelque partie de leurs terres d'aglans, et autre parties de chastagners, et autres parties de noyers, qui seroit un bien public, et un revenu qui viendront en dormant."

28 Palissy, *Œuvres complètes*, 195: "Je voulus quelque fois mettre par estat les arts qui cesseroyent, lors qu'il n'y auroit plus de bois: mais quand j'en eu escrit un grand nombre, je ne seu jamais trouver fin à mon escrit, et ayant tout considéré, je trouvay qu'il n'y en avoit pas un seul, qui se peust exercer sans bois, et que quand il n'y auroit plus de bois, qu'il faudroit que touts les navigations et pescheries cessassent, et que mesme les oiseaux et plusieurs especes de bestes, lesquelles se nourrissent de fruits, s'en allassent en un autre Royaume, et que les boeufs, ni les vaches, ni autres bestes bovines ne serviroyent de rien au pays où il n'y auroit point de bois."

Book 3 and Proverbs, Book 1, 20–28) to be written along the frieze on one area of the grotto "so that ingratitude may be refuted even by insensible and vegetative things … so that men who reject wisdom, discipline, and doctrine, may be condemned even by the testimony of souls vegetative and insensible."[29] Through Palissy's design, the natural world would teach the human about faith. The grotto and garden designs that Catharine Randall terms Palissy's "entexted" structures were described in the *Recepte veritable*, a work that was itself, in Randall's words, "an entryway for the reader to the structure of faith."[30] Palissy's knowledge practice appeared to reflect an emerging Protestant knowledge framework detected by recent scholars in which "religious zeal often served to stimulate the contemporary search for a deeper understanding of nature, which in turn strongly reinforced awe of its Creator."[31]

There was certainly a partisan faith message in the potter's works. Palissy explicitly targeted the lack of aristocratic leadership in forest management but also what he saw as the exploitative practices of Catholic officials. He used his dialogue's interlocutors to pose questions that highlight exploitative ecclesiastical forest management. Palissy had his naïve interlocutor innocently ask: "why do you find it so wrong that forests should be cut down like this? There are several bishops, cardinals, priors, and abbots, monasteries and chapterhouses, who, in cutting down the forests, have made triple the profit."[32] Palissy's mouthpiece responds sharply to this short-sighted notion of profit:

> I cannot detest such a thing enough, I call it not a fault but a curse and a misfortune to all France; because after all the woods are cut down, all arts will have to cease and artisans will have to go eat grass like Nebuchadnezzar.[33]

Moreover, Palissy linked the fate of France's forest directly to contemporary experiences of religious violence. His criticism of Catholic adversaries went further and, as with so much of his knowledge, drew on personal experiences. It included direct criticism of Charles, Cardinal of Bourbon, Bishop of Saintes. Bourbon, Palissy's interlocutor recounts, received permission from the king to exploit the timber resources

---

29 Palissy, *Œuvres complètes*, 173: "à fin que l'ingratitude ne soit redarguee mesme par les choses insensibles et vegatives … à fin que les hommes qui rejetteront Sapience, discipline, et doctrine, soyent mesme condamnez par les tesmoignages des ames vegetatives et insensibles."

30 Catharine Randall, "Structuring Protestant Scriptural Space in Sixteenth-Century Catholic France," *Sixteenth Century Journal* 25 (1994): 341–52 at 343.

31 Walsham, *Reformation*, 358, and fn 94. However, Jitse M. van der Meer, "European Calvinists," is careful to point out that there is diversity of views among Calvinists, not a unified Calvinist natural philosophy.

32 Palissy, *Œuvres complètes*, 194: "Et pourquoy trouves-tu si mauvais qu'on coupe ainsi les forests? il y a plusieurs Evesques, Cardinaux, Prieurs et Abbez, moineries, et chapitres, qui en coupant les forests, ils ont fait trois profits."

33 Palissy, *Œuvres complètes*, 194–95: "je ne puis assez destester une telle chose, et ne la puis appeller faute: mais une malediction, et un mal-heur à toute la France, parce qu'après que tous les bois seront coupez, il faut que tous les arts cessent, et que les artisans s'en aillent paistre l'herbe, comme fit Nabuchodonozor."

of local forests but feared reprisals from the townspeople who enjoyed their livelihood and leisure time there.[34] Under cover of rejecting Calvinist preachers and their teachings, therefore, the bishop, alongside his counsellors,

> decided to win the heart of the people by preaching and presents made to the king's men, and sent into this town of Saintes, and other towns of the diocese, certain monks from the Sorbonne, who foamed, slavered, tormented and twisted themselves, making strange gesture and grimaces, and all their talk did nothing but cry out against these new Christians.[35]

With distraction and persuasion, Palissy lamented that "the poor people patiently allowed their woods to be cut down, and once the woods were thus levelled, there were no more preachers."[36] In Palissy's mind, the loss of the forests and the events of 1546 in which Protestant preachers were driven from the town, pursued by the Bishop of Saintes and the *Parlement* de Bordeaux, were inextricably linked. Bringing his narrative of loss—both of faith and forest—together, Palissy concluded, "this was how the people were deceived of their goods as well as their minds."[37] Saintes was to remain in Catholic hands until the third outbreak of war.

Palissy was by no means the first to voice concerns about the over-exploitation of France's arboreal resources. Indeed, scholarship on the medieval period suggests similar patterns of anxieties about forest exploitation and over-exploitation had arisen during the fourteenth century.[38] By the sixteenth century, however, these concerns, particularly regarding logging and the reproductive capacity of the forests, were reflected in royal legislation and the strengthening of personnel whose responsibilities included combatting abuse of forest entitlements. However, as Michel Devèze has argued and as Palissy was witnessing in Saintes, it seems, these developments overwhelmingly protected the rights of royal, ecclesiastical, and aristocratic elites to the detriment of local communities and their customary expectations to exploit forest resources.[39]

---

34 Palissy, *Œuvres complètes*, 211.

35 Palissy, *Œuvres complètes*, 211–12: "s'aviserent de gagner le Coeur du people par predications et presens faits aux gens du Roy, et envoyerent en ceste ville de Xaintes, et autres villes du Diocese certains Moines Sorbonistes, qui escumoyent, bavoyent, se tourmentoyent et viroyent, faisans gestes et grimaces estranges, et tous leurs propos n'estoyent que crier contre ces Chrestiens nouveaux."

36 Palissy, *Œuvres complètes*, 212: "le pauvre people souffroit patiemment que tous leurs bois fussent coupez: et les bois estans ainsi coupez, il n'y eut plus de predicateurs."

37 Palissy, *Œuvres complètes*, 212: "voila comment le people fut deceu en ses biens, et pareillement en ses esprits."

38 See Danny Lake-Giguere, "*La gestion des forêts royales en Normandie à la fin du Moyen Âge. Étude du Coutumier d'Hector de Chartres*," Master's thesis, University of Montreal, 2014; Danny Lake-Giguere, "The Impacts of Warfare on Woodland Exploitation in Late Medieval Normandy (1364–1380): Royal Forests as Military Assets During the Hundred Years' War," *Journal of Medieval Military History* 16 (2018): 79–98.

39 Devèze, *La vie*, 2:338.

For Palissy, productivity, sustainability and partisan politics were intimately intertwined. The resources of the forest could not be enjoyed without a plan for their longevity, and their exploitation could only occur within a natural philosophical framework that understood God's design, as Palissy himself claimed. Those others, especially Catholics, did not and could not receive that divine knowledge and were thus condemned ultimately to destroy the common wealth of the realm.

Pierre de Ronsard: From Sylvan Destruction to Salvation

Palissy's passionate interventions into the faith politics of the forest would be closely followed by an alternative contribution to these debates, from a firm opponent, the court poet Pierre de Ronsard. The staunch Catholic offers a compelling poetic vision of the forest and specifically of the forest near his home, the Gâtine, as a place of natural beauty and wonder. He argues that forests were a vital source of poetic inspiration, just as they were in the classical world. He recast the woods and rivers that he knew from his childhood to be worthy inspirations and matter for celebration in his poetry, directly comparing the Gâtine forest "my laurel," to the poetic and creative sites of the ancients: "Nestled in your leafy shade/Gâtine, I sing of you/Just as the Greeks by their verses/did of the forest of Erymanthus."[40] Ronsard offered a powerful interpretation of a forest every bit as critical to his emotional wellbeing and poetic lifeforce as those that he had learned to appreciate from classical texts. As such, its survival was paramount to the creative future of France.

With the outbreak of religious fighting in the early 1560s, however, forests fell victim to new menaces. Wars provoked sylvan destruction in multiple ways; soldiers passed through forests, new fortifications and military technologies were built from them, and legal protections were disrupted as brigands and populations drew upon their resources in desperate need. Evidence of some of these acts is found among post-bellum reports submitted by the king's forestry personnel after they surveyed holdings to analyze the consequences of war and when communities sought compensation for their losses. Many had taken advantage of the lax situation to steal timber. In Champagne, near Chaumont-en-Bassigny, in 1564, the inhabitants of Grand and of Moullonvillers formed "an illicit armed gathering through the forest of the prince of Porcian, destroying the tall timber,

---

40 Pierre de Ronsard, *Les œuvres de P. de Ronsard, reveues, corrigées et augmentées par l'autheur* (Paris: Gabriel Buon, 1584), 80, 313: Sonnet: "Saincte Gastine, o douce secretaire:" "mon Laurier," and Ode 15: "A la forest de Gastine," "Couché sous tes ombrages vers/Gastine, je te chante/Autant que les Grecs par leurs vers/La forest d'Erymanthe." Ronsard was well known for amending his works. I have used the 1584 edition, the last published before his death in 1585, but note changes to relevant lines between editions. See Louis Terreaux, *Ronsard, correcteur de ses oeuvres: les variantes des* Odes *et des deux premiers livres des* Amours (Geneva: Droz, 1968).

a large quantity of oaks, causing great loss and disorder."[41] In 1566, the *grand-maître* of Brittany reported in a meeting of the King's Council that the

> forest of Carnouet in Quimperlé, situated along the shore of the ocean, several ships passing there cut and carried away large quantities of wood without anyone knowing who it was ... [and] impossible to prevent them unless the King permitted the guards and foresters to carry arms.[42]

In 1570, Guillaume Mallart, *maitre des forets* in the duchy of Alençon, reported that "there were places in the forest [of Gouffern] ravaged because, during the war, they placed flocks there so that they were not taken by the soldiers."[43]

When the fighting subsided, the forests were also a casualty of the demands of the repair work in its wake. In 1568, for example, the monks of Saint-Pierre-D'Avenay were permitted to take from the forest of Epernay "such a quantity of wood as was necessary for the repair of their church and monastery burned during the troubles."[44] Likewise, the canons, abbot, prior and convents of the churches of Sainte-Croix and Saint-Aignan, Saint-Evert, Saint-Pierre-du-Pont, Saint-Père, Saint-Amy, and Saint-Samson d'Orléans were allowed to cut thirty *arpents* of tall timber from the forest of Orleans to employ "in their repairs of the said churches ruined during the troubles."[45] The forests of France were not just allocated to reinstate Catholic communities but also to prominent individuals. Charles IX gifted president of the *Parlement* of Paris, Christophe du Thou, with "10 *arpents* of wood from the forest of Retz for the re-establishment of mills belonging to Thou, which were burned when the bridge of Charenton was seized by those of the new opinion."[46]

---

[41] AN Z 1E 339, fol. 51v cited in Devèze, *La vie*, 2:235: "en assemblée illicite et à port d'armes, se transportant dans les forets du prince de Porcian, abbattant les bois de haute futaie, une grande quantité de chenes (1300 à 1400 cordes de bois), causant grande perte et désordre."

[42] Bibliothèque nationale (BN) manuscript français 18154, fol. 44 cited in Devèze, *La vie*, 2:235: "forest de Carnouet en Quimperlé étant située le long du rivage de la mer, plusieurs navires passant auprès d'icelles couppent et emportent ordinairement grande quantité de bois sans que l'on puisse savoir qui c'est ... impossible de les en empescher s'il ne plaist au Roy permeitre aux gardes et forestiers qu'il y commectra de porter armes."

[43] BN ms fr 25243, fol. 95 cited in Devèze, *La vie*, 2:236: "il y a eu des endroits de la forest ravages parce que, pendant le temps de guerre, on y a mis les troupeaux afin qu'ils ne soient pris par les gens de guerre."

[44] AN U 548, 31 August 1568, p. 352 cited in Devèze, *La vie*, 2:238: "telle quantité de bois qui leur sers necessaire pour la reparation de leur église et monastère bruslé pendant les troubles."

[45] AN U 548, 29 October 1568, p. 352 cited in Devèze, *La vie*, 2:238: "pour faire jouir les chanoines, abbé, prieur et convent des églises Sainte-Croix et Saint-Aignan, Saint-Evert, Saint-Pierre-du-Pont, Saint-Père, Saint-Amy et Saint-Samson d'Orléans de la coupe de 30 arpens de bois de haute fustaye, à prendre en la forest d'Orléans pour estre employez aux reparations des dites églises ruinées pendant les troubles."

[46] AN U 548, p. 352 cited in Devèze, *La vie*, 2:238: "de 10 arpens de bois à prendre dans la forest de Retz pour le restablissement des moulins audit de Thou appartenans, bruslées lors de la saisie du pont de Charenton, par ceux de la nouvelle opinion."

In asserting regulation of royal forests through the 1560s, *lettres patentes* from Charles IX rescinded a series of rights and permissions due to abuses, complaining, for example, of such wrongdoings by people who

> under colour of some permission that they claim to have, make ash from the branches and little trees that cannot be used for mill wood, dissipate, burn, consume and make great damage to the trees of our forest of our realm so that they are almost totally emptied.[47]

Jean de Bodin de Montguichet was third counsellor of *eaux et forets de la table de marbre de Paris* and *maître en requestes* to Catherine de Médicis. In 1570 he was sent to report on the extent of wartime damage to, and theft from, the king's forests of Normandy, a task that did little to endear him to nearby communities and elite families.[48] His extensive list recorded all manner of destruction including abuse by local residents of their rights to take dead wood from the forests. "They strip the trees near the roots or pierce them and put onion or oil in to make them die so as to cut them down afterwards ... an incredible loss to their advantage."[49] Through such practices, they prevent acorns and beechnuts from reaching maturity, which was, as Bodin reported poetically and pointedly, "the fruit and food of beasts and poor people, the Manna of the Republic, to the point that one only sees from seven years to seven years sufficient qualities of beechnuts and acorns, for trees denuded of branches carry none."[50]

Ronsard's forest of Gâtine was likewise subject to these forces of war through the very period that he was writing. Between April and June of 1570, Guillaume Mallart, écuyer, sieur de Vaufermant, *maitre des eaux et forets de duché d'Alencon*, took a tour through the forests of the region including the Gâtine, reporting that its regular logging had been halted "during the hostilities of war, and because of the passage of men of arms on foot and horseback passing through the land."[51] However, it would be the intensive logging of the domain that occurred in the following years that appears to have spurred

---

47 AN Z1E 341, Lettres de Saint-Germain-en-Laye, July 1567, fol. 150 cited in Devèze, *La vie*, 2:249: "sous couleur de quelque permission qu'ils dissent avoir de nous de faire cendres de branchages et menus bois qui ne peut server à faire bois de moule, dissipent, bruslent, consomment et font si grand desgat des arres qui sont esdites forests de notre royaume qu'elles sont quasi toutes dépeuplées."

48 Devèze, *La vie*, 2:212–3. See also Stuart Carroll, *Noble Power During the French Wars of Religion: The Guise Affinity and the Catholic Cause in Normandy* (Cambridge: Cambridge University Press, 1998), 193–94.

49 BN ms fr 5347, fol. 4v cited in Devèze, *La vie*, 2:240: "ils pellent les arbres prez la racine ou les percent et y mettent de l'oignon ou de l'huile pour les faire mourir afin qu'ils les puissant après coupper ... un dommage incroyable qu'on fait à leur avantage à tous en général."

50 BN ms fr 5347, fol. 6v cited in Devèze, *La vie*, 2:240: "qui est le fruict et nourriture du bestial et des povres gens, la manne de la République, au point qu'on ne voit que de sept ans en sept ans advenir quantité suffisante de faînes et de glands, car les arbres dénués de branches n'apportent rien."

51 BN Ms fr 25243, fol. 85v cited in Devèze, *La vie*, 2:241: "La vuidange [des coupes de la foret de la Gâtine près d'Argentan] n'avait pu ester faicte étant donné le temps d'hostilité et de guerre, et à cause des passages de la gendarmerie et gens de pied et de cheval qui passent par le pays."

some of Ronsard's most significant arboreal interventions, in Elegy 24, in which he laments the logging of the forest that bordered on La Possonnière, his family's estate in the Vendômois. Scholars have considered this work in varied ways: for its contribution to notions of landscape, place, and regionalism, its exploration of the mutability of nature, and for its heavy debt to and imitation of various classical works.[52]

By 1576, Ronsard had returned from court to his native region and may have seen the visible impact of its logging at first hand. The Gâtine was not a royal asset but was instead an aristocratic holding of the heavily indebted Calvinist leader Henri, Duke of Vendôme and King of Navarre. In a 1573 assessment it was measured by notary and surveyor Pierre Lemoyne and in the same year, facing mounting debts, Henri's Council of Vendôme proposed its sale.[53] The Council had recommended Henri sell the Gâtine because it held, among other arboreal species, "the tallest and most beautiful oaks to work."[54] They calculated its value as covering about half of Henri's outstanding debt. Technically, the sale did not inevitably spell the end of the arboreal resource. The forest was apportioned into twelve lots, the rights to log (or to conserve) thus falling to the purchasers.[55] These lots were ceded as compensation against various titles on the forest, including one of fifty *arpents* to Loys de Ronsard, chevalier, sieur de la Possonnière, Ronsard's nephew.[56] Ronsard's extended family appear to have been beneficiaries of this division, which prioritized the economic over the forest's other potential values.

Nonetheless, in Elegy 24, Ronsard took the Calvinist Henri squarely as his target, although unnamed, from the opening lines of the work, clearly situating the king's actions as sordid money-grabbing.[57]

> Whoever first has the hand assigned
> To cut you down, Forest, with a hard axe,
> May he pierce himself with his own stick,
> And feel in his stomach the hunger of Erysichthon ...
> Thus may he swallow his revenues and lands
> And devour himself afterwards with the teeth of war.

---

52 Isidore Silver, *Three Ronsard Studies* (Geneva: Droz, 1978), Ute Margarete Saine, "Dreaming the Forest of Gâtine: Ecology and Antiquity in Ronsard," *Cincinnati Romance Review* 9 (1990): 1–12; Danièle Duport, *Les Jardins qui sentent le sauvage: Ronsard et la Poétique du Paysage* (Geneva: Droz, 2000); Louisa Mackenzie, "'Ce ne sont pas des bois': Poetry, Regionalism, and Loss in the Forest of Ronsard's Gâtine," *Journal of Medieval and Early Modern Studies* 32, no. 2 (2002): 343–74; Susan K. Silver, "'Adieu Vieille Forest …': Myth, Melancholia and Ronsard's Family Trees," *Neophilologus* 86, no. 1 (2002): 33–34; See also Mackenzie, *The Poetry of Place*.

53 Archives départementales des Basses-Pyrenees, E 889. On the sale, René Caisso, "La Vente de la forêt de Gâtine à l'époque de Ronsard," *Humanisme et Renaissance* 4, no. 3 (1937): 274–85.

54 "les plus haultz et beaulx chesnes propres à ouvrager," cited in Caisso, "La Vente," 283.

55 Caisso, "La Vente," 275.

56 Caisso, "La Vente," 276.

57 In the 1623 edition this work gained the title, "Contre les bucherons de la forest de Gastine," which makes its target appear far more generic than contemporary information would suggest.

> May there, to avenge the blood of our forests,
> Always be new interest on new debts
> Owed to the usurer, and that in the end he consumes
> All his wealth to pay back the principal sum ...
> Truly ungrateful people, who do not know how to recognize
> The goods received from you.[58]

In the 1587 edition of Ronsard's *œuvres*, a new addition, possibly added by the poet himself before his death in 1585, was appended to another sonnet composed in 1552 about the forest of Gâtine. This made the target of Ronsard's contempt even more explicit:

> This forest is today half sold by the poor management of the ministers of the Prince. Unhappy are the Princes and Kings, who to furnish their crazy expenditure, sell in a day what Nature could not produce in a thousand years.[59]

Charles IX's legislative efforts from the 1560s signalled a sustained, if largely ineffective, effort at a coherent royal forestry policy, while further regulations in 1573 aimed to conserve French royal domain forests. Henri's decision to sell the Gâtine, a dynastic asset, was not limited by these legal changes, although his actions did run counter to the preservation of forest forms implied in them. Henri's actions were thus legal, but Ronsard's perception of a common good being lost voiced a position increasingly reflected in royal legislation and contemporary publications such as those by Belon and Palissy before him.

Ronsard may well have been particularly disappointed because he expected rather more for the region from this religiously flexible dynasty. His sonnet celebrating the 1551 birth of the Duke of Beaumont, first-born son of Antoine de Bourbon, Duke of Vendôme, tied the family intimately to this region of natural and agricultural abundance: "the Loir be milk, its green ramparts/Transform into an emerald carpet."[60] The staunchly Catholic Ronsard had likely vested high hopes in Antoine, who maintained a rather more ambiguous religious position than his brother, Louis, Prince de Condé, one of the leading Calvinists of the period. Antoine, by contrast, dabbled with a possible return to the Catholic faith of his ancestors. Ronsard may have been hinting at just such a possibility in the final lines of the poem in which he declares:

---

58 Ronsard, *Les œuvres*, 651. Elegy 24: "Quiconque aura premier la main embesongnée/A te couper Forest, d'une dure congnée,/Qu'il puisse s'enferrer de son propre baston,/Et sente en l'estomac la faim d'Erisichthon, ... Ainsi puisse engloutir ses rentes & sa terre,/Et se devore apres par les dents de la guerre./Qu'il puisse pour vanger le sang de nos forests, Tousjours nouveaux emprunts sur nouveaux interests/Devoir à l'usurier, & qu'en fin il consommé/Tout son bien à payer la principale somme ... Peuples vrayment ingrats, qui n'on sceu recognoistre/les biens receus de vous."

59 Ronsard, *Les œuvres en sept tomes*, vol. 1 (Paris: Gabriel Buon, 1578), 167: "Cette forest pour le jourd'huy est demie venduë par le mauvais mesnage des ministres du Prince. Malheureux sont les Princes & les Roys, lesquels pour fournirà leurs folles dispenses, vendent en un jour ce que la Nature ne peut produire en mille ans." See also discussion on the authorship in Silver, *Three Ronsard Studies*, 137–38.

60 Ronsard, *Les œuvres*, 251: "Le Loyr soit laict, son rempart verdissant,/En vn tapis d'esmeraudes se change."

> Here is the day that the child of my master
> Being born into the world, has into the world made reborn
> The first faith and the first honour.[61]

However, any return to the first faith was not to be for Antoine nor the son who would be his heir, Henri, the Duke of Beaumont's younger brother. Ronsard made substantial changes to these final lines in later editions, removing any reference to faith.[62] Henri had doubly disappointed the Catholic poet, not only as the vendor of the Gâtine but also by his Protestantism.

Ronsard thus witnessed a repeated cycle of religious change in both father and son over the course of his active years as a poet, which was reflected in his changing acknowledgements of the family through his works. Henri's life was one not only bound with cycles of conversion but also of fortune. As King of Navarre, he had inherited an impoverished realm, forcing the sale of dynastic assets such as the Gâtine, but in 1584, he would be announced as heir presumptive to the French throne and could look forward to riches to come, not least the forests of the French royal domain.[63] Ronsard may have hoped that his threnodic verse could make Henri value these natural resources and avoid their traumatic devastation, but he had also come to recognize that change was an ever-present feature, both of nature and of human fortune. Such a view is reflected in the last lines of Elegy 24 which draw to the conclusion:

> Oh Gods, true is the philosophy
> That says that all things in the end will perish
> And in changing form will be clothed in another: ...
> Matter remains, and form is lost.[64]

---

[61] Pierre de Ronsard, *Les Amours* (Paris: veuve Maurice de La Porte, 1552), 91: "Voici le iour, que l'enfant de mon maistre,/Naissant au monde, au monde a fait renaistre,/La foy premiere, & le premier honneur."

[62] Changed in the 1578 edition, to "Ce iour nasquit l'heritier de mon maistre./File-luy, Parque, vn beau filet d'honeur,/Puis aille au Ciel de Nectar se repaistre," Ronsard, *Les œuvres en sept tomes*, 1:643.

[63] Interestingly, Henri had abjured his forced Catholic conversion after the St Bartholomew's Massacre of 1574 by making use of a forest. In February 1576, he seized upon an opportunity to escape while on a hunt through the forest of Halatte on the outskirts of Senlis. Ronald S. Love, *Blood and Religion: The Conscience of Henri IV* (Montreal: McGill-Queens University Press, 2001), 69; Vincent J. Pitts, *Henri IV of France: His Reign and Age* (Baltimore: Johns Hopkins University Press, 2012), 75.

[64] Ronsard, *Les œuvres*, 652: "O Dieux, que veritable est la Philosophie,/Qui dit que toute chose à la fin perira,/Et qu'en changeant de forme une autre vestira: ... La matiere demeure, & la forme se perd." See Malcolm Quainton, *Ronsard's ordered chaos: visions of flux and stability in the poetry of Pierre de Ronsard* (Manchester: Manchester University Press, 1980); Silver, *Three Ronsard Studies*, 139–40; Michel Jeanneret, *Perpetuum mobile: métamorphoses des corps et des oeuvres de Vinci à Montaigne* (Paris: Macula, 1997); Silver, "Adieu Vieille Forest."

Nature for Ronsard was always changing form, an idea that he knew from the writings of Antiquity and which was shared by his contemporaries.[65] These ideas were vital to Ronsard's reconciliation and sense of agency in regard to the traumatic loss of the Gâtine.

The religious differences that divided the Catholic author from this "woodcutter," a leading Huguenot, were palpable.[66] It was not the first reference in Ronsard's work to the destructive force of civil war and, specifically, to Huguenot violence on the natural world. In a 1569 work, "The Pine Tree," Ronsard voiced fears about the potential loss of a single pine tree threatened by the approaching Protestant forces of Henri's uncle, Louis de Condé.

> How I trembled recently in cold fear
> That your plant, which is holy to me, would be cut down!
> Alas, I die when I think in these days
> That Blois was taken, and that Tours was threatened.[67]

Here, the poet appeared to intuitively grasp that the loss of the forest was as much due to military operations and fortifications in the region, as to industrial profits. As Devèze has demonstrated, war was a key factor in forest diminution in the second half of the century.[68]

In Ronsard's works, Protestants, in war or penury, could not appreciate the poetic beauty and resource of the Gâtine, for to do so required a particular emotional and spiritual disposition. Elegy 24 develops a myth found in Ovid's *Metamorphosis*, of another king, Erysichthon who, unwise like Henri, felled Ceres' sacred oak tree and was punished with the curse of Famine, leading him to devour not only his daughter but eventually himself. In 1553, Gervaise Sepin, a neo-Latin poet from Saumur, who had written a range of poems celebrating the natural world and specific features of his region, had also taken this myth as inspiration for a poem about the cutting down of a willow tree: "Are you cutting up her body with an axe? You hear the sounds emitted from the tree ... these are the groans and moans of a dying goddess."[69] Ronsard, too,

---

[65] Silver, *Three Ronsard Studies*, 141, and Isidore Silver, "Ronsard's Reflections on Cosmogony and Nature," *PMLA* 79, no. 3 (1964): 219–33. This theme appears elsewhere in Ronsard's *oeuvre*, including his "Hymne de la Mort": "Ce que fut se refaict, tout coulle comme une eau,/Et rien dessus le Ciel ne se void de nouveau:/Mais la forme se change en une autre nouvelle,/Et ce changement là, VIVRE au monde s'appele," Ronsard, *Les œuvres*, 746. For the views of contemporaries on natural resource losses, see Susan Broomhall, "Devastated Nature: The Emotions of Natural World Catastrophe in Sixteenth-Century France," in *Trauma in the Early Modern Period*, ed. Erin Peters and Cynthia Richards (Lincoln: University of Nebraska Press, forthcoming).

[66] As noted by Mackenzie, "Ce ne sont pas des bois."

[67] Ronsard, *Les œuvres*, 785: "Que ie tremblois naguerre à froide crainte/Qu'on ne coupast ta plante qui m'est sainte!/Helas ie meurs quand i'y pense en ces iours/Que Blois fut pris, & qu'on menaçoit Tours."

[68] Devèze, *La vie*, 2:336.

[69] Cited in I. D. Macfarlane, "Neo-Latin Verse: Some New Discoveries," *The Modern Language Review* 54, no. 1 (1959): 22–28 at 25: "In eum quem salices scindentem reperit": "Illique ferro corpora dissecas?/Audis fragores arboris æditos:/Si nescias, sunt hi Dolores/Mortiferae gemitusque Diuæ."

considered the emotions of the natural world in crises, highlighting the tree's physical and emotional pain.

> Listen, Woodcutter, stay your arm awhile
> It is not the woods that you are cutting down,
> Do you not see the blood that gushes forth
> Of the Nymphs who lived beneath the rough bark?
> Sacrilegious murderer ...

He anticipates the varied forms of suffering experienced by the trees and their legendary inhabitants:

> You will feel the ploughshare, the coulter, and the plow:
> You will lose your silence, and gasping with fright
> Neither Satyres nor Pans will visit you again.[70]

Indeed, Ronsard fears that it is love itself that will be lost if the woods are no more: "No more will the amorous Shepherd .../speak of his ardour for his beautiful Janette:/All will become mute, Echo will be without her voice."[71] Ronsard voices the suffering of nature at its devastation but also suggests a concomitant destruction of human affective capacity. For Ronsard, the loss of the Gâtine represents the demise of emotional experience and expression, an affective practice of love, in humans. If they cannot love this forest, can they love at all?

These ideas were connected to the strong sense of place in Ronsard's works, place that was defined as much by its spiritual emotional qualities as its geographical or even conceptual boundaries. Drawing once again upon classical conventions, Ronsard rendered homage to the forest that, bordering on his childhood home, had nourished his emotional turmoils since his youth. In a sonnet first published in *Les Amours* of 1552, the poet paid respect to the therapeutic function of this forest:

> Holy Gâtine, happy secretary
> Of my troubles, who hears the response in your wood
> Out loud, and in a whisper
> The long sighs that my heart cannot silence.[72]

---

[70] Ronsard, *Les œuvres*, 651: "Escoute, Bucheron (areste un peu le bras)/Ce ne sont pas des bois que tu jectes à bas,/Ne vois-tu pas le sang lequel desgoute à force/Des Nymphes qui vivoyent dessous la dure escorce?/Sacrilege meudrier ... Tu sentiras le soc, le coutre et la charrue:/Tu perdras ton silence, et haletans d'effroy/Ny Satyres, ny Pans ne viendront plus chez toy."

[71] Ronsard, *Les œuvres*, 651: "Plus l'amoureux Pasteur sur un tronq adossé, ... Ne dira plus l'ardeur de sa belle Janette:/Tout deviendra muet, Echon sera sans vois."

[72] Ronsard, *Les Amours*, 71: "Saincte Gastine, heureuse secretaire/De mes ennuis, qui response en ton bois,/Ores en haulte, ores en basse voix,/Aux longs souspirs que mon cuœur ne peult taire." By 1584 this is changed to "Saincte Gastine, ô douce secretaire," Ronsard, *Les œuvres*, 80.

This homage to the Gâtine continued in several more works across his œuvre, including his Ode to the Forest of Gâtine.[73] Likewise, his lament, Elegy 24, farewells the forest that has been the training ground for his poetic arts.[74] This quiet secretary that had both heard his troubles and been a source of his inspiration is also made explicitly Catholic. It was the Holy Gâtine, just as the pine tree of his garden was the "plant, which is holy to me." This situated the poem in Ronsard's Catholic worldview, which valued the natural world in a way that, he suggests, Protestants did not. Ronsard's œuvre made these locations not only sacred, poetic sites, in the classical tradition, but also Catholic and aristocratic ones that rejected the economic and industrial imperatives of others.[75] It was a strongly emotional, spiritual space, created by a personal bond to a place experienced through faith behaviours and concepts. Just as place theorists such as Edward S. Casey consider place as space experienced through the lived body, we might consider these places as spaces defined by emotional and spiritual experiences in and through them.[76] Space here became place by Ronsard's positive emotional engagement with it. This was not regionalism in the sense of a shared set of beliefs and cultures with others in this region.[77] Rather, these poetic works speak to Ronsard's very personal relationship with the forest. It evidently did not encompass Henri de Navarre, the Duke of Vendôme who held dynastic rights over it, because for Ronsard, he did not live and experience these spiritual sentiments with nature, like Ronsard suggests he did himself.

Susan K. Silver recognizes the melancholic register of Elegy 24, and Louisa Mackenzie the yearning for a lost past.[78] Yet, there is something specifically connected to place and to nature too in these works, as much as the past. For Ronsard does not see himself as powerless. His works define a specific form of agency for himself. He would make the lost forest live and breathe through his works; his poetry held form and function in conserving nature. As Mackenzie and Silver note, Ronsard argues that his poetry can

---

[73] Ronsard, *Les œuvres*, 313: "... celer je ne puis/A la race future/De combien obligé je suis/A ta belle verdure."

[74] Ronsard, *Les œuvres*, 651: "adieu Vielle forest, le jouet de Zephyre,/Où premier j'accorday les langues de ma lyre."

[75] Mackenzie makes a similar point, "Ce ne sont pas des bois," 355.

[76] Edward S. Casey, "How to Get from Space to Place in a Fairly Short Stretch of Time," in *Senses of Place*, ed. Steven Feld and Keith H. Basso (Santa Fe: School of American Research Press, 1997), 13–52. See also Andreas Reckwitz, "Affective Spaces: A Praxeological Outlook," *Rethinking History* 16, no. 2 (2012): 241–58; and Tim Cresswell's recent argument that the poem itself can create place, Tim Cresswell, "Towards *Topopoetics*: Space, Place and the Poem," in *Place, Space and Hermeneutics*, ed. Bruce J. Banz (Cham: Springer, 2017), 319–31.

[77] Mackenzie, "Ce ne sont pas des bois," suggests that Ronsard defined a kind of regionalism through these works, but, to my mind, it is not clear that Ronsard has in mind any kind of space or place that was to be shared with a broader community.

[78] Silver, "Adieu Vielle Forest," 36; Mackenzie, "Ce ne sont pas des bois," 343; see also Oliver Pot, *Inspiration et mélancolie: L'épistémologie dans les "Amours" de Ronsard* (Geneva: Droz, 1990).

protect and remember the forest.[79] Symbiotically, just as he needs it for his inspiration, the forest and its surrounds need him to memorialize them for future generations.

Ronsard proposes himself as the agent of their ongoing survival, in poetic form. From the very beginning of his poetry career, they were linked, *through* his emotional engagement: "Gâtine, Loir, and you, my sad verses."[80] In "The Pine Tree," he declares confidently: "I will say it, so that this history/will flourish in memory despite the passage of time."[81] This then was not a relationship that can sustain every reader or poet with nature, but one borne of his specific relationship. This relationship could not be replicated, because only Ronsard, the Catholic poet, was the chosen tool of the forest's voice, its pain and its suffering. This concept is embedded in his phrasing, in repetitions of the possessive: "my Gâtine, ... my Vendômois river [the Loir]."[82] Elsewhere, Ronsard recreates Ovid's elegy in his own, possessive manner: "Someone after a thousand years, astonished by my verses/will want to drink at my Loir as at Parnassus."[83] Ronsard's power of emotional management regarding the devastating loss of this forest lies in his ability to conserve it in his poetry.

The ideas that are embedded in Ronsard's Elegy 24 clearly predate the sale of the forest of Gâtine. They are part of long-held intellectual traditions and apprehensions about the mutability of nature, the poet as the one who speaks for and remembers lost nature, and who immortalizes himself through nature. Classical myths and poetic forms form important foundations for Ronsard's work but there were also real-world contexts of religious politics and of actual sales that significantly shaped his *œuvre*. Elegy 24, in particular, is also crafted in the highly individual context of an ageing poet, whose sense of a spiritual site, a Catholic place, was profoundly disrupted by its loss. The forest was for him a resource in another kind of psychosystem, and his interest defined by its faith-sustaining properties for human society, and himself as an individual.

Conclusions

In the battle of religious ideas and practices that swirled across France in the later sixteenth century, the kingdom's forests played an important role. They were enlisted as sites to read the vitality and validity of particular faith positions but also become places where spiritualities were lived and enjoyed, or destroyed by those of opposing

---

79 Mackenzie, "Ce ne sont pas des bois," 351; Silver, "Adieu Vieille Forest," 36.

80 Ronsard, *Les Amours* (1552), 33: "Gastine, Loir, et vous mes tristes vers"; later replaced by "Et vous rochers, les hostes de mes vers," Ronsard, *Les œuvres* (1584), 34.

81 Ronsard, *Les œuvres* (1584), 785: "Je la diray, à fin que telle histoire,/Maugré le temps fleurisse par memoire." Earlier editions have "Je la diray, afin que telle histoire,/En tous endroitz fleurisse par memoire."

82 Ronsard, *Les œuvres*, 303. Ode: "A sa Lyre" "Mais ma Gastine, et le haut crin des bois,/Qui vont bornant mon fleuve Vandomois."

83 Ronsard, *Les œuvres*, 180. Sonnet "Cesse tes pleurs, mon livre:" "Quelqu'un après mille ans de mes vers étonné/Voudra dedans mon Loir, comme en Permesse boire."

views. Forests in general, and particular forests, like the Gâtine, were conceptualized to carry and sustain various spiritual values and experiences, yet they were also material manifestations of God's design and his providence. In this context, regardless of the varied genres or denominations in which spiritual ideas were expressed, productivity, reproductivity, and sustainability were concepts that were founded as much in faith positions as in intellectual ideas and economic realities.

Chapter 12

HOLY WAR, COLD WAR: WAR, COMEDY, AND THE LESSONS OF HISTORY IN THE FILMS OF MARIO MONICELLI

Louise D'Arcens*

ON ASH WEDNESDAY, 2017, two men were apprehended for vandalizing the Cross of Sacrifice, an Australian war memorial in Toowong, Queensland. According to a *Brisbane Times* report on the incident, the men had removed the bronze longsword affixed to the front of the crucifix-shaped monument and "placed it in [sic] an anvil to reshape it into a garden hoe."[1] Although the report's headline labelled the men "religious fanatics," the act had at least three hallmarks of civil disobedience actions carried out by the Plowshares anti-war movement begun in the US in 1980.[2] First, it was a direct action involving the destruction of weaponry; second, the perpetrators were affiliated with the Catholic Worker movement; and, finally, the banner the men hung over the vandalized monument, bearing the phrase "beat swords into ploughshares" and an image of two male silhouettes engaged in that act, clearly alludes to the larger movement's imagery and motto, taken from Isaiah 2:4:

> they shall beat their swords into plowshares,
> and their spears into pruning hooks.
> Nation will not take up sword against nation,
> nor will they train for war anymore.
>
> (NIV)

What marks out this episode in Toowong from other Plowshares acts is the thread of rather literal medievalism woven into it. While the movement's most famous actions have involved inflicting damage on fighter jets and even nuclear weapons—updated versions of the sword—the Toowong pacifists interpreted the biblical edict literally, creating an agricultural tool from a sword, the powerful symbol of the long history of military violence. It is true that a sword need not allude to medieval warfare alone. In

---

* **Louise D'Arcens** is Professor of English at Macquarie University. Her publications include *Comic Medievalism: Laughing at the Middle Ages* (2014), *Old Songs in the Timeless Land: Medievalism in Australian Literature 1840–1910* (2011), *The Cambridge Companion to Medievalism* (2016), and *World Medievalism: The Middle Ages in Global Textual Cultures* (forthcoming 2021).

1 Cameron Atfield, "Religious Fanatics Charged Over Damage to Toowong War Memorial," *Brisbane Times*, March 2, 2017 www.brisbanetimes.com.au/queensland/religious-fanatics-vandalise-toowong-war-memorial-20170302-guosnc.html.

2 See Sharon E. Nepstad, *Religion and War Resistance in the Plowshares Movement* (New York: Cambridge University Press, 2008).

fact Sir Reginald Blomfield, the original designer of the Cross of Sacrifice monuments which spread across the British Commonwealth after the Great War, explicitly eschewed medievalist allusions in his modernist design, aiming "above all, to keep clear of any sentimentalism of the Gothic" which might glorify battlefield sacrifice.[3] But Blomfield's attempts to de-medievalize the sword were lost on the Toowong Plowsharers. Despite an evident awareness of the designer's desire to divorce war deaths from medievalist ideals of chivalric sacrifice, they nevertheless regarded the monument's fusion of sword and cross as a shameful symbol of "the countless wars ... blessed by Christianity" which they claimed post-dated "the conversion of Emperor Constantine" in the fourth century. It would seem, furthermore, that Blomfield's anti-medievalist intentions were thwarted almost from the start. According to *The Brisbane Courier*, at the monument's unveiling on ANZAC Day 1924, the Governor General quoted the first verse of Sir John Stanhope Arkwright's poem "O Valiant Hearts," which honours the "knightly virtue" of the fallen.[4] The sentimentalism of the Gothic exerted its undeniable pull.

Despite its highly localized appearance, the story of the Toowong Cross of Sacrifice exposes a broader truth about the contradictory place occupied by the Middle Ages in modern understandings of warfare. On the one hand, as Allen Frantzen and Stefan Goebel have both amply demonstrated, the medieval period, with its codes of chivalry, has been glorified as the era of martial nobility, used to justify and exalt war, with the Great War of 1914–1918 being a conflict that invoked medieval ethics and iconographies of combat with conspicuous intensity and regularity.[5] On the other hand, the period's powerful association with warfare in the modern imaginary has, as many scholars have noted, underpinned a widespread and unreflective tendency to associate the Middle Ages with a barbarous violence that is coded as specifically pre-modern. Andrew Lynch's account of this is worth quoting at length:

> If "medieval" wars are real, so are "Renaissance" wars, "Reformation" wars, "Enlightenment" wars and "modern" wars generally, and yet, as those terms indicate, the post-medieval is not as strongly identified with war and fighting as the Middle Ages are. Because the modern successfully styled itself as progress in humane learning, religion, science and political institutions, many imaginations of it are strangely dissociated from the history of war and colonial conquest. An early modern battle will primarily be understood as, for instance, part of the Wars of Religion or the English Civil War, not as typifying the "early modern," let alone the "Renaissance," in the way that a twelfth-century Crusade or a battle in the Hundred Years' War seems to typify the "medieval." Even the Great War does not define "modernity" as fully, and was itself heavily disguised with medievalist symbolism ... Conversely, recent military atrocities are readily described as "almost medieval" rather than by reference to any other era, especially our

---

3 Allen Frantzen, *Bloody Good: Chivalry, Sacrifice, and the Great War* (Chicago: University of Chicago Press, 2004), 253.

4 *The Brisbane Courier*, April 26, 1924, p. 7.

5 See Frantzen, *Bloody Good*, and Stefan Goebel, *The Great War and Medieval Memory: War, Remembrance and Medievalism in Britain and Germany, 1914–1920* (Cambridge: Cambridge University Press, 2009).

own; "*almost* medieval" suggests a pitch of barbarism that modernity can never quite reach, and a protective view of modernity in which war horror is anomalous because it belongs properly to the medieval past.[6]

What Lynch points to here is a discursive process in which ideas about war as an event and modern conception of "the medieval" come to mutually define and confine one another. In cinema, this naturalized and popularized assumption has led repeatedly to hyper-realist representations of medieval battle as the gruesome epitome of mud, blood, and death. Some of these representations are for the purposes of spectacle, with little stake in either defending or decrying the violence portrayed. One recent example of this is Justin Kurzel's strongly medievalizing adaptation of *Macbeth*, which foregrounds, in highly stylized scenes of visceral slaughter, combat as a natural tactic in a world where struggles for power are both pitiless and intimate. Others, such as Ridley Scott's Crusades film *Kingdom of Heaven* (2005), attempt representations of medieval battle as a pacifist gesture. Even when taking relish in the intimate and visceral brutality of pre-modern hand-to-hand combat, the underlying ethical purpose is to expose the irrationality, excessiveness, and futility of medieval warfare—and, because the Middle Ages are regarded as the warring era par excellence, the critique implicitly extends to warfare itself.

This chapter will explore two companion films, Mario Monicelli's *Brancaleone's Army/For Love and Gold* (*L'armata Brancaleone*, 1966) and *Brancaleone at the Crusades* (*Brancaleone alle Crociate*, 1970), analyzing how these films, especially *Brancaleone at the Crusades*, use their medieval setting to expose the arbitrary and chaotic nature not just of medieval combat, but of modern combat. Situating the films in the context of the anti-Vietnam War protests sweeping Italy in the 1960s and 70s, which were part of a broader volatile period characterized by Cold War anxiety as well as escalating domestic discord, I will argue that their representation of medieval bellicosity in general and the Crusades in particular draws pointed parallels to the modern West's chaotic incursions into the East and to Italy's state of civil unrest and increasingly repressive government. I will also explore how Monicelli's comic depictions deflate military pretensions then and now, using absurdity, irony, and farce to undercut the chivalric tradition of glorifying war.

Prior to the *Brancaleone* films, Monicelli had already earned a reputation as an anti-war filmmaker as a result of his 1959 film *The Great War* (*La Grande Guerra*), which is widely regarded to be one of the great pacifist war films of the twentieth century.[7] It is celebrated for its portrayal of Italy's role in the Great War through the use of situation comedy and a deflationary neorealist focus on everyday struggle—the two major characteristics of the *commedia all'italiana* that Monicelli was instrumental in shaping. *The Great War* is memorable for its de-romanticized portrayal of two unwilling conscripts,

---

[6] Andrew Lynch, "Medievalism and the Ideology of War," in *The Cambridge Companion to Medievalism*, ed. Louise D'Arcens (Cambridge: Cambridge University Press, 2016), 135–50 at 135.

[7] *La Grande Guerra*, dir. Mario Monicelli. Dino de Laurentiis Cinematografica, Grey-Film, 1959.

Giovanni and Oreste (the endearingly shambolic Vittorio Gassmann and Alberto Sordi), whose friendship grows out of their mutual desire to survive the war. Their lives in the trenches consist of mundane but also highly dangerous duties undertaken at the behest of their arrogant superiors. After a series of picaresque scrapes, the hapless pair is captured and ultimately executed by the Austrians when they refuse to divulge Italian secrets. Their humble and reluctant heroism goes unrecognized at the film's end, however, as their commanders and comrades believe they have deserted. Although Monicelli's refusal of patriotic military historiography attracted some criticism, the film proved to have wide audience appeal and won the Golden Lion at the 1959 Venice film festival. Given the strong association of Monicelli's name with anti-war cinema, it is puzzling that there has been little consideration given to the *Brancaleone* films as anti-war films despite the fact that they, like *The Great War*, are quintessentially anti-heroic picaresque tales that expose the opportunism, violence, and delusionary machismo that propel warfare. It is therefore worth revisiting in order to recognize the role of these films in his anti-war oeuvre, and also to expand the still small corpus of pacifist medievalist films

Starring the impoverished knight errant, Brancaleone di Norcia (played in full declamatory mock-heroic mode by Vittorio Gassman), the films portray his outlandish exploits with the small, scruffy "army" of misfits he gathers around him, which includes in the first film various brigands and vagrants, an orphan boy, a tiny and wizened Jew, and a Byzantine bastard son, and in the second film a blind man, a cripple, a dwarf, a leper (later revealed to be a fugitive princess), a masochistic penitent, a baby, and a witch. Under Brancaleone's blustering and chaotic leadership they embark on a range of adventures that includes falsely (and unsuccessfully) claiming a patrimony bequeathed in a stolen document, following a religious zealot, unsuccessfully attempting to collect ransom for a sham hostage, visiting hermits and stylites, settling the quarrel between Pope Gregory VII and Clement III, setting out on Crusade to the Holy Land (returning a kidnapped heir to his crusading father while there), and repeatedly getting into conflicts great and small along the way.

Just as Oreste and Giovanni in *The Great War* represented the human fodder of modern war, so too Monicelli says that the *Brancaleone* films' cast of misfits allows him to present "history from the point of view of the humble people, the little guy."[8] A key satiric target of the *Brancaleone* films is what Monicelli saw as the apologistic and romanticized way the medieval period has been depicted to the Italian people, and the nationalistic, ethnocentric, and Christocentric implications of these representations. The apparently haphazard structure of the *Brancaleone* films, as well as their earthy palette and the realism of the their hot and dusty mise-en-scènes, are a clear riposte to the immaculate Technicolor Middle Ages of Hollywood's creation, which Monicelli nominated as a particular *bête noire*. Monicelli's critique extended further, moreover, taking aim at what he regarded as academics' airbrushed, "glossy vision" (*visione patinata*) of the medieval

---

[8] Deborah Young, "Poverty, Misery, War and Other Comic Material: An Interview with Mario Monicelli," *Cinéaste* 29 (2004): 36–40 at 38.

period as refined and highly civilized, and replacing it with an Italian Middle Ages that is hierarchical, barbaric, and xenophobic (internally and externally).

> Civilization, truth, and science were on the other side: the side of Islam. That's what the Crusades were all about. We went to occupy places where they were more civilized. Of course, we were repulsed. I wanted to show this was the real Middle Ages in Italy—barbaric and uncivilized, savage, grotesque.[9]

It is not incidental that the director points to wars as the defining events of his "unglossy" counter-historical Middle Ages. Moreover, as I will later argue, it is significant that, in a gesture that bears the possible influence of Sir Steven Runciman's *A History of the Crusades*, Monicelli nominates the religious-military incursions of the Crusades as the events that most succinctly summarize the savagery of the Western medieval past. The realist underpinning impulse is not limited to the narrative, but is also evident in Monicelli's use of framing techniques characteristic of Italian neorealism, in which close-up is eschewed and bodies are embedded in their environments, creating a mise-en-scène that encompasses the characters' life-world.

To say, however, that the *Brancaleone* films simply replace fantasy with social realism would be too simplistic. This is especially true of their visual and aural aesthetic, in which brooding, empty landscapes and deserted towns, again inherited from Italian neorealism, give way to surreal, almost futurist interiors inhabited by a range of cameo characters (often women) in operatically camp costumes designed by Piero Gherardi, costume and design director on a number of Federico Fellini's films, including the oneiric *Juliet of the Spirits* (1965). Some of Monicelli's scenes even reprise the gusting wind that accompany Juliet's spiritual visions in Fellini's film. While these stylized environments seem removed from the mimetic Middle Ages outside, in another way they crystallize the film's "medievalness." The scene in an Italo-Byzantine palace, for instance, where Brancaleone finds himself being whipped by the sexually frenzied Lady Theodora (played by Barbara Steele, an icon of 1960s schlock), is both anachronistic and essentially medieval according to the film's vision of a perverse world dominated by cruelty, pain, and sacrifice. The use, for the dialogue, of a pseudo-archaic, macaronic Italo-Latin of Monicelli's own devising (he says he "invented an Italian that didn't exist") is in keeping with the films' overall comic strategy of offering "uno parodia molto vera," that is a meta-parody in which medieval chivalry and medievalist representation are lampooned by depicting a Middle Ages that is manifestly not real, but nevertheless aims to be true. Monicelli reused this language in his 1984 comedy *Bertoldo, Bertoldino e Cacasenno*, set in ninth-century Veneto. This approach to satiric and parodic truth licenses the creation of a condensed medieval world in which the First Crusade and the Black Death co-exist as temporal indexes of a past epitomized by war and disease.

---

9 Andrea Palazzino, "Il Medievo di Monicelli: una parodia molto vera," *Babel* 15 (2007): 11–16 at 12; Young, "Poverty," 38–39.

Marcia Landy has argued that the *Brancaleone* films are social satires which "explore affinities with contemporary cultural and political life."[10] While Monicelli has explicitly denied that the film satirizes contemporary Italy, elsewhere he has admitted that the film's bottom-up approach to recounting the past corresponds with the socialist and anti-authoritarian perspective that abides across his oeuvre. His displaced satire of the delusional violence of Italian Fascism is subtly present in Brancaleone's occasional maniacal outbursts in which he insists he is "il Duce" of his band. Characters who have power or authority are presented variously as mercurial, cruel, vengeful, exploitative, and arrogant, while warmth and compassion are the preserve of the film's pariah figures, including the Satanist witch Tiburzia, who ultimately sacrifices herself to Death to save Brancaleone during the duel in the desert. The medieval Church fares very badly in both the films' satire of power, being presented as a chief perpetrator of aggression and intolerance. The modality of this satire is largely comic compression; according to Monicelli, "it was easy to find farcical situations" (*situazone farsesche*) in medieval Catholic history,[11] and so disparate historical details such as competing claimants to the papacy, religious asceticism, and trials of faith are condensed into absurd scenes such as the papal face-off in *Brancaleone at the Crusades* where the dispute is resolved by Brancaleone being forced to walk across hot embers by a stylite who adjudicates the outcome. Elsewhere, the tone is bleak and haunting. Arguably the most moving episode across the two films is one in *Brancaleone at the Crusades* titled "The Ballad of Intolerance," in which the itinerant band come across a tree from whose branches dangle dozens of lynched bodies. When Tiburzia, who has the power to speak with hanged people, asks them how they got there, the disembodied voice of one body replies that the village priests and dignitaries rounded them up and killed them for their sins. These "sins" are mostly trifling and non-violent, ranging from an interest in astronomy to eating salami on a Friday, and even, in the case of one figure, simply being a Jew.

Several speeches in this scene give the lie to Monicelli's claim that these films are not commenting on modern Italy, such that this image of medieval atrocity also resonates with the enormities of the twentieth century. When the band first see the tree in the distance, they mistake the corpses for "strange fruit," a phrase immediately identified with the doleful song made famous by Billie Holliday about the lynching of African Americans in the modern South. One cannot, moreover, encounter the image of an executed Jew in a late twentieth-century film without being reminded of the most recent, and most appalling, chapter in the long European history of anti-Semitic persecution. After we learn of the innocent Jew's execution, the voice of another body, claiming to "see afar" into time, says "[t]ravellers, be glad, the world will not forever be intolerant," and offers a sanguine future vision of peace and equality that can only be taken as chillingly ironic in light of the monstrous intolerance of recent European history. The progressivist myth

---

[10] Marcia Landy, "Comedy and Counter-History," in *Historical Comedy on Screen*, ed. Hannu Salmi (Bristol: Intellect, 2011), 177–98 at 181.
[11] Palazzino, "Il Medievo," 15.

of modern civility is further crushed, this time without irony, when the unsettling voice of an especially ghoulish corpse utters an opposing prophesy: "you will be as we are." The use of voiceover for the corpses' speeches in this scene means that their voices float beyond the diegesis, addressing not just the band but history—and, indeed, modernity.

Considering Monicelli's left-wing sympathies, it is not surprising that his brutal Middle Ages would contain allusions to the atrocities perpetrated by the right-wing dictatorships of the Second World War. Images of domestic massacres such as that in the "Ballad of Intolerance" episode would have had strong resonance in an Italy that had for the last few years been engaged in the public commemoration of its anti-Fascist resistance movement, whose members had been ruthlessly and openly slaughtered by Mussolini's forces. Philip Cooke and John Foot have both analyzed the widespread construction of memorials dedicated to resistance martyrs in Italy's town and city squares after the war, including the famous Piazzale Loreto monument in Milan, with Foot affirming that "[t]he biggest surge of resistance monument building ... took place in the 1960s and 1970s" (149).[12] It might at first seem more counterintuitive to suggest that the film's portrayals of medieval violence are also alluding to the Vietnam War, since Italy played almost no active role at all in that conflict and the theatre of war was in a distant part of the world.[13] But it is beyond doubt that, as with other Western European nations in the second half of the 1960s, it was this war that was urgently on the minds of Monicelli's Italian viewers. Although the films were released four years apart, in this context it is more germane to discuss them as a pair, as the loose narrative that arcs across them can be seen to track the escalation of the Vietnam War and the growing momentum of opposition to it. Together they offer a medievalist response to, and allegory of, both the generalized bellicosity of the Cold War era and the specific aggression taking place in Vietnam.

The months immediately leading up to the release of *Brancaleone's Army* were characterized by increasing criticism in Italy of American neo-colonialism in general, and the incursion into Vietnam in particular. It is hardly surprising that this would be the case with Italy's famously robust left wing; but criticism of Vietnam was, as Rebecca Clifford and Nigel Townson have persuasively demonstrated, far more widely expressed. Protest against the war was, moreover, far from just a secular political concern; it was, rather, a significant point of accommodation between the left and Italy's Catholics from at least 1963 on. One of the most influential documents for fostering this shared climate of "spiritual Marxism" was *Pacem in terris*, the encyclical promulgated by Pope John XXIII on April 11, 1963, with its appeal to "all men of good will" (*universis bonae*

---

12 John Foot, *Italy's Divided Memory* (New York: Palgrave Macmillan, 2009), 149. See also Philip Cooke, *The Legacy of the Italian Resistance* (New York: Palgrave Macmillan, 2011).

13 Leopoldo Nuti does note, however, the important role played by the Italian ambassador in Hanoi in Operation Marigold, a diplomatic attempt to bring an end to the war. See Nuti, "The Center-Left Government in Italy and the Escalation of the Vietnam War," in *America, the Vietnam War, and the World: Comparative and International Perspectives*, ed. Andreas W. Daum, Lloyd C. Gardner, and Wilfried Mausbach (Cambridge: Cambridge University Press, 2003), 259–78.

voluntatis hominibus) to denounce the Cold War proliferation of weapons and to reject the concept of "just warfare" as a solution to tensions between nations.[14] In addition to its acknowledgement that Catholics might profitably collaborate with "commendable" and justice-seeking "unbelievers"[15] its much-cited argument that "in this age which boasts of its atomic power, it no longer makes sense to maintain that war is a fit instrument with which to repair the violation of justice"[16] was welcomed by pacifists both within and outside the Church. Although just warfare made a provisional return in Pope Paul VI's Pastoral Constitution *Gaudium et spes*, promulgated in the wake of Vatican II on December 7, 1965, the newer pontiff largely reinforced his predecessor's warnings about the accelerating dangers of war in the nuclear age.

Alongside its prominence in public religious and ethical discourse in Italy, the Vietnam incursion was having a palpable effect on Italian political life in the years leading up to the release of the first *Brancaleone* film. Leopoldo Nuti, a historian of Italy in the Cold War period, has described the Vietnam War as having "disproportionate relevance for Italian domestic and foreign policy" throughout the mid- to late 1960s.[17] In addition to the predictable animosities it intensified between the U.S.-supportive Right and the U.S.-critical Left, significant tensions and what Serge Ricard has called a "tumultuous internal debate"[18] emerged between Italy's centre Left and Far-Left, who in the early- to mid-1960s were in an uneasy coalition. The centre Left's avoidance of a direct condemnation of the conflict was at odds with the Far-Left's outright denunciation, and led to rifts that resulted in high-level governmental resignations.[19] This tension at home in turn affected Italy's and the Vatican's relationships with the U.S., as the mutual need to maintain transatlantic alliances was strained by the growing public disapproval of the war. Visiting representatives of the Johnson administration in mid-1966 encountered vociferous protest, and their attempts to explain the escalation of U.S. bombings in Vietnam were met with derision from the Left, a response that was symptomatic of their nation's general loss of standing across Europe. The war remained a significant focus of parliamentary debate, and complex diplomatic relations between America and Italy continued throughout the 1960s.

Popular objections to the war throughout the 1960s culminated in numerous protests across the nation, including, mid-decade, those held on December 21, 1965. Among the more famous protests of the later 1960s was the 1967 twenty-five-day peace march from Milan to Rome led by Danilo Dolci, the social reformer widely known as the

---

14 *Pacem in Terris*, http://w2.vatican.va/content/john-xxiii/en/encyclicals/documents/hf_j-xxiii_enc_11041963_pacem.html, para. 1.

15 *Pacem in Terris*, paras 159–60.

16 *Pacem in Terris*, para. 127.

17 Nuti, "The Center-Left," 259.

18 Serge Ricard, "Europe and the Vietnam War: A Thirty-Year Perspective," *Diplomatic History* 19, no. 5 (November 2005): 879–83 at 882.

19 Nuti, "The Center-Left," 264–69.

"Italian Gandhi." Dolci's extreme activism on behalf of the poor, and his exposure of the extortions carried out by organized crime syndicates in Sicily, earned him a medieval moniker; none less than Aldous Huxley called him, appositely, "a new St Francis."[20] As with the rest of Western (and parts of Eastern) Europe, 1968 was an intense year of protest in Italy, but the high point was the "hot Autumn" of 1969, in which war protests took place alongside rallies against local terrorism and general student and worker strikes. Anti-Vietnam protest was also registered powerfully in the creative sphere. Italian artists such as Michelangelo Pistoletto, with his mirror installation *Vietnam* (1965) and Pino Pascali, with his work *Le Armi* (1965) which featured military hardware fashioned from junk, were among the members of the Arte Povera movement who mobilized art as commentary about the war.[21] In the theatre, Italy's most famous living playwright Dario Fo's play *Toss the Lady Out* (*La signora è da buttare*, 1967) devoted its second Act to criticizing the foreign policy of the U.S. (the eponymous Lady), with Vietnam as the main focus. Interestingly, Fo's 1965 *Always Blame the Devil* (*La colpa è sempre del diavolo*), the first of his plays to be set in the Middle Ages, not only draws a historical parallel between the Holy Roman Empire and Vietnam-era America, but also features a character called Brancaleone, a thirteenth-century dwarf-devil who, using dark magic, incites a Cathar rebellion which makes him Duke. Tony Mitchell has pointed to the link between the name Brancaleone and organized crime in Southern Italy,[22] and the name could well have been a sly allusion to this kind of endemic corruption. But given Fo's interest in Italian folklore, the name could also conceivably double up as an allusion to contemporary organized crime and a nod to Giovanni Francesco Straparola's mid-sixteenth-century collection of tales *Le piacevole notti* (the Facetious Nights), which feature an ass who presents himself under the name Brancaleone (lion's claw) to appear more fearsome.[23] The play's use of a "medieval" dialect also anticipates, and possibly even influences, the invented Macaronic Italian used in Monicelli's films. The fact that Monicelli admitted that he tried to persuade Fo to play the Byzantine bastard Teofilatto dei Leonzi in the first film suggests that Monicelli saw in Fo a kindred artist for whom the Middle Ages offered a vehicle to criticize the corruption and wide-scale violence of the present.

Of the two films, the first, *Brancaleone's Army*, is not explicit in the parallel it suggests between medieval Italy as envisioned by Monicelli and any specific modern war. Rather, the indeterminate medieval world the characters inhabit is characterized by a general climate of menace, in which conflict can erupt at any time. Following Marcia Landy's argument that Monicelli's historical tragicomic mode "shift[s] emphasis from the agency

---

[20] Aldous Huxley, "Introduction" to Danilo Dolci, *Report from Palermo*, trans. P. D. Cummins (New York: Orion, 1959), ix.

[21] Nicholas Cullinan, "From Vietnam to Fiat-nam: The Politics of Arte Povera," *OCTOBER* 124 (Spring 2008): 8–30 at 14–16.

[22] Tony Mitchell, *Dario Fo: People's Court Jester*, rev. ed. (London: Methuen, 1999), 82.

[23] Giovanni Francesco Straparola, *The Nights of Straparola*, trans. W. G. Waters (London: Lawrence and Bullen, 1894), 2:166–70.

of the characters onto their circumstances,"[24] it would seem the films' hectic mood of constant imminent aggression is in keeping with his key concerns. Although this menacing climate provides opportunities for picaresque misadventure—Brancaleone and his "army" are either thwarted in their plotting or their fighting and set to flight, or else their humiliation of their rivals involves some kind of unedifying spectacle—it also creates in the audience an expectation of imminent conflict that persists throughout the narrative. In this respect it is less an anti-Vietnam film than a Cold War-era comedy, which, like other famous black comedies of the period such as Stanley Kubrick's *Dr. Strangelove* (1964), satirizes the delusional use of aggression and the pursuit of self-interest in a world shaped by the contending forces of panoptic power and anarchy.

Despite its climate of diffuse threat occasionally culminating in unnamed battles and skirmishes, there is nevertheless one conflict that hovers constantly in the background of *Brancaleone's Army*, and that is the Crusades, the defining East-West conflict in modern memory of the Middle Ages. Early into the narrative Brancaleone and his band encounter Zenone, a zealous monk who is leading a motley pilgrim army off to "fight the blacks" in the Holy Land. He urges them to join his ranks, using the Crusader battle-cry "Deus vult" (God wills it) to persuade them. Although they soon desert Zenone's band after he falls through a suspension bridge and into a ravine, they later find themselves in a kind of mock Crusade, defending the Apulian town of Aurocastro against Saracen pirates. Brancaleone's defence of the town is not in the service of any religious or moral ideal, however; rather, "hungry for land and property" he stole the deed to the town and is now attempting to claim it. Defeated first by the Saracens and then by the town's rightful lord, Brancaleone and his army of misfits are ultimately rescued by the miraculously recovered Zenone, and at the film's conclusion are poised to set off to the Crusades.

With their more remote presence in the narrative of *Brancaleone's Army*, the Crusades might not appear to be featuring prominently as a historical analogue for the Vietnam War. And yet just as the Vietnam War is regarded by many as a Cold War "proxy war," that is, a theatre for the larger Communist vs anti-Communist tension, so too in the film the Crusades are a faraway flashpoint of the general bellicosity of the society being depicted. In *Brancaleone at the Crusades*, by contrast, the East as a site of Western incursion is more insistently present. Even though the characters' journey is full of setbacks, diversions, and misadventures, the narrative is dominated by their quest to reach the Holy Land, and their eventual arrival there. There is, of course, a straightforward narrative rationale for this. Not only does the second film's story follow directly from where the first left off, but Brancaleone also needs to travel to Palestine once he has undertaken to deliver the infant son of Bohemond of Sicily to his father in Jerusalem. This narrative rationale need not, however, preclude the idea that the setting is a response to contemporary affairs, especially taking into account the acceleration both of the Vietnam War and of protests against the war between the two films, which

---

24 Marcia Landy, *Cinema and Counter-History* (Bloomington: Indiana University Press, 2015), 110.

fall on either side of the watershed year of 1968. And indeed there is much in the film to suggest that the Vietnam War was on the mind of Monicelli, or at least on those of his writing team Age and Scarpelli (Agenore Incrocci and Furio Scarpelli, who had also written *The Great War*).

As is the case with *Brancaleone's Army*, *Brancaleone at the Crusades* does not aim to offer a historically authentic portrayal of the period in which the film is set. The few key historical events that anchor the film, such as the Gregory VII–Clement III papal rivalry and the arrival of Bohemond in Palestine, were not synchronous, while many other episodes are entirely invented. Monicelli's Middle Ages are, rather, as the director himself has stated, a satirical reminder of the West's history of crudity, violence, and imperialist arrogance. Here it is worth recalling Monicelli's earlier-quoted statement: "[c]ivilization, truth, and science were on the … side of Islam. That's what the Crusades were all about. We went to occupy places where they were more civilized." The "we" in this statement is notable for implying a continuity between the military and colonialist invasions of the past and those of the present. Although he directs this barb more intimately at the Italian people (which might explain the focus on Bohemond, whose Norman family had conquered Southern Italy and Sicily before heading East), in fact his portrayal of their role in the Crusades portrays their ambitions as being the same as, and closely intertwined with, those of rulers from across Christendom, so the "we" implicated in this violent past extends beyond national boundaries to encompass the Christian West.

Notwithstanding the film's wilful, even joyful, ahistoricism, the section of the film set in and around Jerusalem appears to be based loosely on the 1099 Siege of Jerusalem. In a nod to documented history, Brancaleone and his band arrive to find the Crusaders starving outside the city walls, while "the Saracens have wine and cheese." Bohemond admits "half my men are dead, I fear/from fighting Moors and diarrhoea." In addition to the amusing, deflationary zeugma in its second line, this statement is typical of the mock-heroic nature of the entire Crusades episode, the dialogue of which is declaimed almost entirely in rhyming couplets. It is in this episode that we encounter the clearest analogy between the Crusades and public discourses about the Vietnam War at the end of the 1960s and into 1970, when the film was being made. In the dialogue between Bohemond and Brancaleone it is possible to hear echoes of the sentiments expressed at such mass protests as the Moratorium to End the War in Vietnam (October 15, 1969) and the Moratorium March on Washington (November 15, 1969), which gave expression to public outrage at the futility of this seemingly interminable war of attrition. Even though the 1099 siege was, in historical retrospect, early into the Crusades, Bohemond's speech about the exhaustion of his troops and his own sense of demoralization is the speech of someone a long way into a pointless and ill-fated war:

> I never dreamed at first
> That this Crusade could be accurs'd
> If I could, I'd let it be
> And return to Sicily
> …
> Should Jerusalem not fall,
> We'll skedaddle, one and all.

When Brancaleone reminds him of the religious mission motivating the Crusades, he expresses doubt about both their divine mandate and their likelihood of success:

> You speak truly, but I fear
> God may to the Moors' side veer.
> Has he shown the way ahead
> To our colleague Mohammed?
> You are right to voice distress,
> We are in an awful mess.

The film's first viewers in 1970 and 1971 could, moreover, easily have been struck by the familiarity of the Saracen Emir's pacifist injunction, "let us end this useless war/and agree to fight no more." The Muslim civility he embodies is expressed in his rejection of the Christians' bellicosity. His proposal of a chivalric tournament replaces mass slaughter with the contained and codified spectacle of the lists. This proposal also enables the episode to devolve into slapstick, as Brancaleone, now exposed as a commoner and thus desperate to prove himself a natural knight, unleashes his frenzied and unorthodox battle moves on his Saracen opponents, eventually killing them all and winning Jerusalem for the Christians, a victory that exposes the violence close beneath the surface of the Christians' pretended adherence to chivalric codes. The film does not dwell on this victory, however, but moves on somewhat abruptly. One can only speculate as to the reasons for this, and whether the film's viewers could have been expected to know that after conquering Jerusalem the victorious Crusaders went on infamously to massacre the city's Muslim and Jewish inhabitants. The film's wilful drift from its historical moorings perhaps makes such speculation redundant; but given that in the year before the film's release the public had had its eyes opened to such U.S. atrocities in Vietnam as the My Lai massacre (committed in March 1968 but suppressed until November 1969), it might have been too raw and too obscene to pursue the analogy between Vietnam and the Crusades far enough to depict the 1099 massacre. In any case, the film jumps almost immediately to the final scene in which Brancaleone wanders the dunes of Palestine alone. His final showdown with the scythe-wielding figure of Death, a manic homage to the solemn, existential chess game between Death and Antonius Block, the returned Crusader in Ingmar Bergman's *The Seventh Seal* (1957) aligns Brancaleone with one of cinema's greatest portrayals of a disillusioned war veteran.

Although the story appears to end with an optimism typical of the picaresque, with its hero whistling the film's jaunty theme song to himself as he swaggers into the desert, having fallen on his feet yet again, in fact it is also an entirely open-ended and even unsettling conclusion. Having just won Jerusalem for the Crusaders in single combat, he has moved on without explanation, and without any of the loyal band who followed him through so such mishap and hardship. His duel with Death suggests that his desertion has little to do with a renunciation of combat; rather, having finally been ennobled for his services to the Crusaders, he now appears to have turned knight errant (though without a horse), wandering with his sword across his shoulders. Yet as both a chivalrous and a picaresque figure, an indeterminate future lies ahead of him. As the scene cuts to a final encircling aerial view of Brancaleone, he is a tiny figure with only heat and emptiness stretching before him, as well as the possible reappearance of Death, who has been only temporarily warded off. Just as Monicelli's intended original viewers lived in a world shaped both by a controversial neo-colonial war and by the ongoing threat of nuclear war, the medieval climate of imminent, haphazard violence and its uncertain consequences is not fully dispersed at the film's conclusion, despite the apparent cheerfully bombastic marching music that takes us to the credits.

Brancaelone at the Crusades' presentist use of the Middle Ages should not, however, be reduced to simply being a commentary on the Vietnam War. The years between the two films saw the international instability being compounded by a significant acceleration of internal unrest in Italy known as the Years of Lead (anni di piombo, 1969–1980), which were characterized by periods of fractious, repressive, and corrupt government, general strikes, political assassinations, domestic terrorism, and the emergence of extremist politics on both the Right and the Left. Within the generalized state of exception, protests were both allied with and opposed to these extremist movements. As I have discussed elsewhere,[25] in the creative response to this political climate, the Middle Ages loomed surprisingly large. Monicelli was only one among a number of his compatriots who, influenced by the account offered by Antonio Gramsci in his *Prison Notebooks*, saw in the Italian Middle Ages both a reflection of the present and a model for an alternative future. For them it was a period in which a hegemonic medieval culture, buttressed by the relationship between the Catholic Church and the feudal order, was contested by a resilient folk culture characterized by ribald buffoonery and anti-authoritarianism.

The most discussed proponent of this view was Dario Fo, in his *Mistero Buffo* (1969), a subversive interpretation of the medieval mystery cycles that, in using farce to ridicule the powerful, pays tribute to the buffonic "theatre" developed by St Francis and his guerilla successors such as Gherardo Segarelli.[26] At the same time, moreover, that Monicelli was making his *Brancaleone* films, the radical left-wing Italian film maker Pier Paolo Pasolini's concern for those systemically excluded from prosperous, bourgeois Italy, led him, like Monicelli, back through time to an exploration of the fringe-dwellers of pre-modern Italy. In the first of his medievalist films, *The Hawks and the Sparrows* (*Uccellini e Uccellacci*), released in 1966, two characters of the modern Italian underclasses are transformed into buffoonish Franciscan friars, who unsuccessfully preach to the hawks not to attack the sparrows. *The Hawks and the Sparrows* was followed by Pasolini's Trilogy of Life, which contains his versions of *The Decameron*, *The Canterbury Tales*, and *The Arabian Nights*, released in the early 1970s. In the first two of these films, Pasolini selects episodes from these famous late medieval frame tales which enable him either to celebrate the irrepressible sexual jouissance and the

---

25 See Louise D'Arcens, "Dario Fo's *Mistero Buffo* and the Left-Modernist Reclamation of Medieval Popular Culture," in *Medieval Afterlives in Popular Culture*, ed. Gail Ashton and Daniel T. Kline (New York: Palgrave Macmillan, 2012), 57–70; and "The Thunder after the Lightning: Language and Pasolini's Medievalist Poetics," *Postmedieval* 6, no. 2 (2015): 191–99.
26 Dario Fo, "Mistero Buffo," trans. Ed Emery, in *Plays: 1*, intro. Stuart Hood (London: Methuen, 1992).

scatological grotesquery of medieval corporeal existence (*The Decameron*), or, in a more Gramscian vein, to dramatize the struggle between medieval people's transgressive natural appetites and the ecclesiastical-feudal regimes that seek to subject these bodies to surveillance, repression, and punishment (*The Canterbury Tales*). The concern for the marginalized in Pasolini's medieval films corresponds closely to Monicelli's stated desire, as cited earlier in this chapter, to portray "history from the point of view of the humble people, the little guy." Monicelli makes good on this intention in his representations of war across the centuries: both *The Great War* and the Brancaleone films show the audience world-historical events as experienced by those who gain little and lose much from the wars waged by authorities and institutions, such as churches, armies, and governments. The larger historical events that find their way into the Brancaleone films, the Crusades and papal schism being the two most conspicuous ones, shape and play out on the minor stage of the characters' smaller lives to unfortunate and even tragic ends. Lorenzo Codelli, and Marcia Landy after him, have both identified this tendency as a broad counter-historical strategy in Monicelli's work.[27]

First and foremost, Monicelli's Brancaleone films are comedies which delight audiences with their Cervantean mock-heroic deflations, their farcical plots, and their vividly anachronistic, picaresque Middle Ages. But they are also films which, along with the *The Great War*, use comedy to expose how human precarity in times of conflict has been a harsh reality across many centuries, especially for those with little say over the political and economic forces that determine their lives. Andrew Lynch's argument that "it is rare to see the use of medievalism to contest the basic association of fighting with goodness and with struggle towards a worthwhile goal"[28] throws into relief the singularity of Monicelli's undertaking. For viewers whose own lives called them to cope with deep turmoil at the local level, the menacing threat of global conflict, and an unjust neo-colonial war in which world orders faced off against one another, these medievalist films present a world which, despite being amusingly distant, was also unsettlingly familiar.

---

[27] Lorenzo Codelli, "Mario Monicelli: 1915–2010," *Positif* 600 (2011): 56–57 at 56; Landy, "Comedy and Counter-History," 17. Tommaso di Carpegna Falconieri characterizes Monicelli's representation as that of "un medievo degli emarginati, dei poveri, dei cavalieri ridicoli." See Tommaso di Carpegna Falconieri, *Medioevo militante: La politica di oggi alle prese con barbari e crociati* (Torino: Einaudi, 2011), 131.

[28] Lynch, "Medievalism," 148.

SELECT BIBLIOGRAPHY

Arnould, Paul. "Introduction. Forêts: entre nature et société." *Bulletin de l'Association de géographes français* 78 (2001–2002): 107–9.

Aubrey, Elizabeth. "Reconsidering 'High Style' and 'Low Style' in Medieval Song." *Journal of Music Theory* 52, no. 1, Essays in Honor of Sarah Fuller (Spring, 2008): 75–122.

Barker, Simon. *War and Nation in the Theatre of Shakespeare and his Contemporaries.* Edinburgh: Edinburgh University Press, 2007.

Batt, Catherine. *Malory's Morte Darthur: Remaking Arthurian Tradition*. New York: Palgrave, 2002.

Birchwood, Matthew, and Matthew Dimmock, eds. *Cultural Encounters between East and West, 1453–1699*. Newcastle-upon-Tyne: Cambridge Scholars, 2005.

Bonanno, George A. *The Other Side of Sadness: What the New Science of Bereavement Tells Us about Life After Loss*. Ann Arbor: University of Michigan, 2009.

Bouquet, Damien, and Piroska Nagy. *Medieval Sensibilities: A History of Emotions in the Middle Ages*. Translated by Robert Shaw. Cambridge: Polity, 2018.

Brandsma, Frank, Carolyne Larrington, and Corinne Saunders, eds. *Emotions in Medieval Arthurian Literature: Mind, Body, Voice.* Cambridge: Brewer, 2015.

Broomhall, Susan. "Feeling Divine Nature: Natural History, Emotions and Bernard Palissy's Knowledge Practice." In *Natural History in Early Modern France: The Poetics of an Epistemic Genre*, edited by Raphaële Garrod and Paul J. Smith, 46–69. Leiden: Brill, 2018.

Bruckner, Matilda Tomaryn. "Fictions of the Female Voice: The Women Troubadours." *Speculum* 67, no. 4 (1992): 865–91.

Burton, Jonathan. *Traffic and Turning: Islam and English Drama*. Dover: Delaware University Press, 2005.

Caisso, René. "La Vente de la forêt de Gâtine à l'époque de Ronsard." *Humanisme et Renaissance* 4, no. 3 (1937): 274–85.

Cayley, Emma, and Ashby Kinch, eds. *Chartier in Europe*. Cambridge: Brewer, 2008.

Cole, Penny J. *The Preaching of the Crusades to the Holy Land, 1095–1270*. Cambridge, MA: Medieval Academy of America, 1991.

Cooke, Philip. *The Legacy of the Italian Resistance*. New York: Palgrave Macmillan, 2011.

Cresswell, Tim. "Towards *Topopoetics*: Space, Place and the Poem." In *Place, Space and Hermeneutics*, edited by Bruce J. Banz, 319–31. Cham: Springer, 2017.

Crofts, Thomas, and Robert Allen Rouse, "For King and Country: Reading Nationalism in Popular English Romance." In *A Companion to Medieval Popular Romance*, edited by Raluca L. Radulescu and Cory James Rushton, 79–95. Woodbridge: Brewer, 2009.

Curtis, Michael. *Orientalism and Islam: European Thinkers on Oriental Despotism in the Middle East and India*. Cambridge: Cambridge University Press, 2009.

D'Arcens, Louise. "Dario Fo's *Mistero Buffo* and the Left-Modernist Reclamation of Medieval Popular Culture." In *Medieval Afterlives in Popular Culture*, edited by Gail Ashton and Daniel T. Kline, 57–70. New York: Palgrave Macmillan, 2012.

Davis, Kathleen. *Periodization and Sovereignty: How Ideas of Feudalism and Secularization Govern the Politics of Time*. Philadelphia: University of Pennsylvania Press, 2012.

Davlin, Mary Clement. *A Journey into Love: Meditating with the Medieval Poem "Piers Plowman."* Los Angeles: Marymount Institute, 2008.

Dell, Helen. *Desire by Gender and Genre in Trouvère Song*. Woodbridge: Brewer, 2008.

Devereaux, Rima. *Constantinople and the West in Medieval French Literature: Renewal and Utopia*. Gallica 25. Cambridge: Boydell & Brewer, 2012.

Donoghue, Daniel. *How the Anglo-Saxons Read Their Poems*. Philadelphia: University of Pennsylvania Press, 2018.

Downes, Stephanie, Andrew Lynch, and Katrina O'Loughlin, eds. *Emotions and War: Medieval to Romantic Literature*. London: Palgrave, 2015.

———. *Writing War in Britain and France, 1370–1854: A History of Emotions*. London: Routledge, 2018.

Duport, Danièle. *Les Jardins qui sentent le sauvage: Ronsard et la Poétique du Paysage*. Geneva: Droz, 2000.

Edelman, Charles. *Shakespeare's Military Language: A Dictionary*. London: Athlone, 2000.

Findley, Brooke Heidenreich. "Reading Sincerity at the Intersection of Troubadour/Trobairitz Poetry: Two Poetic Debates." *Romance Quarterly* 53, no. 4 (Fall, 2006): 287–303.

Foot, John. *Italy's Divided Memory*. New York: Palgrave Macmillan, 2009.

Frantzen, Allen. *Bloody Good: Chivalry, Sacrifice, and the Great War*. Chicago: University of Chicago Press, 2004.

Fuchs, Barbara. *Mimesis and Empire: The New World, Islam, and European Identities*. Cambridge: Cambridge University Press, 2001.

Fuchs, Barbara, and Emily Weissbourd, eds. *Representing Imperial Rivalry in the Early Modern Mediterranean*. Toronto: University of Toronto Press, 2013.

Fussell, Paul. *The Great War and Modern Memory*. Oxford: Oxford University Press, 1975.

Garrison, Jennifer. "Chaucer's *Troilus and Criseyde* and the Danger of Masculine Interiority." *The Chaucer Review* 49, no. 3 (2015): 320–43.

Garrison, John S., and Kyle Pivetti. *Shakespeare at Peace*. London: Routledge, 2019.

Getz, Faye. *Medicine in the English Middle Ages*. Princeton: Princeton University Press, 2001.

Gill, Paul E. "Politics and Propaganda in Fifteenth-Century England: the Polemical Writings of Sir John Fortescue." *Speculum* 46 (1971): 333–47.

Goebel, Stefan. *The Great War and Medieval Memory: War, Remembrance and Medievalism in Britain and Germany, 1914–1920*. Cambridge: Cambridge University Press, 2009.

Goodman, Jennifer Robin. *Chivalry and Exploration, 1298–1630*. Woodbridge: Boydell, 1998.

Goodrich, Peter H. "Saracens and Islamic Alterity in Malory's 'Le Morte Darthur'." *Arthuriana* 16, no. 4 (2006): 10–28.

Harris, Sharon M. "Feminism and Shakespeare's Cressida: '*If* I be false ....' " *Women's Studies: An Interdisciplinary Journal* 18 (1990): 65–82.

Heffernan, Carol Falvo. *The Orient in Chaucer and Medieval Romance*. Woodbridge: Brewer, 2003.

Heller, Henry. *Labour, Science, and Technology in France, 1500–1620.* Cambridge: Cambridge University Press, 1996.
Hoffman, Donald L. "Assimilating Saracens: The Aliens in Malory's *Morte Darthur*." *Arthuriana* 16, no. 4 (2006): 43–64.
Jackson, William E. *Ardent Complaints and Equivocal Piety: The Portrayal of the Crusader in Medieval German Poetry.* Lanham: University Press of America, 2003.
Jardine, Lisa, and Jerry Brotton. *Global Interests: Renaissance Art Between East and West.* Ithaca: Cornell University Press, 2000.
Jorgensen, Paul A. *Shakespeare's Military World.* Los Angeles: California University Press, 1956.
Kay, Sarah. *Courtly Contradictions.* Palo Alto: Stanford University Press, 2001.
King, Ros, and Paul J. C. M. Franssen, eds. *Shakespeare and War.* Basingstoke: Palgrave Macmillan, 2008.
Koebner, Richard. "Despot and Despotism: Vicissitudes of a Political Term." *The Journal of the Warburg and Courtauld Institute* 14 (1951): 275–302.
Lake-Giguere, Danny. "The Impacts of Warfare on Woodland Exploitation in Late Medieval Normandy (1364–1380): Royal Forests as Military Assets During the Hundred Years' War." *Journal of Medieval Military History* 16 (2018): 79–98.
Landy, Marcia. "Comedy and Counter-History." In *Historical Comedy on Screen*, edited by Hannu Salmi. Bristol: Intellect, 2011, 177–98.
Leitch, Megan G., and Cory James Rushton, eds. *The New Companion to Malory.* Cambridge: Brewer, 2019.
Love, Ronald S. *Blood and Religion: The Conscience of Henri IV.* Montreal: McGill-Queens University Press, 2001.
Lynch, Andrew. "Medievalism and the Ideology of War." In *The Cambridge Companion to Medievalism*, edited by Louise D'Arcens, 135–50. Cambridge: Cambridge University Press, 2016.
———. *Malory's Book of Arms: The Narrative of Combat in* Le Morte Darthur. Cambridge: Brewer, 1997.
———. "'What cheer?': Emotion and Action in the Arthurian World." In *Emotions in Medieval Arthurian Literature: Body, Mind, Voice*, edited by Frank Brandsma, Carolyne Larrington, and Corinne Saunders, Arthurian Studies 83, 47–53. Cambridge: Brewer, 2015.
Mackenzie, Louisa. "'Ce ne sont pas des bois:' Poetry, Regionalism, and Loss in the Forest of Ronsard's Gâtine." *Journal of Medieval and Early Modern Studies* 32, no. 2 (2002): 343–74.
MacLean, Gerald, ed. *Re-Orienting the Renaissance.* Basingstoke: Palgrave, 2005.
Magennis, Hugh. *Images of Community in Old English Poetry.* Cambridge: Cambridge University Press, 1996.
Maier, Christoph T. *Crusade Propaganda and Ideology: Model Sermons for the Preaching of the Cross.* Cambridge: Cambridge University Press, 2000.
Manion, Lee. *Narrating the Crusades: Loss and Recovery in Medieval and Early Modern English Literature.* Cambridge: Cambridge University Press, 2014.
Marlowe: Plays and Poems. Edited by M. Ridley. London: Dent, 1955.
Marx, C. William. *The Devil's Rights and the Redemption in the Literature of Medieval England.* Cambridge: Brewer, 1995.
Matar, Nabil. *Islam in Britain, 1558–1685.* Cambridge: Cambridge University Press, 1999.

Matteson, Kieko. *Forests in Revolutionary France: Conservation, Community, and Conflict, 1669–1848*. Cambridge: Cambridge University Press, 2015.
McKinstry, Jamie. *Middle English Romance and the Craft of Memory*. Cambridge: Brewer, 2015.
Miller, Dean A. *The Epic Hero*. Baltimore: Johns Hopkins University Press, 2000.
Miller, William Ian. *Bloodtaking and Peacemaking: Feud, Law and Society in Saga Iceland*. Chicago: University of Chicago Press, 1990.
Nall, Catherine. *Reading and War in Fifteenth-Century England: From Lydgate to Malory*. Cambridge: Brewer, 2012.
Nepstad, Sharon E. *Religion and War Resistance in the Plowshares Movement*. New York: Cambridge University Press, 2008.
Page, Christopher. *Voices and Instruments of the Middle Ages: Instrumental Practice and Songs in France 1100–1300*. London: Dent, 1987.
Paterson, Linda, Luca Barbieri, Ruth Harvey, Anna Radelli, and Marjolaine Ragain. *Singing the Crusades: French and Occitan Lyric Responses to the Crusading Movements, 1137–1336*. Cambridge: Brewer, 2018.
Philippides, Marios, and Walter K. Hanak, *The Siege and the Fall of Constantinople in 1453: Historiography, Topography, and Military Studies*. Farnham: Ashgate, 2011.
Porter, Roy. *The Greatest Benefit to Mankind: A Medical History of Humanity from Antiquity to the Present*. London: HarperCollins, 1997.
Quainton, Malcolm. *Ronsard's Ordered Chaos: Visions of Flux and Stability in the Poetry of Pierre de Ronsard*. Manchester: Manchester University Press, 1980.
Radulescu, Raluca L. "'Oute of mesure': Violence and Knighthood in Malory's *Morte Darthur*." In *Re-Viewing "Le Morte Darthur": Texts and Contexts, Characters and Themes*, edited by K. S. Whetter and Raluca L. Radulescu, 119–31. Arthurian Studies 60. Cambridge: Brewer, 2005.
———. *Romance and its Contexts in Fifteenth-Century England: Politics, Piety, and Penance*. Cambridge: Brewer, 2013.
Rawcliffe, Carole. *Medicine and Society in Later Medieval England*. Stroud: Sutton, 1995.
Reichl, Karl, ed. *Medieval Oral Literature*. Berlin: De Gruyter, 2012.
Rigby, Steve. *Wisdom and Chivalry: Chaucer's "Knight's Tale" and Medieval Political Theory*. Leiden: Brill, 2009.
Robinson, Benedict. *Islam and Early Modern English Literature: The Politics of Romance from Spenser to Milton*. New York: Palgrave MacMillan, 2007.
Saunders, Corinne, Françoise Le Saux, and Neil Thomas. *Writing War: Medieval Literary Responses to Warfare*. Woodbridge: Brewer, 2004.
Simpson, James. "Pecock and Fortescue." In *A Companion to Middle English Prose*, edited by A. S. G. Edwards. Woodbridge: Boydell & Brewer, 2004, 271–88.
Tao, Hongyin. "A Usage-Based Approach to Argument Structure: 'Remember' and 'Forget' in Spoken English." *International Journal of Corpus Linguistics* 8 (2003): 75–95.
Tiller, Kenneth J. "En-graving Chivalry: Tombs, Burial, and the Ideology of Knighthood in Malory's Tale of King Arthur." *Arthuriana* 14 (2004): 37–53.
Tolan, John Victor. *Saracens: Islam in the Medieval European Imagination*. New York: Columbia University Press, 2002.
Trembinski, Donna. "Trauma as a Category of Analysis." In *Trauma in Medieval Society*, edited by Wendy J. Turner and Christina Lee. Leiden: Brill, 2018, 13–32.

Trilling, Renée. *The Aesthetics of Nostalgia: Historical Representation in Old English Verse.* Buffalo: University of Toronto Press, 2009.

Trotter, D. A. *Medieval French Literature and the Crusades (1100–1300).* Geneva: Librairie Droz S. A., 1988.

van der Eijk, Philip. *Medicine and Philosophy in Classical Antiquity: Doctors and Philosophers on Nature, Soul, Health and Disease.* Cambridge: Cambridge University Press, 2005.

Vandeventer, Tory. "Laying Siege to Female Power: Theseus the 'Conqueror' and Hippolita the 'Asseged' in Chaucer's the *Knight's Tale*." *Essays in Medieval Studies* 23 (2006): 31–40.

Waldron, R. A. "Langland's Originality: The Christ-Knight and the Harrowing of Hell." In *Medieval English Religious and Ethical Literature: Essays in Honour of G. H. Russell*, edited by Gregory Kratzmann and James Simpson. Cambridge: Brewer, 1986, 66–81.

Wallace, David. *Chaucerian Polity: Absolutist Lineages and Associational Forms in England and Italy.* Stanford: Stanford University Press, 1997.

Walsham, Alexandra. *The Reformation of the Landscape: Religion, Identity, and Memory in Early Modern Britain and Ireland.* New York: Oxford University Press, 2011.

Warner, Lawrence. "Jesus the Jouster: The Christ-Knight and Medieval Theories of Atonement in 'Piers Plowman' and the 'Round Table' Sermons." *The Yearbook of Langland Studies* 10 (1996): 129–43.

Weisl, Angela Jane. *Conquering the Realm of Femeny: Gender and Genre in Chaucer's Romance.* Woodbridge: Brewer, 1995.

White, Robert S. *Pacifism and English Literature: Minstrels of Peace.* London: Palgrave, 2008.

Young, Deborah. "Poverty, Misery, War and Other Comic Material: An Interview with Mario Monicelli." *Cinéaste* 29 (2004): 36–40.

Zumthor, Paul. *Toward a Medieval Poetics.* Translated by Philip Bennett. Minneapolis: University of Minnesota Press, 1992.

INDEX

Abraham, 121–23
adventure(s), viii, 3, 17, 46–47, 49, 51–62, 70–73, 139, 171–76, 202
Aeneid, 176
Aers, David, 120
agency, 36, 51, 53–56, 61–62, 178, 194, 196, 207
Akbari, Suzanne Conklin, x
Albertus Magnus, 133
Alliterative *Morte Arthure*, xiii, 69, 152–56
  Robert Thornton's copy, 153
Amadis of Gaul, 172–73
ami, 115–16
  amie, 115
Anderson, Perry, 178
anger, 29, 31–36, 43, 53, 65, 67–69, 74–78, 134, 140–1, 145
anticipatory grief, 71, 73–74, 77–78
anti-Semitism, x–xi, 204
anxiety, 43, 49, 128, 201
Arabian Nights, The, 211
Arcite, 3, 12, 45–46, 48–55, 57–58, 61–63
Aristotle, 132
Arnould, Paul, 180
Arnoldus de Villa Nova, 132
Arthur, King, xii, xiii, 2, 3, 29–44, 67–69, 73–79, 131–49, 153–57, 168, 176
Ash Wednesday, 199
Augustine, St, 114, 133

ballate, 106, 108
Balan, 70–73, 135, 138–39, 151, 152
Balin/Balyn, 70, 135, 138–39
Bartholomaeus Anglicus, 133–34
Battle of Maldon, The, 3, 7, 83–100
  The Battle of Maldon (historical event), 1
behaviour, 3–4, 13, 36, 45, 60, 70, 75, 78, 83–87, 94, 98, 113, 175
Belon, Pierre, 6, 181–82, 184, 192

De arboribus coniferis resiniferis, aliis quoque nonullis sempiterna fronde virentibus, 181
Les remonstrances sur le default du labour & culture des plantes, & de a cognoissance d'icelles, 181
Berel, Sir, 68, 136
Bernart de Ventadorn, 102, 106
Beowulf, ix, 3, 83–100
  Robert Zemeckis' 2007 film, ix
Best Years of Our Lives, The (film), 14
Béthune, Conon de, 108–9
betrayal, 74, 87, 95
Bevis of Hampton (romance), 176
boasts, 75, 84–87, 103
Bartholomaeus Anglicus, 133–34
  De proprietatibus rerum, 133–34
Boccaccio, 47–56
  Teseida, 48–55, 61
Boethius, 50–51, 54
  Chaucer's *Boece*, 50–51
Boldrewood, Rolf, x
Bors, Sir, 79, 136, 146, 168
Brancaleone films, 6–7, 201–4, 211–12
  Brancaleone at the Crusades, 201, 204, 208–9
  Brancaleone's Army/ For Love and Gold, 201, 205, 207–9
  Great War, The (film), 6, 201–2, 209
breath/breathing, 5, 131–49
Brief Encounter (film), 23
Brotherhood, 51, 73
Brown, Peter, 48, 50
Burrow, John, 48
Burton, Jonathan, 177
Bruckner, Matilda, 102, 115

Cador, Sir, 68–69, 79, 136
canso, 102–7, 112
canzone, 106

Capystranus (romance), 171
Casablanca (film), 23
Caxton, William, 80, 134, 170, 175
  The History of Godefrey of Boloyne and of the Conquest of Iherusalem, 170, 175
  The Lyf of the Noble and Crysten Prynce, Charles the Grete, 170, 175
ceremony, 29–43, 168
chance, 50–55, 60, 152
  chance encounters, 23
chanson(s), vii, 4, 101–18, 171
chansons de croisade, 4, 106, 108, 110, 113–17
Charlemagne, 171–72, 176
Charles VI, king of France, 34, 38
Charles VII, king of France, 157
Charles IX, king of France, 189–90, 192
Charles of Orléans, 42
Chartier, Alain, 5, 151, 157–58
Chaucer, Geoffrey, xi, xiii, 31, 45–63, 134
  Canterbury Tales, The, 45, 47–49, 52, 54, 60, 154, 212
  Franklin's Tale, 58
  Knight's Tale, 3, 12, 49–54, 57, 62, 154
  Legend of Good Women, 60
  Man of Law's Tale, The, 58–59
  Prioress's Tale, x–xi
  Tale of Sir Thopas, The, 52
  Troilus and Criseyde, 2, 30
chivalry, xiii, 6, 132, 135, 169–72, 175, 200, 203
Christ, xi, 1, 4, 119–29, 143
Christology, 120
Clark, Ronald W., 117
Clifford, Rebecca, 205
Codelli, Lorenzo, 212
codes, 83–84, 92, 98
  codes of conduct, 4
Cold War, 201, 205–6, 208
Columbe, 70–72
combat, 65, 67–72, 76, 121, 123–24, 136, 200–201, 210
conflict, ii, 1–4, 7, 9–11, 17, 21–22, 25, 29, 111, 119, 123, 126–29, 135, 144, 149, 179, 200, 205–8, 212

Conon de Béthune, 108–9
Constantine of Africa, 133, 176, 200
Cooke, Philip, 205
counter-giving, 96
courtly love, 45, 51, 84, 105, 169
cowards, 4, 85–87, 94, 159
Cressida, 10, 23–25
Creton, Jean, 35–37
Criseyde, 2, 31–36, 42, 54
Chrétien de Troyes, x, 58
  Conte du Graal, x
Crofts, Thomas H., 176
crucifixion, 4, 119–21, 123
Crusades, the, 1, 4, 167–71, 201, 203–4, 208–12
  crusade motifs, 167
  crusade songs, 101, 103, 118
  crusade propaganda, 106, 113
  crusading rhetoric, 167
crying, 66, 140

Dad's Army (BBC sitcom), 20–21
Dante, 106, 161
Davis, Kathleen, 178
Davlin, Mary Clement, 120
death, 4, 11–12, 14, 16, 18, 65–74, 76–79, 119–20, 123–29, 134–36, 139–40, 144–48, 201
  deathbed, 67, 77–80
  death books, 135, 144
  death scene(s), 3, 67, 73
  great death(s), 74, 79–80
Decameron, The, 211–12
Dekker, Thomas, 15
  A Larum for London, or the siedge of Antwerpe: with the vertuous actes and valorous deedes of the lame Soldier (play, attributed to Dekker), 15–16
  The Shoemaker's Holiday (play), 16
despair, 47, 51, 53, 58–62, 115, 142
destiny, ix, x, 18, 24, 46–55, 58, 60, 62, 138
Devèze, Michel, 187, 194
Diomede (Greek prince), 33, 42
Dolci, Danilo, 206–7
dole, 65–80, 135, 140–41, 145–46, 148

Don Quixote, 172
Donoghue, Daniel, 98
Dr. Strangelove (film), 208
duty, 96, 98, 100, 110, 112

Edward III, king of England, 42, 153
Edward IV, king of England, 152, 155–56
Elaine of Astolat, 78, 145
Elaine of Corbenic, 142
Elizabeth I, queen of England, 14, 177
   Elizabethan drama, 177
   Elizabethan literature, 9
   Elizabethan stage, 177
Emelye (Chaucer), 3, 45–63
   Emilia (Boccaccio), 12, 51, 55–58
emotion(s), vii, 1–3, 5, 7, 9, 11, 29, 30–32,
   34, 37–38, 41–44, 45, 47–54, 56–58,
   60, 62, 65–71, 73–79, 102, 106, 108,
   117, 122, 128, 131–37, 139–41,
   146–48, 195
   emotional community, 67
   emotional experience, 3, 65–66, 68, 74,
      79, 132, 135, 195
   emotional life/lives, 11–12, 23, 25,
      31, 132
   emotional loss, 66
   emotional regime(s), 69–70
   emotional response(s), 31–32, 36, 68, 117
Engels, Friedrich, 170
environment, xiv, 61, 179
Erasmus, 19

Fall, the, 121, 123, 125
fall of Constantinople, 167–68, 170–73, 176
fear, 10, 35, 47, 59, 62, 134
Fellini, Federico, 203
   Juliet of the Spirits (film), 203
fellowship, 67, 71, 146, 169
field of combat, 67, 76
Field, P. J. C., 169
Fierabras, 170, 175–76
fin'amors, 4, 102, 107, 110
Findlay, Brooke Heidenreich, 102
Finke, Laurie A., x
Fo, Dario, 211

Always Blame the Devil (play), 207
Mistero Buffo (play), 211
Toss the Lady Out (play), 207
Foot, John, 205
forest(s), 6, 46, 57, 86, 142, 179–98
Fortescue, John, 155–56, 158–59
   De laudibus legum Anglie, 156
   De titulo Edwardi Comitis Marchiae, 155
   Defensio juris domus Lancastria, 155
   De natura legis Naturae, 155
   On the Governance of England (also
      known as the *Monarchia*), 156
fortune, 47, 50, 159, 193
Four Daughters of God, 125, 128
Francis of Assisi, St, 75, 207, 211
   Prima vita, 75
Frantzen, Allen, 200
Frederick II, 169
French Wars of Religion, 180
Friedman, Jamie, 50
freedom, viii, 47, 48–51, 57–59, 61–62
Froissart, Jean, 34, 37
Fuchs, Barbara, 177
Fussell, Paul, 10

Galahad, Sir, 143–44
Galen/Galenic, 68, 76, 132–34
Gareth, Sir, 38, 66, 68, 70, 74, 80, 137,
   146, 156
Gawain/Gawayne, Sir, 38–42, 69, 73–80,
   136, 143, 146–47
   Gawain-poet, xiii
gemunan, 85–91, 93–94, 96, 98–100
Geoffrey of Monmouth, xiv, 153
   Historia Regum Britanniae, 153
George, St, 174
genre, 101–18
Gilbert de Tournai, 113
Gilbertus Anglicus, 134
giving voice(s), 5, 157, 160, 162
God, xiii, 4, 6, 22, 95–96, 108–18, 119–22,
   124–28, 133, 145, 171, 183, 208, 210
Goebel, Stefan, 200
Goodman, Jennifer, 177
Goodrich, Peter, 169

Goody, Jack, 92, 94–96, 98
Gower, John, xiii, 134
grace, 119, 143, 147
Great Depression, viii
greve, 66
Gohory, Jacques, 184
Gospel of Nicodemus, 125
Grail, the, 142–44, 156
   Grail knights, 143
   Grail Quest, 5, 73, 135, 142, 147–49, 169
   Grail romances, 169
Gramsci, Antontio, 211
   Prison Notebooks, 211
Great War, the, viii, xii, 200–201
Greek(s), 2, 24–25, 30–32, 132–33, 154, 167, 169, 176, 188
Grocheio, Johannes de, 106
Guenevere/Guinevere, Queen, 2–3, 30–31, 38–43, 71, 80, 140, 142, 146, 148, 156
guilt, 76, 91
Guy of Warwick (romance), 176

Hamel, Mary, 168–69
Handlyng Synne, 125
Harris, Sharon M., 24
harrowing of Hell, 119–21, 122–25, 127
Hayward, John, 34–36, 38
heart/body topos, 111–12
heaven, 109–10, 114, 120, 122–23, 126–27, 143, 148
Hector, 13, 32
Heng, Geraldine, 171–72
Helen of Troy, 23–24, 32
hell, 119, 123, 125–28, 175
Heller, Henry, 184
Henri II, king of France, 182
Henri IV, king of France, 193
Henri, Duke of Vendôme and King of Navarre, 191
Henry IV, king of England, 31, 33–36, 38, 42
Henry IV Part One (*1 Henry IV*), 12, 16–17, 22
Henry IV Part Two (*2 Henry IV*), 16–17
Henry V (play), 7, 11
Henry V, king of England, xiii, 2, 18–20, 154–56

Henry VI, king of England, 155–56
Henry VIII, king of England, 168
hero, xii–xiii, 77, 86, 151, 172, 210
   epic hero, 85
   romance hero, 46, 57
   heroic action, 67, 69, 86
   heroic code, 83–85, 95
   heroic world, 83
Hippolyta, 12, 18, 20, 47, 56
Hippocrates, 132
Historia Regum Britanniae, 153
Hoccleve, Thomas, xiii
Hoffman, Donald L., 169
Holliday, Billie, 204
honour, ix, 22–23, 85, 91, 109, 113, 138
Hundred Years' War, 42, 168, 200
Huxley, Aldous, 207

Iliad, 68, 176
imagery, 4, 9, 13–14, 25, 119–20, 123–27, 134, 168, 199
imagination, 65, 134, 158, 163
In Which We Serve (film), 11
Incarnation, the, 119–23, 126
interiority, 50, 56, 135
Irving, Edward, 84
Isabelle de Valois, 2, 30–31, 33–43
Isidore of Seville, 133–34
Isode, 140–42, 145

Jackson, William, 101
Jerusalem, 5, 115, 119, 124–25, 168–69, 208–10
joust, 4, 123, 128–29, 139

Kay, Sir, 68–69
Kempe, Margery, 124
kenosis, 122
Kingsley, Charles, x
Kingdom of Heaven (film), 201
knighthood, 132, 135, 140, 163, 168–69
Knight's Tale, the, 3, 12, 49–54, 57, 62, 154
Kolve, V. A., 48

lament, 66, 69–70, 72–73, 138–39, 146, 148–49
Lamorak, Sir, 5, 66–67, 136, 138, 140, 149
Lancelot, Sir, xiii, 2–3, 30–31, 38–42, 68, 71, 73, 75–80, 135–36, 138, 140–49, 156–57
Landy, Marica, 204, 212
Langland, William, 4, 119–26, 128–29
Las Sergas de Esplandían (Garcí Rodriguez Ordóñez de Montalvo), 173
Launceor, 69–73
Laȝamon's *Brut*, xiv, 43
Le Morte Darthur, xiii, 1, 3, 5, 7, 30, 65–70, 73–74, 79–80, 84, 131, 135, 149, 156, 168
  "Tale of Balyn Le Sauvage", 71, 73, 135, 137–38
  "Tale of the Sankgreal", 142
love, xi, 3–5, 7, 9–25, 32–33, 37, 47, 51–57, 59, 61–63, 70, 74, 91, 102, 108, 112–13, 115–17, 122–24, 127–29, 132, 135, 140, 142, 145, 149, 195
  adulterous love, 42
  courtly love, 45, 51, 84, 105, 169
  God as Love, 122
  God's love, 119, 123
  love songs, 101–18
  romantic love, 74
  tragic love, 71
  true love, 71, 123
  unreturned love, 66
loyalty, 3–4, 41, 83, 85, 159, 163
Lucifer, 1, 4, 119–29
Lydgate, John, 153–54
  Siege of Thebes, 154
  Title and Pedigree of Henry VI, The, 154
  Troy Book, 153
Lynch, Andrew, 1, 7, 29–30, 41, 43, 45, 65–67, 70, 79, 84, 131–32, 138, 200, 212
  Emotions and War, 7, 45
  Malory's Book of Arms, xiv, 42, 65
lyric tradition, 102

Mackenzie, Louisa, 196
Magennis, Hugh, 84
Mallart, Guillaume, 189–90
Malory, Thomas, xiii, 1, 3, 31, 40–43, 65–80, 135–48, 151, 155, 168–69, 175
Mancall, Peter C., 180
Manion, Lee, 171
Mann, Jill, 54
Mareuil, Arnaut de, 102, 106
Marx, Karl, 170
Médicis, Catherine de, 184, 190
memory, 65, 73, 85, 90, 92, 94, 96–98, 134, 148, 156, 180, 197
  memories, 6, 66, 80, 86, 89, 91–92, 94, 97, 99
  moral memory, 87
mercy, 19, 42, 123, 126, 128
  Mercy (in *Piers Plowman*), 125
Merlin, 71, 73, 137
Metlitzki, Dorothy, 171
Mézières, Philippe de, 168
Miller, Mark, 61
Milton, John, 21
Mitchell, Tony, 207
Monicelli, Mario, 7, 201–7, 209, 211–12
  Bertoldo, Bertoldino e Cacasenno (film), 203
Montmorency, Anne de, 184
Mordred, xiii, 38, 76, 79, 153
Moses, 123
mourning, 3, 65–68, 70–74, 78–80, 135

Nicholas, St, 174
Njáls saga, xiii
Nolan, Barbara, 54
nuclear war, 211
  nuclear age, 211
  nuclear weapons, 199
Nuti, Leopoldo, 206

Ottoman Empire, 5, 167–72, 174, 176–77
  Ottomans, 168–70, 177

pacifism, 19
Palamon (Chaucer), 3, 12, 45–57, 61–63
  Palemone (Boccaccio), 51, 53, 55–56
Palomides, 5, 138, 140–41, 149

Palissy, Bernard, 6, 183–88, 192
    Recepte veritable, 184, 186
Pascali, Pino, 207
passion(s), 13, 24, 35, 55, 57, 61–62, 68, 131, 135, 140–42, 145, 147, 149
    Christ's passion, 124–25
Pasolini, Pier Paolo, 211–12
    Hawks and the Sparrows, The (film), 211
    Trilogy of Life (film series), 211
Paterson, Linda, 101, 103, 105, 117
peace, xiv, 2–3, 5, 9, 16, 19, 22–23, 29–32, 34, 37, 38, 43, 65, 88, 131–32, 135, 144, 148, 204
    feeling of peace, 29, 38, 43
    Peace (in *Piers Plowman*), 125
    Western peace, viii
Pearsall, Derek, 123
Percival, Sir, 142–43
    Percivale, 66–67
Piers Plowman, 1, 4–5, 119–29
Pistoletto, Michelangelo, 207
Plowshares, 199
Pope Gregory VII, 202, 209
Pope Gregory IX, 169
Pope John XXIII, 205
    Pacem in terris, 205
Pope Paul VI, 206
post-traumatic stress disorder (PTSD), 14, 16, 75–76
Priamus, 136, 169
private feeling(s), 29, 31, 33
protest(s), 201, 205–9, 211
prowess, 47, 66, 135, 137–41, 148–49
    knightly prowess, 5, 132, 141, 147
    physical prowess, 138
    military prowess, 22
    secular prowess, 144
public ritual(s), 30, 32–33, 37
Pugliatti, Paola, 14
punishment, 75, 125, 127–28, 212

Quadrilogue Invectif, 5, 151–63

Randall, Catharine, 186
Reddy, William, 117

remembering, 4, 85, 87, 90–96, 98–100
returned soldiers, 15–16
revenge, 3, 21, 34, 42, 52, 67–70, 75–76, 78–79, 88, 96, 146
    historical revenge, 176
rhetoric, 3, 23–24, 70, 72, 75, 160
Ricard, Serge, 206
Richard II, king of England, 2, 10, 30, 33, 35, 153
Richard Coer de Lyon (romance), 176
Rigby, Steve, 55
ritual(s), 29–33, 36–39, 43–44, 67, 79–80
roaming, 3, 45–63
Roman de Thebes, 154
romance, xii, 5, 11, 31, 47, 51, 56, 60–62, 68, 132, 167–78
    romance epic, 171–72, 175, 177
    romance framework, 47, 52, 54
    romance genre, 33, 56–57, 171
    romance hero, 46, 57
    romance heroine, 47, 56, 59, 60–62
    romance literature, 31
    romance tradition, 45, 53, 55, 58
    romance tropes, 46, 51
Rome, xii, 140, 148, 153, 206
Ronsard, Pierre de, 6, 188, 191–97
Round Table, 3, 7, 67, 69, 71, 77–78, 80, 168
Rosenwein, Barbara, 45, 67
Rouse, Robert Allan, 176
Rowland, Meg, 169
Runciman, Sir Steven, 203
Russell, Bertrand, 117

salvation, 119–21, 124, 188
Salvation History, 121
Saracen(s), 5, 168–69, 171–77, 208, 210
Shichtman, Martin, x
Scott, Walter, ix
Sege off Melayne, The (romance), 171
Seventh Seal, The (film), 210
Shakespeare, William, 2, 9–12, 14, 16, 18–20, 23–25
    All's Well that Ends Well, 10–11, 21, 23
    Antony and Cleopatra, 10, 25
    Comedy of Errors, The, 9

Macbeth, 25, 201
Midsummer Night's Dream, A, 18
Much Ado about Nothing, 10, 21–22
Othello, 10, 22–23, 25
Pericles, 16
Romeo and Juliet, 10
Troilus and Cressida, 10, 23
Twelfth Night, 16
shame, 3, 10, 40, 77, 91
Shippey, Tom, 93
shock, 65–66, 75–76, 134, 141
Silver, Susan K., 196
sin, 1, 4, 119–29, 144
sincerity (topos), 102–3
sirventes, 108–10
slander, 22–23, 161
Spearing, A. C., 48
Spenser, Edmund, x, xiii, 172–73
   Faerie Queene, xiii, 173–74
Song of Roland, 171
sorrow, 3, 31–32, 36, 65–71, 74–75, 108, 126, 134, 140–41, 145
Stanzaic *Morte*, 146–48
Straparola, Giovanni Francesco, 207
   Le piacevole notti (the Facetious Nights), 207
swoon(s), 5, 66, 68, 72, 74, 78, 134–35, 139–42, 144, 147, 149
   swooning, 3, 5, 66, 74, 78, 144–45, 147

Tao, Hongyin, 99
Tasso, Tarquato, 172–73, 175
   Gerusalemme liberate, 175
tears, 5, 11, 19, 35–36, 41–43, 69–70, 75, 135, 140–41, 146, 148–49
Tennyson, Alfred, xii–xiii
   Idylls of the King, xiii
Thebes, xii, 12, 154, 158
Theseus, 12, 18, 46–50, 56, 60, 62–63, 154
tomb narration, 67, 70–74, 79
Townson, Nigel, 205
Trial of Chivalry, The (play), 16
tragedy, 47, 80, 135, 138–39

trauma, xiii, 3, 10, 17, 45–47, 49–53, 57, 61–63, 75
Treaty of Troyes, 157
Trembinski, Donna, 75
Trevisa, John, 133–34
Trinity, the, 119, 121–27
Tristram, Sir, 5, 66, 68, 71, 135–38, 140–42, 145, 149, 156, 169
Trojan War, 1, 30
Troy, xii–xiii, 23–24, 31–33, 43, 153, 176
Troilus, 2, 10, 23–25, 30–33, 42
Trotter, D. A., 109
troubadour(s), 101–5, 108
trouvère, 101–2, 104, 110, 114–15, 117
Turk(s), x, xi, 168–69, 171–72, 174–75, 177

Usk, Adam, 34, 36
Utz, Richard, x

values, viii, xiv, 23, 67, 85, 92, 180, 191
   chivalric values, 67, 172
   cultural values, 84
   ethical values, 167
   social values, 95
   spiritual values, 198
Vatican II, 206
vengeance, 23, 68–69, 75, 77, 79, 96, 176
Vietnam War, 205–11
   My Lai massacre, 210
Vincent, Diane, 172
violence, ii, ix, xi, 10, 13, 22, 25, 32, 35, 51, 75, 89, 124, 128, 145, 152, 200–202, 204–5, 207, 209–11
   anti-social violence, 16
   cultural violence, 23
   military violence, 199
   religious violence, 186
Virgin Mary, 110
Visions of Daniel, 176
vital spirit(s), 65, 68, 74, 78, 132–34, 136–37, 139–40, 144–48

Walsham, Alexandra, 179–80
war(s), vii–xiv, 1–3, 5–7, 9–14, 17–26, 29–31, 40–44, 45–55, 65, 68, 74–77, 79, 92, 124, 128–29, 131, 135, 140, 146, 148–49, 179, 187–90, 194, 199–212
   civil war, 5, 12, 18, 21, 77, 147, 151–63, 194, 200
   external war, 152–54, 156–57
   prisoner(s) of war, 3, 12, 16, 47, 61
   trauma(s) of war, 47, 50–53, 61–62
   war bride, 2, 18, 25
   war captive, 45–46
   war literature, vii–xiii
   war widow(s), 11–12, 25
   war wives, 2, 10
Wars of the Roses, 168
warfare, xi, 3–4, 13, 42–43, 86, 131, 137, 145, 200–202, 206
   medieval warfare, 29, 199
warrior(s), ix, xiii, 4–5, 31, 51, 68–69, 84, 95, 171, 173, 175
Watt, Ian, 92, 94–96, 98
weeping, 3, 17–18, 34, 36–39, 69, 74, 139–41, 147–48, 160
White, T. H., xiii
Wilcox, Helen, 11
Wille (in *Piers Plowman*), 120–123, 127
William of Tyre, 175
Winchester Manuscript, 39, 69–70, 78
Windeatt, Barry, 48
Woods, William F., 48
words spoken, 84, 86, 95
Wordsworth, William, x
Wynkyn de Worde, 134